CAROL ROBERTSON

THE LITTLE BOOK

BOOK

MOVIE LAW

of

AMERICAN BAR ASSOCIATION
Defending Liberty
Pursuing Justice

16 15 14 13 12   5 4 3 2 1

Library of Congress Cataloging-in-Publication Data

Robertson, Carol, 1948–
    The little book of movie law / Carol Robertson.
        p. cm. – (Little book series ; 7)
    Includes bibliographical references and index.
    ISBN 978-1-61438-470-0 (alk. paper)
1. Motion pictures–Law and legislation–United States.
2. Motion pictures–United States–History. I. Title.
    KF4298.R63 2012
    343.7309'9–dc23

                            2012014340

To Stephan and Tess,
my wonderful research assistants,
thanks for sharing so many films.

Table of Contents

Introduction

My childhood memories are infused with movies and movie lore. They have formed a significant part of my life since I was a small child and my older brother took me and my sister to the movies to assuage our sorrow over the loss of our grandfather—and to take us off our grieving mother's hands for a few hours. We saw a Western—who knows which one. It doesn't matter. What is important is that for several hours, we three children were able to lose ourselves in another world and to forget for a moment the harsh reality of our own. That is the power of the cinema.

I grew up in the Mountain West and what otherwise might have been long weekends of boredom were instead filled pleasurably by the Saturday matinee at the Chief Theater in Pocatello, Idaho (where Judy Garland was born in a trunk in *A Star is Born* (1954)). I spent summers at my grandmother's home in a small Wyoming town and several times a week she would give us 50 cents to see a movie at the Strand Theater—25 cents for the admission, 20 cents for popcorn and a soft drink, and 5 cents for a Milk Nickel ice cream treat for the walk home. She was not very good at judging the subject matter of films and I am sure that my sister and I saw many that would have been more appropriate for adults than grade school girls. She owned a hair salon and all winter she would save the movie magazines for me to read when I came for the summer so that I was able to keep up with the lives of all my favorite stars.

And these were many: Rock Hudson as he appeared in all those comedies with Doris Day, James Dean (*Rebel without a Cause* (1955) and *Giant* (1956)), Paul Newman (*The Long Hot Summer* (1958)), Warren Beatty (*Splendor in the Grass* (1961)), and Robert Redford (*Butch Cassidy and the Sundance Kid* (1969)). I majored in French in college, dreaming of living in the fantasy Paris of Audrey Hepburn and *Sabrina* (1954) or that of

Leslie Caron in *Gigi* (1958)), while viewing all the New Wave movies shown at my university's student center—*Jules et Jim* (1962), *Tirez sur le pianist* (*Shoot the Piano Player*) (1960), and of course, *À bout de souffle* (*Breathless*) (1960), with the very sexy Jean-Paul Belmondo.

I have come to realize that I am not alone in my love of films and that many lawyers share the same passion, some even more so than I. In my research, I discovered an opinion written by Judge Alex Kozinski of the Ninth Circuit Court of Appeals—a well-known movie buff—ruling on an antitrust claim involving a chain of movie theaters, in which he hid the titles of over 200 movies. He was aided by his law clerk who went on to become an entertainment lawyer. And some of the best movies have law or legal cases as subjects—such as *To Kill A Mockingbird* (1962), *Twelve Angry Men* (1957), *Breaker Morant* (1980), and *Dead Man Walking* (1995), or have great actors (and actresses—such as Susan Sarandon in *The Client* (1994)) in lawyer roles. Spencer Tracy almost made a career out of portraying lawyers or judges—as in *Adam's Rib* (1949), *Inherit the Wind* (1960), *Judgment at Nuremberg* (1961), and his last movie, *Guess Who's Coming to Dinner* (1967), to name a few.

What surprised me most when I began to research this book—wanting to choose cases that would illustrate a legal point specific to the movie industry or that would tell a compelling story about the business—was how many cases exist that meet those criteria. I thought that my choices would be limited. Au contraire. I was left with a difficult triage, starting from a list of over one hundred worthy cases. I discovered that passions run high in the motion picture business and what in another industry would be, perhaps, a mundane contract dispute or a property rights matter, takes on greater importance because of which actor or director or what film was involved. The cases are replete with a desire for involvement, a wish to become famous, and a hope of bringing to the screen a favorite novel or play.

We see this passion from the very first days of the industry. Independent movie producers—not to be deterred by the strong-arm tactics of men such as Thomas Edison and others who sought to control the business through enforcement of their patent rights—at a risk to their very lives, headed out to California to shoot the movies that they wanted to make. A filmmaker reads a gripping story about a chariot race and decides to film it on a beach in New Jersey, but fails to obtain the rights that he needs from the book's publisher. Actors and actresses, at first leery of an industry viewed as inferior to the stage, are soon lured by the promise of steady work, as well as possible fame, wealth, and stardom. But early on a rift develops between the industry moguls, seeking control and profits, and the artists—the actors, the directors, the screenwriters—wishing to preserve the integrity of their creative work. Hence, a silent film actress pushes back when she is fired for showing too much independence in how she would perform her roles. Another actress sues because she is not permitted to choose the parts she will perform under the restrictive Hollywood studio system. Another fights back when the studio pulls a part from her and tries to push her into an inferior role. A producer sues because he is shut out of a movie—based on a Shakespeare play—which he has wanted to make for a very long time. A director sues because her film is edited in such a way that it has destroyed her creative vision.

Through movies we also witness the development and changes in society and culture from the early 20th Century to the 21st. Whereas in 1915, censorship of movies was viewed as normal and legitimate, by the 1960s, it was perceived as a restraint on First Amendment rights and as stifling creativity and the visual arts. Through movies and the history of the industry, we see changes in American society from the Progressive Movement through the Second World War and the Cold War years, witnessing, for example, the very personal devastation that the McCarthy and HUAC hearings caused individual movie producers, directors and screenwriters. And of course, Hollywood has been known for its scandals since the beginning—whether the trial of Roscoe "Fatty" Arbuckle or the love affairs, marriages and divorces of famous stars (from Mary Pickford and Douglas Fairbanks to Roberto Rossellini and Ingrid Bergman to Elizabeth Taylor and Richard Burton)—any of which could be and sometimes have been the subject of their own movies.

So get out your popcorn, find a comfortable chair and prepare yourself for thrills, passion, heartbreak and laughter, as you enter into the legal world of cinema.

THE LITTLE
BOOK
of
MOVIE LAW

Part I

The Early Days of the Cinema
A Period of Invention

It is amazing that in just a few short years between 1890 and 1920, the cinema was invented and developed from an arcade-type amusement to an art form, and had become a significant international business. Various historical, legal, and technological developments fostered the growth of cinema both as entertainment and as art. The development of modern industry in the late nineteenth century led to the expansion of urban areas, not only in the United States but also in other countries. This created in turn ready-made audiences for the motion picture houses that grew up in these new boom towns. In the United States, a wave of immigrants from southern and eastern Europe, living mostly in large cities, enjoyed the new silent pictures as a form of entertainment. These small theaters, known as nickelodeons, showed a wide variety of short films, mainly comedies, such as the early films of Roscoe "Fatty" Arbuckle,[1] which had a definite slapstick style, as the new technology transferred popular vaudeville acts to film.

On the legal front, what was initially a free-for-all, where inventors and film producers competed ruthlessly, gradually became more and more regulated. Both patent and copyright protections were extended to the new motion pictures. Censorship at the local and state level became prevalent. And enforcement of the Sherman Antitrust Act, enacted in 1890, ulti-

---

1. *See* Intermission 2, Sex and Crime in 1920s Hollywood.

mately provided a check on what otherwise would have quickly become a lasting monopoly.[2]

Of course, the cinema's beginnings were well before 1890. Movies would not have come into being without the many inventors who actively contributed in this early period, each building on the others' inventions. As early as the 1870s and even before, various inventors were experimenting with cameras for taking photographs that could be shown on other devices at varying speeds to create a sensation of movement. For example, the Zoetrope, a device containing a series of drawings on a narrow strip of paper inside a revolving drum, providing an illusion of movement, was invented in 1833.[3]

Several inventions in the field of photography—such as an 1888 Kodak camera that made photographs on rolls of sensitized paper, and the first celluloid roll film invented by George Eastman in 1889 and intended for still cameras—were quickly utilized in the new motion picture machines.[4] In October 1878, *Scientific American* published a series of pictures depicting a horse in full gallop. The photos were taken by an English-born photographer, Eadweard Muybridge, who had used multiple cameras to do motion studies of the running horse. His goal was something very different from creating a new "moving picture" for its own sake. Muybridge's client, California businessman Leland Stanford, had enlisted Muybridge to take the photos in order to settle a bet with one of Stanford's business colleagues. Muybridge's twelve pictures enabled Stanford to win.[5]

A Frenchman, Étienne-Jules Marey, inspired by Muybridge,

---

2. Thompson, Kristin & Bordwell, David, *Film History: An Introduction*, 2d Ed., McGraw Hill, 2003, New York, New York, p. 11.

3. Thompson & Bordwell, pp. 14.

4. Thompson & Bordwell, pp. 14-15.

5. Starr, Kevin, *California: A History*, Modern Library 2005 (Modern Library Paperback Edition 2007), p. 145.

used a different technology—a photographic gun—to study birds in flight.[6] Marey was also the first inventor to use the flexible film stock that had become available with a box-type camera, utilizing an intermittent mechanism to display a series of still photographs at rapid speed.[7]

One of the most prolific of the early inventors was Thomas Edison. After inventing electricity, the incandescent light bulb (still in use today), the phonograph, and other modern technologies, Edison, with his assistant William K. L. Dickson, turned to motion pictures in the late 1880s.[8] Edison had seen Marey's box camera during a trip to France and asked Dickson to produce a comparable device. Using the new Eastman film stock, Dickson created a camera called a Kinetograph, and a new machine, called a Kinetoscope, which was a viewing box for the photographs shot with the Kinetograph camera. His use of the Eastman film was particularly innovative: Dickson cut the film into one-inch-wide strips (35 millimeters), spliced them to create a long strip, and punched four holes on either side of each frame so that toothed gears could pull the film through the camera and the Kinetoscope viewing box. This new application of what had been sheets of photographic film has since become the norm in the film industry; his original film stock—35 millimeters with four perforations per frame—can be shown on a modern film projector.[9]

Edison and Dickson then went into film production. They built a film studio, called the "Black Maria," in New Jersey, where Edison had his laboratory, and began production in early 1893. Those early films were truly shorts—lasting approximately

---

6. Thompson & Bordwell, p. 15.
7. Thompson & Bordwell, p. 16.
8. Thompson & Bordwell, pp. 16-17.
9. Thompson & Bordwell, p. 17.

twenty seconds each (the longest length of film that the Kinetoscope could then hold). They consisted of moving displays of performances by entertainers, such as acrobats or dancers. In 1894, Edison opened his first performance venue to show his work and also premiered his machine in Paris and London.[10]

In the meantime, other inventors were at work. In France, Louis and Auguste Lumière—whose family company, Lumière Frères (the Light Brothers), was a very successful European manufacturer of photographic plates—entered the motion picture business in 1894, when a local Kinetoscope exhibitor asked them to produce a short film that would be less expensive than the films he was receiving from Edison. In response, the Lumière brothers designed a little camera that they called a "Cinématographe," which utilized 35-millimeter film, with an intermittent mechanism that they modeled after the sewing machine (another recent invention).[11]

In London, the parlor that had leased Kinetoscope machines from Edison had become such a popular venue that its owner asked a local photographic equipment manufacturer, R.W. Paul, to make some extra machines.[12] Because Edison only supplied films to exhibitors who had leased his machines, Paul also had to create a camera and to make films to be shown on his copycat kinetoscopes.

Paul chose a different business model than Edison. Edison only leased his machines to exhibitors, thus enabling him to collect royalties from exhibitors who used them. This delayed the progress of the film industry in the United States because only licensed films could be shown on the machines and these were

---

10. Thompson & Bordwell, p. 19.

11. Thompson & Bordwell, pp. 18-19.

12. Edison had failed to patent the Kinetoscope outside the United States, thus allowing copies to be made and sold in England. Thompson & Bordwell, p. 19.

in short supply. Paul sold the machines as he made them, much as the Lumière Brothers did in France, which enabled films from multiple suppliers to be shown. This allowed the film industries in those two countries to grow at a more rapid pace than in the United States.

Meanwhile, other technologies were introduced. One of the most important was the "Latham Loop," invented by Woodville Latham and his sons.[13] Motion picture cameras and projectors then in use were limited to using a short stretch of film that lasted only a couple of minutes because the tension from a longer, heavier roll of film would cause it to break. The Latham Loop was a simple device that created slack, which relieved the tension, allowing the film to feed through the projecting machine with a regular, uniform movement, resulting in much longer films. The Latham Loop is still in use today in film projectors. "So important was the technique that a patent involving it was to shake up the entire film industry."[14]

With continuous new developments, the popularity of the Kinetoscope was fading. Edison took an interest in another projector, invented by Thomas Armat in 1886, originally called the "Phantoscope" and renamed the "Vitascope." He entered into a venture with Armat, agreeing to both manufacture the device and supply films to exhibitors using it. It was then publicized as "Edison's Vitascope."[15]

By the late 1890s, Dickson had terminated his relationship with Edison and formed a new business venture with Her-

---

13. Patent No. 707,934, submitted June 1, 1896, granted August 26, 1902. Musser, Charles, *The Emergence of Cinema: The American Screen to 1907*, Chapter 5, "Early Motion Picture Companies," Note 6, University of California Press, 1994.

14. Thompson & Bordwell, p. 20. The case was *Motion Picture Patents Co. v. Universal Film Mfg. Co.*, 243 U.S. 502 (1917). *See* discussion at Reel 1, The Edison Patent Cases.

15. Thompson & Bordwell, p. 20.

man Casler, who had patented a flip-card device that he called the "Mutoscope." They formed a new business, The American Mutoscope Company, and began showing films made for this machine. By 1897, theirs was the most popular film company in the United States.[16] It specialized in two types of exhibition—peep shows for individuals and projection parlors for general audiences. It changed its name to American Mutoscope and Biograph, to reflect this double role in peep shows and projected films. In the early 1900s, the company had two "claims to fame" in the newly born film industry—from the legal perspective, as we shall see, as the sparring partner for more than a decade in legal disputes with Thomas Edison—and in the creative arena, as the employer of one of the most significant silent film directors, David Wark (D.W.) Griffith, and the first stars, the "Biograph" girls, among whom the most famous was Mary Pickford.[17]

By the early 1900s, "the invention of cinema was largely completed."[18] But the creative process in the development of film as an art form was just taking shape. Unfortunately, the battles for what came to define cinema as a business in some respects discouraged this artistic development and at the same time determined who would control and profit from that business. This conflict would dominate the legal landscape for decades to come. And not surprisingly, intellectual property law, in particular patent rights, played a big part in this changing business and legal landscape.

In the course of examining the early film industry, particularly in the United States, it is critical to note that the broad

---

16. Thompson & Bordwell, p. 28.
17. Griffith's first film made in California, *The Thread of Destiny* (1910), starred Mary Pickford and was filmed in Mission San Gabriel. Starr, *California*, p. 275.
18. Thompson & Bordwell, p. 21.

protections that patent law provided to inventors encouraged the development of the technology through which motion pictures could be produced and exhibited, while at the same time discouraging the artistic process. This was due to the fact that strong patent protections held by men such as Thomas Edison discouraged others from remaining in the business. Because Edison in particular aggressively pursued and controlled so many patents, and also because he was so litigious, he dissuaded many competitors and would-be competitors. And the fact that he controlled through his patents not just the equipment on which films were made and exhibited but also the films that actually could be made and shown resulted in a narrow and hampered creative perspective.[19]

It was other film producers, not Edison, who looked upon filmmaking not just as a technology to show moving pictures but as a means to tell a story, to entertain an audience, to thrill and to excite. That is the story of the cinema—but not something that Edison understood—and unfortunately for the first decade of the twentieth century, film production in the United States was slowed and restricted because Edison used his patent rights as a blunt club to stifle the creativity of his competitors. By the end of the first decade of that century, certain exhibitors and producers, calling themselves the "Independents," who were willing to ignore Edison's claims and his threats of litigation, rebelled. They used illegal equipment and film stock. Some fled to the West Coast, to California, which seemed remote enough to evade Edison's New Jersey lawyers. This in turn led to the birth of Hollywood as the new home of the U.S. film industry.[20]

---

19. Wallace, Harold Scott, *Competition and the Legal Environment: Intellectual Property Rights in the Early American Film Industry*, University of Connecticut, October 1998, p. 4, found at digitalcommons.uconn.edu/cgi/viewcontent.cgi?article=1324+context=econ_wpapers.

20. Starr, *California*, pp. 274-276.

The Troll Under the Bridge
The Edison Patent Cases

Edison v. American Mutoscope Company, 110 Fed. 660
(S. D.N.Y. 1901); *Edison v. American Mutoscope Company*,
114 Fed. 926 (2d Cir. 1902); *Edison v. American Mutoscope
& Biograph Co.*, 144 Fed. 121 (S. D.N.Y. 1906); *Edison v.
American Mutoscope & Biograph Co.*, 151 Fed. 767
(2d Cir. 1907); *Motion Picture Patents Co. v. Universal
Film Mfg. Co.*, 243 U.S. 502 (1917)

> **Trolls exist. They steal your socks,
> but only the left ones. What's with that?**
>
> Gobber, in *How to Train Your Dragon* (2010)

In Scandinavian fairy tales, the innocent traveler learned to
beware of bridge trolls—fearsome, ugly, gnome-like crea-
tures that lurked under bridges demanding a toll before the
traveler would be allowed to cross. In technology circles,
the term "patent troll" is used to refer to a person who files
for broad patent rights on new technologies (or who acquires
these rights from poor inventors) and then seeks out unwitting
persons it claims are infringing on those patents and, if the
alleged infringer refuses to pay an often unreasonable license
fee, files an infringement lawsuit.[1] Because of the costs associ-

---

1. A patent for an invention is the grant of a property right to the inventor, which
is issued by the U.S. Patent and Trademark Office. The term of a new patent is usually twenty years from the date on which the patent application was filed. *See* www.
uspto.gov/web/offices/pac/doc/general/whatis/htm.

ated with such a suit, and the fact that patent trolls frequently are not the original inventor but rather companies whose sole *raison d'être* is to acquire and hold patent rights, patent trolls are frequently accused of chilling innovation and technological experimentation.[2]

Thomas Edison was, in modern parlance, a patent troll. Now, he and his defenders would have argued that he was simply a very inventive person who contributed tremendously to innovations in film technology and that the industry would have been slower to develop without his many contributions. This may have been the case, although comparable contributions were made by inventors other than Edison, and much of the range of patented technologies that Edison controlled were either invented by his assistant Dickson (such as 35-millimeter film) or were acquired by Edison from others (such as the Vitascope). In any event, due to Edison's strong role in the development of film technology, he actually may have slowed the growth of the industry in the United States.[3]

At the same time as Edison was engaged in aggressive patent litigation against his competitors, French, British, and Italian film companies were leaders throughout the world in creating the modern film industry. In fact, it can be argued that, without the so-called Independents, who defied Edison's litigation threats, and the outbreak of World War I, which disrupted the European momentum, the U.S. movie business would have been obliged to play catch-up behind those more innovative European markets for many years. With the onset of the Great War in August 1914, "the growing Hollywood film industry stepped in to

---

2. *See* Steiner, Tracy, and Guth, Stephen, "Beware Patent Trolls," FindArticles, Business Management Quarterly, Fall 2005, found at http://findarticles.com/p/articles/mi_hb3266/is_3_46/ai_n29219090/, last viewed July 23, 2011.

3. Thompson & Bordwell, p. 12.

fill the gap in supply, expanding its distribution system abroad. By the war's end, American films had an international grip that other countries would struggle, usually with limited success, to loosen."[4] However, this success was despite Edison and not because of his contributions to develop the industry during those years. By 1919, the industry had successfully relocated to Hollywood and the courts had intervened in several important cases to end the monopoly power that Edison had previously held over the industry.[5]

Since the late nineteenth century, Edison, through the corporate entities he controlled, the Edison Company and Edison Manufacturing Company, worked diligently to control the new film industry and to force its competitors out of business through litigation over its patent rights. Edison filed for broad rights covering the technologies behind motion picture cameras, film projectors, and even the film stock used in those devices. In June 1891, Edison and his partner, Dickson, filed two patent applications for his "Kinetograph" camera and for the "Kinetoscope" peephole-viewing device. In January 1892, the Patent Examiner rejected Edison's patent claims, stating that these were similar to the contributions of others[6] and the technology behind those devices had been anticipated by the patents of other inventors. On December 29, 1893, Edison's lawyers filed a new set of claims, which again were rejected on October 18, 1895. Not to be dissuaded, they inserted substitute specifications and, in December 1896, the Patent Office accepted Edison's patent claims.

In August 1897, the Patent Office finally issued Edison a pat-

---

4. Thompson & Bordwell, p. 12.

5. *See* Reel 4, The End of the Edison Monopoly.

6. To obtain a patent, the invention must be new; a patent can be denied if there is "prior art."

ent for his motion picture camera.[7] In the application, Edison made three claims for an apparatus capable of capturing by photography moving objects, another for the projector, and a fifth for the photographic film used in the camera. "The prospect of Edison obtaining patent rights clearly intimidated other players in the young industry. His substantial resources and mythic status made Edison a formidable opponent in the courtroom. Most early competitors were extremely small and lacked the necessary capital to wage lengthy legal battles."[8]

From the point that Edison's patent was issued, his lawyers aggressively took action, filing twenty-three patent infringement suits against manufacturers, as well as motion picture producers, distributors, and exhibitors, forcing them to obtain licenses. Those unable to pay the fees were shut down. These suits created financial uncertainty in the new film industry and deterred outside investment in film production.[9]

After early patent cases went in Edison's favor, most companies that could do so agreed to pay a license fee to Edison in order to continue making and exhibiting films in the United States. However, one company resisted: the rival business formed by Edison's former assistant, Dickson, American Muto-

---

7. Patent No. 589,168, issued August 1897. According to the patent grant, the kinetographic camera's purpose was: "producing pictures representing objects in motion throughout an extended period of time, which could be used to exhibit the scene including such moving objects in a perfect and natural manner by means of a suitable exhibiting apparatus." This apparatus was also described as having a continuous intermittent movement. The camera was further described: "a camera in which the film is wound from one reel to another intermittently past the lens, between which and the film a disk perforated near the edges revolves, bringing the apertures between the lens and the film when the latter is at rest, and the solid part between them when it is in motion, producing successive exposures, by which photographs of moving objects may be taken, at equal distances, in a line, upon the film, with great rapidity."

8. Wallace, *Competition and the Legal Environment*, p. 4, citing Musser, Charles, *The Emergence of Cinema: The American Screen to 1907*, from the series *History of the American Cinema*, Vol. One, New York, Scribner 1990, p. 6.

9. Wallace, p. 7.

scope Company (later known as American Mutoscope & Bio-graph Co., or simply "Biograph"). Biograph argued that its camera, a roller-driven device, did not use the same mechanism and relied on different patents from those that Edison was claiming (whose technology was based on sprocket gears). Biograph was the only real competitor with the financial strength to push back at Edison. Biograph had challenged Edison's early applications for patents for the Kinetograph and the Kinetoscope devices.[10]

In May 1898, Edison filed suit against Biograph for infringement of his camera patent. In this first suit, Biograph argued that cameras such as the Kinetograph had been in use for more than two years prior to the time when Edison had amended his patent application in 1896. Therefore, its right to the patent should have been barred. The court rejected this argument, noting that Edison had initially made a mistake in his original patent application by trying to claim rights to the manner in which his device was to be used rather than the apparatus itself, but that he had corrected that error when he amended his patent application.

Biograph also referenced the prior art on which Edison's device was based—Marley's phenakinoscope, the "Photographic Gun" that was described in the June 1882 issue of *Scientific American*.[11] But the court also rejected that argument, relying on the Patent Office's determination that Edison's application presented "the first complete disclosure of an apparatus by which can be produced a series of photographs on a continuous film, by the use of which a reproduction of an animate scene may be obtained." Even though Edison did not invent the lens, the camera, the film, or the instantaneous exposure, he put them

---

10. Wallace, p. 7.
11. *See* Part I, The Early Days of the Cinema—A Period of Invention.

all together to create the means of putting the film in front of the lens at the right speed to take the photograph at the right moment in order to exploit the illusion of movement.

Biograph's efforts to emphasize the uniqueness of its own camera and film did not impress the court. Because Biograph's equipment did virtually the same thing—even though the court acknowledged that the means that Biograph used to achieve this effect in its camera were not the same as those covered by Edison's patent—it was the functional equivalent of Edison's device. Thus, the court found for Edison. The court stayed this decision to allow Biograph to appeal.[12]

While the appeal was pending, however, the lower court decision, although not enforced, had a chilling effect on the film industry. Biograph's equipment used a different technology from that used in other camera systems that were closer to Edison's and, if the court had found Biograph's camera to infringe on Edison's patents, then others did not see how they could ever prevail against an Edison lawsuit. In the interim, Biograph ceased filmmaking, producing instead only films of news events. However, Edison did not capitalize on the time—from mid-July 1901 to mid-March 1902, a period of eight months—when he had market dominance to press his business advantage. Rather than use this windfall afforded by the district court to invest in big movie productions that would seal Edison's dominance, the company instead produced inexpensive news events and copied European films in order to minimize costs. Nothing the company did served to advance the U.S. film industry and the delay allowed the French and the Italians to gain worldwide dominance.[13] In fact, Edison did not really believe that the film industry had a

---

12. Edison v. American Mutoscope Company, 110 Fed. 660 (S. D.N.Y. 1901).
13. Wallace, p. 10.

future. He saw these inventions as merely an adjunct to his more favored invention, the phonograph.

In March 1902, the appellate court reversed the lower court decision, holding that Edison's patents were invalid because they were too broad, embracing more than what Edison had actually invented, assuming that he had actually invented anything.[14] Looking askance at Edison's claim that he essentially held patent rights over all aspects of motion picture technology, the appellate court more closely examined Biograph's claim that the various steps in moving picture production had all been accomplished long before Edison came into the picture. The court asked whether this was in fact "prior art," possibly negating the "novelty" of Edison's patent claims.

In addition, the court was concerned about the breadth of Edison's claims. As the court noted, "any combination of the means to 'capture a moving image on a camera lens' at a high enough rate of speed to secure the result of persistence of vision," would be covered by Edison's patent claims. The court came to the conclusion that Edison was not a pioneer in either the large sense of having been the sole inventor of all that, nor in the limited sense in which he would have been if he had also invented the film. He did not invent the film, the court pointed out. Eastman had done this. When one broke down the claims provided in Edison's patent application, it became obvious that other inventors had been there before Edison and had anticipated key components of Edison's devices. The court concluded that Edison had utilized the film invented by Eastman, which earlier inventors had lacked, and perfected the devices in existence at the time to accommodate the film, and in that manner had satisfied "the conditions necessary for commercial suc-

---

14. Edison v. American Mutoscope Company, 114 Fed. 926 (2d Cir. 1902).

cess." However, the court continued, this did not entitle him, under patent law, "to a monopoly over all motion picture cameras capable of utilizing the film."

This decision improved the prospects for Biograph and other film producers who had been waiting out the litigation and it had a temporary positive effect on the industry. Both Edison (who now had to create more competitive products, having lost his monopoly over production) and Biograph created more ambitious, longer films during this next period. But in the patent arena, Edison was not to be deterred. His attorneys revised his patent claims and resubmitted applications, which were approved on September 20, 1902.[15] On the basis of these reissued patents, Edison again brought suit against Biograph (in November 1902) for patent infringement. This new litigation had a renewed chilling effect, as people again waited to see what result would issue this time.

In March 1906, the circuit court ruled in favor of Biograph.[16] Edison had claimed that in his application for the reissued patent, he had narrowed the claims to fit the appellate court decision—or so he insisted. The court found that he had, in fact, retained the same broad claims from his original patent application, but had added specific detail, for example, in describing how the camera would work. Based on the appellate court's decision with respect to Edison's original patent, and noting the similarity between the claims in that patent and the reissued patent, the court concluded that Edison's invention "if there be one," would be very narrow. In fact, the court wondered, if only "a moderate amount of mechanical ingenuity" was required to perfect the details of a device that had already been designed

---

15. Patent Reissue No. 12,037 for a kinetographic camera and Patent Reissue No. 12,038, for the film.

16. Edison v. American Mutoscope & Biograph Co., 144 Fed. 121 (S. D.N.Y. 1906).

and was in public use, had Edison actually done anything that amounted to an invention? However, after carefully examining prior patents, the court finally concluded that Edison's device did show invention in the means by which intermittent movement occurred while the film was passing in front of the lens (allowing the mechanism to work smoothly, accurately, and rapidly and thus alleviating a trembling or jerky appearance in the reproduced pictures). Accordingly, the court determined that the claims in the reissued patent were valid.

However, in view of the prior art, Edison's patent had to be narrowly construed in considering an infringement claim, and confined to the specific feeding mechanism described in Edison's application. In light of this interpretation, the court determined that Biograph's camera, although operationally similar to the one covered by Edison's patent, had a different feeding device from the sprocket wheel used in Edison's device. Edison's camera employed this sprocket wheel to engage the film and carry it along across the lens with an intermittent motion. On the other hand, the Biograph camera used two rollers to pull the film across the lens, while responding to a vibrating clamp in the opposite side—a sort of "rake-through" process. The court found that these mechanical devices for accomplishing film movement were essentially different and, therefore, the Biograph camera did not infringe. Biograph had a second alternate camera, called the Warwick camera, which used a sort of bifurcated fork with studs to pull the film through holes in the opposite edges of the film. Because Edison's invention was limited to the specific sprocket device described, the court found that Biograph's Warwick camera did not infringe either.

Of course, Edison promptly appealed the decision, arguing, with a straight face, that the litigation was causing a "high state of uncertainty in the industry." The appellate court agreed with the lower court that, because of differences in parts, in action, and in result, the Biograph camera did not infringe on Edison's patents.[17] However, the court did overturn the lower court's ruling with respect to the Warwick camera, finding that the bifurcated fork with studs was "the fair equivalent" of the wheel with sprockets, and that it therefore infringed.

This ruling with respect to the Warwick camera, while saving Biograph's device, had a "devastating effect" on producers other than Biograph who used equipment that resembled the Warwick camera. It was unfortunate. At the time, there was a boom in the movie industry with exhibitors clamoring for more and more films, and instead of producing these, the industry was battling Edison over patent rights. Although losing against Biograph with this decision, Edison had just affirmed his rights in the technology that was the most practical for making motion pictures—a camera using a sprocket wheel device. Edison immediately began notifying producers and exhibitors of his rights and collecting license fees.[18]

There was, however, one patent out there that Edison did not own or control—the patent for the Latham Loop[19] which was the practical device that alleviated the tension problem in film projectors. In 1908, Edison again sued Biograph, this time claiming that Biograph was infringing his patents in film stock. Biograph turned around and strategically improved its position by acquiring the patent rights to the Latham Loop. In addition, Biograph formed an alliance with the Armat Moving Picture Company to gain legal access to its projector patents.[20] With these new rights in hand, Biograph countersued Edison, claim-

---

17. Edison v. American Mutoscope & Biograph Co., 151 Fed. 767 (2d Cir. 1907).

18. Thompson & Bordwell, p. 39.

19. *See* discussion in Part I, The Early Days of the Cinema—A Period of Invention.

20. Wallace, pp. 18-19.

ing that Edison's use of the Latham Loop in his cameras and projectors was infringing.

The competition between these two rivals grew more intense. With each of them owning a broad library of patent rights, they set up rival patent licensing associations in early 1908: The Association of Edison Licensees and the Association of Biograph Licensees. Edison Association members paid licensing fees to Edison and agreed to do business exclusively with each other. The Biograph Association received funds from foreign companies that wanted to bring films into the American market.[21] What this meant effectively was that Edison's group controlled the camera and film stock industry and Biograph controlled the projection world.[22]

Finally the parties called a truce and in late 1908 together formed the Motion Picture Patents Company (MPPC), a patent pooling and licensing association, in which each party (Edison and Biograph) were equal owners. Other members were movie producers and exhibitors who were licensees of either Edison or Biograph. Parties who contributed patents to the enterprise (largely Edison and Biograph) received license fees from the venture, in relation to the number of patents contributed. Only licensed companies could make films with equipment under MPPC licenses. Only licensed distributors were allowed to release the films. And exhibitors had to pay fees for the privilege of showing films. The MPPC also had an exclusive arrangement with Eastman Kodak for film stock. Those who attempted to make films without paying fees to the MPPC were sued. Several companies attempted to work around the MPPC, arguing that the cameras they were using employed different

---

21. Thompson & Bordwell, p. 39.
22. Wallace, p. 19.

mechanisms from those under MPPC patents. The MPPC actually hired detectives to visit movie parlors to gain evidence that films not licensed through the MPPC were being shown using the Latham Loop technology.[23] Between 1909 and 1911, the MPPC brought suits against nearly all of these independent producers and exhibitors for using alleged patent infringing technology.[24]

In 1917, the U.S. Supreme Court ruled against the MPPC, on the grounds that the technique of the Latham Loop had been anticipated by earlier patents.[25] According to the facts of that case, in 1912, the MPPC had entered into an agreement with Precision Machine Company to manufacture projectors using the Latham Loop. These projectors were to be used solely for exhibiting motion pictures using Edison's patented camera equipment. A "patent notice" was attached to each machine, referencing Patent No. 12,192, one of the reissued Edison camera patents, and stating that the machine could only be used to show films made with the Edison camera. This particular patent expired on August 31, 1914.

In November 1914, Prague Amusement Company leased a playhouse and acquired the projector that was kept there. In late 1914, Universal Film Manufacturing Company made two films that were sold to Prague for exhibition in the playhouse. These were shown in March 1915. The MPPC sent notice letters to Prague and Universal, telling them that showing the unlicensed films on a projector using the Latham Loop was an infringement of the MPPC's patents. The MPPC also filed suit the same day. The lower court held that Prague had an implied license to show the films on the machine because the license

---

23. Thompson & Bordwell, p. 39.
24. Thompson & Bordwell, p. 40.
25. Motion Picture Patents Co. v. Universal Film Mfg. Co., 243 U.S. 502 (1917).

fee had been paid when the equipment was manufactured. The case made its way to the U.S. Supreme Court. At the time, it was universally acknowledged that the Latham Loop was the only mechanism with which modern motion pictures could be successfully projected.

In deciding this case, the Court relied on three fundamental principles: First, the scope of any patent is limited to the invention described in the claims contained in the patent application and nothing more. Second, the patent holder receives nothing from the issuance of a patent that he did not have before, that is, the only effect of a patent is to prevent others from producing or selling what he invented. Third, the purpose of the patent laws is not to create private fortunes for patent owners but rather "to promote the progress of science and the useful arts."

Using these principles, the Court concluded that the owner of a patent was not entitled, by putting a notice on the machine made using patented technology, to extend its patent monopoly by restraining the use of the machine to materials, such as films, that are not part of the patented technology.[26] Thus, the restriction was invalid. The Court did not stop there, however, but rather summed up by stating that "this restriction would give to the [MPPC] such a potential power for evil over an industry which must be recognized as an important element in the amusement life of the nation." And the Court concluded that to allow such a broad patent enforcement right to the MPPC "would be gravely injurious to the public interest." The Court essentially told Thomas Edison, "Go back under your bridge and do something useful for society; quit trying to promote your own private fortune at the expense of the public well-being." In other words, stop spoiling the fun.

---

26. 243 U.S. at 516-517.

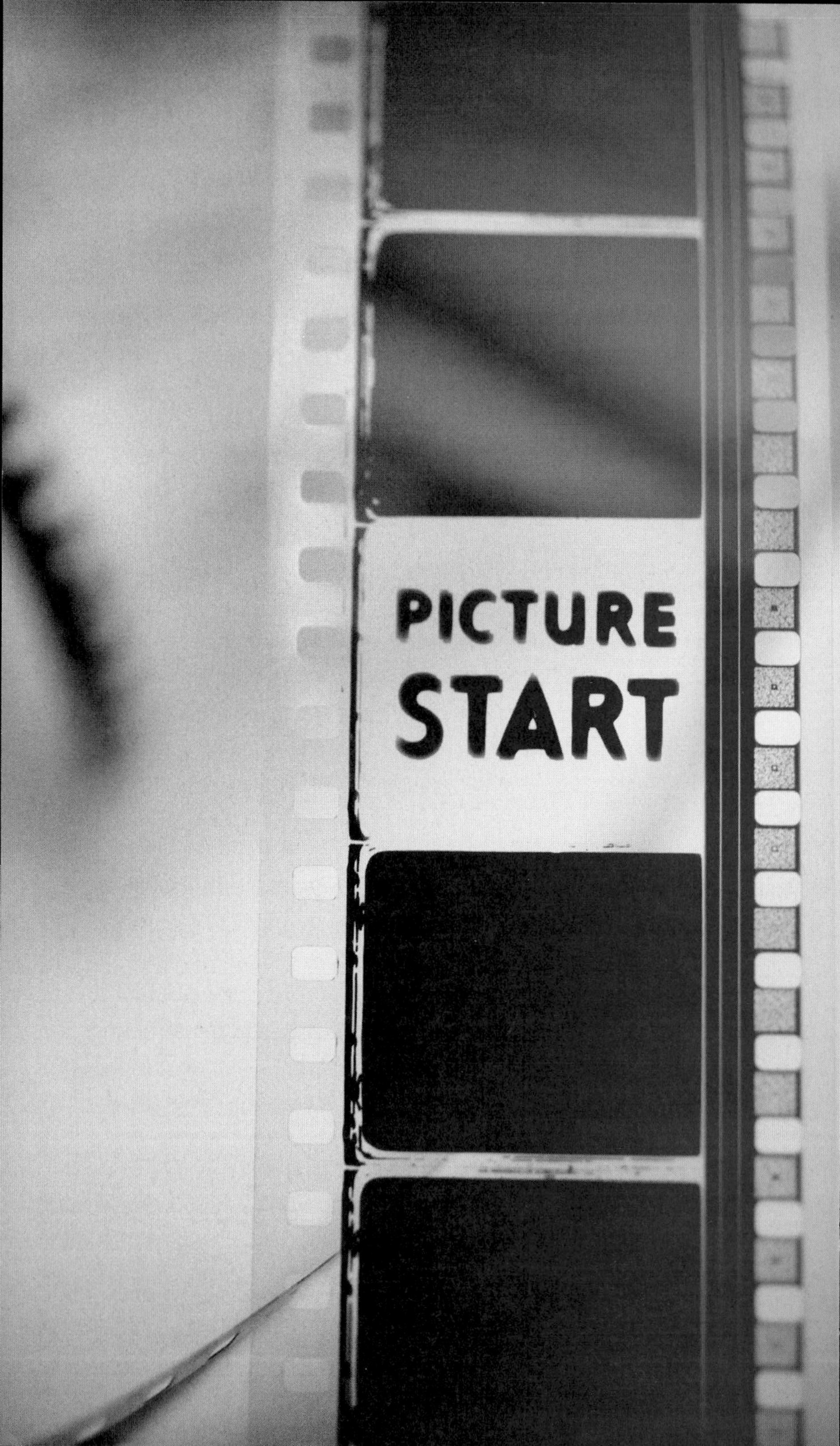
PICTURE
START

Trading Places

Edison and the Nascent Copyright Protection for Film

Edison v. Lubin, 119 Fed. 993 (E. D.Pa. 1903);
rev'd 122 Fed. 240 (3d Cir. 1903); *American Mutoscope & Biograph Co. v. Edison Mfg Co.*, 137 Fed. 262 (D.N.J. 1905)

> **Randolph Duke: Money isn't everything, Mortimer.**
> **Mortimer Duke: Oh, grow up.**
> **Randolph Duke: Mother always said you were greedy.**
> **Mortimer Duke: She meant it as a compliment.**
>
> Ralph Bellamy as Randolph Duke and Don Ameche as Mortimer Duke, from *Trading Places* (1983)

Anyone who owns or rents a movie DVD is familiar with the FBI warning that appears before the film credits, alerting the viewers that the film that they are about to see is protected by U.S. Copyright Law. No reproduction or commercial use of the movie is allowed. Ironically, Edison and the American Mutoscope & Biograph Company (Biograph) were able to use the strong protections afforded to them as patent holders by the U.S. Patent Law in effect at the time to keep competitors at bay for more than a decade. But as they developed and improved on technologies for motion pictures, they had initially no copyright protection for the content of the films that they were producing with that equipment. It is difficult to imagine, but motion pictures were not listed in the creative works covered by copyright law in the early days of the cinema.[1] How could this be? In the late 1890s and early 1900s, when early film producers were first telling stories through film, the copyright law that then protected artistic expression had been put in place earlier in the nineteenth century, when no one dreamed of a motion picture as a form of art. In fact, copyright law was expanded only in 1870 to cover still photographs. At the time, moving pictures were barely imaginable and certainly not within the minds of those responsible for drafting copyright law revisions.[2]

As a result of limited copyright protection, "free riding"— blatant duplication of others' film prints—was rampant.[3] Film producers took such steps as they could to protect their work. Both Edison and Biograph registered their movies with the U.S. Copyright Office by submitting paper prints of their films. They believed that the law could and should protect the films by judging the underlying prints to be the equivalent of still photographs. It was largely an uphill battle to convince the courts to allow such protection. Although common-law rules sometimes were liberally interpreted by the courts to prevent blatant infringement, because the protection was piecemeal and uncertain, those seeking to copy the films produced by another usually succeeded.[4]

In 1902, Edison sued Sigmund Lubin, accusing him of selling duplicated copies of his films, particularly his popular

---

1. Copyright protection for motion pictures was not provided until the law was amended in 1909. March 4, 1909, 62nd Congress, 2nd session; Public Law, No. 303, added motion picture photoplays and motion pictures other than photoplays to the list of works for which a copyright could be claimed.

2. *See* Steiner, Tracy, and Guth, Stephen, "Beware Patent Trolls," FindArticles, Business Management Quarterly, Fall 2005, found at http://findarticles.com/p/articles/mi_hb3266/is_3_46/ai_n29219090/, last viewed July 23, 2011.

3. Wallace, p. 21.

4. Wallace, p. 22.

actuality, *Kaiser Wilhelm's Yacht, Meteor, Entering the Water.* Edison's filmmaker had taken a series of 4,500 pictures on a celluloid sheet, each of which was slightly different from its predecessor and successor, which in their totality represented Kaiser Wilhelm's yacht "Meteor" as it was christened and launched. (Movie viewers' tastes were less demanding at that time than they are today.) Edison sent the celluloid sheet to the Department of the Interior, to be copyrighted to Edison, as the owner, as a photograph, entitled "Christening and launching Kaiser Wilhelm's Yacht, 'Meteor.'" Edison placed a copyright notice on copies of the film, one inscribed on a celluloid plate fastened at the front of the series and one at the end of the sheet.

From one end of the marked copies, about one-third was detached by an unknown person, and this segment fell into Sigmund Lubin's hands. Lubin claimed to not know that the film had been copyrighted. The portion of the film in question showed part of the launch. Lubin made a negative of the purloined copy and from this duped new copies of the film, which of course were exact reproductions of Edison's copyrighted one. He sold these to exhibitors.

Edison relied on his filing of the film print with the Copyright Office in the lawsuit that he brought against Lubin for copyright infringement. Unfortunately, the lower court did not agree and ruled against Edison, holding that "a series of photographs, arranged for use in a machine for producing a panoramic effect" was not entitled to copyright protection as a photograph. The court determined that each and every one of the 4,500 photographs, no matter how or for what purpose one or the other may have been linked to the others, was required to be separately registered. In addition—and this was the problem—each had to be inscribed with a copyright notice.

Of course to do this would have been impractical in a motion picture, as it would have destroyed the quality of the movie viewing experience. (Imagine how that would have looked to the viewer.) And the court recognized this. But the court did not believe that it could interpret existing law otherwise. If the law was defective because it could not be used to protect a motion picture, then Congress should address the deficiency. "In the absence of any expression of the will of Congress," the court said, it was unwilling to guess how film should be treated.

Edison, of course, appealed. However, while waiting for the appellate court to render its decision, his company restricted its filmmaking activities with respect to original subjects, assuming that Lubin and other free-riders would simply copy the films.[5]

In April 1903, the appellate court reversed the lower court decision, granting Edison an injunction against Lubin's copying.[6] The court noted that the negative and its positive reproduction represented a similar act and event—the launch of the yacht. It determined that "to require each of the numerous undistinguishable pictures to be individually copyrighted, as suggested by the [lower] court, would, in effect, be to require copyright of many pictures to protect a single one."[7] The court viewed motion pictures as progress in the development of the photographic art and believed it to be inconceivable that Congress, in deciding to extend copyright protection to photographs, would not have chosen to afford protection to that progress. "While such advance has resulted in a different type of photograph, yet it is none the less a photograph—a picture produced by photographic progress."[8]

---

5. Wallace, p. 23.
6. Edison v. Lubin, 122 Fed. 240 (3d Cir. 1903).
7. 122 Fed. at 241.
8. 122 Fed. at 242.

This decision put a stop to the more blatant and egregious duping activities, at least on the domestic front. Foreign films lacked copyright protection, however, and were considered to be fair game. The copying of these films "continued to be a popular and lucrative practice."[9]

This decision did not stop the practice of movie "remakes," however. Edison apparently believed that he should benefit from copyright protection, but that his arch-rival, Biograph, should not. In the early 1900s, Biograph was earning a reputation for high-quality story films directed by artists such as D.W. Griffith and starring quality actresses, who were known as "Biograph" girls. Edison found it to be easier, instead of developing original screenplays, to have his film production company, Edison Manufacturing Company, simply "remake" the most popular Biograph movies. Biograph released its first-run films to an exclusive group of theaters that subscribed to its motion picture service. Edison Manufacturing would produce remakes that it supplied to rival exhibitors.[10]

Biograph had made a film entitled "Personals." It depicted a scene at Grant's Tomb in New York City and represented a French gentleman who had inserted an advertisement stating his desire to meet a handsome girl at Grant's Tomb at a certain time, with the ultimate object of finding a wife. In the film, the man appears at Grant's Tomb and is set upon first by one woman, then another, and eventually by several more, who so aggressively pursue him that he is forced to flee. He runs away from them but they follow in close pursuit. The chase is shown as taking place at several locations, until the Frenchman is overtaken by one of the women, who finds him hiding out and, at the point of a pistol, forces him to yield.

9. Wallace, p. 25.
10. Wallace, p. 25.

Biograph copyrighted the film. Edison Manufacturing also produced a motion picture that it called "How a French Nobleman Got a Wife Through the New York Herald Personal Columns," with a plot remarkably similar to Biograph's film. Biograph sued Edison Manufacturing for copyright infringement, seeking an injunction against its remake on the grounds of plagiarism.[11]

Edison Manufacturing demurred, asking the court to dismiss the suit because Biograph had no cause of action. Edison's lawyers argued, on the basis of *Edison v. Lubin*, that copyright law only protected against the physical duplication of a film. They also argued that Biograph's film had been shot with several cameras, which was then edited from a number of negatives, into a single film. Biograph had registered the resulting film as a single photograph when, according to Edison, it should have filed for protection of each of the original (pre-edited) films individually. The court denied Biograph's motion for an injunction. It noted that Edison Manufacturing had "merely borrowed" Biograph's idea and made other similar photographs of its own.[12] However, the court was interested not only in the form of expression—a photograph or series of photographs—but also the purpose of copyright law: to protect not only the representation but rather the expression of an idea. In this respect, a film, even if taken with several cameras and then edited into one "photograph," merited copyright protection as the expression of the author's ideas and conceptions embodied in one story.

However, in this case, Edison had not just made a copy of Biograph's film; he had made his own film at several locations

---

11. American Mutoscope & Biograph Co. v. Edison Mfg Co., 137 Fed. 262 (D.N.J. 1905).

12. 137 Fed. at 263.

near Grant's Tomb and in New Jersey. He used different actors wearing different costumes. Although the two films had similar features, Edison's was not exactly like Biograph's. Edison's lawyers argued that the film was therefore original because it carried his own expression as to how the story of the French nobleman should be carried out.

Although the court refused to grant Biograph an injunction, the court made clear that a series of films integrated into one through the editing process could be treated as the equivalent of a single photograph, and therefore merited protection under existing copyright law. As the decision did not achieve Biograph's goal, however, of stopping Edison from making imitations of its successful films, Biograph changed its business practice. Instead of providing subscriptions to its exhibition service, the company sold prints of its films once they were completed to distributors. In this manner, Edison was no longer able to remake Biograph films in time to compete with their first runs in movie parlors. Edison's company was therefore forced to compete with Biograph by creating its own original screenplays. And Biograph from that point on filed for copyright protection for its films both as photographs and also as dramatic compositions.

The Great Race
The "Ben Hur" Case

Harper Brothers v. Kalem Company,
169 Fed. 61 (2d Cir. 1909); aff'd *Kalem Company
v. Harper Brothers*, 222 U.S. 55 (1911)

> **Messala: It goes on. It goes on, Judah.
> The race—the race is not—over.
> [dies]**
>
> Stephen Boyd, as Messala, from *Ben Hur (1959)*

When I was a small child, my local parochial school gave the entire student body the afternoon off so that we could attend a matinee performance of the very popular movie, *Ben Hur* (1959), directed by William Wyler and starring Charlton Heston in the title role and Stephen Boyd as his rival, Messala.[1] Juda Ben Hur was the hero of a novel written by General Lew Wallace in 1880. In the novel, Ben Hur, a Judean aristocrat during the reign of the Roman Emperor, Tiberius, is enslaved because of the betrayal of his Roman friend, Messala. Bitter, once he regains his freedom, Ben Hur seeks out Messala to avenge the wrong. However, after encountering Jesus and witnessing his crucifixion, Ben Hur is redeemed. But he is nevertheless obliged to do battle with Messala, thus leading to the climax of the story, an epic chariot race between Ben Hur and Messala.

What many may not realize is that this movie was not the first film based on the Lew Wallace novel. Before this panoramic

---

1. The film was a popular success and won an unprecedented eleven Academy Awards.

production, there was a 1927 MGM movie, filmed in Italy, as well as a very early silent film, produced in 1907 by the Kalem Company. The 1907 film was also unprecedented, not in the motion picture world, but in the legal world, as it resulted in a precedent-setting decision by the U.S. Supreme Court. For this 1907 movie was based on the Lew Wallace novel, but, unlike the 1959 film, it was made without the permission of the author's estate or that of Harper Brothers, the copyright owner.

A stage play was made from the novel, under license from Harper Brothers. Kalem engaged a screenwriter, Gene Gauntier, to read the novel and to write a description of certain scenes from it, from which Kalem produced and exhibited the film in 1907. Gene Gauntier was a silent film actress, writer, director, and producer. She supplemented her actor's salary by writing screenplays. She was connected with both Biograph and Kalem. In her 1928 memoirs, she remarked that, at the time, the film industry infringed on everything: "up to now no one had seemed to know just where they stood."[2] Kalem did not reproduce the entire story in the Lew Wallace novel (it was only a one-reel version), just certain of the more dramatic scenes, including Ben Hur as a slave in the galley of a Roman ship and, of course, the famous chariot race, which was filmed on a beach in New Jersey.[3] Further, Kalem did not actually exhibit the film but rather licensed its use to movie parlors.

---

2. "Blazing the Trail: Gene Gauntier Again," *Woman's Home Companion*, Volume 55, Number 10, October 1928, page 7.

3. In her 1928 memoirs, Gene Gauntier describes shooting the chariot scene: "In five days after the idea was conceived we were at Sheepshead Bay taking the first scenes. In three days more it was finished and in the developing tanks. Just compare that with the two years or more that Metro-Goldwyn spent on the stupendous *Ben Hur* which recently dazzled the public and which represented several trips to Italy and an investment of millions." Gene Gauntier, "Blazing the Trail," *Woman's Home Companion*, Volume 55, Number 10, October 1928, page 7. *See* discussion in Menefee, David W., *The First Female Stars: Women of the Silent Era*, Greenwood Publishing Group, 2004, pp. 71-73.

Harper Brothers sued Kalem for copyright infringement.

The copyright law at the time[4] gave the author of a book not only the sole right to print it, but also the sole right to dramatize it and, in such case, the sole right to perform that dramatization publicly. The issue, then, that the court had to confront was whether the film, *Ben Hur*—which was essentially a series of photographs (as interpreted by the then copyright law)—was a dramatization of the novel, *Ben Hur*, and thus in violation of Harper Brothers' copyright, or not. And, as a corollary, did this movie violate Harper Brothers' sole right to dramatize the book? Finally, was the exhibition of the film—again which was essentially at the time considered to be a series of photographs projected in rapid succession on a screen—a public performance of a dramatization of the novel? Big questions for a court in 1908. A whole new way of looking at the world.

The circuit court determined that the film (that is, the "photographs") only represented the artist's (that is, the photographer's or movie producer's) idea of what the author had expressed in words in his novel and therefore did not infringe on the copyrighted book or the dramatization.[5] However, the court also stated that when the film was projected to a viewing audience, it did become a dramatization, which infringed on the copyright of the novel's author, as well as his right as the owner of the copyrighted drama. As this was a silent film (talkies had not yet been introduced), the court also felt obliged to note that it was not necessary that there be both speech and action to constitute a dramatic performance.

Kalem had argued that because "moving pictures only express the artist's conception of the author's ideas as

---

4. The Copyright Act of 1909, §4952, Rev. Stat. U.S.
5. A stage play had been made of the novel which was the basis for Kalem's screenplay.

expressed in the words of the copyrighted book or dramatic composition, they cannot be said to infringe the author's rights." The court did not buy this argument, ruling in favor of Harper and pointing out that over the prior fifty years the types of works entitled to copyright protection had expanded, not contracted. In 1891, the court noted as an example, authors were given the exclusive right to dramatize their copyrighted works.

Kalem appealed to the U.S. Supreme Court, which in 1911 issued its landmark ruling in the case. Justice Holmes delivered the Court's decision. The Court for the first time legally recognized that motion pictures could be a medium for artistic expression, ruling that they were definitely a dramatization of the writer's work. Part of the problem was that films were silent; in that sense they could be viewed more as moving pictures rather than as a dramatic expression, like a play. But Justice Holmes rejected this limitation, providing a stunning affirmation of the artistic expression in silent movies: "Action can tell a story, display all the most vivid relations between men, and depict every kind of human emotion without the aid of a word ... The essence of the matter ... is not the mechanism employed, but that we see the event or story lived."[6]

Kalem argued that pictures of scenes in a novel could be made and exhibited without infringing the copyright, and could be copyrighted themselves. Justice Holmes noted, however, that even if a derivative film could be copyrighted, "it does not follow that the use of the photos in motion [that is, the exhibition of the film] does not infringe the author's rights." Kalem further argued that it had not produced the representation, that is, the exhibition or dramatization of the film, but merely had sold the film to distributors. Therefore, it could not be liable for infringe-

---

6. 222 U.S at 61.

ment. But the Court held that a person, such as Kalem, who produces a film and offers it for sale for exhibition, even if not the person exhibiting the film, can infringe the author's copyright. As Justice Holmes noted, Kalem had advertised the film as a dramatic reproduction of *Ben Hur*, thereby contributing to the infringement and was therefore liable for infringement.[7]

The Kalem case was a critical advancement in legal thinking about films and what role they would play in the twentieth century. If movies were merely photographic images and if they had continued to be treated as such, the motion picture business might not have developed into the industry that we know today. In order to create a film that was longer than one reel (about 15 minutes of play time), a large-scale capital investment was required. But no one would have been willing to make such an investment without being assured of the legal rights to the resulting work. By the second decade of the twentieth century, the industry was ready for this investment. The years following 1910 witnessed tremendous growth in the film industry, seeing the production of some of the great works of the silent film era, such as D.W. Griffith's, *The Birth of a Nation* (1915), and even MGM's authorized remake of *Ben Hur* in 1925.[8]

---

7. This is the theory of contributory infringement that would be relied on almost a hundred years later by the Supreme Court in holding Grokster liable for copyright infringement in *Metro-Goldwyn-Mayer Studios v. Grokster, Ltd.*, 545 U.S. 913 (2005). *See* discussion at Reel 28, The Pirates of the Internet.

8. *See* description of MGM's investment in Note 3 above.

The Empire Strikes Back
The End of the Edison Monopoly

United States v. Motion Picture Patents Co.,
247 U.S. 524 (1918)

> **Louis: My God! The Dukes are going to corner the entire frozen orange juice market!**
> **Ophelia: Unless somebody stops them...**
> **Coleman: ...or *beats* them to it.**
> **[all turn and look at him]**
> **Coleman: Egg-nog?**
>
> Dan Aykroyd, as Louis, Jamie Lee Curtis, as Ophelia, and
> Denholm Elliott, as Coleman, in *Trading Places* (1983)

The second decade of the twentieth century brought big changes to the movie industry. As discussed in the first chapter, competition among the various movie producers and patent holders was so intense in the early part of the century that it caused a drag on the momentum of the industry in the United States—allowing foreign companies, such as Pathé in France—to gain market share and to take the lead internationally. Recognizing that this hostile environment was becoming a distraction and harming everyone's business, the major players— Edison, Biograph, and Vitagraph—formed the Motion Picture Patents Company (MPPC) in 1908. Each party contributed its patents to the enterprise in return for a share of the license fees collected.[1]

The MPPC hoped to control all three phases of the movie business: production, distribution, and exhibition. This new company, which was commonly known as "The Trust," quickly gained monopoly control over the industry, issuing licenses for equipment under its patents to a small group of just ten member producers.[2] Under MPPC rules, only companies holding licenses for MPPC patents could make films. Only licensed distributors could release these films and theaters showing the films paid a weekly fee to the MPPC.[3] In addition, Eastman Kodak agreed to sell film stock only to MPPC members, who in turn agreed to purchase film only from Eastman Kodak.[4] Because Eastman Kodak was at the time the supplier of most of the industry's film stock, this severely limited the ability of movie producers who did not belong to the MPPC to access a critical resource.[5] This arrangement and other exclusive agreements like it gave The Trust virtual control over the entire U.S. film market and enabled it to block the entry of new producers.

The threat of litigation for patent rights enforcement restrained many potential newcomers from entering the market, at a time when this young industry should have been bur-

---

1. Thompson & Bordwell, p. 39. In June 1907, Kalem was admitted to the Motion Picture Patents Company. In her memoirs, Gene Gauntier, the silent film actress, screenwriter, and director, described the prevailing view of this organization in the early twentieth century, stating that it "was bitterly assailed as the moving picture trust of its day." Besides Kalem, Vitagraph, Edison, and Biograph, Selig, Lubin, Pathé, Melies and Essanay were also members, according to Gauntier. "Blazing the Trail: Gene Gauntier Again," *Woman's Home Companion*, Volume 55, Number 10, October 1928, page 7.

2. Starr, *California*, p. 274. *See* The American Experience, People & Events: The Business of Movies, found at http://www.pbs.org/wgbh/amex/pickford/peopleevents/e-business.html.

3. Thompson & Bordwell, p. 39.

4. Fellow, Anthony R., *American Media History*, Cengage Learning, 2009, p. 219.

5. The American Experience, People & Events: The Business of Movies, found at http://www.pbs.org/wgbh/amex/pickford/peopleevents/e-business.html.

geoning with innovators and creative ideas. Any producer who used a film camera without paying a fee to the MPPC risked a costly court battle.[6] And since the MPPC also had control over patents covering film projectors, including the Latham Loop patent essential to the functioning of virtually all projectors,[7] even movie parlors were restricted in the films they could present.

Very early on an underground market formed. As discussed in the opening introduction,[8] rather than submit to the demands for onerous licensing fees, some producers, such as Carl Laemmle (the founder of Universal Studios), calling themselves the "Independents," using patented equipment (but refusing to pay fees) with imported film stock, continued to make films.[9] They always had to be one step ahead in a cat-and-mouse game with detectives hired by the MPPC to catch and shut down any illegal uses. These were often unscrupulous thugs who used hardball tactics instead of legal process, confiscating unlicensed equipment, stealing machinery and supplies, intimidating casts, and causing "accidents" that destroyed negatives.[10] In addition, MPPC producers refused to deal with any movie theater that showed films made by an independent producer.

Between 1909 and 1911, the MPPC brought lawsuits against nearly all of these independent producers, largely by claiming patent rights in the cameras or in the projectors used to show the films. Because every projector by that time utilized the Latham Loop, it was impossible for any exhibitor to avoid using this patented technology.[11] But between 1911 and 1919, several events stopped the MPPC in its tracks.

---

6. Thompson & Bordwell, pp. 39-40.
7. Thompson & Bordwell, p. 40. *See* Reel #2.
8. *See* Part I, The Early Days of the Cinema—a Period of Invention.
9. Fellow, p. 219.
10. Fellow, p. 219.
11. Thompson & Bordwell, p. 40.

First, many of the Independents installed their operations in Hollywood, where the distance enabled them to make films without the intrusions of the MPPC thugs.[12] One early independent producer described the atmosphere in those early days:

> "The Patents Company hired goons for gunmen. If they saw a bunch of people working, and it wasn't one of their companies, they'd shoot a hole through the camera. Without the camera you couldn't work, and cameras were impossible to get. The reason we came to places like California was to get away from these goons. Around Chicago and New York, your life was in your hands if you went out with a camera. . . . And so we sneaked out to California and hid away in little places. We worked in areas where you could see everything around you, and we stationed sentinels."[13]

By 1915, 60 percent of U.S. produced films were made in Hollywood.[14]

Second, two significant legal actions put a halt to MPPC activities. The first of these was the Supreme Court ruling against the MPPC, invalidating its patent for the Latham Loop.[15] Then, in a final blow, in 1912, the U.S. government began proceedings against the MPPC, alleging that it was a trust operating in restraint of trade—in violation of the Sherman Antitrust Act[16]—

---

12. One of the first film companies to install itself in California was Selig in the winter of 1907-08. "Not only did the Selig staff appreciate the reliably good weather of Los Angeles, they also relished the distance from the subpoena servers constantly being dispatched by the lawyers hired by Edison Laboratories to initiate suits against producers" who were unwilling to pay "licensing and reel footage fees." Starr, *California*, pp. 274-275.

13. Filmmaker Allan Dwan, quoted in Brownlow, Kevin, *The War, The West, and The Wilderness*, Alfred A. Knopf, New York, 1979, p. 237.

14. Fellow, p. 219.

15. *See* discussion at Reel 1, The Edison Patent Cases.

16. The Sherman Antitrust Act, July 2, 1890, ch. 647, 26 Stat. 209, 15 U.S.C. §§ 1–7.

and the U.S. Supreme Court rendered its decision against the MPPC in 1918.

The MPPC defended itself in this latter action using a novel argument. Because the motion picture business was really that of dramatic representation and because dramatic representation was really "the practice of an art," the control of the movie industry was therefore "the control of an art and not of trade, or of anything, which is the subject of commerce." This was definitely the height of chutzpah from a group of businessmen who produced peep shows for the entertainment of working class immigrants in nickelodeons, strictly for profit. The Court was not fooled. It ruled that the motion picture industry was a business like any other and needed to be regulated and its activities judged as such.

The MPPC's second line of defense was, not surprisingly, its reliance on its patent rights. The Antitrust Act—which at the time was still in its infancy, having been enacted into law in 1897—did not repeal patent laws and the monopoly that those laws confer on inventors. The Court noted that patent laws do not give inventors the right to make, use, or sell the products of their inventions but rather they take away, for a limited time while the patent is in effect, the right that others might have to make, use, or sell the patented article. This was an important distinction.

The Court differentiated between the "monopoly" created by the patent laws—the exclusive right to make or sell a patented article—and the monopoly condemned by the antitrust laws. Rights under the patent law are those to make or sell or to withhold from sale, as well as the right to impose reasonable and legal conditions to the sale by others. The Court saw competition in business as a race, which all may enter and where anyone can, by exerting his powers, gain over the other competitors and win all the prizes. But he must do this without "unfair jostling or hampering of others." Where one of the competitors has a patent right, he may use it as any other form of property. But if he uses it as a weapon to disable a rival or to drive him from the field, he may not do so for any greater purpose "except to the extent of protecting his exclusive right."

In other words, the patent holder may enforce his exclusive rights but only in his "proper field of trade." He may not try to extend that field beyond what is proper by employing "unfair practices." In that respect, where business persons enter into agreements whose end is to preserve to the owners of the patent the exclusive sale of the patented article, with a *legal* intent to assert "proper control over sales to be made," this would not be condemned as a restraint of trade. But where the purpose of the agreement was to create "undue or unreasonable restraints of trade," then the fact that one or more of the persons who were parties to the agreement owned patents would not prevent a finding of a conspiracy to restrain trade.

The Court acknowledged that the MPPC members had a "noble" motive to "allay bickering and recriminations among themselves," and to improve the industry by their control over it, as well as to make money for themselves—something they frankly admitted. But, as the Court pointed out, the primary purpose of the MPPC was all-encompassing domination and control over all aspects of the motion picture business and in this respect the members had gone too far. There was not one aspect of the business that they did not influence. The Court noted that, by the time the government brought its case against the MPPC, only one independent film producer was left. Every theater was required to pay a royalty to the MPPC for the use of the projector in that theater, even if the machine had been owned by the exhibitor before the MPPC was formed. And the MPPC retained and exercised the power to recall any film acquired by an exhibitor if the MPPC determined that the exhibitor had violated the terms of its agreement.

To illustrate its point, the Court used an analogy from agriculture. The owner of a patent for a handle of a plow could acquire the rights to the rest of the plow design, or could enter into an agreement with the holder of the patent for the plow body, without fear of a violation of antitrust law. But this did not mean that a combination among the owners of the patents to all the plows, reapers, and other farm equipment, as well as the dealers in this equipment (who were not actual patent owners) for the purpose of monopolizing trade in agricultural products would be tolerated. Owning a patent in such a case would not be a defense to the charge of unlawful combination. The Court saw this to be the same for the motion picture business.

The Court would have been willing to uphold the MPPC members' right to enforce their patents if the combination had been limited and if their agreements had a real relation to the protection of their patent rights. But because their combination was so much broader, with the goal of asserting control over the entire motion picture industry, the Court determined that the MPPC placed an unreasonable restraint on trade and that the members' combination and agreements were therefore illegal.

By the time the Court rendered its decision against the MPPC, the situation had already changed, for two reasons. For one, a patent holder enjoyed a monopoly over the patented article for a limited time (at the time, seventeen years[17]) and by the time of the decision, many of the patents claimed by the MPPC had expired or were soon to expire. And second, the independent producers had already succeeded in their battle with the

---

17. In 1861, the term of a utility patent was extended to seventeen years, 12 Stat. 246, 249.

MPPC. While the MPPC members had busied themselves with protecting their narrow turf, churning out reliable one-reel films with predictable plots, the independents, along with foreign filmmakers, were creating quality feature-length movies, which would become the new standard.

In California, where many had relocated, they benefited from consistently good weather and open land, wide areas where they had a choice of shooting scenes on natural scenic locations near to their bases, or of constructing immense studio lots where they could install entire cities.[18] Moreover, these producers were able to capitalize on the talents of the recognizable performers that they featured in more than one film. It was the turn of these newly minted Hollywood moguls to lead the way to the next stage in the development of the motion picture industry. The studio system came into being and the star system was born. Hollywood now stood in place of Thomas Edison as the center of the motion picture industry.

---

18. Starr, *California*, pp. 274-275.

Part II

The Silent Era— 1915–1929

Risqué Films and Scandal in the Industry

In the years between the development of filmmaking equipment and the establishment of the Hollywood film empire, movies changed dramatically. Originally one-reel shorts, the films became more sophisticated, with complex plots, sympathetic characters, and artistic expression. The earliest motion pictures portrayed scenes of historic importance, such as Edison's popular film showing the launch of a yacht. Many early filmmakers borrowed heavily from vaudeville acts. Some of the earliest films of Charles Chaplin, Harold Lloyd, Buster Keaton, and Roscoe "Fatty" Arbuckle were not much more than comedic acts, acrobatic performances, and physical—so-called "slapstick"—comedies. Buster Keaton, for example, started as a child in a vaudeville act with his parents. Moving to film when he hooked up as a young man with Fatty Arbuckle in the late teens was a natural evolution.[1]

Many of these early movies had a familiar plot: Fatty, portraying a bumbling, yet well-meaning hero, is in love with an attractive young woman, who loves him back. But for various reasons, such as the hostility of a father or the actions of a rival, the romance is almost ruined by an interloper. Arbuckle, with the assistance of Keaton, manages to foil the rival, but only

---

1. Bourne, Mark, Review, "The Best Arbuckle/Keaton Collection," Image Entertainment, found at http://www.dvdjournal.com/reviews/b/bestarbucklekeaton.shtml, last accessed October 15, 2011.

after a series of more and more outrageous stunts, including pie throwing, back flips, and whackings with umbrellas, pans, lamps or whatever else is at hand. Arbuckle, meanwhile, is disguised in a woman's dress or perhaps garbed as a child (which defies any sense of reality given that he weighed 300 pounds, although he did have a cherubic face). The action finally culminates in a fight among the entire cast, with Arbuckle, amazingly light on his feet, doing acrobatics to the general amusement and amazement of the audience, while in the end saving the day and winning the girl.

Hollywood movies also evolved in other respects. Where early films were often suggestive "peep shows" with partially clothed women and virtually no plot, they became fully developed stories, perhaps melodramas and tragicomedies, with villains lashing young women to railroad tracks, only to be saved at the last minute by the hero. But by the beginning of the 1920s, movies had become full narratives and audiences could expect a wide range of entertainment from the feature films shown in their local movie parlors, whether romantic comedies, romances, serious dramas, westerns, or even tragedies.[2]

2. Starr, *California*, pp. 277-278.

Intermission 1

Scandals in Hollywood: Selling Movies and Hiding the Foibles of the Stars

The Progressive Era is distinguished as a period in American history where reformists believed that government could and should take measures to protect its citizens from harmful things. To the good, this era witnessed, for example, the enactment of food safety laws.[1] However, national Prohibition—in which the consumption of alcoholic beverages was banned in the entire country—was also a major accomplishment of that period.[2] Movies were another area where reformists saw a need for action.

By the early 1920s, Hollywood was the film capital of the world, its name to be emblazoned on the side of a hill for all to see.[3] Almost all movies made in the United States at the time were filmed or produced in Hollywood or its environs. The industry bolstered its reputation as the world leader by luring to Southern California some of the best actors and directors from Europe, such as Greta Garbo and Hedy Lamarr, and Ernst Lubitsch and Josef von Sternberg. Hollywood prided itself on the sheer number and variety of films that were produced there. Movies were at that time one of the most popular forms of mass entertainment. Hollywood motion pictures had evolved in a delicious way since the early days of the industry. They had become urbane and sophisticated. They exuded glamour, exoticism, and above all sex appeal. Prominent examples were the sex comedies and domestic dramas of Cecil B. DeMille, such as *For Better or Worse* (1919) and *Why Change Your Wife* (1920), presenting "adultery as a frivolous, even glamorous, pastime,"[4] and the sophisticated society comedies of Ernst Lubitsch, which were not overtly sexual but suggestive enough, with sexuality just beneath the surface, cleverly hidden by a veneer of politeness, and double entendres.[5] The most famous of these were *The Marriage Circle* (1924), *Lady Windermere's Fan* (1925) and *So This is Paris* (1926). Another producer of the time, Erich von

Intermission 1 (continued)

Stroheim, released *Blind Husbands* in 1919, treating a married woman's flirtation with another man as commonplace, if just a little risqué.[6]

These types of films—swashbuckling adventure films, romantic comedies with infidelity (or suspected infidelity) as a common theme, dramas showcasing the morals (or lack of) and manners of the rich, and "tales of flaming youth" discovering love in risqué settings—appealed to newly urbanized audiences.[7] These motion pictures were a reflection of the time, the Roaring Twenties, with "bootleg liquor, jazz music, flappers and wild parties."[8] And Hollywood created grand, plush movie palaces, whose decorations carried out themes of exotic locales such as ancient Egypt or China, in which to project their works.[9]

Hollywood was also the home of the stars—luminaries such as Rudolph Valentino and Mary Pickford, Douglas Fairbanks and Charles Chaplin. The fan culture in Hollywood developed early on and, in fact, even before the industry's decampment to Southern California.[10] Initially, the actors who performed in the earliest silent feature films did not receive screen credit, and received relatively low weekly wages. They were seen as expendable. But as audiences saw the same performers again and again, they started to demonstrate preferences for their favorites. Actors became "stars" and devoted audiences were their "fans." Because screen credits did not divulge the names of performers in the roles, the audiences provided them. For example, Florence Henderson, who was featured in a number of films directed by D.W. Griffith at Biograph, became known as the "Biograph Girl," in keeping with a quote from a contemporary film reviewer: "the chief honors of the picture are borne by the now famous Biograph Girl, who must be gratified by the silent celebrity she has received."[11]

Companies soon saw the value in exploiting this audience demand, using the stars to leverage publicity for their films. Movie studios "whetted" the appetites of fans for more new films by creating an image for their stars.[12] "Actors were larger than life on screen, . . . Publishers issued fan magazines to satisfy public curiosity about stars' likes, dislikes, hobbies and idiosyncrasies."[13] Movie magazines such as *Photoplay* were extremely popular, allowing fans to follow the daily lives of their favorite actors. Hollywood and its stars came to symbolize the '20s—the extravagance, the glamour, and the fun. Another film star of the time, Gloria Swanson, who was frequently cast in the sex comedies produced in the late 1910s and early 1920s by Cecil B. DeMille, such as *Male and Female* (1918) and *Why Change Your Wife* (1920), was representative of the glamorous Hollywood star. Representing the excesses of the period, Swanson was reputed to bathe in a solid gold bathtub.[14]

"The fabulous mansions of stars . . . with swimming pools, tennis courts, waterfalls, and private golf courses were the stuff of daydreams for countless moviegoers, who conflated 'real life' with 'the pictures.'"[15] Tom Mix, the famous silent film cowboy, was one of the most flamboyant of the stars, wearing patent leather boots and diamond-studded pants. He was representative of "an age that welcomed exaggeration . . . and adored unrestrained showmanship."[16] He put his name on top of his house in six-foot-high letters.[17] His press agent regularly put out autobiographical articles about his life that had a distant relationship with the truth, and "set no limit on their audience's gullibility."[18] "They're here for entertainment," Mix is quoted as saying, "So I give them a reel out of one of my pictures."[19] Allan Dwan, an early film producer, described how Mix took a train to New York, booking a private boxcar for his horse Tony. In New York, he rode the horse down Broadway, stopping traffic. Everyone loved it.[20]

Two still famous names stand out—Rudolph Valentino and Mary Pickford. Valentino came to fame in *The Four Horsemen of the Apocalypse* (1921), which chronicled the lives of a South American family during World War I. Valentino played the romantic lead, that of the doomed lover, and became an instant star. He was signed by Paramount and cast as the "Latin Lover" in a number of popular films, including *Blood and Sand* (1922). Hundreds of grief-stricken fans flocked to his funeral when he died prematurely in 1926.[21]

Mary Pickford had a more lasting fame. She was known as

Intermission 1 (continued)

America's sweetheart. And she was one of the few movie actors of her generation to be able to capitalize on her popularity to gain a fortune as well.[22] Fans filled the movie houses to see her films. She was known as the "girl with the golden curls."[23] Born Gladys Louise Smith in 1892 in Toronto, Canada, she went to New York at age fifteen hoping to perform on Broadway. Unable to break into the New York theatrical world, at the suggestion of a stage producer, she opted for the last resort for serious actors of her day—moving pictures. Hoping that this would be a short interlude before she could make it on Broadway, she approached the most successful movie director of the time, D.W. Griffith, for a job acting in a film he was making for Biograph. She was soon identified as the new "Biograph Girl"[24] with a beginning salary of $100 per week. She quickly doubled that while at Biograph, because of her growing popularity. She left a short time later and, by moving from company to company, she was soon making ten times her original salary. In 1916, she went to work for Adolph Zukor's Famous Players, where in just three years, she had her own production unit where she shared creative control with Zukor. In 1919, she joined with two of the most popular actors of the day, Douglas Fairbanks and Charles Chaplin, and the director, D.W. Griffith, to form a new movie studio, United Artists.[25]

In 1920, she and Fairbanks married to the great happiness of their fans. They were the queen and king of Hollywood—the world's first international superstars. Their "castle" was Pickfair, a large hilltop estate in Beverly Hills, a wedding gift from Fairbanks to his new wife. It was what California historian Kevin Starr called "the White House of Hollywood: the very essence of glamor and respectability (as envisioned in the movie kingdom)."[26] He has noted that "an entire generation of aspiring middle-class Americans took its cues in the matter of domestic living from what Mary Pickford and Douglas Fairbanks were up to at Pickfair."[27]

On stage and offstage, Hollywood fostered a myth of elegance, of material success, and its stars exemplified the dreams of many Americans. They were adored. But one aspect of the myth that Hollywood struggled to maintain, to keep polished, was that these stars in their personal lives were just as pure and wholesome as they seemed in their public personas, with solid reputations and good family lives. This was a reputation that Hollywood publicists worked overtime to maintain. And their task was not easy. For behind the scenes, the lifestyles of industry moguls and performers were often less than upright. Over the decade, Hollywood was rocked with scandals that showed less palatable aspects of these peoples' lives, including sex scandals, murder charges, alcoholism, and corruption. In this atmosphere, film producers found it harder and harder to hide behind the wholesome façade that they had built for their stars.

Mary Pickford, idolized by her public, childlike on stage, with tumbling curls, bright eyes, and sweet manners, illustrated the dichotomy. When she married the film hero, Douglas Fairbanks, the couple's fame knew no bounds. They were the perfect couple, even though, away from the public eye, they had engaged in a torrid affair while still married to their first spouses. In 1917, the couple, accompanied by Charles Chaplin, toured the country, drumming up support for the war effort by selling Liberty Bonds, while all the while hiding their illicit relationship from the public. In 1920, after quietly divorcing their respective spouses, they married and everyone seemed to overlook that small detail, at least until Fairbanks strayed again—this time into the arms of a British socialite, Lady Sylvia Ashley. After starring together in a disastrous production of *The Taming of the Shrew* (1929), Pickford and Fairbanks separated, retired from acting, and finally divorced in 1936.

Divorce was not the worst of the scandals that lurked beneath the surface in Hollywood and that occasionally erupted and were met with public outcry against a corrupt industry. William Desmond Taylor, a director, was found murdered under suspicious circumstances that revealed affairs with well-known actresses.[28] Actor Wallace Reid killed himself in 1923 and it was widely rumored that his death was due to a drug overdose.[29] Nothing, however, compared with the case of Roscoe "Fatty" Arbuckle,

Intermission 1 (continued)

who was accused of raping and murdering a movie starlet following a raucous party in a hotel room in San Francisco.[30]

The sensationalized murder trial of Arbuckle was fuel for a fire that was already burning. The public increasingly saw Hollywood as a place of excess and decadence. Reformers demanded that the movie business clean up its problems or risk outside regulation, much as the alcoholic beverage industry had come to be regulated by Prohibition in 1919. Rather than risk this outcome, Hollywood moguls decided to self regulate, forming the Motion Picture Producers and Distributors of America (MPPDA) in 1922, bringing in William Hays, then postmaster general under President Harding and an elder in the Presbyterian Church, to clean up the industry. Hays used pressure tactics to convince film producers to remove offensive content from their movies and to insert "morals clauses" in their contracts with actors. Even though Roscoe Arbuckle was acquitted of the charges against him, Hays nevertheless ordered that his films be banned.[31] Hays instituted the "Formula," a vague list of "Don'ts and Be Carefuls," which eventually was replaced in the early 1930s with the Production Code.[32] This established production standards under which henceforth movies were to be made. Called the "Hays Code," or simply, the "Code," it would change the nature of filmmaking in Hollywood for almost half a century.

But the movement toward Code enforcement was slow to come, even then. With the stock market crash of 1929 and the onslaught of the Great Depression, filmmakers, facing a harsh economic environment, turned to the two commodities that sold in good times and in bad—sex and violence. To keep audiences in their theaters, they put aside for the time being thoughts of self-regulation.

1. See Robertson, Carol, *The Little Book of Coffee Law*, Chapter Three: "I Like My Coffee Fully Leaded— Adulterated Coffee."

2. Ratified in 1919 by Constitutional Amendment, repealed in 1932 by the 21st Amendment. *See* Robertson, Carol, *The Little Red Book of Wine Law*, Case 2: "When is Wine Not a Beverage?"

3. Hollywood, located to the east of downtown Los Angeles in the foothills of

the Santa Monica Mountains, became a mecca for studio moguls. Starr, *California*, p. 176.

4. Thompson & Bordwell, p. 146.

5. Thompson & Bordwell, pp. 158-159.

6. Thompson & Bordwell, p. 146.

7. Starr, *California*, p. 278.

8. Thompson & Bordwell, p. 146. *See also*, "Hollywood History: American Film in the Silent Era," found at http://web.viu.ca/davies/HollywoodAsHistory.htm.

9. Friedman, Nancy, *Art of the State: California*, Harry N. Abrams, Inc., New York, 1998, p. 98.

10. Thompson & Bordwell, p. 41.

11. Thompson & Bordwell, p. 41, quoting Gunning, Tom, "D.W. Griffith and the Origins of the American Narrative Film: The Early Years at Biograph," Urbana: University of Illinois Press, 1991, pp. 219-220.

12. Thompson & Bordwell, p. 132.

13. The American Experience, PBS, Mary Pickford, found at http://www.pbs.org/wgbh/amex/pickford/peopleevents/e_fans.html.

14. Digital History, *Hollywood As History*, "The Rise of Hollywood and the Arrival of Sound," site developed through collaborative partnership of the University of Houston, Chicago Historical Society, The Gilder Lehrman Institute of American History, et. al., found at http://www.digitalhistory.uh.edu/historyonline/hollywood_history.cfm#rise, last accessed November 2, 2011.

15. Friedman, p. 98.

16. Brownlow, p. 301.

17. Digital History, *Hollywood As History*

18. Brownlow, p. 301.

19. Told to Brownlow by Yakima Canutt, the silent film stuntman, quoted in Brownlow, p. 301.

20. Brownlow, p. 309.

21. Thompson & Bordwell, p. 150.

22. Mary Pickford and Charles Chaplin were making thousands, even tens of thousands of dollars a week by the 1920s. Thompson & Bordwell, p. 73.

23. The American Experience, PBS, Mary Pickford, found at http://www.pbs.org/wgbh/amex/pickford/peopleevents/p_pickford.html.

24. The American Experience, PBS, Mary Pickford, found at http://www.pbs.org/wgbh/amex/pickford/peopleevents/p_pickford.html.

25. Starr, *California*, p. 277.

26. Starr, *California*, p. 277.

27. Starr, *Inventing the Dream: California Through the Progressive Era*, Oxford University Press, 1986, p. 337.

28. Starr, *Inventing the Dream*, pp. 327-328.

29. Thompson & Bordwell, p. 146.

30. Starr, *Inventing the Dream*, pp. 325-326. *See* Intermission 12: The Arbuckle Case: Sex and Crime in 1920s Hollywood.

31. "Adolph Zukor decided to cut his losses. Impounding a million dollars' worth of Arbuckle comedies already filmed, Zukor ordered Arbuckle blacklisted from any further work." Starr, *Inventing the Dream*, p. 327.

32. Thompson & Bordwell, pp. 146-47.

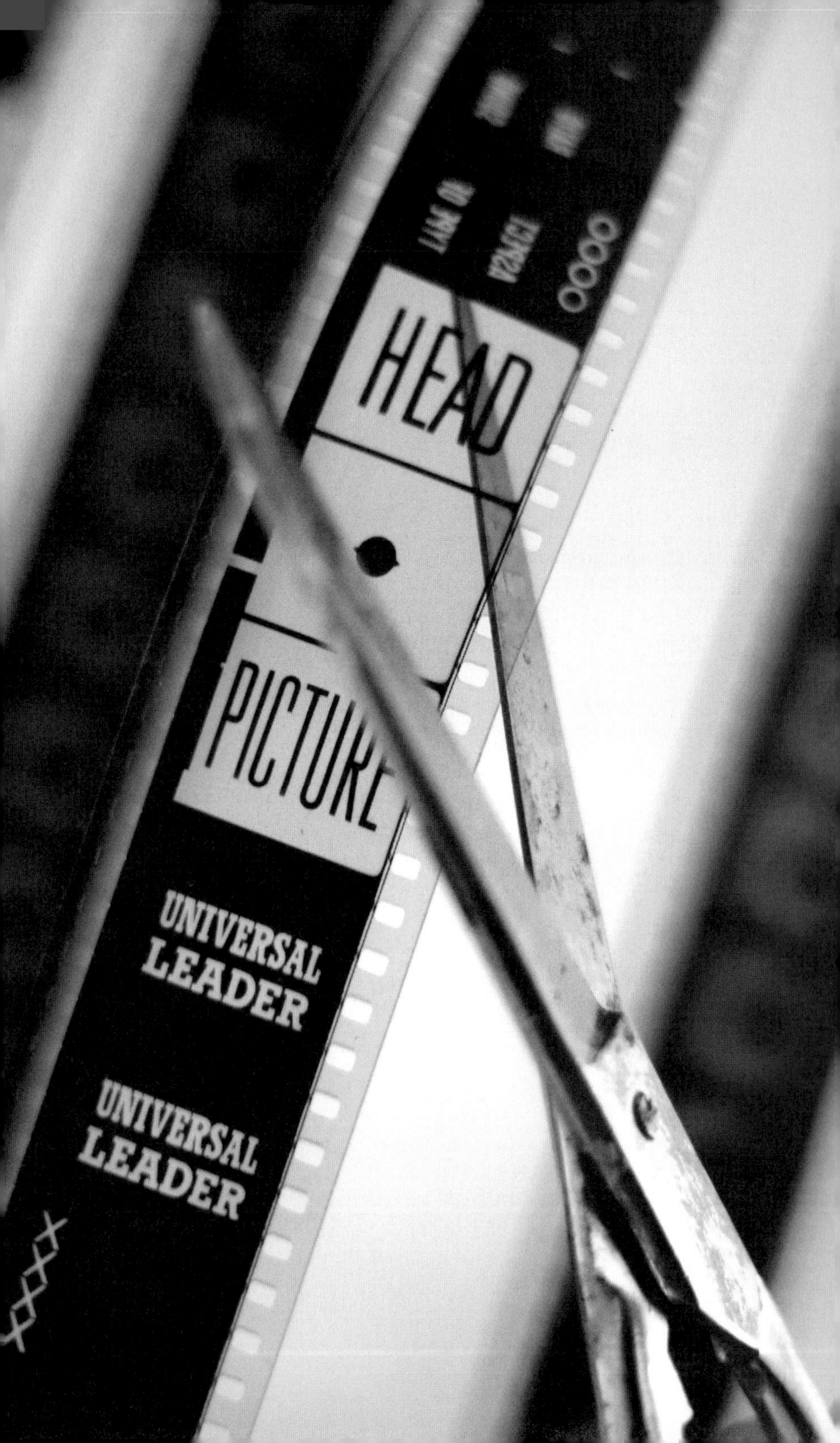
HEAD
PICTURE
UNIVERSAL
LEADER
UNIVERSAL
LEADER

This Film Is Not Yet Rated
Censorship of Movies

Mutual Film Corporation v. Industrial Commission of Ohio, 236 U.S. 230 (1915)

> **Harold Hill: Mothers of River City, heed that warning before it's too late! Watch for the telltale signs of corruption! The minute your son leaves the house, does he rebuckle his knickerbockers below the knee? Is there a nicotine stain on his index finger? A dime-novel hidden in the corncrib? Is he starting to memorize jokes from Captain Billy's Whiz-Bang? Are certain words creeping into his conversation? Words like "swell" and "so's your old man"? If so my friends, ya got trouble!"**
>
> Robert Preston as Professor Harold Hill,
> from *The Music Man* (1962)

O ne subject of debate that came up frequently in the early days of the cinema was the purpose of movies: were they merely entertainment without serious social benefit, were they a form of artistic expression, were they a form of social commentary and thus a necessary benefit to society, or, finally, were they some combination of all of these? In connection with this debate, a strong desire to control an industry that up to then had been able to flourish without significant restriction in terms of content became prevalent. The very ambivalent view that people had of movies led to efforts at censorship.[1]

---

1. Thompson & Bordwell, p. 40.

As early as 1908, the mayor of New York closed down all of the city's nickelodeons, which religious groups viewed as evil places where young people could be led astray.[2] The cinema became a cultural battlefield. In 1907, Chicago, for example, established one of the first censorship boards.[3] A censorship board was created in New York City in 1909 by a group of concerned citizens. The group called itself the National Board of Censorship.[4] Pennsylvania enacted its law in 1911; Ohio and Kansas followed in 1914, and Maryland in 1916.[5]

Censorship under state laws worked generally in this manner: film distributors would submit a copy of the movie and its script to the local review board, accompanied by the required fee. Then they would have to wait until the board had reached its decision and issued a license for exhibition. Although some censors were diligent and advised the distributors of their decision within a short time after the submittal, others took their time. This aggravated distributors tremendously, for they had no idea when a film could be premiered in a given state, or if it would be allowed to be shown at all. This created a logistical as well as a financial burden.[6]

In the 1910s and 1920s, two methods were used to distribute films. The first was via a nationwide release at the same time. Film producers licensed a print of the film to a local distributor for certain regions (usually larger than a single state). It was

---

2. "Movies, because of their mass appeal, their attractiveness, and their influence, were believed to hold 'a special capacity for evil,' an ability to sway people in ways unimaginable in older media. Because of the potential for harm, both the public and the legal culture had no problem accepting that movies needed and deserved prior restraint." Wittern-Keller, Laura, and Haberski, Raymond, *The Miracle Case: Film Censorship and the Supreme Court*, University Press of Kansas, 2008, p. 17.

3. Wittern-Keller & Haberski, p.12.

4. Thompson & Bordwell, p. 40.

5. Wittern-Keller & Haberski, p.16.

6. Wittern-Keller & Haberski, p.17.

the custom for film producers to release all prints of a film in all theaters on the same day, known as the release day. By doing so, because the films had never been shown to the public before that day, the appeal of the film was greater. This print would be shown in theaters in a particular region until it fell apart. For more expensive feature-length films, producers preferred a "road show" release, because it was more lucrative. For these, producers would enter into formal agreements with theater owners—usually those of the more upscale theaters where the ticket prices were higher. After the road show exhibition was completed, the producers would schedule a second release in a wider range of markets. Most producers chose a combination of both methods in order to maximize profits.[7] But whichever method was used, the desire of the distributors for a uniform release date was frustrated by the whims of local censors.

In 1913, Mutual Film Company, a regional film distributor in three Midwest states, began a campaign to overturn film censorship statutes. Mutual Film bought, sold, and leased films produced in states other than Ohio, as well as European and other internationally produced motion pictures. At the time it brought its case, it had at least 2,500 reels of films that it had intended to exhibit in Ohio and elsewhere which had been impossible to do because they were tied up with the Board of Censors in Ohio. The company argued that it was physically impossible for the censors to review and approve all of these films quickly enough to enable the company to do its business and that the delays limited its ability to make a profit.

Ohio's statute, enacted in 1913, was similar to many of the others in the country. It formed a board of censors whose duty was to review and approve all films intended to be exhibited.

7. The American Experience, People & Events: The Business of Movies, found at http://www.pbs.org/wgbh/amex/pickford/peopleevents/e_business.html.

The board also had the power to arrest anyone who showed a film that had not been approved in the state. Mutual Film argued that these laws infringed on its First Amendment right of freedom of expression.[8] At the time, courts had little sympathy for filmmakers' arguments on these grounds. Even though in other contexts attempts to censor newspapers or literary expression might have been deemed to be unconstitutional, movies were not viewed in the same light. They were perceived to be special—to be an almost hypnotic form of entertainment, without any redeeming artistic or literary merit. Predictably, Mutual Film lost its case in the lower courts and the matter was brought before the U.S. Supreme Court.

At the Supreme Court, Mutual Film had essentially three arguments. First, that the statute imposed an intolerable burden on interstate commerce. Second, that it violated Mutual Film's freedom of speech under the Ohio constitution (which provided similar protection to that in the U.S. Constitution). Third, that it delegated legislative power to an unelected board of censors.

The Supreme Court's decision against Mutual Film Corporation was unanimous. On the first point, the Court gave very short shrift to the argument that the law placed an unreasonable burden on interstate commerce. According to the Court, because the films were to be exhibited in Ohio and the law only sought to regulate films "to be publicly exhibited and displayed" in that state, it had no impact on the exhibition of films in other states. And even if there was a burden, because of the special character of movies, regulation was not unreasonable. As Justice McKenna stated, because movies could "be used for evil," examining them prior to showing them seemed to be a necessary control. As he said, "[t]heir power of amusement, and it

---

8. Wittern-Keller & Haberski, p.26.

may be, education, the audiences they assemble, not of women alone nor of men alone, but together, not of adults only, but of children, make them the more insidious in corruption by a pretense of worthy purpose. . . . There are some things which should not have pictorial representation in public places and to all audiences." He concluded, "We would want to shut our eyes to the facts of the world to regard the precaution unreasonable or the legislation to effect it a mere wanton interference with personal liberty."

The Court also perfunctorily dismissed the delegation of legislative power argument. Mutual Film had argued that because the statute had provided no standard for what is "educational" or "moral" or "harmless," the decision was left to the "arbitrary judgment, whim and caprice" of the individual unelected censors. The Court disagreed. Although these terms could be considered to be vague, they gained precision and meaning "from the sense and experience of men."

Likewise, the Court rejected the notion that movies should be entitled to free speech rights, much like a newspaper or a book. They were, Justice McKenna stated flatly, "a business pure and simple, originated and conducted for profit . . . not to be regarded, . . . we think, as part of the press of the country or as organs of public opinion." It is worth noting that, at the time, no one in the film industry would have considered a free speech argument as viable. Few would have thought to try to convince the Court that there was any intellectual or artistic value in films.

Although the result in this case, and the fact that it was a unanimous decision of the nine Justices, might surprise many people today, accustomed as we are to a Court that affords broad individual rights, including free speech, to businesses and corporations, most people of the era in which the *Mutual*

Film Corporation case was decided would likely have agreed with the decision. Not only did no one, including most film-makers, view a movie as a work of art at the time, most would have agreed with the Court that moviemaking was a business, "pure and simple." Moreover, Americans were then accustomed to seeing censorship in plays and other theatrical productions. Commercial speech had no First Amendment protection nor did anyone expect that it should. This case was much in sync with that historic period. In the Progressive Era (between the late 1990s and into the 1920s), engaged citizen groups felt very much entitled to actively regulate human behavior—whether it was the days of the week when people could shop (leading to Sunday closing laws), what they drank (bringing about National Prohibition of alcoholic beverages), or the films that they watched.

The amazing thing about the *Mutual Film Corporation* decision was that it endured, far outlasting the era in which it was decided. If it represented a rational approach to censorship of the film industry at the beginning of the twentieth century, it nevertheless played a very restrictive role in the development of that industry over the next forty years. Long after movies came to be appreciated as works of art and commentaries on society and human nature, the courts continued to uphold the efforts of sometimes very parochial film censors to restrict and control their exhibition. It was not until the 1950s—in a very different social and political time—that the Supreme Court was willing to reconsider the issues that were raised in the *Mutual Film Corporation* case.

Intermission 2

The Arbuckle Case: Sex and Crime in 1920s Hollywood

At the height of the Roaring Twenties, Hollywood was rocked with a sex and crime scandal that has since become a legend in Hollywood history—the Arbuckle case. No one better illustrates the ephemeral nature of Hollywood fame than Roscoe "Fatty" Arbuckle, who went from being one of the most popular and well-paid actors in Hollywood history to public disgrace in a matter of days, when he was arrested for the rape and murder of a movie starlet in a room at the St. Francis Hotel in San Francisco.[1]

Arbuckle started in vaudeville as a child and by the time he reached his twenties, he was a famous performer in early cinema, generally in outlandish slapstick comedies.[2] His stardom was amazing for he was seriously overweight—weighing between 250 and 300 pounds for most of his adult life—yet surprisingly graceful and agile. He was known for his great flexibility as a performer. Because of his weight, he was called Fatty, a nickname that he detested.[3] From 1914 on, he created, produced, and directed the comedies in which he starred. By 1919 he was at the apex of his career. In 1919, he accepted a $1 million per year contract for six feature films at Paramount.[4]

Exhausted after making three films in rapid succession, in 1921, Arbuckle was persuaded to join a party at the St. Francis Hotel in San Francisco, complete with starlets and "bathtub gin" (illegal alcohol—this occurred during Prohibition). Several days after the drunken revelry at the hotel, one of the partygoers, a movie starlet named Virginia Rappe, died from acute peritonitis. Several supposed eye witnesses accused Arbuckle of rape and manslaughter in connection with the death and he was arrested. From then on he was the subject of a frenetic media circus, where local newspapers were fed scraps of information from unscrupulous prosecutors. The horde was led by William Randolph Hearst. Hearst whipped up a public frenzy against

Intermission 2 (continued)

Arbuckle to sell newspapers and filled his columns with lurid, largely invented "details" about the case.[5] The news of Arbuckle's arrest shocked the country. Theater owners pulled his films[6] and Paramount suspended his contract.

The facts were something different and more mundane than the press made them out to be. According to Arbuckle's testimony, Miss Rappe left the room where everyone was assembled and it was only some time later that Arbuckle found her on the bathroom floor of his suite. Thinking that she was just severely inebriated, he said he helped her to the bed and called hotel officials for assistance.[7] She was taken to a hospital and died several days later. The eye witness against Arbuckle, Maude Delmont, had a history of setting up famous rich men with young women for blackmail. When the young woman would accuse the man of rape, Delmont would demand money in exchange for an agreement on the part of the accuser to keep silent.[8] With Arbuckle, things went wrong when Rappe died, possibly from an overdose of illegal gin. Delmont then went to the police and made her accusations against Arbuckle.

Arbuckle was also caught up in the political ambitions of the San Francisco district attorney, Matthew Brady, who was planning a run for higher office. He pushed forward with a murder trial, despite the unreliability of his main witness against Arbuckle, Delmont.[9] Arbuckle was tried three times. The first trial, on November 15, 1921, turned into a media circus. Delmont was unable to testify because of a prior arrest for bigamy. The jury hung, with an 11-1 vote for acquittal. The lone holdout juror later stated that she had made up her mind before the trial began and was unwilling to change her mind, despite the weakness of the prosecution's case. Because his attorneys were so certain he would be cleared at the second trial, held in January 1922, they did not have Arbuckle testify. This was a mistake—the vote was 10-2 for conviction. The final trial took place in March and April 1922. The jury returned its not guilty verdict in six minutes and publicly apologized to Arbuckle for the harassment he had suffered at the hands of the media and the prosecutors.[10] Arbuckle was acquitted but his career was in ruins.

In a personal statement given after the first trial, Arbuckle said, "My only connection with this sad affair was one of merciful service, and the fact that ordinary human kindness should have brought upon me this tragedy has seemed a cruel wrong. I have sought to bring joy and gladness and merriment into the world."[11] Just two years after signing his big deal with Paramount, Arbuckle was no longer a viable star. He became, as he called it, the "goat," the symbol of everything the outraged nation saw as wrong with Hollywood.[12] Even after his acquittal, doubts remained about his innocence. Several years before, a similar charge of rape had been leveled against Arbuckle from events that allegedly occurred at a Boston party. Rumor was that studio heads managed to quash it. Arbuckle himself obliquely referred to the incident in a letter to Joseph Schenck, a friend and the producer of some of his earlier films. "Tell Mr. Zukov," he wrote, "before passing judgment to remember the Boston party. He knows what a shakedown is. .."[13]

---

1. To this day, tour guides in San Francisco point out the hotel as the place where Fatty Arbuckle was accused of murdering a young woman after a night of carousing.

2. "Biography: The Life Story of Roscoe 'Fatty' Arbuckle," found at http://www.callmefatty.com/id2.html, last accessed December 7, 2010.

3. Ibid.

4. Ibid.

5. *See* http://www.callmefatty.com/id14.html, last accessed December 7, 2010. The headlines in San Francisco newspapers tried and convicted him before he ever set foot in court. On September 10, 1921, only five days after the party, for example, the *San Francisco Bulletin* boasted this headline "'Get Roscoe,' Dying Girl's Last Words." In the body of the story, the paper claimed that Arbuckle had called her a "bum," asserting that he didn't even know who she was. "Arbuckle Quiz in Girl's Death," *The Bulletin*, September 10, 1921, found at http://www.callmefatty.com/id16.html, last accessed December 7, 2010.

6. In Medford, Massachusetts, for example, the town's mayor notified motion picture houses that Arbuckle films were barred. In Memphis, Tennessee, the Board of Censors revoked its permission to show Arbuckle films until he had cleared himself of all charges. "Many Towns Place Ban on Arbuckle Movies," *The Bulletin*, September 12, 1921, found at http://www.callmefatty.com/id20.html, last accessed December 7, 2010.

Intermission 2 (continued)

7. "Arbuckle's Side of the Story," found at http://www.callmefatty.com/id11.html, last accessed December 10, 2010.

8. "World of Criminal Justice." 2 vols. Gale Group. (2002.), quoted in "The Case Against Arbuckle," found at http://www.callmefatty.com/id12.html, last accessed December 7, 2010.

9. "The Case Against Arbuckle," found at http://www.callmefatty.com/id12.html, last accessed December 7, 2010.

10. Ibid. "Acquittal is not enough for Roscoe Arbuckle. We feel that a great injustice has been done him. We feel also that it was only our plain duty to give him this exoneration, under the evidence, for there was not the slightest proof adduced to connect him in any way with the commission of a crime." Quoted in "The Trials of Roscoe 'Fatty' Arbuckle," found at http://www.callmefatty.com/id10.html, last accessed December 7, 2010.

11. *Movie Weekly*, December 31, 1921, quoted in "Arbuckle's Side of the Story," found at http://www.callmefatty.com/id11.html, last accessed December 7, 2010.

12. Arbuckle never rose to the same level of fame although he was gradually able to reenter the movie business. On the cusp of signing a new contract with Warner Brothers, he died in his sleep at the age of 46. "Biography: The Life Story of Roscoe 'Fatty' Arbuckle," found at http://www.callmefatty.com/id2.html, last accessed December 7, 2010.

13. Academy of Motion Picture Arts & Sciences, Margaret Herrick Library, Zukor file, "Correspondence," found at "Arbuckle's Side of the Story," http://www.callmefatty.com/id11.html, last accessed December 7, 2010

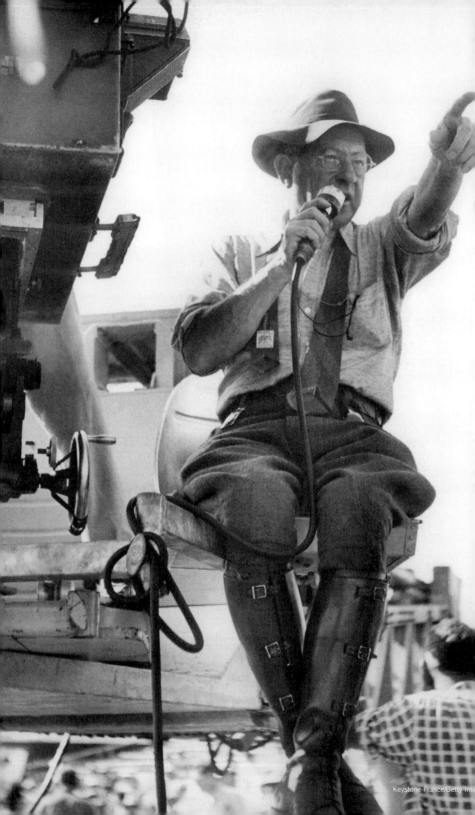

A Star Is Born

Goudal v. DeMille Pictures Corp.,
118 Cal. App. 407, 5 P. 2d 432 (2d Dist. 1931)

All right, Mr. DeMille, I'm ready for my close-up.

Gloria Swanson, playing Norma Desmond,
from *Sunset Boulevard* (1950)

From the time he first arrived in Los Angeles in late 1913 to film the western, *The Squaw Man* (1914), Cecil Blount DeMille had a reputation as an exacting and tyrannical director.[1] He wore military-style outfits, including jodhpurs and riding boots, with a directing style "like a general on campaign."[2] He was quoted telling a new assistant, while welcoming him to his private bungalow on the Paramount set, that "the floor slants down and to the left. I'm placing you in the left side office at the end of the hall, so you can watch the heads as they roll by." He is reputed to have told a film crew: "You are here to please me. Nothing else on earth matters."[3] He was also known for projecting glamorous actresses into sophisticated roles that launched and sustained their careers, until they ceased to be beautiful and glamorous, at which time he jettisoned them. Gloria Swanson was a case in point—she was considered one of the top stars in Hollywood and she owed her fame to DeMille, but she was also embittered by her fall from grace.[4]

---

1. Starr, *California*, p. 275-276.
2. Starr, *California*, p. 276.
3. Internet Movie Database, Cecil B. DeMille Biography, Trivia, found at http://www.imdb.com/name/nm0001124/bio#trivia, last accessed July 1, 2011.
4. Gloria Swanson played the role of the aging diva in 1950 in Billy Wilder's *Sunset Boulevard*, in which DeMille makes a brief appearance playing himself, as her former director.

One silent film star who learned of DeMille's tyranny the hard way was Jetta Goudal. She was a successful silent film star who, like Charley Chase, is known only to the most ardent film buffs today.[5] Yet, in the 1920s, she was an acclaimed box office draw, the star of several successful DeMille films. Born Juliette Henriette Goudeket, she was a European stage actress who left war-torn Europe in 1918 and settled in New York, aspiring to perform on Broadway. She shortened her name and gave herself a French ancestry to make herself more attractive to New York audiences, calling herself Jetta Goudal. Before long, she became part of the nascent film industry and headed west to Hollywood, where she appeared in several financially and critically success-ful films at Paramount—*Open All Night* (1924) and *Salome of the Tenements* (1925). When her contract with Paramount was cancelled, she signed a one-year contract with DeMille in May 1925, giving DeMille an option of four yearly extensions of the contract term, which he exercised twice. Two films that she made with DeMille—*White Gold* and *The Forbidden Woman*—were selected by the National Board of Review as among the best films of 1927.[6]

Despite her success as an actress, she butted heads with DeMille too frequently. She insisted on portraying her roles as she thought best and this temperament conflicted with the pro-ducer's absolutist approach to filmmaking. He tolerated her for a time—largely because of her skill and popularity—but finally,

---

5. Charley Chase is respected as a "great" of silent films by silent film fans. In the early days of the cinema, he was a very successful actor, appearing in comedies with Charles Chaplin and Roscoe Arbuckle, and as the star of memorable one-reel films produced by the Hal Roach Studios, directed by Leo McCarey, in the late 1910s and early 1920s. Among his most memorable films are *Mighty Like a Moose* (1926), *Crazy Like a Fox* (1926), and *Movie Night* (1929). Internet Movie Database, Charley Chase (1893-1940) found at http://www.imdb.com/name/nm0153713/, last accessed July 1, 2011.

6. Internet Movie Database, Jetta Goudal Biography, found at www.imdb.com/name/nm0332135/bio, last accessed December 15, 2011.

citing her "temperamental" outbursts on the set that delayed production and, as DeMille claimed, cost the studio "thousands," he terminated her contract early, in September 1927.

Goudal sued in California Superior Court, arguing that DeMille had wrongfully terminated the contract. The trial court determined that Goudal had not breached her contract and that her discharge was not justified. She was awarded $34,531.23 in damages. DeMille appealed.

DeMille argued that Goudal had refused to perform her parts as requested by the directors. This argument was based on many incidents that he claimed had occurred during filming, where Goudal, instead of unquestioningly performing as directed, called attention to inconsistencies and possible improvements in the performance that was called for, as it appeared to her. In some cases, this resulted in a change being made by the director without argument. In other cases, the change was made after some argument between them. In many instances, when the director did not make the requested change, it appeared that Goudal took the question up with DeMille himself, and many times, in fact "in a substantial number of cases," according to the court, he agreed with her and ordered that the changes be made. Sometimes, however, he disagreed. DeMille argued that this behavior by Goudal was a refusal to perform her parts as required by the contract.

Was Goudal compelled by the contract to go through her scenes "as a mere puppet responding to the director's pull of the strings, regardless of whether he pulled the right or wrong string"? the court asked. Or did the contract require her to "give an artistic interpretation of her scenes, using her intelligence, experience, artistry, and personality to the ultimate end of securing a production of dramatic merit"? By its phrasing of the questions, the court provided the answers: a film actor was not to be treated as a "mere puppet." The court expressed its belief that, by suggesting ways to improve scenes, "when made in good faith," Goudal was only acting in the interest of the employer. It appeared from the testimony at trial that DeMille welcomed Goudal's interventions and, in fact, in many instances encouraged them. At the commencement of her contract, DeMille apparently informed Goudal that "he did not want mannequins to work for him," that he "wanted thinking people" in his films, and that "if she would explain to him why she wanted to do a thing in a particular way, he would appreciate it." And by the facts he apparently had allowed her great leeway in this respect, until one day he did not.

DeMille also claimed that there was unexcused tardiness and that her behavior had caused numerous and costly production delays. However, the instances that DeMille brought up at trial all had explanations and, the court believed, were not at all Goudal's fault. In fact, one instance was explained by the fact that DeMille had failed to deliver a script to Goudal. The court noted also that most of the alleged breaches occurred before May 1927, when DeMille for the second time had notified Goudal that he was extending her contract for another year, and after Goudal had completed filming seven of the eight movies that she had agreed to make for DeMille.

The court expressed its disbelief at the disparity between DeMille's argument that Goudal had persistently breached the contract with the studio's unilateral decision, after all those breaches supposedly occurred, to turn around and "voluntarily avail itself" of its option to renew Goudal's contract for another year. It was, the court said, "difficult to reconcile as sincere." If DeMille was so dissatisfied with Goudal prior to May 1927, as he asserted he was, then why on earth did he exercise his option and secure her services for another year? This was even more curious, the court noted, when under a new contract provision voluntarily inserted by DeMille, Goudal was to earn $39,000 more than she had earned during the prior year. The court saw the exercise of the option as a confirmation by DeMille that, contrary to his assertions at trial, he was satisfied with Goudal's performance and did not believe her to be in breach.

Moreover, the court noted, the contract that Goudal had signed was for personal services of a "special, unique . . . extraordinary and intellectual character," to be rendered "conscientiously," and "artistically." The court found "sincere efforts by the artist to secure an artistic interpretation of the play," which could easily, as the court saw it, "involve the suggestion of changes" that, even if "insistently presented," would not amount to willful disobedience and, in fact, could be viewed as compliance with the contract requirements.

The court concluded that Goudal had not refused to perform and that there had been no willful misconduct on her part.

DeMille had also tried to prevent Goudal from recovering damages by arguing that, after her discharge, she should have sought other employment. But the trial court had already taken that factor into account when it deducted $3,000 from her recovery to account for the fact that, after January 1, 1928, she should have known that she was not going to be rehired by DeMille and should have sought other work. Given this, the appellate court saw no reason to overturn the calculations of the trial court.

Although Goudal won her case against DeMille, in a sense winning this battle caused her to lose the war. She had had the temerity to sue an important movie mogul. And she had been active in the work of the newly formed actors' union, Actors' Equity, in its goal of forcing the industry to accept a closed shop (could this have been DeMille's real reason for firing her?). These two marks against her caused many Hollywood studios to steer clear of Goudal after the lawsuit was decided. It may also be that her foreign accent, which would not have been a factor in silent pictures, prevented her from obtaining roles in talkies (although this did not impede the careers of other foreign stars such as Marlene Dietrich or Greta Garbo, who both easily made the transition into talking films). In any event, after 1928, Goudal's film appearances were limited. In an era where stars appeared in multiple movies in a given year, Goudal only had one role—in *The Cardboard Lover*, produced by William Randolph Hearst and Marion Davies—in 1928 and in 1929, she made only *Lady of the Pavements*, directed by D.W. Griffith. In 1930, Jacques Feyder directed Goudal in her only French language film, *Le Spectre Vert*. In 1932, she made her last film appearance, starring with Will Rogers in *Business and Pleasure*. She then pursued other interests until her death in 1985.

Despite the fact that no one other than serious silent film fans may know who Jetta Goudal is today, she is famous among legal scholars who know her as the actress who took on the legendary Cecil B. DeMille. But even though she does not have the current following she may deserve, she nevertheless has a star on the Hollywood Walk of Fame on Hollywood Boulevard— a testament to the time when she was not obscure; she was a star.

Intermission 3

Silent Stars in Hollywood: Famous Actors Attract Followers

It seems to be the case that whenever a movie actor becomes a "star," he or she attracts fans and would-be writers who offer the actor a great idea for a movie. Since the silent era, this has been a problem, afflicting even two of the greatest stars of that era—Charles Chaplin and Harold Lloyd.

The Little Tramp as Hitler

Charles Chaplin was in his time one of the most powerful actors and filmmakers in Hollywood. He was famous for his comedic timing, his creativity, and, of course, for his "Little Tramp" character, which he debuted in American cinema in 1914, and which has been called "the best-known comedic figure of the twentieth century."[1] Chaplin was born in London, England. Orphaned at ten, he became a vaudeville performer to survive. On a United States' tour in 1912, he was given a film contract with Mack Sennett, director of the Keystone Studios.[2] Immediately popular with American audiences, winning their hearts as the hard luck but dignified Little Tramp, Chaplin soon was commanding a high salary. By the time he joined Mutual Film Corporation in 1915, he was earning $10,000 a week— an unheard of sum for a film actor at that time. At Mutual, he did some of his most brilliant work, including *Easy Street* (1916) and *The Immigrant* (1916). In 1919, he joined Mary Pickford, Douglas Fairbanks, and D.W. Griffith to form United Artists.[3] At United Artists, he made several of his best and most famous films, including *The Kid* (1921), *Gold Rush* (1925), *City Lights* (1931), *Modern Times* (1936), and *The Great Dictator* (1940).

This latter film, which Chaplin wrote, directed, and produced, was his first talking picture, as well as one of his most successful films. It was also the only major feature film released before the United States entered World War II that openly satirized Adolf Hitler.[4] In the film, Chaplin plays two characters: a poor

Intermission 3 (continued)

Jewish barber (the Little Tramp character) and a fascist dictator, Adenoid Hynkel.[5] Chaplin was very proud of his accomplishments in this film and was greatly embarrassed when his friend, Konrad Bercovici, sued him for plagiarism after the film was released, demanding $6,450,000.

Bercovici claimed that he had first suggested to Chaplin the idea of having the Little Tramp play Hitler in the 1930s, after Hitler had come to power in Germany. He also maintained that he had a verbal contract with Chaplin for the production of a series of films, including *The Great Dictator*, under which he was entitled to 15 percent of the gross profits from these movies. At the trial in April 1947, Chaplin testified that he had been thinking about playing Hitler for some time.[6] He had a scrapbook from 1936 that contained several news stories that compared Hitler's mustache to that worn onscreen by the Little Tramp.[7] He also testified that he never made oral contracts. At the settlement conference in May 1947, Bercovici dropped his claim to $500,000, but Chaplin refused to consider paying any amount over $100,000. Bercovici finally agreed to accept $95,000 plus $5,000 in attorneys' fees to settle the case.[8]

Chaplin insisted that he alone had written the film's script, but that he had settled the case to avoid the continued notoriety and negative headlines in the newspapers. The lawsuit had attracted international attention and, although Bercovici eventually settled for a relatively small sum compared to his initial demand, people interpreted the payment as an admission by Chaplin that he had stolen Bercovici's work. It has been suggested that Chaplin probably could have made Bercovici go away sooner by paying him for his idea for a film treatment. But it seems that Chaplin was not the compromising sort, and it appears that this suit was not the only one that he faced. In her 1998 biography of Chaplin, writer Joyce Milton describes Chaplin's strategies for avoiding service of process. "Even the waiters at Chaplin's favorite restaurants were on the alert for process servers and hustled him through the kitchen if one appeared. If all else failed,

Chaplin resorted to hiding out with friends and donning disguises."[9] She tells the story of how federal marshals sat in Chaplin's private office at the studio one time for an entire day while he hid in a nearby closet.[10]

In a lawsuit with a better outcome for Chaplin, Films Sonores Tobis, the producers of René Clair's À nous, la liberté! (Liberty for Us!) (1931), claimed that Chaplin had borrowed the conveyor belt sequence from Clair's film in his movie, Modern Times (1936). However, Clair refused to join in the suit, stating that if any borrowing had taken place, he would be flattered because he had borrowed from Chaplin. He stated, "My romance is a typical Chaplin romance, only lacking his genius." Without Clair's cooperation, Tobis was forced to drop its suit.[11]

"Step Right Up and Call Me Speedy"

Harold Lloyd, known as "Speedy" after a line in his popular movie, The Freshman, fared better when he was accused of appropriating another's idea. Having also come from a poor family, Lloyd was very protective of his property rights, even to the point of litigiousness. He gave as good as he got.

Lloyd had immigrated to California with his father in 1913, when he was twenty years old. There he met the silent film producer, Hal Roach, which was a lucky break that changed his life. He joined with Roach in the production of several very popular comedies under a production agreement with the French film company, Pathé. Wanting to create a familiar character like Chaplin's Little Tramp, he soon settled on the "Harold with the glasses" persona—an average likeable young man who overcomes obstacles thrown at him to win out in the end. His popularity grew. He made one of his finest films, The Freshman, in 1925. His movies relied mostly on visual gags and he had a rough time transitioning to sound films. Although his later movies, as a result, were less successful (and some, such as The Sin of Harold Diddlebock (1947), directed by Preston Sturges and financed by Howard Hughes, were money losers), he had managed his money well while he was at the height of his career. When he retired from the motion picture business to concentrate on his many

Intermission 3 (continued)

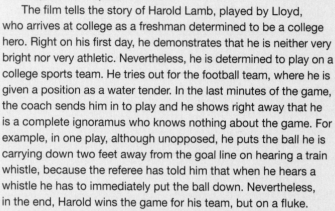

hobbies—cars, dog breeding, and photography—
he was a tremendously wealthy man. When he
died in 1971, he left an estate valued at $12 million.

Lloyd's very successful film, *The Freshman*, was
the subject of a major court case.

The film tells the story of Harold Lamb, played by Lloyd,
who arrives at college as a freshman determined to be a college
hero. Right on his first day, he demonstrates that he is neither very
bright nor very athletic. Nevertheless, he is determined to play on a
college sports team. He tries out for the football team, where he is
given a position as a water tender. In the last minutes of the game,
the coach sends him in to play and he shows right away that he
is a complete ignoramus who knows nothing about the game. For
example, in one play, although unopposed, he puts the ball he is
carrying down two feet away from the goal line on hearing a train
whistle, because the referee has told him that when he hears a
whistle he has to immediately put the ball down. Nevertheless,
in the end, Harold wins the game for his team, but on a fluke.

The movie was very successful, making Lloyd and Pathé
somewhere between $1 and $2 million by the time Harry
Witwer filed his lawsuit against Lloyd in 1929. Witwer had
written a short story called "The Emancipation of Rodney" that
he claimed to have shared with Lloyd's representatives before
The Freshman was shot. This story was about a college freshman,
Rodney Benham, who is very smart but wants to be popular and
believes he can achieve this by playing sports. He has devised
a mathematical game-winning formula for football. At the end
of the story, Rodney finds the girl of his dreams and also wins
the college football game using his formula. Because there were
comparable elements in both the story and the movie (such as
a football game)—even though Lloyd testified that he had not
read the story—the trial court found in favor of Witwer.

On appeal, the Ninth Circuit reversed, ruling in favor of
Lloyd.[12] Although the general plot lines of the two works were
similar, the court found that the mere resemblance between
the two would not necessarily show that one was pirated from

the other. Moreover, the elements that were similar, such as the football game, were neither new nor novel. There were sufficient differences even in the football scenes that the ordinary observer would not think them the same at all. In the story, Rodney wins the game because he has come up with a game-winning strategy; in the movie, Harold wins the game despite his utter lack of skill.

One fact that the court particularly found relevant was Lloyd's style of filmmaking. Lloyd's representatives had testified at the trial that Lloyd worked without a script when he was filming a scene. The plots were developed ad hoc on the set: someone would throw out an idea, such as a gag in the football game in *The Freshman*, and Lloyd would act on it, to try it out (he performed many of his own stunts). Given that method of operating, the court determined that it was very unlikely that Lloyd would have borrowed from a script or story, even if he had read it.

1. Starr, *California*, p. 277. *See* The American Experience, People & Events: Charlie Chaplin (1889-1977), found at www.pbs.org/wgbh/amex/pickford/people events/p_chaplin.html.

2. Sennett's Keystone Studios was most famous for its popular Keystone comedies and especially those featuring the "Keystone Cops," which were filmed in the streets and avenues of early twentieth century Los Angeles. Starr, *California*, p. 275.

3. Starr, *California*, p. 277.

4. Both Hollywood and the U.S. government exhibited reticence in speaking against Hitler and the Nazi regime in Germany prior to the U.S. entry into World War II in 1941. *See generally*, Larson, Erik, *In the Garden of Beasts: Love, Terror, and an American Family in Hitler's Berlin*, Crown, New York, NY, 2011.

5. Stratton, David, review: "The Tramp and the Dictator," *Variety*, February 21, 2002. The film was nominated for five Academy Awards, including Best Picture.

6. "Law Library—American Law and Legal Information," found at http://law.jrank.org/pages/3002/Bercovici-v-Chaplin-1947.html.

7. Milton, Joyce, *Tramp: The Life of Charlie Chaplin*, DaCapo Press, 1998, p. 368. "A number of people had suggested to Chaplin that 'the Fuhrer, after all, sported a version of the Charlie Chaplin mustache,' and the remarkable physical resemblance between the world's funniest man and the world's scariest had already been noted by political cartoonists and pundits."

8. "Law Library—American Law and Legal Information," found at http://law.jrank.org/pages/3002/Bercovici-v-Chaplin-1947.html.

9. Milton, *Tramp*, p. 363.

10. Milton, *Tramp*, p. 363.

11. Gehring, Wes D., *Personality Comedians as Genre*, Greenwood Publishing Group, 1997, p. 54.

12. Harold Lloyd Corporation v. Witwer, 65 F. 2d 1 (9th Cir. 1933).

Part III

The Development of Sound Cinema— 1929–1945

It is difficult today to imagine a time when sound in cinema did not exist, when films with sound were a rarity and the more commonplace motion pictures were silent. Yet for many today, watching a great silent film, such as *Greed* (1924) or *City Lights* (1931), is a strange experience; even though the viewer may appreciate the artistry in the film, something familiar— that is, voice—is missing. Some are annoyed that they have to read captions when viewing a silent film; these same people are also often irritated when watching a modern foreign film in a language they do not understand because they have to read the subtitles. Others among us do not mind subtitles, finding them to be, at most, frustrating because we know that important dialogue is missing from the translated text at the bottom of the screen. And for some of us, there is a comfort in watching a good silent movie because we can concentrate on the film using only one sense—the visual—without being distracted by dialogue.

There is a myth that sound in films appeared almost overnight; in other words, that there was a bright line between the day when people only watched silent films and the next, when all theaters presented talkies. There is also a legend that the arrival of sound ruined the careers of otherwise great actors, such as the Latin Lover with a squeaky voice or the glamorous star who had a Brooklyn accent or an incomprehensible foreign accent. This myth was perpetuated in the 1952 film, *Singin' in the Rain.* In this movie, two vaudevillian actors, played by Gene Kelly and Donald O'Connor, have made careers performing in silent films. Kelly's character, Don, becomes famous for his portrayals of screen lovers, cast alongside a blonde bombshell, Lina (played by Jean Hagen). They are in the midst of filming when a studio executive rushes in to stop the shoot because *The Jazz Singer* (1927) has just been released and there will be no more silent films. Unfortunately, Lina proves to have a terrible voice and the producers are in despair because she is the star and must be in the film. In the meantime, Don (Kelly) has fallen in love with an extra, Kathy (played by a perky Debbie Reynolds) who, of course, can act, dance, and sing with a beautiful voice.

In fact, there was no landmark event that brought sound to the pictures. As early as the 1890s, Thomas Edison tried to perfect his "kinetophone," which was a combination of his kinetoscope invention and his phonograph machine.[1] But there was little appetite in the United States to convert film studios and movie theaters to show sound films when the technology was first developed because silent movies were very successful and easy to film and because converting theaters to sound was very expensive. Also, syncing sound to film proved to be a challenging task.

However, the studio heads at Warner Brothers, which was struggling financially, saw sound as a vehicle to differentiate it from its stronger rivals. In 1926, Warner released a film of *Don Juan*, with a synchronized film score.[2] *The Jazz Singer*, released in 1927, did not turn movies toward sound all at once, but it was a very popular movie. *The Jazz Singer* was not a complete "talkie." It was shot as a silent film, but with a few brief

---

1. Crafton, Donald, *The Talkies: American Cinema's Transition to Sound, 1926-1931*, University of California Press, 1999, p. 9.
2. Crafton, pp. 10-11.

scenes inserted where direct sound is introduced, for example, when Al Jolson, the popular recording star who played the title role, talks to his mother and sings some songs. "The film demonstrated forcefully . . . the importance of star voices in the sound film, the appeal of popular music, and the potential rewards for adding dialogue and singing to otherwise silent films."[3]

Meanwhile, in Europe, the German company, Tobis Klangfilm, had a large number of patents for film sound technology. The company set up facilities throughout Europe to produce movies in the local languages. It was very successful in France, through its Société des Films Sonores Tobis (Tobis Sound Films Company). Tobis demanded substantial royalties for the use of its technology.[4] This created competition for U.S. film studios for the European and international market and pushed forward the movement into sound films.

Much like the recent advances in 3D technology in films such as *Avatar* (2009), however, where followers created films with 3D features in order to capitalize on the enthusiasm for this innovation, many of the early sound films produced in 1929 and 1930 were not great. They were "hastily cobbled together" to meet the demand for more talking pictures.[5] These movies demonstrated all of the problems with trying to integrate sound into film, particularly films developed initially as silent movies that were reshot as talkies: static, poorly written scripts, bad recordings, and inauthentic speaking voices that resulted from forcing the actors to speak directly into a microphone.[6]

The changeover to sound occurred gradually over a four-to-five-year period following the release of *The Jazz Singer*,

---

3. Crafton, p. 12.
4. Crafton, p. 420.
5. Crafton, p. 14.
6. Crafton, p. 14.

as theaters revamped for the new talking pictures. But once momentum was gained, the film industry assimilated quickly.[7] Exhibitors rapidly wired their theaters for sound, so that by the time the stock market crashed in October 1929, most theaters in the United States were able to show the new talking pictures. This proved to be a lucrative development, drawing greater numbers of people into movie parlors. By 1931, "sound production had been standardized,"[8] and by 1932, the conversion to sound in the United States was virtually complete.[9]

But silent films did not disappear. They were produced well into the 1930s in the United States and in other countries. Some of the finest movies of the 1930s by famous Japanese filmmakers, such as *An Inn in Tokyo* (1935) directed by Yasujirô Ozu, and *Apart from You* (1933) and *Street Without End* (1934) by Mikio Naruse, were silent films. However, those purists who favored the artistry of the silent film over talking pictures were in a losing battle. One of these was Charles Chaplin, who mounted a campaign against the movement toward talking pictures. He argued that silent films could, and should, be allowed to coexist with sound pictures. He was, of course, self-interested in this battle because his Little Tramp character, which had evolved from mimes in Chaplin's music hall/vaudeville days, was best suited for silent representation. In 1931, he released *City Lights*, which was a great movie but which met with a less than enthusiastic reception because it did not have sound. Moreover, sound films brought in from Europe, such as *Der blaue Engel* (*The Blue Angel*) (1930), proved that movies with sound could be artistic as well as popular.[10]

---

7. Crafton, p. 7.
8. Crafton, pp. 6-7.
9. Thompson & Bordwell, p. 195.
10. Crafton, p. 17.

Two world events occurred just as sound was introduced that changed movies and affected the appetites and tastes of the movie-going public—the Great Depression, which lasted through most of the 1930s, and World War II, which dominated the 1940s. Because sound had been introduced just before the stock market crashed and the economy tumbled, American film producers were able to create through new film genres an ambiance that allowed moviegoers to momentarily escape the poverty and want that daily surrounded them. "Hollywood can be said to have helped stabilize the nation by offering intensities of psychological release for the stress everyone was experiencing."[11] These were the now familiar movie genres: gangster films, extravagant musicals, and comedies (that depended on dialogue for humor rather than acrobatics), which made actors such as Edward G. Robinson and James Cagney, directors such as Busby Berkeley, and comedians such as the Marx Brothers and W.C. Fields the new box office draws. Historian Kevin Starr points out that this decade also saw the ascendancy of the western, such as *Stagecoach* (1939), which represented "renewed hope in America."[12] The rise of the Nazis in the 1930s and the descent of Europe into world war in the early 1940s enabled American movie studios to assert their dominance over the international film market, providing those studios with substantial revenues from distribution. It did not hurt either that in the 1930s, Tobis Klangfilm lost an important lawsuit against Western Electric, which ended its monopoly from its patents over European sound technology.[13]

11. Starr, *California*, p. 278.
12. Starr, *California*, p. 278.
13. Crafton, p. 418.

You Can Cheat an Honest Man

Yadkoe v. Fields, 66 Cal. App. 2d 150 (2d Dist. 1944)

If a thing is worth having it's worth cheating for.

W.C. Fields, from *My Little Chickadee* (1940)

W.C. Fields was one of the most popular film comedians in the 1930s, known particularly for his quick and often sarcastic wit (some would have called it mean-spirited), as well as a running gag, made credible by his large and bulbous nose, that he was constantly inebriated. Like so many comedians of his generation, he came out of the music hall and vaudeville tradition. He was born in Philadelphia and quit school as a child to work with his father selling vegetables from a horse cart. His father was an alcoholic who beat him and, when he was eleven, he ran away from home, becoming a juggler in Atlantic City. By the time he was in his twenties, he was in London, performing on stage with Sarah Bernhardt and in Paris, appearing with Maurice Chevalier at the Folies Bergère. In 1915, he was picked up by the Ziegfield Follies and then he moved to film, performing in several of D.W. Griffith's movies. He relocated to Hollywood, settled into a Burbank mansion, and proceeded to make dozens of films, where he generally played a misanthrope with a love of alcohol, which apparently was not a stretch from his off-stage personality.[1]

---

1. W. C. Fields, Biography, Internet Movie Database, found at http://www.imdb.com/name/nm0001211/bio, last accessed July 1, 2011.

As a popular actor, Fields attracted his share of fans, including those who wanted to get into the film business themselves and who saw an avenue by providing the famous actor with an idea, a synopsis, or a "pitch" for a movie. Harry Yadkoe was one such fan. After writing a series of admiring letters to Fields, pitching various gags, skits, comedy routines, dialogue, and other ideas, he saw the film, *You Can't Cheat an Honest Man* (1939) and was furious when he realized that Fields had used in this movie the material that Yadkoe had provided to him for his consideration.

In August 1938, when he learned that Fields was ailing, Yadkoe wrote him an enthusiastic letter, enclosing a script, telling Fields, "To say that I rate you as the greatest of comedians is putting it mildly you old rascal you. There isn't a greater master of mimicry, buffoonery, or what have you on the stage radio or screen." He continued, "When I read in a daily paper that a medico tried to limit your liquid refreshment [that is, whiskey], I knew the millennium was here. Bill without his refreshment. Egad! What next? Is there no Justice? Gazooks." And then he concluded with what would be for Fields fateful words. "Whatever you think the enclosed . . . script is worth is OK with me 'Bill.' Pardon a young man's brashness in addressing you so familiarly, but I know you'll understand."

In September, Fields (or more likely Fields's representatives) replied to Harry Yadkoe, telling him, "Thanks for the snake story. I shall use it in conjunction with one I have either on the radio or in a picture . . . if you would like to submit a couple of scripts gratis and I am able to use them, who knows, both parties being willing, we might enter into a contract." The letter continued, "my reason for injecting the vile word 'gratis' is that we get so many letters from folks who if we even answer in the negative, immediately begin suit for plagiarism. Whilst we have never had to pay off, they sometimes become irritating to no end."

Harry responded several times and in October 1938 sent Fields "some scenes and dialogue" for his next picture, *You Can't Cheat an Honest Man*, concluding "P.S. Get that contract ready, Bill."

Yadkoe was soon to learn that it was actually possible to cheat an honest man, assuming that he saw himself as an honest—or at least a trusting—man. He sued Fields in California Superior Court where the trial court awarded him $8,000 for the value of the material he had submitted to Fields that Yadkoe claimed was used in the film. Fields appealed, contending that "from the mass of material" that Yadkoe claimed to have submitted to Fields, Fields used very little—only four items.

Yadkoe claimed that he had sent Fields a "snake story" that Fields used in *You Can't Cheat an Honest Man*. In the episode, a woman fainted each time Fields used the word "snake" and each time she fainted a glass of whiskey would be ordered, ostensibly to be used to treat the lady having the fainting spell, but which the character played by Fields would drink. Yadkoe testified that he had sent Fields a story line in which Fields would arrive home, "bragging" about "how he had conquered the snake, how he beat it wrestling, and as he does so this woman hears the mention of snakes and faints, and as she faints, he gives her a drink of liquor and takes a drink of liquor himself and goes right on talking about snakes and the same thing happens and he takes another drink."

Yadkoe also testified that he suggested a scene where a big game hunter (Fields) tells rules of "how to hunt big game, never to use high-powered rifles on lions, just look them in the eye and sort of hypnotize them"; the only wild animals not included in the lesson were crocodiles, who were "not worthy of a big game hunter's attention"—they were to be ignored. In *You Can't Cheat an Honest Man*, a character named Blacum, an animal trainer, hypnotized animals, but ignored crocodiles.

Fields argued in his appeal that Yadkoe's material did not merit protection because it was not his "property," that there was no value in the use of the material even if it were original, literary, or worthy of protection. Yadkoe disagreed. He maintained that he was the original author and owner of the literary material that Fields used without his permission and that he, Yadkoe, as the owner was entitled to the reasonable value of this use of his material. In legal terms, Yadkoe was using copyright theories to claim compensation from Fields. He was arguing that this material was "the product of the mind," that as such it was entitled to copyright protection, that Fields used a substantial portion of Yadkoe's material without his permission in the film, and finally that this use was not a "fair use" under copyright law.

The appellate court disagreed with Yadkoe on this theory. What Yadkoe had presented to Fields were ideas or concepts, not the expression of those ideas. And ideas cannot be copyrighted. However, the court nevertheless concluded that Yadkoe was entitled to recover compensation from Fields based on contract law. As the court saw it, the evidence presented in the correspondence between Yadkoe and Fields showed that Fields expressly accepted the material that Yadkoe submitted in his first letter to Fields, and invited Yadkoe to submit more. The only item missing from what the court viewed as an "express contract" between the two men was the amount or rate of compensation to be paid.

Having reached this conclusion, however, the court then decided the amount of Yadkoe's recovery based on those same "property right" arguments that Yadkoe had made and that the court had just shot down. Yadkoe had a property right in the appropriated material, the court stated. "While we recognize that an abstract idea as such may not be the subject of a property right, yet, when it takes upon itself the concrete form which we find [here] . . . it is our opinion that it then becomes a property right subject to sale. Of course, it must be something novel and new . . . While it is settled that there can be no property right in an abstract idea, there may be literary property in the form in which ideas are expressed." This was an odd theory, to say the least. Copyright law did not apply, except when it did.

As the owner of this "property," as the court viewed the facts, Yadkoe had made an offer to sell it to Fields. Absent an express agreement by Fields to pay a certain amount for Yadkoe's material, the court needed to determine whether Fields's use of Yadkoe's property would raise an obligation to pay him some amount for such use. This raised the question of value. Was it the value of the material itself or the value of the use? The court determined that the material had intrinsic value outside of its potential use. Given that, the court ruled that the jury was correct in awarding a sum to Yadkoe to properly compensate him for Fields's use of the material that Yadkoe had submitted to him.

It is hard to determine exactly what legal theory the court decided to use to ensure that Yadkoe received some compensation for the ideas he so willingly gave to Fields. It seems clear that the court wanted to show Yadkoe that, in fact, you can't cheat an honest man, or at least an honest fan, and expect to get away with it in California. And one would hope that Fields learned to beware of enthusiastic fans sending friendly "get well" letters. They should be treated like crocodiles and ignored.

A Dangerous Woman

De Havilland v. Warner Bros. Pictures,
67 Cal. App. 2d 225 (2d Dist. 1944)

> **Scarlett: You'd rather live with that silly little fool who can't open her mouth except to say "yes" or "no" and raise a passel of mealy-mouthed brats just like her.**
> **Ashley: You mustn't say unkind things about Melanie.**
>
> From *Gone with the Wind* (1939), with Clark Gable as
> Rhett Butler, Vivien Leigh as Scarlett O'Hara, Leslie Howard
> as Ashley Wilkes, and Olivia de Havilland as Melanie Hamilton

By the 1930s, Hollywood had settled into a structure for film production that gave enormous power to the eight studios that dominated the filmmaking industry: Paramount, Loews (generally known under the name of its production subsidiary, MGM), Fox, Warner Brothers, RKO, Universal, Columbia, and United Artists[1]—all companies (with the exception of RKO) that remain familiar names in the movie business today. Under what was known as the "studio system," everyone involved in the film production industry—screenwriters, directors, actors, technicians, and support functions—were salaried employees of the corporately owned studios.[2] Movie stars were signed to seven-year contracts for a fixed salary, which

---

1. Thompson & Bordwell, p. 213.
2. Starr, *California*, p. 276-277.

was frequently relatively low because the actors entered into these agreements at the start of their movie-making careers, before they became famous. During the contract term, studios could put the stars into as many or as few films as the producers chose, without any input from the artists and without regard to their professional development or maturing acting skills. Actors, as can be imagined, were generally dissatisfied with these arrangements but had little clout to change them.

To add to the actors' unhappiness, studios also had the right to lend out their services to other production houses for individual film projects. Much of this "horse trading" occurred during the 1930s and early 1940s, and many successful Hollywood films of the time were made with performers on loan from other studios. The borrowing producer was often willing to pay a high price to the lending studio to obtain the services of a sought-after star for a film. Under the actors' contracts, however, the studios were entitled to retain 100 percent of the compensation received for their services, while the artists continued to receive only the salary that was set out in their contracts at the time of signing. The actors had only the extra work and none of the monetary rewards derived from this practice.

In the early years of the history of the cinema, few stars, with the exception perhaps of a Mary Pickford or a Charlie Chaplin, would have been powerful enough to demand different treatment. Although they were frustrated with a situation that essentially left them powerless against the whims of the studio moguls and even though they longed to be independent of the burdensome contracts, most actors accepted their position in the system and did not cause trouble. Those who did suffered consequences. They were tarnished with the reputation of being "difficult" and their pushiness often had the contrary result of fewer and less challenging roles made available to them. And if they refused to perform, they were subject to suspension under the terms of the contract.

This right of the studios to "suspend" any actor who failed, refused, or neglected to perform the services required by the producers particularly rankled, even as it served to keep even the most recalcitrant stars in line. The suspension, without pay, would continue until the actor returned to the studio and agreed to resume work. In addition, any suspension time would then be added to the contract term. In other words, if an actor became ill or refused to take a part in a film, the studio had the right to cut off the actor's salary until he or she agreed to return and then to lengthen the contract term. For example, if the suspension lasted for four months, at the end of the original seven-year contract term, the studio would be entitled to add on an additional four months. Multiple suspensions over the life of a contract could potentially extend its term almost indefinitely.

By the mid-1930s, several popular stars tried to challenge the system. Most notable were two who had a reputation for being independent—James Cagney and Bette Davis. Cagney had become popular by playing tough-guy roles in gangster movies in the 1930s, such as *The Public Enemy* (1931) and *Angels with Dirty Faces* (1938).[3] Not wanting to be type-cast in these roles, he campaigned unsuccessfully with his studio, Warner Brothers, for more varied parts. Twice he refused roles and was suspended and twice he was forced to return, albeit with a higher salary. In 1936, Cagney left Warners, convinced that he could get better acting roles by working outside the studio system. However, he found that no one was willing to engage him. Because they all benefited from the status quo, studios feared that allowing a single actor, even one as popular as Cagney, to deviate would

---

3. Internet Movie Database, James Cagney, found at http://www.imdb.com/name/nm0000010/bio.

open the floodgates to other disgruntled actors to do the same and disrupt the contract system that was so profitable for them all.[4] Cagney reluctantly returned to Warner Brothers, where he remained until the 1940s, when he left to form his own production company with his brother, William.[5]

If Cagney represented the "bad boy" actor, he had a female counterpart in Bette Davis. In 1932, she signed a seven-year contract with Warners, where she made between five and seven films a year.[6] By the mid-1930s, she had two critically acclaimed performances under her belt, that of Mildred Rogers in *Of Human Bondage* (1934) (made while Davis was on loan to RKO) and as Joyce Heath in *Dangerous* (1935). This latter performance brought her a Best Actress Academy Award in 1936.

Davis soon became dissatisfied with her situation at Warners. Even though she had rapidly become one of the most highly regarded actresses of her day, Warners only offered her what she considered to be small, insignificant parts.[7] Her situation, and that of other popular screen stars, was ameliorated somewhat by the arrival, in 1936, of the Music Corporation of America (MCA), a music booking agency, and its new West Coast head, a publicist named Lew Wasserman,[8] who began to represent stars such as Davis, Gene Kelly, Joan Crawford, Jimmy Stewart, and Ronald Reagan.[9] In his aggressive representation of

---

4. *Hollywood Renegades Archive*, Cagney Productions, The Society of Independent Motion Picture Producers, found at http://www.cobbles.com/simpp_archive/cagneys.htm.

5. Ibid. *See also*, Corliss, Richard, "Spanking Stars Who Misbehave," TIME, Thursday, August 24, 2006, found at http://www.time.com/time/arts/article/0,8599, 1328848,00.html.

6. Bette Davis: The Official Website, Biography, found at http://www.bettedavis.com/about/bio.htm.

7. Ibid.

8. Thompson & Bordwell, p. 336.

9. Film Reference: *Writers and Production Artists, Lew Wasserman—Writer*, found at http://www.filmreference.com/Writers-and-Production-Artists-Vi-Win/Wasserman-Lew.html.

his clients, Wasserman was able to obtain better financial terms from the studios. He is credited with putting an end to the ability of the major studios to use long-term contracts to stifle the independence of actors and directors.[10] But his was not an overnight success, as Bette Davis's story demonstrates.

In 1936, Davis was offered what she considered a more suitable film role in England and decided to take it, even though it meant breaking her exclusive studio contract with Warner Brothers. Warner Brothers sued her, in England, where the court—viewing her as an unreliable, temperamental star—failed to appreciate the source of her intransigence. Her lawyer's description of her complaints—that she could be suspended without pay for refusing a part, that she could be required to play any part within her abilities regardless of her personal beliefs, that she was expected to take inferior roles that were beneath her skills, and that adding time to the length of her contract for each period of suspension amounted to involuntary servitude—fell on deaf ears. Her case was viewed not as a search for better roles but as a simple dispute over money. Warner's barristers, for their part, successfully portrayed her as a spoiled celebrity who only wanted a bigger salary. She lost her case and was forced to return to Warners.[11] However, due to the assistance of Wasserman, Warners offered her a new contract for a higher salary and, more importantly, better roles. In 1939, she received her second Best Actress Academy Award for her performance in *Jezebel* (1938).[12] In 1942, Wasserman set her up in her own production company, B.D. Inc., and negotiated new terms to her contract with Warners, which included a 35 percent

---

10. Ibid.

11. Corliss, "Spanking Stars Who Misbehave."

12. Internet Movie Database, Awards for Bette Davis, found at http://www.imdb.com/name/nm0000012/awards.

share of profits for each film in which she had a starring role in addition to her usual fee.[13] By then, she was one of the highest paid actresses in Hollywood,[14] but she was still subject to the studio contract system.

In the end, this nefarious system was not broken by a popular tough guy such as Cagney or a reputably temperamental star such as Bette Davis, but rather by a Hollywood actress known for her demure, well-mannered attitude and for her ladylike performances, such as that of Melanie Wilkes opposite the wild cat Scarlett O'Hara in *Gone with the Wind* (1939)—Olivia de Havilland.

In May 1936, de Havilland signed the standard studio contract with Warner Brothers. This agreement was for an initial term of fifty-two weeks, but gave Warners the right to extend the term for all or any of six successive periods of fifty-two weeks each, for a total term of seven years. She initially played ingénue roles, such as Elsa in *The Charge of the Light Brigade* (1936), the kind-hearted fiancée of Errol Flynn, and again as Errol Flynn's love interest, Maid Marian, in *The Adventures of Robin Hood* (1938). She soon felt constricted by playing essentially the same role in each film and asked for more challenging work. The only interesting parts seemed to come to her when she was on loan to other studios, such as the role of Melanie in *Gone with the Wind*, which was produced by David O. Selznick. For her performance in that film, she was nominated for an Academy Award. She was nominated a second time for her performance in *Hold Back the Dawn* (1941), but Warners continued to cast her in passive ingénue roles. As she noted in a 2006 inter-

---

13. Thompson & Bordwell at p. 336.
14. Bette Davis: The Official Website, Biography.

view,[15] she realized that Warners was not going to give her the work that she wanted and that she was being relegated to "doing indifferent work" in a series of "indifferent films." She started to refuse parts and, as a result, was put on suspension. When the initial term of her contract expired in May 1943, Warners added six additional months to the term as "suspension time," which the studio claimed the right to do under the terms of the agreement. At that point, Warners loaned her to RKO for *Government Girl* (1943), which made her unhappy, but she "went ahead and did it." But when Warners again tried to loan her out to Columbia for what she thought could be a disastrous film, she refused. And once again, she found herself on suspension.[16]

It was at this point that Martin Gang, her agent and lawyer, told her that it was illegal for studios to keep actors tied to studio contracts for longer than seven years and suggested that she could sue Warners. She asked to see the statute and, after reading it, told her lawyer to "go after Warner Brothers."[17] It was a courageous move that had immediate consequences. "Oh, they blacklisted me," de Havilland told an interviewer in 2010, but she continued, "I did not care. The main thing for me was to do the work I wanted to do, where I wanted to do it and hopefully give others the same opportunity."[18]

No one thought that de Havilland would win, at least not at the lower court level, given the tremendous power of the stu-

---

15. Interview with Olivia de Havilland, October 5, 2006, Washington, D.C., "The Last Belle of the Cinema," Academy of Achievement: A Museum of Living History, Olivia de Havilland, Legendary Leading Lady, found at http://www.achievement.org/autodoc/page/deh0int-1.

16. Ibid.

17. Copetas, A. Craig, "'Gone with the Wind' Star Olivia de Havilland Is Feisty at 94," *Bloomberg*, September 15, 2010, 4:00 PM PT, found at http://www.bloomberg.com/news/2010-09-15/-gone-with-the-wind-star-de-havilland-feisty-at-94-recalls-studio-fight.html.

18. Ibid.

dios in Southern California, where the trial took place.[19] But in March 1944, the trial judge ruled in her favor. Warners immediately appealed. Oral arguments took place in September 1944, and the appellate court rendered its decision in December of that year.

The case turned on the interpretation of the California statute governing personal service contracts that de Havilland's lawyer had shown her. The facts were not in dispute. De Havilland's contract gave Warners the right to suspend her for any period or periods when she failed or refused to perform her services. She was to receive no compensation while suspended until she agreed to resume work under the contract. The agreement also afforded Warners the right to extend the term, at its option, for a time equal to the periods of suspension. After December 1939, there had been several such suspensions, including a one-month suspension while de Havilland was ill. Each time, Warners exercised its right under the contract to extend the term of the agreement. These facts were affirmed by both parties. Neither did Warners claim that de Havilland had breached the contract through bad faith. She testified demurely on the stand that she had refused several roles because they were not suited to her abilities.[20] But the contract did not allow for any such discretion on her part. According to the terms of the agreement, Warners was to be the sole judge of the suitability of roles and de Havilland was only to do as she was told.

The only question before the court was whether the provi-

---

19. 2006 de Havilland Interview.

20. In Copetas' 2010 interview with de Havilland, she told him that, after visiting her lawyer on the momentous day when she filed her lawsuit, she went directly to Bergdorf Goodman to buy an outfit for her court appearance. "I needed the right outfit," she told Copetas, "I needed to use all my theatrical skills." It was a "simple and demure black-silk suit, a black hat and a black veil, which I, of course, tied beneath my chin when I testified," she said. Copetas, "'Gone with the Wind' Star Olivia de Havilland Is Feisty at 94."

sions of the contract that allowed Warners to extend the term for each period of suspension were valid under California law and effective in binding de Havilland beyond the seven years from the date she began to perform services under it. If the terms were lawful, then de Havilland owed another six months of service to Warners under the contract. If the provisions violated the applicable statute, then the contract had expired in May 1943 and was no longer enforceable.

The statute in question, California Civil Code Section 1980, had been amended in 1931 to provide that a contract for personal services could not be enforced against an employee "beyond a term of seven years from the commencement of services under it." This law contained an additional proviso with respect to contracts for "exceptional services," which the parties agreed would include acting in films. This proviso contained a similar seven-year term limitation: "for a term not beyond a period of seven years from the commencement of service under it." In 1937, this section of the California Civil Code was repealed, but a new section was added to the California Labor Code (Section 2855) which contained substantially the same wording as the former Civil Code Section, with minor language changes. The appellate court determined that this new Labor Code Section was essentially the same as the former Civil Code Section which was in effect in May 1936 when de Havilland began services under her contract.

The applicable provisions of Labor Code Section 2855 read as follows:

> "A contract to render personal service, other than a contract of apprenticeship . . . may not be enforced against the employee beyond seven years from the commencement of service under it. Any contract, otherwise valid,

to perform or render service of a special, unique, unusual, extraordinary, or intellectual character, which gives it peculiar value and the loss of which cannot be reasonably or adequately compensated in damages in an action at law, may nevertheless be enforced against the person contracting to render such service, for a term not to exceed seven years from the commencement of service under it."

Warners defended the legality of its actions, based on its lawyers' reading of the language in the 1931 amended statute to the effect that a contract for "exceptional services" could be enforced against an employee for seven years of *actual service* even though this would result in requiring the employee to render services over a period of more than seven calendar years. Warners argued that the former Civil Code Section 1980 had always made an exception for contracts of apprenticeship, as did the Labor Code section, and that when this statute was amended in 1931, a similar exception was created for contracts for "exceptional services." The effect of this change, they argued, was to take contracts for "exceptional services" out of the general limitation of seven years and to state a special rule for these types of contracts. They interpreted the statute in this manner despite the seemingly clear language in Civil Code Section 1980 that contracts for exceptional services "may nevertheless be enforced against the person contracting to render such service for a term *not beyond a period of seven years from the commencement of service under it*" (emphasis added).

It made no sense to have the proviso at all, Warners contended, if the phrase "for a term not beyond a period of seven years" meant the same thing as "beyond the term of seven years," which was how the paragraph relating to contracts for services of a general nature was phrased in the Civil Code Section. They argued that the legislature must have intended a different meaning and effect and this was, they claimed, in the use of the word "term." According to their interpretation, "term" was not used in the sense of a mere lapse of time because the word "period" was also used. Instead, they maintained, this usage referred to a "term" established by the contract (that is, with extensions to it to account for suspensions).

The court could not accept this argument, noting that, for Warner's interpretation to be correct, the proviso would have to be modified to give it the clear meaning that Warners was attempting to impute to it, so that it would be understood to read, "for a term not beyond a period of seven years *of actual service* from the commencement of service under it." However, the legislature had not used the words "of actual service" when the statute was amended in 1931 nor when the Labor Code provision was enacted and the court believed that this raised an insurmountable problem for Warners. When language seems to be clear on its face, it is not necessary to search for hidden meanings. As the court noted:

> "The substitution of years of service for calendar years would work a drastic change of state policy with relation to contracts for personal services. One would expect that such a revolutionary change, even as applied to a particular class of contracts, would be given expression in clear and unmistakable terms. It is difficult—in fact, too difficult—to believe that a purpose which could have been expressed so simply and clearly was intentionally buried under the camouflage of uncertainty and ambiguity."[21]

---

21. 67 Cal. App. at 232.

The court conceded that the provision was "ineptly phrased," but noted that the legislature had further revised the ambiguous language—"for a term not beyond a period of seven years"—when this law was carried over to the Labor Code in 1937, so that at the time of the decision, the statute read more clearly "for a term not to exceed seven years from the commencement of service under it."

However, the court did agree with Warners that there had to have been some purpose for the exception for contracts for "exceptional services" or otherwise why would the legislature have felt compelled to add it? If the proviso for this type of personal service contract meant the same thing as the clause related to contracts for services of a general nature, then it would have been unnecessary. The answer, the court believed, lay in the remedies for breach of a contract for exceptional services afforded by other California statutes.

Both parties had conceded that before the 1931 amendment, employees who had contracted for the exclusive services of artists could enforce their contracts for a term of two years by means of an injunction preventing these artists from rendering services to others. The court noted that before 1919, another section of the California Civil Code (Section 3423) had prevented injunctive relief for breach of any contract that would not otherwise be "subject to specific performance," that is for which a damages remedy was available. In 1919, Section 3423 was amended to create an exception for contacts for exceptional services, such as the de Havilland contract, which provided for a rate of compensation to the artist of at least $6,000 per year. Even though the 1931 change to Civil Code Section 1980 did not allow employers to enforce contracts for exceptional services beyond seven years, the amendment did make clear that the contract could be enforced during that seven-year term against the artist by means of an injunction (where damages for breach could not be readily fixed). According to the court, providing this clarity as to the enforceability of a contract for exceptional services would have been a sufficient reason for the addition of the exception created in the 1931 amendment to Section 1980.

The court concluded that, where the legislature had acted to put a maximum term of seven years on a personal service contract, the court could not essentially second-guess whether this limitation infringed on the right of a studio to have the exclusive services of an actor for a period of seven years of service. Accordingly, the court affirmed the lower court's judgment against Warner Brothers, ruling that Warner's attempted extensions of de Havilland's contract due to her suspensions were invalid and ineffective in extending the term and binding her beyond May 5, 1943, seven years after her services to Warner Brothers commenced.

Warners appealed the decision to the California Supreme Court, which declined to take the case.

De Havilland's principal worry when she brought her lawsuit against Warners was whether, as a result of challenging the authority of a major studio, once she was released from her contract, other studios would refuse to work with her, as they had with James Cagney. She was pleasantly surprised. After the decision, she performed some of her most memorable and challenging roles. Paramount offered her the starring role in *To Each His Own* (1946) and Universal engaged her to star in *The Dark Mirror* (1946).[22] She played a mentally ill woman in *The Snake Pit* (1948) and was rewarded with an Oscar nomination. She won Best Actress Academy Awards for her performance in

---

22. 2006 de Havilland Interview.

To Each His Own and for her portrayal of Catherine Sloper in *The Heiress* (1949).

The "de Havilland decision," as it has come to be known, had a lasting impact on the movie industry as a whole. In her 2006 interview, de Havilland admitted being especially pleased about the difference the decision made for the Hollywood actors who returned to the studios in 1945, after their World War II military service. Without the benefit of this ruling, these men faced coming back to work at the same salaries that they had received before the war, even though their services were much more valuable by 1945. The war years would have counted as periods of "suspension" under these men's contracts, which would have tacked several more years to their terms. But because Olivia de Havilland stood up to Warner Brothers, as she noted with pride, "all those chaps, those brave, splendid young men, were able to negotiate new contracts."[23]

After the ruling in favor of de Havilland, she and other Hollywood actors were free to work at any studio on projects that suited them, and to negotiate their own fees. This shift in the balance of power in the film industry gave greater influence in Hollywood not just to actors but also to writers and directors, and their agents, and forever changed the way the studios did business. This decision was one of several events in the post-World War II years that weakened the power of the moguls who controlled the major production houses in the first half of the twentieth century, and ultimately destroyed the studio system they had created.

---

23. Ibid.

The Studios' Last Stand

United States v. Paramount Pictures, 334 U.S. 131 (1948)

Gordon Gekko: It's a zero sum game, somebody wins, somebody loses. Money itself isn't lost or made, it's simply transferred from one perception to another.
Michael Douglas, as Gordon Gekko, in *Wall Street* (1987)

B y the end of World War II, the major Hollywood studios had virtual control over the entire filmmaking industry. At the time, there were eight large companies that dominated all aspects of the movie business, from production to distribution to exhibition. Five of these were called the "Majors" (or the "Big Five"). They were Paramount, Loews (generally known by the name of its production company, MGM), 20th Century Fox, Warner Bros., and RKO. Each of these companies was vertically integrated, that is, each had a production business, a theater chain, and an international distribution operation. The other three studios, which were smaller than the Big Five, were called the "Minors" (or the "Little Three"). These were Universal, Columbia, and United Artists. There also were some independent production firms, such as Samuel Goldwyn and David O. Selznick, but for the large part, these eight firms were the ones that called the shots in the industry.[1]

Even though, to the casual observer, there were ostensibly

---

1. Thompson & Bordwell, p. 214.

a large number of movie studios in the 1940s, there actually was very little competition among the Majors, the Minors, and the independents. The Big Five provided the bulk of the popular feature films for the mainstream movie theaters. The other three supplied additional films, largely to smaller theaters that were not part of the Majors' business structure. And the independents either made a few select "prestige films" that were distributed by the Majors, or produced low-budget "B" movies, such as westerns and crime thrillers.[2]

During the 1930s and 1940s, the eight major Hollywood studios had managed to keep competitors from entering the film business, largely through their control of distribution channels and because of their guaranteed outlet for their films in their own theater chains.[3] This situation since before World War II had caused concern with the U.S. government, which opened an investigation and filed suit against a number of studios in 1938 under the Sherman Antitrust Act.[4] The government accused the Majors of violating that law's provisions by colluding to monopolize the film business. The Minors were also accused of violating the law by cooperating to exclude other filmmakers from the market. This original case was settled in 1940, under a Consent Decree that entitled the government to reinstate the suit if, in the three-year period following the settlement date, the Department of Justice determined that the actions taken by the studios to comply with the Consent Decree were inadequate.

One of the biggest concerns to the government was the practice of "block-booking." This was a system that the studios employed to control the manner in which films were distributed into theaters. The studios would offer films in blocks to theaters

---

2. Thompson & Bordwell, p. 218.
3. Thompson & Bordwell, p. 327.
4. 15 U.S.C. §§1, 2.

before they were actually produced. This practice prevented competitors from bidding on single films on their individual merits. In other words, the right to exhibit one premium film was conditioned on the theater's agreement to take one or more other features that were included in the block of films offered. The Majors loved block-booking as it ensured the profitability of more of their pictures and took risk out of production. By booking whole packages of films in this manner, the bigger budget, "star-studded" feature film could carry the weaker pictures.[5]

The original Consent Decree had four main features. First, it prevented the Majors from block-booking short film subjects along with feature films. Second, it allowed the Big Five to continue to block-book feature films, but the block size was limited to five films. Third, the practice of "blind buying," which forced theaters to take films sight unseen, was outlawed and replaced with bimonthly screenings at "trade shows," where representatives of theater owners could actually see the films before they were booked. And, finally, it created an administrative board to enforce the Decree's requirements.[6]

In 1943, after determining that the Majors had not met the requirements of the Consent Decree, the Justice Department reinstated its lawsuit. There were three groups of defendants: the "producer/distributor/exhibitors," which consisted of the Majors; the "producer/distributors," who were the Minors; and the "distributors," who engaged only in the distribution of motion pictures. The government charged that the producer defendants had attempted to monopolize and had succeeded in monopolizing the production of motion pictures. The government also charged that all of the defendants as distributors had conspired to restrain and monopolize interstate trade in the dis-

5. Thompson & Bordwell, p. 327.
6. 66 F. Supp. 323.

113

tribution and exhibition of films, as well as to monopolize the exhibition of motion pictures in most of the larger cities in the country. And, finally, it complained that the vertical combination of production, distribution, and exhibition of films in which the Majors engaged violated the Sherman Antitrust Act.

The case was tried in 1945 and, in 1948, after a three-judge district court panel ruled in favor of the government, holding that the studios had violated antitrust laws, the case reached the U.S. Supreme Court. Justice Douglas delivered a lengthy opinion laying out the many, many ways in which the studios had violated the laws, including the myriad unfair means that the Majors, by use of block-booked films and otherwise, even after the Consent Decree, continued to keep independent films out of the first-run movie theaters, and conversely kept independent theater owners from obtaining rights to exhibit the best feature films produced by the major studios. Further, the Court also believed that the Little Three studios, although they did not own theaters, had cooperated with the Majors to keep other filmmakers from the market.

Because the practice of block-booking prevented competitors of the Majors from bidding for single feature films on their independent merits, the Court found that the practice "added to the monopoly of a single copyrighted picture that of another copyrighted picture" that had to "be taken and exhibited in order to secure the first." This was not right and served no public purpose. "Where a high quality film greatly desired is licensed only if an inferior one is taken, the latter borrows quality from the former and strengthens its monopoly by drawing on the other." Justice Douglas made clear that films could still be put out for sale in blocks or groups as long as there was no requirement—express or implied—of the purchase of more than one film.

The Court also considered an entire host of other studio practices that it considered to be anticompetitive. For example, Justice Douglas agreed with the district court that the industry had engaged in price fixing. No film was ever sold to a movie theater owner. Instead, the right to show the film was established through a copyright license. When these licenses were issued, the producers/distributors imposed minimum prices for admission to a film showing. All of the licenses to movie theaters had substantially uniform prices, all established by agreement with the theater owners, whether in a master license agreement, a franchise agreement, or a joint operating agreement made by the five Majors with each other. As a result, all of the theaters owned by a particular defendant in a given geographic region would charge the same minimum admission price. The other three studios, the Minors, likewise, charged the same minimum fee to exhibitors to whom they licensed the right to show their films. Justice Douglas affirmed the district court's findings that this price fixing occurred in two fashions: a horizontal scheme among all the studios and a vertical conspiracy between each distributor and its licensees. This latter was based on the express agreements among the parties and the former was inferred from the pattern of price fixing observed through the evidence presented by the government at the trial.

The studios argued that as copyright owners—much like patent owners—they were entitled to grant a license that fixed the price at which the film could be shown, much as a patent owner can grant a license for the manufacture of a patented article and fix the price at which the patent licensee can sell the patented article. Justice Douglas disagreed. He started from the opposite perspective. As far as the antitrust laws were concerned, a price-fixing combination was illegal *per se* and not even a patent holder is entitled to restrain competition in an entire industry through licenses containing price-fixing agreements. Given that restriction on patent owners, then the owner of a copyright would be subject to the same constraint.

Another area where the studios had managed to stifle competition was in film "clearances." The studios justified this practice because it was designed to protect a movie theater's revenue stream. This was a guaranty by a distributor that it would not allow a theater's competitors to show a film at the same time or soon after its initial release in the first theater. The district court had found that in practice this system of clearances was so broad as to restrain competition. It had therefore proscribed the distributors and theater owners from creating any system of clearances or from enforcing any clearance against theaters that were in substantial competition with them beyond what was necessary to protect the initial run of the film. The distributors asked the court to also allow them, in determining when to grant a clearance and for how long, to take into account a fair return to the theater owner. But the district court had rejected this additional discretion and the Supreme Court affirmed this decision, perceiving the practice as essentially asking a fox to guard the hen house. This would have been a first step toward allowing distributors to grant clearances to their own theaters while disfavoring the theaters of competitors, and all the while justifying the limitations they were placing on their competitors as necessary to protect the revenues of their own theaters. "That is too potent a weapon to leave in the hands of those whose proclivity to unlawful conduct has been so marked," Justice Douglas remarked.

The theaters also had a practice of pooling profits, sharing them among themselves according to agreed-upon percentages. In addition, some of these agreements restricted the ability of the parties to acquire other competitive theaters without first offering them for inclusion in the joint pool. This eliminated competition among the members of the group and increased competition by the pool against the few nonmember independent theaters. Justice Douglas saw these as "bold efforts to substitute monopoly for competition." The Court prohibited future acquisitions of interests in independent theaters unless the studio could demonstrate that the reason for acquiring the theater was "innocent." The Majors also were required to terminate their joint ownership of theaters and to divest themselves of their theater chains.

The studios used a variety of contracts to control the market, such as "formula deals" and master agreements. A "formula deal" was a licensing agreement in which the license fee for a specific motion picture was calculated for the theaters covered by the agreement by a percentage of the national gross revenues earned by that film. Paramount and RKO had made formula deals both with independent chains and with "circuits" of qualified theaters. (A "circuit" was a group of more than five theaters controlled by the same person.) The inclusion of theaters within a circuit into a single agreement left no opportunity for other theater owners to bid for the first-run films in their respective geographic areas. Master agreements covered the showing of a film in two or more theaters in a particular circuit and allowed the owner of the theaters to allocate the rental to be paid for the film among the theaters as it saw fit and to exhibit the film on a performance schedule that it chose and left all the other terms of the agreement to the entire circuit.

The Supreme Court agreed with the district court that these types of agreements were unlawful restraints of trade in two respects. First, they prohibited bidding for films theater by theater, thus eliminating the opportunity for the small competitor to obtain the best choice of first-run features and putting a premium on the size of the circuit. As such, these agreements worked to stifle competition by "diverting the cream of the business to the large operators." Second, the pooling of purchasing power of the entire circuit in bidding for films was a misuse of monopoly power insofar as it combined the theaters in small towns with competitive situations.

The studios also used a variety of contract terms to discriminate against small independent theaters in favor of large affiliated circuits. For example, a contract could be suspended if a theater within a circuit remained closed for more than eight weeks, allowing reinstatement for the theater without liability on reopening. For independent theaters, contracts were terminated for failure to continuously operate and reinstatement, if allowed at all, required payment of a hefty fee. A circuit theater was allowed deductions in film rent also if double bills were played. No such favors were bestowed on independent theaters. The circuit theaters received other favors, such as extended runs and unlimited playing time. Foreign films and those of independent producers could be excluded from circuit theaters. The studio owners blamed theater owners for this practice, claiming it had been foisted upon them. The Court was unimpressed with this denial. Noting that "acquiescence in an illegal scheme is as much a violation of the Sherman Act as the creation and promotion of one," the Court found that all of these practices constituted illegal discrimination against small independents.

Once the Court had sorted out all the ways in which the studios had managed to stifle competition, its problem was to craft a solution that would put a halt to the anticompetitive behaviors. The district court had issued an order requiring that films be licensed on a competitive bid basis. Films were to be offered to all theaters in each geographic area. The license for the desired run was to be granted to the highest responsible bidder unless all offers were rejected by the studio. The licenses were to be offered and taken theater by theater and picture by picture. Justice Douglas was suspicious of this remedy.

One way of telling that this solution was seriously flawed was by looking at which party found it to be acceptable. In this case, the only parties who favored the remedy were the Majors themselves. Everyone else—the Minors, the independent producers and distributors, and the Department of Justice—opposed it. Justice Douglas agreed with these parties' objections. At first blush it might have seemed like a commendable system because it would have allowed the small independent operators, who up to then had been excluded from the game, to freely participate. But Justice Douglas believed that it would ultimately prove to be unworkable as a remedy because it would involve the courts too deeply in the daily operation of the motion picture business. More importantly, its benefits were at best "dubious" and at worst could result in the very favoritism that the courts were attempting to avoid. Further, it was doomed to fail by its very nature because in most cases the "highest responsible bidder" would doubtless prove to be the party "with the greatest purchasing power," i.e., the theaters controlled by the Majors. It might even result in the court-assisted elimination of the independents, perversely increasing the studios' "strategic hold on the industry" and "the concentration of economic power in the industry"—the very situation that the courts were trying to remedy.

So, if competitive bidding wasn't the answer, then what was? As Justice Douglas saw it, the problem was this concentration of power, the monopoly held by a few studios and theater owners. At the time the case was brought in 1945, the five Majors held interests in more than 17 percent of the theaters in the United States. These theaters paid 45 percent of the total domestic film rental fees received by the eight dominant studios. In the ninety-two cities of the country with populations over 100,000, at least 70 percent of all the first-run theaters were affiliated with one or more of the five Majors. In thirty-eight of these cities, there were no independent first-run theaters.

However, despite the evidence of a restrained competitive market, no single studio owner among the five Majors could be deemed to have a monopoly over the industry. The district court had believed that under the law it could not treat the five as collectively holding a monopoly. Furthermore, even where a single Major owned all of the first-run theaters in a town, there was not enough proof that the studio had acquired all these theaters for the purpose of creating a monopoly. The root of the difficulties, the district court had believed, lay not in theater ownership but in the studios' unlawful practices. Therefore, the court did not feel that it could require the five Majors to completely divest their theater holdings. It did, however, issue an order to prevent them from expanding their current theater holdings.

Justice Douglas did not have such a benign view of the studios' motives. To him, at least with respect to the five Majors, it was "clear . . . that the aim of the conspiracy was exclusionary, . . . in other words, the conspiracy had monopoly in exhibition for one of its goals." He believed that it was not sufficient to measure monopoly in terms of size or extent of holdings: "It was the relationship of the unreasonable restraints of trade to the position of the defendants in the exhibition field (and more particularly in the first-run phase of that business)." Even if the studios fell short of achieving a monopoly, they had created an unreasonable restraint of trade and without appropriate sanctions "would be reward[ed] from the conspiracy through retention of its fruits." As Justice Douglas saw it, it was the duty of the courts to undo what the conspiracy had achieved. Accordingly, the Court sent the case back to the district court to structure a remedy that would correct this problem and achieve a workable remedy.

On remand, the district court ordered that the five Majors divest themselves of their theater chains (the "Paramount Decree").

The *Paramount* decision had a beneficial impact on movie production due to the greater competition that resulted from the studios' divestiture of their theater chains. Theater owners could fill all or part of their program schedules with independent films without repercussions. Independent film producers proliferated after the decision. As a result of this decision, coupled with that of the California court in the *de Havilland* case,[7] which knocked down the studio contract system, stars and directors began to break away from studios to form their own production companies. In addition, the block-booking practice had protected the studios from the full impact of unpopular or low quality movies. The *Paramount* decision's ban on this practice meant that studios could no longer count on one or two strong films to carry the mediocre ones. Each motion picture had to stand on its own merits. "As a result, studios concentrated on fewer, but more expensive, films. Because they were enabled to compete, smaller studios had greater incentive to produce larger budget films."[8]

Smaller independent theaters also benefited from the decision because they had access to a wider variety of films. But, at the same time, they had to compete with each other for first-run rights to the smaller number of movies that were being released. Even though the widespread use of practices that restrained trade was halted by the *Paramount* decision, local theaters

---

7. *See* Reel 8, A Dangerous Woman.
8. Thompson & Bordwell, p. 327.

continued to cooperate among themselves, limiting the number of theaters in a given city where the same film would play. One senses that even today there is not a lot of competition for a moviegoer's business because admission prices among theaters in many towns have remained relatively uniform.

But, finally, the decision had a lesser impact on the distribution side of the industry. It was and remains prohibitively expensive to build a large distribution system and the studios already had theirs in place. Independent producers did not have the wherewithal or ability to replicate such an extensive nationwide network. Therefore, virtually all independent filmmakers continued to rely on the eight established corporate studios to distribute their films. As a result, despite the *Paramount* decision and the industry changes that resulted from it, a small number of movie studios continue to dominate the motion picture business, at least with respect to film distribution, and this side of the business continues to have the lowest risk and the highest revenues. The bulk of box office revenues continue to fall into the pockets of the few.

Part IV

The Post-War Era—1945–1960

The post-World War II era saw massive shifts on a global scale. The War had inflicted enormous damage on the infrastructure and economies of Europe, Japan, and the USSR and these countries were sidelined into an immense rebuilding effort. The United States, on the other hand, had come out of the war years as a prosperous country and eager to reinstate its position as a global leader. Great political shifts took place. In Great Britain, the empire was waning and in 1947, India and Pakistan became separate countries, independent of Britain. Between 1957 and 1962, a number of African countries also gained their independence. The USSR under the totalitarian control of Josef Stalin began a process of "liberating" (taking control of) its neighbors to the west, and as Winston Churchill described it, an "iron curtain" fell to separate those countries and Western Europe.

In the United States, the feeling that communists (in the form of the Soviet monolith) were taking over the world led to an era of suspicion and fear. Beginning in the late 1940s, intelligence agencies investigated persons suspected of being spies against the U.S. government. A congressional committee was formed to determine the extent of communist infiltration into government, schools, and business,[1] and the country generally adopted a "cold war" mentality.

This was also the era where "teens"—young people between the ages of fourteen and twenty who had their own taste in music and movies—became a separately identifiable and impor-

---

1. The House Un-American Activities Committee, or HUAC.

tant demographic. Television became a constant in many American homes,[2] and teens were an important audience, both as viewers and as consumers, susceptible to the ubiquitous advertisements for food, beverages, and other consumer products. And the location of these consumers changed, for post-war America saw enormous growth in homebuilding outside of metropolitan centers, in new "suburbs."

These developments were reflected in the cinema of the era. Given the prosperity within the U.S. economy, Hollywood and its films continued to reign supreme over both the domestic and international film markets. In 1946, a box office record of over $1.5 billion in movie ticket sales shows the strength of the industry at the time.[3]

But clouds were on the horizon for the movie business. The *Paramount* decision in 1948 had required the studios to divest their theater holdings, thus depriving them of a major source of revenue, and the advent of television gave an incentive to potential audiences to stay home instead of frequenting movie theaters, leaving movie producers with fewer outlets for their films. How many young people—who in prior years in the summer months would have headed to a matinee at the local movie theater—instead now stayed home with their friends to watch "American Bandstand" on the little box in their rec rooms?

Color had already been introduced into cinema in the 1930s, but to compete with television, Hollywood produced more and more of its films in color in the 1950s. The two competing technologies were Technicolor (a three-strip dye process perfected in the 1930s) and Eastman Color (which used a single-strip

---

2. Americans owned 32 million television sets by 1954 and by 1960 90 percent of American homes had at least one television set. Thompson & Bordwell, p. 328.

3. Thompson & Bordwell, p. 326.

color film).[4] Technicolor produced movies with a richer color but Eastman color was easier to use and by the late 1960s Eastman was the preferred technology.[5] However, Eastman prints tended to fade, especially if they were hastily processed and films of that era now tend to have a faded image.[6]

During the same time period, Hollywood began to present films targeted to segmented audiences: family films, "teen" movies for the new youth culture (such as the "Gidget" movies, other surfing films, and "rebel" films, such as those with the hot star, James Dean), juvenile films (such as Disney movies) for younger audiences, and art movies, many of which were imported from abroad and distributed by U.S. distributors, for the more sophisticated audiences, especially in large cities such as New York and in college towns.[7]

This was also the heyday of the drive-in movie theater. These were easy to construct—an empty parking lot with a big screen, a speaker on a stand at each parking space (which was clipped to the inside of a slightly lowered car window), a concession stand, and sometimes a playground for the children. Drive-ins made it possible for young suburban families to throw pillows and blankets in the back of the family station wagon, pack a picnic supper, and head out to the movies. When the sun set and the movie started, after watching the cartoon feature, the little ones could pile into the back of the wagon under the blankets and sleep, while their parents could cuddle up in the front seat to enjoy the movie. It was not the most aesthetic of experiences: the sound from the box speakers in the car window crackled and screeched, it sometimes would rain, mak-

4. Thompson & Bordwell, p. 328.
5. Thompson & Bordwell, p. 329.
6. Thompson & Bordwell, p. 329.
7. Thompson & Bordwell, pp. 333-334.

ing viewing almost impossible, and the picture quality was not good. But drive-ins filled an unmet need. "During the 1950s, about one-quarter of box office income came from drive-ins."[8]

When I was a little girl, my parents would often take me and my sister to the drive-in movies in the summertime. We were allowed to play after dark with other neighbor children and to watch the cartoon and maybe the first feature (many drive-ins showed two and sometimes three features every night). And the highlight of a fun evening would occur at the beginning, for as we drove in the entrance, my father would pause and honk his horn at one of the cars parked in the back of the "theater," to embarrass my teenaged older brother who would be installed there with his girl friend. The drive-in was truly an experience for family members of all ages.

8. Thompson & Bordwell, p. 334.

The Iron Curtain Descends

Shostakovich v. Twentieth Century Fox Film Corp.,
196 Misc. 67, 80 N.Y.S. 2d 575 (N.Y. Sup. Ct. 1948);
aff'd 275 A.D. 692, 87 N.Y. S. 2d 430 (1949)

**Before, he was evil and my enemy;
now, he is evil and my friend.**

Richard Burton as Alec Leamas, in
The Spy Who Came in from the Cold (1965)

As the Cold War took shape in Western Europe and America in a strategic conflict with Josef Stalin's aggressive government in the USSR, Hollywood entered the fray with films that highlighted the good in America and the bad in repressive communist regimes. One of these films was entitled, appropriately, *The Iron Curtain* (1948). This movie was based on a true story about the defection of a Soviet code specialist named Igor Gouzenko.

Gouzenko, played by Dana Andrews in the film, was, after careful training, assigned to the Soviet embassy in Ottawa, Canada, during World War II. In 1945, he defected with 109 pages of material that outlined steps taken by the Soviets to obtain secret information about nuclear bomb technology and that implicated several high-level members of the Canadian government. It disclosed that numerous "sleeper cells" of Soviet agents had been established throughout North America. This incident and the disclosures, publicized by American columnist Drew Pearson in 1946, with the revelation that sleeper cells of communists were

131

living among Americans, caused great consternation within the governments of the United States, Canada, and Great Britain, and contributed to the Red Scare that was occupying the minds of Americans at the time.

The film, directed by William Wellman, dramatized the incident but also provided a human dimension as the history of a man who has lost his way in a frightening world, as he moves from the certitude of his position and beliefs into a new reality of uncertainty and questionable loyalties. The movie was shot in black and white in Ottawa, during a gray Canadian winter, and the music used in the film score reinforces the tension and the feeling of menace.

As Gouzenko (Andrews) works side-by-side with his Russian compatriot, Vinitov, in deciphering and formulating code messages at the embassy, loud music is played at Vinitov's insistence, in order to prevent eavesdropping. The music selected—scored by the head of Twentieth Century Fox's music department, Alfred Newman—is that of four internationally renowned Soviet composers—Dmitri Shostakovich, Sergei Prokofiev, Aram Khachaturian, and Nicholai Miaskovsky.

When the film was released in 1948, all four signed (or were ordered to sign?) a letter of protest to the filmmakers that their music had been used without permission, appropriated by means of a "swindle" to accompany an "outrageous picture." The gravamen of their complaint was that the music was used without their consent and that they never would have allowed its use in a film, particularly one that was so blatantly anti-Soviet.

The four composers then brought suit against Fox in New York court, seeking an injunction to prevent the continued use of their music in a motion picture that did not reflect their views and that suggested their approval and endorsement of, and participation in the production of, the film, which of course was not the case. They argued that the film made it appear that they were disloyal to their country, in essence defaming them. Their legal case was difficult to establish, however. They could not rely on copyright law because the works selected by Newman were not subject to copyright in the United States and were in the public domain.[1] The composers therefore tried to persuade the court using a combination of "moral rights" and defamation types of arguments to prove their case.[2] Although a number of countries, most notably France, and some states within the United States recognize and protect an author's "moral rights" (in French, "droit moral"), unfortunately in New York in 1948, this was not the case. "Moral rights," where they are protected, are unrelated to copyright or other ownership rights in a work. A moral right transcends these legal rights and is separate and distinct from copyright or other intellectual property laws; it permits the author of a work to retain control over it for personal reasons.[3]

The court in the *Shostakovich* case, however, felt uncomfortable in using any nonstatutory basis for granting the requested injunction, because it saw that using any of the composers' arguments would be inconsistent with the existing body of U.S.

1. A work of authorship is in the "public domain" if it is no longer under copyright protection or if it failed to meet the requirements for copyright protection. Works in the public domain may be used freely without the permission of the former copyright owner. U.S. Copyright Office FAQs, found at http://www.copyright.gov/help/faq/ faq-definitions.html. See, "Golan v. Holder: Should Shostakovich be Public Domain?" IMSLP Journal found at http://imslpjournal.org/golan-v-holder-should-shostakovich-be-public-domain/, and discussion at Reel 30, A Foreign Affair: *Golan v. Holder*.

2. They suggested four grounds for issuing the injunction: 1) invasion of their right to privacy under the New York Civil Rights Law, 2) publication of libelous material, 3) deliberate infliction of injury without just cause, and 4) invasion of their moral rights. See, Rabin, Susan, "Moral Rights and the Realistic Limits of Artistic Control, GOLDEN GATE UNIVERSITY LAW REVIEW, Vol. 14, Issue 2, Article 9, 1984, p. 449, found at http://digitalcommons.law.ggu.edu/cgi/newcontent.cgi?article=1350&context=ggulre v&sei-redir=#search="196+misc+67+shostakovich".

3. *See* discussion at Reel 26, The Sculptor: *Huston v. La Cinq*.

intellectual property law.[4] In fact, the court sidestepped the moral rights issue, stating "in the absence of any clear showing of the infliction of a willful injury or of any invasion of a moral right, this court should not consider granting the drastic relief asked" due to the unsettled state of moral rights law in the United States.

The composers had cited one statute, New York's civil rights law, in arguing that Fox had violated their right of publicity, but the court gave short shrift to this argument, as the use of these composers' works in the film was for artistic purposes and not for advertising purposes, as the statute, in the court's view, required.

The court focused its attention primarily on the defamation claim that the composers had made: that the portrayal of the espionage activities of the representatives of the USSR in Canada and the defection of one of those representatives (Gouzenko) presents a theme with which the composers disagreed. And yet, because their musical compositions were used in the film's score, and in fact their names appear in the opening credits, the film created a "false imputation" that they had cooperated in creating the movie and that they had been "disloyal to their country." The composers urged the court to consider that the use of their names and music "necessarily implied" their consent or collaboration in the production because "the people at large know that living composers receive payment for the use of their names and creations in films." But the court concluded that there were no grounds for any such contention. The use of the composers' music was not an endorsement of the movie.

There was no such necessary implication otherwise, partic-

---

4. *See* Rosenthal Kwall, Roberta, "Copyright and Moral Right: Is an American Marriage Possible?" I Vand L. Rev. 8 at p. 28 (1985).

ularly "where the work of the composer is in the public domain and may be freely published, copied or compiled by others." Although the court did not say as much, the composers had a difficult case to make under defamation theories because they could not establish an essential element of a defamation case in the United States—that the use of the works exposed the composers to "contempt or public ridicule, to the detriment of [their] professional standing."[5]

Of course, detriment to professional standing was probably the least of these composers' worries at the time. They more likely than not feared something much more severe in their home country. Shostakovich in particular had endured great hardship under Stalin's dictatorship in Russia. During the 1930s and 1940s, he had suffered from ugly political attacks in the official Soviet newspaper, *Pravda*. His music, deemed to be subversive to the communist state, was banned in the Soviet Union in 1948, even as it was internationally acclaimed, and performances of his works were prohibited in Russia until after Stalin's death in 1953.[6]

Therefore, at the time *The Iron Curtain* was released, Shostakovich and the other composers were under severe scrutiny by their government. The release of the film presented a significant threat to these men, whose liberty and even their very lives were at stake. It is highly unlikely that any of the composers saw the movie; it is more likely that their "protests" were sent and the lawsuits filed on their behalf to demonstrate their

---

5. DaSilva, Russell J., *Droit Moral and Amoral Copyright: A Comparison of Artists' Rights in France and the United States*, 28 BULL. COPYRIGHT SOC. 1. 16-17 (1980). Interestingly, these composers brought an action in France and succeeded in their arguments that the film was a violation of their "droit moral." As a result, the exhibition of the movie in France was halted. Judgment of Feb. 19, 1952, [1952[D. Jur. II 204 (Cour d'appel Paris). *See* Rabin, p. 459.

6. Dmitri Shostakovich, Biography, Internet Movie Database, found at http://www.imdb.com/name/nm0006291/bio.

loyalty to the Stalinist regime (and even to save themselves from sentencing to a gulag or execution).

Ironically, at the same time this case was being fought in the New York courts under the shadow of the purges of artists then taking place in the Soviet Union, writers and directors in Hollywood were coming under scrutiny from their own government, through the investigations conducted by the House Un-American Activities Committee (HUAC). In America, a "blacklist" was being created of persons whose activities or ideas were considered to be "subversive."[7]

---

7. *See* Reel 11, The Way They Were: The Un-American Activities of the House Un-American Activities Committee.

Intermission 4

Moral Rights: A Different Way of Viewing Artistic Works

In the United States, intellectual property rights dominate and those who are not able to establish a case for violation or infringement of those rights often have no legal recourse when their "work" is taken, altered, or otherwise damaged. This is not the case in many other parts of the world. In a number of nations there are laws that, to varying degrees, protect authors' rights in their works. This right is commonly referred to as the "moral right" ("droit moral") of the author in his or her creation.[1] A moral right is not viewed in the same context as a property right and is not treated in the same manner. It does not involve a monetary or financial interest but is, rather, a human right. Thus, an author may sell, license, or otherwise transfer some or all of her property rights in her work, but she still will retain her moral right at least in those countries that recognize and respect such a right. "Recognition of moral rights is well established in Europe, deriving largely from judicial decisions of French courts since the middle of the 19th Century."[2]

In France, in particular, because it is viewed as vested in the person of the artist and not solely in the work created by that artist, the sense of the droit moral is so strong that it cannot be transferred or waived and it remains the author's right forever. The concept of a droit moral derives from 19th Century Napoleonic law, the rules of which were codified in France in 1957. But even though France has some of the strongest protections, other Western European and Latin American countries also have codified various versions of the concept of moral rights.[3]

A moral right encompasses within it a number of different values—that of personal expression and that of the uniqueness of the individual creation. Moral rights are spelled out in various iterations but generally include a "right of integrity," a "right of attribution," and a "right of disclosure."

Intermission 4 (continued)

The first of these is also sometimes referred to as the right to respect for the work which "lies at the heart of the moral right doctrine."[4] Under this principle, the author is entitled to prevent anyone from distorting, cutting, or mutilating the work or otherwise doing anything t o it that would misrepresent the author's intended expression. This right has been used to prevent use of the work in any context or format if the author does not approve. For example, in the *Shostakovich* case,[5] the composers could have prevented the use of their music in the score of the movie, *The Iron Curtain,* based solely on their disapproval of the context in which their works were presented, even though the compositions were in the public domain and lacked copyright protection. In the *Huston* case,[6] the heirs of John Huston were able to prevent the exhibition in France of a colorized version of their father's film, *The Asphalt Jungle* (1950), even though they had no copyright, because that version was considered to be a mutilation or distortion of the work.

The "right of attribution" in its most simple form is the right of the author to be identified as the creator of a work. However, this right also can be used to protect the creator against other abuses, such as attributing to that author a work created by someone else. The author can also rely on this right to prevent others from being identified as the creator or a cocreator of one's own work and to publish anonymously or under a pseudonym.

The third moral right, the "right of disclosure," affords to the author the sole right to decide when the work is complete and ready for publication as well as the right to retract a work from publication and to prevent its distribution. This right also has been used to prevent excessive criticism of a work as well as ad hominem attacks (attacks on the author's personality as opposed to the work).

In the Berne Convention for the Protection of Literary and Artistic Works,[7] an international copyright treaty, the moral rights of integrity and attribution were expressly included in Article 6bis.[8] This Article provides that the author retains rights of authorship "independently of the author's economic rights"[9] and can object

138

to any distortion, mutilation, or other modifications of, or other derogatory action in relation to, that work, which would be prejudicial to his honor or reputation. These rights continue after the author's death.[10]

The means of claiming such rights under the Berne Convention are governed by the country where protection is claimed. The United States did not sign on to the Berne Convention until 1988, however, and at the time the treaty was adopted, and legislation was drafted to implement it, Congress determined that the minimum standards of moral rights required by Article 6bis would be satisfied without further statutory revision. Basically, Congress had assessed the legal landscape of moral rights laws in the United States and concluded that the patchwork of common laws and state statutory schemes (where they existed) provided substantially equivalent protection as Article 6bis. The other signatories to the Berne Convention seem to have accepted this.[11] Since the Berne Convention was adopted, other than limited legislation in 1990 that provided moral rights of attribution and integrity to authors of narrowly defined works of visual arts,[12] there has been very little movement to create greater moral rights protection in the United States than what otherwise existed prior to the implementation of the Berne Convention.

1. Self, Henry L., "Moral Rights and Musicians in the United States, 2003-2004," *Entertainment, Publishing and Arts Handbook* 165 (2003), found at http://www.lavelysinger.com/MoralRights.pdf.
2. DaSilva, Russell J., *Droit Moral and Amoral Copyright*, 16-17.
3. DaSilva, Russell J., 16-17.
4. Self.
5. *See* Reel 10, The Iron Curtain Descends.
6. *Huston v. La Cinq. See* Reel 26, The Sculptor.
7. Berne Convention for the Protection of Literary and Artistic Works of September 9, 1886, completed at Paris on May 4, 1896, revised at Berlin on November 12, 1908, completed at Berne on March 20, 1914, revised at Rome on June 2, 1928, at Brussels on June 26, 1948, at Stockholm on July 14, 1967, and at Paris on July 24, 1971, and amended on September 28, 1979.
8. By the Rome Amendments in 1928, Berne Convention, Article 6bis.
9. Berne Convention, Article 6bis (1).
10. Berne Convention, Article 6bis (2).

Intermission 4 (continued)

11. *See* H.R. Rep. No. 100-609, at 37 (1988), Final Report of the Ad Hoc Working Group on U.S. Adherence to the Berne Convention 29, reprinted in 10 Columbia Law J & Arts 513 (1986).

12. These rights, following the model suggested in the Berne Convention, guarantee to authors of so-called fine arts and exhibition photographs the right to claim or disclaim authorship in a work; limited rights to prevent distortion, mutilation, or modification of a work; and the right, under some circumstances, to prevent destruction of a work that is incorporated into a building. The Visual Artists Rights Act of 1990 (VARA), 17 U.S.C. § 106A. Moral rights are also protected indirectly by state tort, privacy, and publicity laws.

The Way They Were
The Un-American Activities of the House Un-American Activities Committee

Cole v. Loew's, Inc., 76 F. Supp. 872 (S.D. Cal. 1948);
Loew's, Inc. v. Cole, 185 F. 2d 641 (9th Cir. 1950)

> **Marcus Licinius Crassus: The enemies of the state are known, arrests are being made, the prisons begin to fill.**
> From *Spartacus* (1960), screenplay by Dalton Trumbo

The cold war period in the United States was very unlike that which had immediately preceded it and the years that followed. As Charles Dickens wrote in *A Tale of Two Cities*, "It was the best of times; it was the worst of times." In the post-war period, the United States entered a period of prolonged prosperity and the Hollywood film industry experienced several decades in the 1950s and the 1960s—after the Paramount decision—where independence and creativity abounded. The best of times. But it was also a time of great uncertainty and chilling fear among the American public. As Josef Stalin began annexing Eastern European countries under the Soviet Union, creating an "Iron Curtain" separating the largely democratic Western nations from the totalitarian Eastern bloc, people grew fearful and distrustful. Soviet spies were uncovered and more could still be in hiding in the much talked-about "sleeper cells," ready to take over the American government and undermine people's freedoms. It was the worst of times. Dalton Trumbo, the screenwriter and one of the "Hollywood Ten" referred to below, called this era the "Time of the Toad."[1]

It was an anxious time, but ironically, in the end, the movement that created the greatest threat to American liberties was not of Soviet origin but rather arose right from within our government, in the U.S. Congress, in the form of Senator Joseph McCarthy of Wisconsin in the U.S. Senate and the House Un-American Activities Committee (HUAC), under Representative Parnell Thomas. And the eyes of the Committee members were on Hollywood.

During the 1940s, a large number of Hollywood actors, screenwriters, and directors had been sympathetic to the Soviet Union and the communist cause. They were idealists. Some of these had joined the American Communist Party.[2] This was not all that surprising because, during World War II, the Soviet Union was an American ally in the battle against Hitler.[3] However, before American soldiers had even returned home from the war effort following the Armistice, politics in the United States had already veered sharply to the right and this placed many of these same writers, actors, and directors in a vulnerable position.

When the HUAC hearings began in 1947, a large number of witnesses from Hollywood were subpoenaed. So-called "friendly" witnesses intimated that there were communists actively involved in the production of Hollywood movies. These witnesses were given a hospitable reception by the HUAC, while the "unfriendly" witnesses, many of them screenwriters, were

---

1. Starr, *California*, p. 280.
2. Thompson & Bordwell, p. 326.
3. California historian Kevin Starr points out that a number of movies made during the war years, such as *Action in the North Atlantic* (1943) with Humphrey Bogart (and a screenplay by John Howard Lawson, one of the Hollywood Ten) showed a pro-Soviet sentiment. Starr, *California*, p. 280.

treated with hostility and suspicion. Under a barrage of sharp questions from Committee members, they were barely allowed to speak. Several refused to admit or deny that they were communists, stating that their First Amendment right of freedom of expression protected them and their work. This was not what the Committee wanted to hear. Ten of these men were cited for contempt of Congress and briefly imprisoned. They came to be known as the "Hollywood Ten": scriptwriters John Howard Lawson, Dalton Trumbo, Albert Maltz, Alvah Bessie, Samuel Ornitz, Herbert Biberman, Ring Lardner, Jr., and Lester Cole; director Edward Dmytryk, and producer Adrian Scott.

Initially the studios were inclined to support their employees. After all, among these ten were the most prolific and reliable screenwriters in Hollywood, having authored many of the best scripts filmed. Four had received Academy Awards for their work.[4] The screenwriter Dalton Trumbo, for one, had signed with MGM (Loew's Inc.) one of the most lucrative contracts in the industry at the time, carrying a $3,000 per week salary.[5]

Lester Cole, for another, was also very well-regarded. It was true that, as one of the organizers of the Screen Writers Guild, the first and probably the most radical of the Hollywood guilds established in the 1930s, Cole's politics were more to the left of the mainstream. He had joined the American Communist Party in 1934. But he had proved his worth to Hollywood, having worked for almost every major studio. Just before he received the HUAC subpoena, requiring him to testify before Congress, he had signed a contract with Loew's, calling for a salary of $1,300 per week. He had just been assigned to write one of

---

4. Donald Ogden Stewart, Sidney Buchman, Ring Lardner, Jr., and Howard Koch. *See* Ceplair, Larry, and Englund, Steven, "The Hollywood Ten: From the Blacklist to Prison, November 1947-June 1950," *The Inquisition in Hollywood: Politics in the Film Community, 1930-1960*, Chapter 10, p. 333.

5. Thompson & Bordwell, p. 335.

MGM's biggest productions, *Zapata*, and he was on the verge of a promotion to writer-producer. He was at the peak of his career in the film industry. But as Cole and the others soon learned, no one man is, and no ten men—whatever the level of their skill—are, indispensable to a huge industry overflowing with talent.[6] Thus, despite the value that these men had brought to their studios, they were thrown overboard. The studios believed that they had to placate and "silence the baying patriotic wolves."[7] The Ten were put on suspension by their studio employers and blacklisted by the industry.

These men still believed that it was a matter of free speech and that no employer could impose a "political opinion test for employment."[8] They failed to realize that the studio heads no longer cared about "why" the Ten had refused to provide testimony to the HUAC. It was perceived as a question of behavior: "how" had they acted before the Committee and had they "brought disrepute" onto the studios? What the studio heads thought about the HUAC and the anticommunist mood of the country did not matter. For example, Louis B. Mayer, head of Loew's (MGM), did not ever say that he had decided to let Cole go because he was a communist; whatever his "real reasons, the formal justifications for the institution of the blacklist had to be framed in 'moral terms.'" The studio heads had already decided to cut their losses.[9] MGM did not actually fire Cole and Trumbo, but rather indefinitely suspended their contracts and stopped their paychecks. Thus, by the end of 1947, "for the first time in the history of the American film industry, ten perfectly capable experienced screen artists found themselves at the end

---

6. Thompson & Bordwell, p. 336.
7. Thompson & Bordwell, p. 326.
8. Thompson & Bordwell, p. 327.
9. Thompson & Bordwell, p. 328.

of their professional careers as a consequence of their political beliefs."[10] By the end of 1947, the Hollywood Ten had become "nonpersons" as far as the film industry was concerned.

Hollywood went into a defensive posture, attempting to prove its patriotism to the HUAC and to the public at large. The studios turned out numerous patriotic films[11] that warned people of the dangers of communism. These films were for the most part not successful but the studios believed that they served the purpose.

In the same month (December 1947), the HUAC voted contempt of Congress citations against the Hollywood Ten and a federal grand jury indicted them. Cut loose by the studios and with most people in Hollywood cowering before the power of the HUAC and hostile public opinion, these men each had to mount a defense, all the while without even the funds to live on and to maintain their families. They filed civil suits against the studios and in turn faced criminal trials. All in all, the Ten filed eight civil suits against the studios charging breach of contract and conspiracy to blacklist.[12]

Cole's case against Loew's was one of the most hopeful, because he won at the trial court level. In January 1948, after his dismissal by Loew's, Cole filed suit against the studio for breach of contract in California Superior Court in Los Angeles. Loew's filed to move the case to federal district court and this petition was granted. The case was heard in a jury trial before Judge Yankevich.

Cole claimed that Loew's had no right to suspend him or

---

10. Thompson & Bordwell, p. 331.

11. *See* Reel 10, The Iron Curtain Descends.

12. Ceplair & Englund, p. 350. These were *Cole v. Loew's, Inc., Scott v. RKO, Trumbo v. Loew's Inc., Lardner v. Twentieth Century Fox, Maltz v. Loew's Inc.*, and *Young v. Motion Picture Association.* Some of these were dropped and some were settled out of court, and several were successful at the trial court level but then overturned on appeal.

to stop payment of his salary and he sought a declaratory judgment from the court stating so. Judge Yankevich from the beginning refused to hear any testimony questioning the constitutional validity of the HUAC or its right to subpoena witnesses such as Cole. The only question he was willing to consider was whether Cole's conduct before the Committee was such that the suspension and refusal to pay his salary was warranted. At the conclusion of the trial, the jury came back with a verdict against Loew's, determining that the studio had no right to suspend Cole's employment or compensation and ordering reinstatement as well as awarding $75,600 in back pay. Unfortunately, Cole was never to see this money. Loew's appealed.

Cole contended that his conduct before the HUAC had been "political" and that California law forbade an employer from coercing or influencing the political activities of its employees. But the appellate court noted that, if Cole had willfully refused to answer questions of a congressional committee, then he was guilty of contempt of Congress, which was a misdemeanor under federal law, and a conviction could lead to potential imprisonment.

The court further referred to Cole's contract, which provided that the employee agreed to conduct himself "with due regard to public conventions and morals."[13] The court determined that if a person chose to conduct himself in such a manner as to be guilty of a misdemeanor that could send him to prison, then he could hardly be said to be behaving "with due regard to public conventions." However, the court also noted that this question of Cole's conduct, which it viewed as inherent to the

---

13. This was one of the "morals clauses" that studios began inserting into contracts in the 1920s under pressure from William Hays for an entirely different reason. *See* Intermission 1, Scandals in Hollywood: Selling Movies and Hiding the Foibles of the Stars.

case, had not been presented at trial and therefore the jury had not been able to rule on it. The court also concluded that as a matter of law in 1947 it was entirely possible that, by refusing to state whether or not he was a member of the Communist Party (where the public viewed communism and communists as "evil"), Cole had breached his agreement with the studio.

Cole also argued that the studio executives, prior to the HUAC hearing, had led him to understand that the course of action he chose—neither admitting nor denying his party affiliation—would not be regarded as a breach of his contract. His counsel submitted facts to support this contention. First, while the HUAC hearings were taking place, Cole was offered an amendment to his contract, extending its term, guaranteeing him more work, and increasing his rate of compensation. This agreement was signed in August 1947. In October 1947, the attorneys for the "unfriendly" witnesses, which included Cole, sent a letter to the Committee giving notice that they would move to quash the subpoenas because the investigation was an unlawful attempt to control the content of motion pictures and to censor them. Loew's did not object to this action. Meanwhile, Paul McNutt, counsel to the Motion Picture Producers Association during this time, held press conferences and gave radio interviews related to the hearings that were critical of the HUAC investigation. On the basis of this background, and especially McNutt's statement, Cole claimed to have reasonably been led to believe that the studio would not object to the conduct that he demonstrated as a witness before Congress.

The court disagreed. Even though the studios had showed some hostility or unhappiness with the Committee hearings, the court did not believe that this provided Cole with his employer's implied consent to go so far as to be cited for contempt of Congress. "He was plainly ill advised to go to the extreme which he did," the court said. Cole also argued that, even if the studio was not pleased with his behavior before Congress, it promptly put him back to work without discharging him. It was only after a public uproar arose—a consequence of the actions of the writers who refused to testify—that industry executives determined to try to save themselves by throwing these writers "under the bus." Cole also pointed out that after the hearings, he was allowed to work on the screenplay for the film *Zapata*, which was then in production, and to collect his weekly compensation. The jury had seen this as a waiver by the studio of Cole's behavior. But the appellate court disagreed. It viewed the studio's delay as a natural response, because it would have needed a reasonable time to determine a course of action. And furthermore, this was irrelevant to the right of the employer to enforce the contract.

Accordingly, finding that the "net effect" of the HUAC hearing was to make Cole a distinct liability for the studio, the court reversed the jury verdict, ruling in the studio's favor.

Cole was not alone. None of the Ten fared well, whether in the civil cases they filed or in the criminal proceedings. Despite their defense that the HUAC did not have a right to interrogate them on the basis of their political beliefs, they were all convicted of contempt of Congress, and sent to prison. Lawson, Trumbo, and Scott served their terms in Ashland, Kentucky. Cole was sentenced to one year in the federal prison in Danbury, Connecticut, where he served his time with Ring Lardner.[14]

---

14. Ceplair & Englund, p. 356. The authors recount the following anecdote: "Cole and Lardner were pleasantly surprised one day to find that a new inmate in Danbury was none other than their old acquaintance, Parnell Thomas [former Chairman of the HUAC]. The New Jersey congressman had been sentenced for padding his office payroll. Lester Cole happened to pass the former HUAC chairman, now busily at work in the prison's chicken coop. Cole said something of a political nature, to which Thomas replied, 'I see you are still speaking radical nonsense.' Said Cole, 'And I see that you are still shoveling chicken shit.'"

In 1947, the thrust of the HUAC hearings had been to demonstrate that Hollywood films were filled with communist ideas.[15] By the time the Hollywood Ten had served their sentences and were released from prison, the mood in Hollywood had worsened. In the intervening time, China had fallen to the communists, the Rosenbergs had been tried as Soviet spies and sentenced to death, and American troops were fighting in the Korean War. "The fate of the Hollywood Ten turned out to be only a small foretaste of the political, professional and human destruction that was to occur in Hollywood. The jailing of successful screen artists shattered the pervasive illusion that Americans could not be punished for their political beliefs and activities."[16]

When the HUAC hearings resumed in 1951, after several years' hiatus, this time with the goal of exposing all communists in the film industry, people ran scared and friends turned on friend and foe alike. Former communists and those accused of having been party members were encouraged to save themselves by naming others. Some did, among them actor Sterling Hayden and directors Edward Dmytryk and Elia Kazan.[17] Prominent actor Edward G. Robinson, facing a dark cloud of suspicion over his successful career, testified at his own request before the Committee, providing documents and records.[18] Even those who did not name others sat back quietly, hoping to avoid notice. No one in Hollywood objected to the witch hunt that was taking place. Even the Screen Actors Guild voted to ban communists from their organization.[19]

Those who refused to testify were blacklisted; those who

---

15. Thompson & Bordwell, p. 326.
16. Ceplair & Englund, p. 361.
17. Thompson & Bordwell, p. 326.
18. Ceplair & Englund, p. 364.
19. Ceplair & Englund, p. 368.

named others generally survived with their careers intact but with their reputations tarnished: they so feared losing their careers and their income that they cooperated.[20] While these individuals continued to thrive in Hollywood, for the Hollywood Ten and those who followed on the blacklist, their lives and their careers were shattered. Some, such as Jules Dassin, managed to revive their careers by relocating abroad. And others wrote under pseudonyms.[21]

Lester Cole, once in a lucrative writer-producer position at MGM, came out of prison to work in a warehouse[22] and then as an assistant copywriter in the advertising department at a mattress manufacturer at a salary of $400 per month.[23] Cole eventually went back to screenwriting, albeit under an assumed name. When he was sent to prison, his unfinished script was completed by John Steinbeck and the film, directed by Elia Kazan, was released as *Viva Zapata* (1952), starring Marlon Brando. Under the assumed name of Gerald L.C. Copley, he wrote the script for *Born Free* (1966). Dalton Trumbo wrote the script for *The Brave One* (1956) under the assumed name of Robert Rich, which won him an Oscar for Best Screenplay (under that pseudonym).[24] In 1960, Otto Preminger declared that he would give Trumbo screen credit for his script for *Exodus*. Kirk Douglas did the same for Trumbo's screenplay for *Spartacus* (1960), which Douglas later described as "one of the proudest decisions" of his life.[25]

---

20. Ceplair & Englund, Chapter 11, "The Devastation: HUAC Returns to Hollywood, 1951-53," p. 377.

21. Thompson & Bordwell, p. 326.

22. Ceplair & Englund, Chapter 11, p. 378.

23. Ceplair & Englund, Chapter 10, p. 357.

24. Thompson & Bordwell, p. 326-327.

25. Douglas, Kirk, "Kirk Douglas on Trumbo," Letter to the Editor, *The New York Times*, Thursday, December 29, 2011, page A26, found at http://www.nytimes.com/2011/12/29/opinion/kirk-douglas-on-trumbo.html, last accessed December 30, 2011.

The blacklist was ended. But these were only a few success-es. Most of those who were blacklisted never resumed their careers.

The atmosphere in Hollywood remained poisonous long after the 1950s and the industry suffered from the distrust and wasted talent. Sterling Hayden and Elia Kazan eventually admit-ted that they had thrown their colleagues to the wolves in order to save themselves. The resentment toward them, and toward others who had given names during the hearings, lingered for decades,[26] to the extent that at the 1999 Academy Awards when Kazan was honored with a lifetime achievement award, some attendees remained seated and refused to applaud him.[27]

The effects were felt into the 1960s and to this day. The Writ-ers Guild engaged in a long-standing dispute with the studios over the issue of withholding screen credit for writers who had taken the Fifth Amendment during the HUAC hearings.[28] In fact, it was only in late 2011 that the Guild restored the screenwriting credit to Dalton Trumbo for William Wyler's *Roman Holiday* (1953).[29]

---

26. Thompson & Bordwell, p. 326.

27. Biography for Elia Kazan, Internet Movie Database, found at http://www.imdb.com/name/nm0001415/bio.

28. *Variety*, December 28, 1966, quoted in Harris, Mark, *Pictures at a Revolution: Five Movies and the Birth of the New Hollywood*, The Penguin Press, New York, 2008, p. 206.

29. Itzkoff, Dave, "Dalton Trumbo's Screenwriting Credit Restored to 'Roman Holiday,'" *The New York Times*, Dec. 20, 2011, found at http://artsbeat.blogs.nytimes.com/2011/12/20/dalton-trumbos-screenwriting-credit-restored-to-roman-holiday/, last accessed December 22, 2011. Trumbo wrote the screenplay while in exile in Mexico, but the work was attributed to a "front" writer, Ian McLellan Hunter. On December 15, 1992, the Board of Governors of the Academy of Motion Picture Arts and Sci-ences voted to change its records and credit Trumbo with the Best Screenplay award given to *Roman Holiday* in 1954. The Oscar was presented to Trumbo's widow on May 10, 1993. News Release, July 18, 2005, "'Great To Be Nominated' Enjoys a 'Roman Holiday,'" Academy of Motion Pictures Arts and Sciences website, found at web.archive.org/web/20071008054115/http://www.oscars.org/press/pressreleases/2005/05.07.18.html, last accessed December 22, 2011. In a letter that was posted on the Guild's website, Ian McLellan Hunter's son, Tim Hunter, wrote that the movie "was tangible proof of a friendship, a symbol on celluloid of many friendships, and

And it took a federal court in 1966 to force the Directors Guild to abandon the anticommunist loyalty oath that it had imposed on its members at the height of the Red Scare.[30]

the manifestation of a pact between friends during a time of political persecution." The president of the Writers Guild of America, West, Chris Keyser, is quoted as follows: "It is not in our power to erase the mistakes or the suffering of the past. But we can make amends, we can pledge not to fall prey again to the dangerous power of fear or to the impulse to censor, even if that pledge is really only a hope. And, in the end, we can give credit where credit is due." News Release, December 19, 2011, "A Gift of Justice for the Holidays: Dalton Trumbo's Screenplay Credit Restored to 'Roman Holiday,'" Writers Guild of America, West, website, found at http://www.wga.org/content/default.aspx?id=4782, last accessed December 22, 2011.

30. Zion, Sidney E., "US Court Voids A Loyalty Oath," *The New York Times*, July 15, 1966, found at http://select.nytimes.com/gst/abstract.html?res=F50716 F63559117B93C7A8178CD85F428685F9&scp=1&sq=Zion,%20Sidney%20E.,%20 %E2%80%9CUS%20Court%20Voids%20a%20Loyalty%20Oath&st=cse, last accessed December 30, 2011; "Directors Guild is Ordered to Drop Oath Requirement," *The New York Times*, January 28, 1967, found at http://select.nytimes.com/gst/abstract. html?res=F30C14FF3D5D107B93CAAB178AD85F438685F9&scp=1&sq=Directors%20 Guild%20is%20Ordered%20to%20Drop%20Oath&st=cse, last accessed December 30, 2011. *See*, Harris, *Pictures at a Revolution*, p. 206, note 9.

Intermission 5

Movie Censorship Reprised: The Legion of Decency and The Code

I was raised in a very strict Roman Catholic family. Every week my parents received and read a Catholic newspaper that published movie ratings. It was in very fine print—movies never fell off the list although others were added. The list started with the most benign—those receiving the Catholic Legion of Decency's A1 rating, "approved for all"—and ended with those that had received a "C, condemned," rating. I do not recall what movies made it to the top of the list in the A1 category; those titles obviously weren't interesting. I was much more intrigued by the films that received the dreaded C. What was there about those films that made it a sin to see them? What sordid features did they contain that had condemned them? The titles sometimes seemed so innocent. I recall the movie that always headed the top of that list (the list was in alphabetical order)—*And God Created Woman* (1956). What could have been wrong with that biblical reference, I wondered, not realizing until much later that it was the title of a French movie with the sex idol, Brigitte Bardot. Further down the list appeared *Baby Doll* (1956) and *Breathless* (1960).

The Legion of Decency was formed in the 1930s by leaders of the Catholic Church as a protest against what they viewed as lax enforcement of the Hollywood Production Code by the Motion Picture Producers and Distributors of America (MPPDA).[1] The Code had been instituted at a bad time for movie producers. With many experiencing significant financial difficulties and some falling into bankruptcy with the onset of the Great Depression, the last thing they needed was a self-inflicted restriction on using the two film subjects that they knew would boost box office numbers, sex and violence.[2] But outspoken pressure groups were outraged by films that they believed promoted loose moral standards. Gangster movies such as *The Public Enemy* (1931) and *Little*

Intermission 5 (continued)

Caesar (1931), featuring popular "tough guy" actors such as James Cagney and Edward G. Robinson, had become very popular and were sure winners at the box office. Even though the "heroes" were killed at the end, these films "were seen as glorifying criminals."[3] Worse, immoral sexual behavior also seemed to be glorified: films such as *Baby Face* (1933), starring Barbara Stanwyck, presented positive images of loose women who "traded sexual favors for material gain," lived in sumptuous apartments, and wore elegant clothes.[4] Mae West, one of the most popular and successful performers of the 1930s whose dialogue was particularly "salacious," was a "top moneymaker" for Paramount.[5] Other certain box office winners were the light comedies of Ernst Lubitsch, which were filled with sexual innuendo. His very popular *Trouble in Paradise* (1932), which at once seemed to glorify loose sexual morals and criminal activity, is an example. It tells the story of Gaston Monescu (played by Herbert Marshall)—a gentleman thief—and Lily (played by Miriam Hopkins)—a pickpocket—who, in a very amusing opening scene, fail to successfully steal from each other and then join forces in an attempted swindle of a wealthy woman in Paris—all in an engaging mélange of comedy, sexual dalliances, and thievery. The two lovable scoundrels go unpunished in the end and the audience wouldn't have had it any other way.

These types of films, although successful financially for the industry, were a source of consternation to reformers. Criticism of movie content grew and religious and other leaders asserted pressure on the industry to reform itself or be reformed. The Legion of Decency encouraged Catholics to take a "pledge" to patronize only those movie theaters that showed wholesome films and, under pain of sin, to boycott any condemned movies. Studio heads paid attention. Because many moviegoers, especially in urban areas, were Catholics, and because of the weakness in box office receipts, the studios did not feel they could afford to alienate this large group of consumers. As a result, the MPPDA announced the establishment of the

Production Code Administration (PCA) to oversee and enforce movie content according to the Code. Beginning in 1934, only films that had a Production Code seal could be shown in MPPDA member-owned theaters.[6] Member studios that released films without a seal were subject to a $25,000 fine.[7]

As a result, post-Code films became more suggestive while overt sexual scenes disappeared.[8] Extreme violence was implied but occurred only off-screen. Gangster films still featured criminals as protagonists, but the plots were devised to demonstrate that, in the end, crime does not pay. *Angels With Dirty Faces* (1938), for example, chronicles the lives of two tough kids growing up in New York, one of whom as an adult goes straight and becomes a priest, and the other, a gangster. The gangster, Rocky (played by James Cagney), is idolized by the neighborhood children. When he is sentenced to die in the electric chair, the priest (played by Pat O'Brien), persuades Rocky to pretend to be terrified before his execution, so that the kids will think of him as a coward and will not continue to see him as a role model.

This state of affairs for the U.S. film industry continued through the war years. However, as the movie business changed from a studio system to a freer structure in the postwar era, the practice of self-censorship and the power of the Legion of Decency began to unravel. The *Paramount* case did much to bring about this change.[9] The Production Code was enforced by means of the rule that no theater belonging to a MPPDA member could show a film that lacked a Production Code seal. Once the major studios, under court order, divested themselves of their theater chains, then cinemas were free to show any film they chose.[10] Before, the Hollywood studios had been able to use the requirement of a Code seal to keep independent films out of the U.S. market because these often had more risqué subject matter than the standard features produced at the time by the major studios. Once theaters were free to show what they wanted, with or without Production Code seals, more independent and foreign films came into theaters and these frequently had more

Intermission 5 (continued)

"adult" subject matter. Now, the theaters would not have chosen to show these movies if there had been no demand for them. But in the postwar years, audience tastes were also changing.

Public demand for films with more sophisticated themes was high. Certain American directors, such as Otto Preminger and Billy Wilder, provided these. And foreign films were also popular. These movies frequently had problems obtaining a Hollywood seal, even when they contained neither overt sexual content nor extreme violence. *The Bicycle Thief* (1948) is a case in point. This is a gritty story of a down-on-his-luck man in postwar Rome trying to find work to support his wife and small son. He finally gets a job as a poster hanger, but he needs a bicycle or he cannot do the job. He hocks his wife's few pieces of good linen and with the money buys a bicycle. On his first day of work, the bicycle is stolen. He and his son search everywhere for the thief but with no luck. At the end of the film the desperate father steals another bicycle but is caught by an angry crowd. In the last scenes, this poor man has now lost everything, including his pride and the respect of his son.

In 1949, the New York film importer, Joseph Burstyn, obtained the rights to distribute this Italian movie in U.S. theaters. It opened in New York and was immensely popular both with audiences and critics. Warner Brothers noticed the attention the film was receiving in New York and decided to book the film for its theaters in other parts of the country. Burstyn sent a print of the movie to the PCA to obtain a seal. Its head, Joseph Breen,[11] ordered two cuts to be made to the film, one of a scene that showed the little boy relieving himself against a wall and the other providing a very brief look inside a brothel. The movie's producer, Vittorio De Sica, refused to approve the cuts. Both scenes were viewed as essential to the movie's plot, and the development of its characters. The scene with the young son, for example, demonstrated the desperation of the father—so determined to locate his stolen bicycle that he forgot about even the most basic needs of his little boy.

Denied the seal, the movie could not be distributed nationally. Breen's refusal to award a seal to this particular film provoked an outcry. Burstyn ran ads attacking the PCA's position.[12] Despite the lack of a seal, the film won an Oscar for best foreign film in 1949 and an award as the "Best Foreign Film of the Year" from the New York Film Critics Circle. Ironically, the movie that could not get a Production Code seal had passed muster with the restrictive New York film censors and had even obtained a "B" rating ("objectionable in part") from the conservative Legion of Decency.[13]

Along with changing tastes in the postwar years, new competition, in the form of television, was affecting box office revenues.[14] Hollywood had to consider how to attract and keep its audiences. "One way of competing with television, which had extremely strict censorship, was to make films with more daring subject matter."[15] Consequently, the studios themselves began producing motion pictures that did not meet Code standards. Otto Preminger was notorious for ignoring the Code. When his movie, *The Moon Is Blue* (1953), was denied a seal, his distributor, United Artists, released it anyway, as well as his later film, *The Man With the Golden Arm* (1955), where Frank Sinatra played the role of a musician with a drug addiction.[16] Other films, such as Billy Wilder's *Some Like It Hot* (1959), with Marilyn Monroe, received a seal even though, by their content, in an earlier day they likely would not have.[17]

However, as the PCA loosened its standards, giving seals to films such as *Some Like It Hot* and *Baby Doll* (1956), the Catholic Legion of Decency did not suspend its activities or loosen its standards for approval. Both these movies, for example, received a "C" rating. The Legion also condemned foreign imports, such as Jean-Luc Godard's gangster film, *À Bout de Souffle (Breathless)* (1960), with Jean Seberg and Jean-Paul Belmondo, which to the Legion's eye was unacceptable because it contained both sex and violence. *Baby Doll* in particular upset church leaders because it dealt with illicit sex. Based on a Tennessee Williams play, the movie portrays Archie, a cotton gin owner, who married

Intermission 5 (continued)

a seventeen-year-old virgin, "Baby Doll" Meighan, but agrees to wait until she is twenty before consummating the marriage. As her birthday approaches, a rival gin owner, angry because Archie had burned down his gin, avenges himself on Archie by seducing Archie's wife. The film has unpleasant scenes of a scantily clad Baby Doll, sleeping in a crib, and of a leering Archie.

Nevertheless, the PCA had awarded its seal because there was no overt sexual activity on screen and this decision incensed Catholic leaders. In December 1956, in St. Patrick's Cathedral in New York City, Cardinal Spellman condemned the film in a sermon, telling the congregation gathered that day that he was shocked by the release of the movie and that he found it to be "deplorable" that Hollywood had approved *Baby Doll* for release in U.S. movie theaters.[18] He called on all Americans, Catholic and non-Catholic alike, to boycott the movie, as a "moral and patriotic duty." For people to refuse to attend this film, he said, would be "an indictment of those who defy God's laws and contribute to corruption in America."

But Spellman's attack only demonstrated how tenuous a hold the Catholic Church and the Legion of Decency had on filmmaking by the 1950s. It is true that Cardinal Spellman's stand against the movie and the resulting boycott by Catholics kept it out of many theaters and therefore, by some standards, the church's effort was successful. However, it also demonstrated the weakened influence that the church had over the industry. For, even though many Catholics boycotted *Baby Doll*, the movie was shown in a sufficient number of theaters during its run to remain among the box office top ten grossing films for two months.[19] And the church's failure to shut down the film, as well as the controversy provoked by its opposition to *The Miracle* several years earlier,[20] had weakened the ability of the Catholic Church and its Legion of Decency from that point to effectively censor movies in the United States.

1. Known as the "Hays Code" after Will Hays, the head of the MPPDA, who had put it in place in 1930. The Code was an outline of moral standards with respect to the depiction of crime, sex, and violence in films. Thompson & Bordwell, p. 216.

2. Wittern-Keller & Haberski, p. 21.

3. Thompson & Bordwell, p. 233.

4. Thompson & Bordwell, pp. 216-217.

5. Thompson & Bordwell, pp. 216-217.

6. Wittern-Keller & Haberski, p. 22.

7. Thompson & Bordwell, p. 217.

8. Thompson & Bordwell, pp. 216-217. Would *Gone With the Wind* have been the same movie if Rhett Butler (played by Clark Gable) had not been able to speak his famous line, "Frankly, my dear, I don't give a damn"? Yet that was almost the case. Thompson and Bordwell inform us that, before the release of the film, the MPPDA had initially required that that particular line be cut due to its "profanity." Only after a lengthy controversy did the MPPDA back down.

9. *See* Reel 9, The Studios' Last Stand, discussing *United States v. Paramount Pictures*, 334 U.S. 131 (1948).

10. Thompson & Bordwell, pp. 335.

11. Described "as 'an altar boy with brass knuckles' . . . and 'a professional Catholic' . . ." he ruled as the industry's Code enforcer into the 1950s. Wittern-Keller & Haberski, p. 22.

12. Wittern-Keller & Haberski, p. 56.

13. Wittern-Keller & Haberski, p. 56.

14. Wittern-Keller & Haberski, p. 49.

15. Thompson & Bordwell, pp. 335.

16. Thompson & Bordwell, pp. 335.

17. Thompson & Bordwell, pp. 335.

18. Wittern-Keller & Haberski, p. 154.

19. Wittern-Keller & Haberski, p. 156.

20. *See* Reel 12, The Cardinal—The Catholic Church and Movie Censorship.

The Cardinal
The Catholic Church and Movie Censorship

Joseph Burstyn, Inc. v. Wilson, 343 U.S. 495 (1952)

> **Cardinal Glennon:**
>   **You're not afraid of me.**
> **Stephen Fermoyle: No.**
> **Cardinal Glennon:**
>   **Why not? Most people are.**

John Huston as Cardinal Glennon and Tom Tryon
as Stephen Fermoyle in *The Cardinal* (1963)

As enforcement of the Code weakened and public taste for films with more sophisticated subjects increased, the time was ripe for another legal challenge to movie censorship laws. Surprisingly, the 1915 *Mutual Film Corporation* decision had not been overturned and had remained good law for almost fifty years. Even more surprising was that the film that finally led to a successful challenge to this decision was not one with overt violence or offensive sexual content, but rather a gentle, almost religious, story—*Il Miracolo* (*The Miracle*) (1948), an Italian film produced by Roberto Rossellini and Federico Fellini.

The Miracle tells the story of a simple-minded peasant woman in rural Italy who works as a day laborer to support herself. One day, while she is tending goats in the hills, she encounters a bearded stranger who resembles the statues of Saint Joseph that she has seen in the local church. He plies her with wine and she becomes more and more infatuated with him. The scene fades away and in the next scene "Saint Joseph" is gone and the woman wakes alone. She wanders down the hillside and encounters two priests, one of whom assures her that saints can appear to humans. Later, when she discovers she is pregnant, she announces to the village inhabitants that she is carrying Saint Joseph's child. The villagers mock her and she flees into the mountains. When the baby is due, she goes into an abandoned mountain chapel, where she gives birth to a son. Her love for this child transforms her and she becomes beautiful.

The movie had a mediocre response when it was released in Italy and to drum up support, Rossellini presented it at the Venice Film Festival in 1949, where the American film distributor, Joseph Burstyn, first saw it and acquired the U.S. distribution rights.

This film was an unlikely candidate for a landmark Supreme Court ruling on censorship in films. How and why did a simple film about an uneducated peasant woman become a "cause célèbre" in the fight against censorship? The picture provoked outrage from the beginning, as it was seen as mocking the Catholic doctrine of virgin birth. But there are several reasons why this outrage and the controversy that the film provoked ultimately led to a hearing before the U.S. Supreme Court.

Certainly, one reason was its distributor, Joseph Burstyn, already famous for having taken on Joseph Breen, head enforcer of Hollywood's Production Code, in order to gain national distribution for another Italian film, *The Bicycle Thief* (1948).[1] At the time of this controversy, one of Breen's associates stated that Breen had viewed Burstyn's application for a Hollywood

---

[1] *See* Intermission 5, Movie Censorship Reprised: The Legion of Decency and The Code

seal for *The Bicycle Thief* as a "trial balloon" rather than a case in its own right.[2] As an independent distributor of foreign films, Burstyn was frustrated by how censors in various states inhibited his ability to import quality foreign films from abroad and show them to a wide audience.[3] Burstyn may have been itching for a fight.

Another reason was in the person of the film's director, Roberto Rossellini. Political and cultural sensibilities in the United States had progressively veered to the right in the post-World War II years. Uncertainty over the growth of communism in Europe and Cold War tensions, as well as frightening political uprisings in various parts of the world, including Europe, with the perceived rise of left-wing governments in France and Italy, and the fear-mongering of Senator Joseph McCarthy and the House Un-American Activities Committee (HUAC),[4] led to a conformity of opinion in the American public and a distrust of anything "foreign." And Rossellini was not only one of those "foreigners" in the abstract but a specific subject of controversy as the result of his illicit affair with the very popular screen actress Ingrid Bergman in 1949, when she went to Italy to film *Stromboli* (1950). The affair, and her subsequent abandonment of her husband and daughter to have Rossellini's child and to live in Italy with him, had undermined her up to then wholesome image (she had been nominated for an Oscar in *The Bells of Saint Mary's* (1945) in which she played a nun).

The "moral guardians" of the American press and the Catholic clergy spoke out vehemently against the two sinners and the public was outraged. "Clearly 1950 was no time for a Rossellini

---

2. Wittern-Keller & Haberski, p. 58.
3. Wittern-Keller & Haberski, p. 54.
4. *See* Reel 11, The Way They Were—The Un-American Activities of the House Un-American Activities Committee.

film that American Catholics might interpret as insulting their faith," to be brought into the United States.[5]

And, finally, the Catholic Church played a big role in fanning the flames of opposition against the movie. The Legion of Decency gave the film (and the two other movies that had been packaged with *The Miracle* for exhibition together) a condemned rating, "the first film the Legion had designated as 'sacrilegious.'"[6] The Archdiocese of New York had officially spoken out against the movie as "an open insult" to the Catholic faith.[7] All sides were joined for battle.

While Burstyn, who like other movie distributors had been frustrated by the New York film censors since he entered the business in the 1930s,[8] may have been hoping at some point to find a film with great artistic merit with which to challenge censorship laws, it is doubtful that when he first previewed *Il Miracolo* in Italy in 1948, he saw it as a vehicle for such a challenge. He thought, when he acquired the U.S. distribution rights, that this film would likely be uncontroversial for New York State censors and he was right. The censors passed the film without issue. In December 1949, he packaged the film, which was very short (only 40 minutes) with two others as a triptych called *Ways of Love* and booked it for exhibition in the New York Paris Theatre.[9] The films opened to critical acclaim.

It was at this point, however, when powerful Catholics,

---

5. Wittern-Keller & Haberski, p. 64.
6. Wittern-Keller & Haberski, p. 65.
7. Wittern-Keller & Haberski, p. 66.
8. Wittern-Keller & Haberski, p. 24. According to these authors, Burstyn hated having to ask permission from censors to show a film in New York. He said, "Every time I had to submit a film for censorship, I felt that I was in an illegitimate business and that being in this business was a crime."
9. "The Paris had been built two years before by the Pathé Company, a French film producer and distributor as a venue to showcase the best European films" in New York. Wittern-Keller & Haberski, p. 64.

including the Archdiocese, the Legion of Decency, and Edward T. McCaffrey, the City's Commissioner of Licenses, came out against the film. McCaffrey threatened to pull the Paris Theatre's business license if *The Miracle* was not removed from the *Ways of Love* triptych. At Burstyn's insistence, the Paris's management refused to remove the film and McCaffrey "suspended" the theater's operating license.[10] McCaffrey also threatened to suspend the license of any other theater that tried to book the movie.[11] Burstyn, with the Paris Theatre, sued to prevent McCaffrey from suspending theater licenses.

The public outcry both for and against the movie was huge. "Lines snaked around the block despite the wintry weather," with viewers anxious to see the film, once McCaffrey was ordered to withdraw the suspension.[12] In support of the film, the New York Film Critics named *Ways of Love* the best foreign film of 1950.[13] The Catholic Church for its part urged a boycott and the theater was picketed.[14] In January 1951, under pressure from Catholic authorities and assailed with hundreds of letters and telegrams from people both protesting and supporting the movie, the New York Board of Regents (who administered New York's censorship statute), ordered Burstyn to appear before a hearing it had called to consider rescinding Burstyn's license from the censorship board.[15] After viewing *The Miracle*, the Regents determined that the movie was sacrilegious and

---

10. Wittern-Keller & Haberski, p. 64.

11. Wittern-Keller & Haberski, p. 65.

12. Wittern-Keller & Haberski, p. 66.

13. Wittern-Keller & Haberski, p. 65.

14. Wittern-Keller & Haberski, pp. 69-70.

15. New York's censorship statute was contained in its Education Law: The statute made it unlawful "to exhibit or to sell, or lease, or lend for exhibition at any place of amusement for pay or in connection with any business in the State of New York any motion picture film or reel . . . unless there is at the time in full force and effect a valid license or permit [from] . . . the education department." McKinney's N.Y. Laws, 1947 Education Law §129.

two weeks after this hearing, Burstyn's exhibition license was revoked.[16] Burstyn appealed the Regents' decision in the New York courts.[17]

Burstyn argued that the Regents had violated his First Amendment rights. He maintained that New York's censorship law was void for vagueness and was a prior restraint on his right of free speech. Had he been a newspaper editor, these would have been winning arguments. But since the *Mutual Film Corporation* decision,[18] no court had ruled that movies were entitled to such constitutional protection. "No gambler would have bet on Burstyn: legal precedent was solidly contrary to his position that movies should be free of prior restraint."[19] And it did seem that he had a losing case. In May 1951, the appellate division unanimously ruled against him. So he took his case to New York's highest court, the Court of Appeals, but this court also upheld the Board of Regents' decision. Burstyn's First Amendment arguments had gone nowhere, even with the help that he had garnered from various advocacy groups, such as the American Civil Liberties Union.[20]

Burstyn filed an appeal with the U.S. Supreme Court. His attorneys argued that the film had been incorrectly banned and this action violated both the Establishment Clause and the Free Speech Clause of the First Amendment to the U.S. Constitution. They believed and argued to the Supreme Court that, in taking

---

16. Wittern-Keller & Haberski, p. 74.

17. Wittern-Keller & Haberski, p. 84.

18. *Mutual Film Corporation v. Industrial Comm'n of Ohio*, 236 U.S. 230 (1915). *See* Reel 5, This Film is Not Yet Rated—Censorship of Movies.

19. Wittern-Keller & Haberski, p. 84.

20. The ACLU was eager to go to court in this case, not just because they saw it as presenting a good First Amendment argument, but also because the group was concerned about the growing influence of special interest groups, such as the Legion of Decency, which had become very vocal in speaking out against a number of films, both those that were domestically produced, such as Otto Preminger's and Billy Wilder's movies, and also foreign films. Wittern-Keller & Haberski, p. 82.

action against the film, the Regents had favored one religious group over others and, in fact, "had caved to Catholic pressure."[21]

On May 26, 1952, the Supreme Court issued its opinion in a unanimous decision, written by Justice Tom Clark.[22]

The New York statute allowed the state's Board of Censors to ban a film if it was found to be "sacrilegious."[23] In evaluating the merits of Burstyn's arguments that this law violated his First Amendment rights, the Court had to consider whether it should overturn the *Mutual Film Corporation* decision. In *Mutual Film*, the Court had determined that films were entertainment— that was all—and not akin to the press, where a free exchange of ideas was necessary and where prior restraint (that is, preventing the publication of those ideas) was intolerable. Justice Clark noted that the world was very different in post-World War II America than it had been in 1915 when *Mutual Film* was decided. He wrote, "It cannot be doubted that motion pictures are a significant medium for the communication of ideas. They may affect public attitudes and behavior in a variety of ways, ranging from direct espousal of a political or social doctrine to the subtle shaping of thought which characterizes all artistic expression. The importance of motion pictures as an organ of public opinion is not lessened by the fact that they are designed to entertain as well as to inform."

The Court then considered the continued relevance of

---

21. Wittern-Keller & Haberski, p. 97.

22. Justice Clark, who had been appointed to the Supreme Court by President Truman, had been the President's attorney general and in that capacity had overseen the federal antitrust action that led to the *Paramount* decision. United States v. Paramount Pictures, 334 U.S. 131 (1948). Wittern-Keller & Haberski, p. 94. *See* Reel 9, The Studios' Last Stand.

23. The statute required the state's Board of Censors to promptly examine every motion picture submitted to them and "unless such film . . . is obscene, indecent, immoral, inhuman, sacrilegious, or is of such a character that its exhibition would tend to corrupt morals or incite to crime," to issue a license to show the film. McKinney's N.Y. Laws, 1947, Education Law §122.

another principle from the *Mutual Film* decision—that motion pictures were not entitled to First Amendment protection because they were made for profit; they were "a business pure and simple," not intended to be regarded "as part of the press of the country or organs of public opinion."[24] Justice Clark recognized that this view of films simply as vehicles for entertainment accorded well with public opinion in 1915, but times had changed and public opinion had changed too. As he noted, "that books, newspapers, and magazines are published and sold for profit does not prevent them from being a form of expression whose liberty is safeguarded by the First Amendment. We fail to see why operation for profit should have any different effect in the case of motion pictures."

Finally, the Court demolished the third and final justification from the *Mutual Film* decision for treating films differently from books or newspapers: the concern over the potential harm that made movies special. Because motion pictures could be used for "evil" as well as for good, the Court in *Mutual Film* had determined that requiring that they be examined and approved prior to exhibition was a necessary and reasonable control. Justice Clark concluded that, even if it is the case that movies present a risk of harm, especially for society's youth, this does not mean that all motion pictures should be denied First Amendment protection. It did not justify the broad censorship that New York's statute allowed. The Court concluded that motion pictures are entitled to First Amendment protections and, to the extent that this ruling was inconsistent with the *Mutual Film* decision, that decision was overturned.

This did not mean that no censorship of films would be allowed at all. The Court recognized that there may be an

---

24. 236 U.S. at 244.

"exceptional case" where a prior restraint would be an acceptable burden. But New York's law was too broad in that it required advance permission to exhibit any motion picture. With respect to *The Miracle*, the Court noted, New York would have a "heavy burden" to demonstrate that the film represented "such an exceptional case."

The Court then turned its attention to the basis on which the Regents had revoked Burstyn's license to exhibit *The Miracle*—that the film was "sacrilegious." Justice Clark noted that "the state has no legitimate interest in protecting any or all religions from views distasteful to them . . . . It is not the business of government in our nation to suppress real or imagined attacks upon a particular religious doctrine, whether they appear in publication, speeches or motion pictures." In considering the term "sacrilegious," which was the sole standard used by the Board in revoking the movie's exhibition license, the Court concluded that the term was "impossibly ambiguous."

However, the ruling in the *Burstyn* decision was narrow. The Court left open the possibility, for example, that prior restraint might be acceptable if a film were deemed to be "obscene." Likewise, Justice Clark intimated that, by censoring *The Miracle* because some considered it to be "sacrilegious" for mocking the Catholic belief in the virgin birth, the state of New York violated the First Amendment's requirement of separation of church and state. However, he did not believe that he needed to consider that issue to support his ruling in favor of Burstyn because it was sufficient that the statute was unconstitutionally vague and that it infringed on the First Amendment rights of free speech and free press. The *Burstyn* decision had the effect of putting movie censors in states other than New York on notice that their statutes also were subject to challenge and ultimately this led to the dismantling of those laws.

It is important to clarify the debate that the movie provoked. It would be simple to classify this controversy as a battle between Catholics, who hated the film, and Protestants, who loved it. But that was not the case, for there were non-Catholics who also found the film to be offensive and many Catholics who waited in lines to see it, despite the warnings from the church leaders. This was rather a dispute between the hardcore prelates, in the person of Cardinal Spellman, who had developed a personal animosity to the film, and in the form of the Legion of Decency, versus others, including many Catholics, who believed that the film had been badly judged and who wondered if part of the rancor from the pulpit was directed as much at the film's director, Roberto Rossellini, as at the film itself. Justice Frankfurter, in his concurring opinion, quoted a number of Catholic commentators who spoke out in favor of the movie. One noted that there was "blasphemy" in the picture, "but it was the blasphemy of the villagers, who stopped at nothing, not even the mock singing of a hymn to the Virgin, in their brutal badgering of the tragic woman."[25] Allen Tate, a Catholic poet and critic, wrote, "The picture seems to me to be superior in acting and photography, but inferior dramatically . . .. In the long run, what Cardinal Spellman will have succeeded in doing is insulting the intelligence and faith of American Catholics with the assumption that a second-rate motion picture would in any way undermine their morals or shake their faith."[26]

Interestingly, this case was the first time that the Supreme Court justices watched a movie before issuing an opinion. It

---

25. Spaeth, Otto L. "Fogged Screen," *Magazine of Art*, Feb., 1951, p. 44; *N. Y. Herald Tribune*, Jan. 30, 1951, p. 18, col. 4, quoted in Frankfurter concurring opinion, 343 U.S. at 515, fn. 21.

26. *The New York Times*, Feb. 1, 1951, p. 24, col. 7, quoted in Frankfurter concurring opinion, 343 U.S. at 515, fn. 24.

was reported that, as they filed out of the viewing room, Justice Minton opined that "if he had paid any money to see the film, it would have been too much." In terms of movie quality, many critics have preferred other Rossellini films over *The Miracle*, such as *Rome, Open City* (1945) or *Paisan* (1946). Ironically, this motion picture might have been forgotten if it had been judged on its merits rather than for the controversy that it provoked.

The Players
Idea Submission Cases

Golding v. R.K.O. Pictures, Inc., 35 Cal. 2d 690 (1950)
and *Weitzenkorn v. Lesser*, 40 Cal. 2d 778 (1953)

> **Griffin Mill: I was just thinking what an interesting concept it is to eliminate the writer from the artistic process. If we could just get rid of these actors and directors, maybe we've got something here.**
>
> Tim Robbins, as Griffin Mill, in *The Player* (1992)

In a creative writing seminar I attended at The University of California, the professor told the class that we should beware if we hoped to sell a movie idea to Hollywood, because it was a nest of vipers. He urged us to seek out other outlets for our creative inspiration because the pros in Hollywood would take what we had to offer and pay us a pittance, if anything.

Cases from the courts in California seem to confirm this cynical advice; they are filled with stories of would-be writers and producers who had an inspiration that they believed would be the next blockbuster film. Those who act on the impulse to sell it to a studio often learn a hard lesson—their idea is more often than not going to be rejected. Later, when they see a movie that oh so closely resembles the story plot that they submitted, they are angry, sometimes justifiably so. And then they sue, especially if they have any proof that the studio had access to their idea or had agreed to pay them if they sent in their concept or treatment.

175

Cases chronicling the complaints of would-be screenwriters and want-to-be movie producers, charging plagiarism, or alleging that an "agreement" or understanding between the plaintiff and a studio existed, are plentiful. And that is because the California courts have bent over backwards to give them hope. Two cases in particular stand out: *Golding v. R.K.O. Pictures* and *Weitzenkorn v. Lesser.*

The *Golding* case involved a plagiarism claim. Samuel Golding and Norbert Faulkner were two established writers who had written a play entitled "The Man and His Shadow." They neither published it nor did they register it with the U.S. Copyright Office. But the Pasadena Playhouse produced the play in 1942 and, after making a few revisions, the two men submitted it to R.K.O. Pictures for consideration as a movie screenplay. A producer at R.K.O. received the manuscript. He happened at the time to be looking for a movie script where the action would take place on board a ship because a boat happened to be available on the studio lot. But after holding on to Golding's and Faulkner's script for several weeks, R.K.O. sent it back to the authors, informing them that the studio was not interested in the play after all.

In August 1943, R.K.O. released a motion picture entitled *The Ghost Ship*, and Golding and Faulkner sued R.K.O. alleging that the studio had based this film on their play, "The Man and His Shadow." At trial, the play was read to the jury and they also viewed the film. They returned a verdict in favor of the authors and awarded them $25,000 for plagiarism. R.K.O. appealed and the case went before the California Supreme Court in 1950.

There were similarities between the two works. In both the play and the movie, the action took place on board a ship. In the movie, the ship was a freighter, the "Altair." Tom Merriam signs on to the ship as a third officer, under Captain Stone. At first the two men get along. Stone sees Merriam as a younger version of himself and Merriam considers Stone as the first adult to treat him as a friend. But after a couple of strange deaths of crew members, Merriam begins to think that Stone is a psychopathic madman obsessed with authority. When Merriam confronts Stone, Stone admits that he had caused the deaths of some of his crew because the men were disrespectful. When Tom has the captain brought up on official charges, Tom is expelled from the ship.

He is eventually returned to duty, but the rest of the crew then shun him and will not help him as he pleads for his life when he is threatened by Stone. Only one person believes Tom; the rest assume that he has a grudge against the captain. However, when Tom's defender is found dead, it dawns on the others that Captain Stone may in fact be a murderer. The captain, realizing that he is about to be uncovered, loses his mind and brings about his own death.

The action in the play takes place on a pleasure cruise and the captain is an imposter whose true identity is about to be revealed. The play has the same basic plot as the film: it is a chronicle of a paranoid ship's captain, obsessed with his position and authority, engaged by an adversary aboard his ship and defeated by that same opponent and by his own mental collapse. But despite these similarities, there also are substantial differences between the two. Besides the fact that the action in the play takes place on a luxury cruise ship, not a freighter, the cast in the film—crew members—was different from the cast in the play—other passengers. R.K.O. argued that the similarities were coincidental and that the differences demonstrated that no plagiarism had taken place.

But the authors insisted that the court should focus on the basic dramatic situation between the captain and his antagonist, which was the same in both the movie and the play. This, they claimed, was the truly original and valuable feature of it. The majority of the justices agreed with the authors, ruling that what R.K.O. had copied was their "literary property," that is, "the fruits of a writer's creative endeavor," which "extend to the full scope of his inventiveness" and may include any number of features, "the entire plot, the unique dialogue, the . . . emotional appeal or theme of the story, or merely certain novel sequences or combinations of otherwise hackneyed elements." It all turned on the "novelty" of the work. "It is . . . only the product of the writer's creative mind which is protectible."

To prove whether the resemblance between the two was a mere coincidence or plagiarism, the court considered the interplay between two factors: proof of access and proof of similarity. Where there is a strong similarity, an author may not have to demonstrate that much more. On the other hand, where there is strong evidence of access, less proof of similarity is required. The court determined that, even though there were many differences between the two works, "the core of the . . . play constituted the truly original and valuable feature of it." Therefore, even though R.K.O. *could have* obtained the story from another source," the court did not think that to be likely. The authors had demonstrated that the film's producer had access to their play. They also showed that he was noted for taking ideas and having his own staff writers "make" his stories. He was quoted as saying, "Well, Golding, I don't have to buy my stories. I don't have to lay out money for originals." Without expressly saying so, the court seemed most offended by the cavalier attitude that the studio had taken with the authors. "The evidence of opportunity and, indeed, inclination to pirate" the two men's literary property, the court noted, was "clearly supported by the evidence."

178

Moreover, the fact that the jury viewed the film and heard the play and then returned a verdict in favor of the authors seemed sufficient evidence to the court that the "average observer" would find the two works to be similar and would reach the conclusion that one was copied from the other.

Justice Traynor dissented. He took issue with the majority's finding that the writers had a "property interest" in the "dramatic core" of the play. To him, this was insufficient under California law to create a property interest. More was required; to wit, "a concrete form in which the circumstances and ideas have been developed, arranged and put into shape." Justice Traynor noted, "themes, ideas and plots in books or plays are a common fund from which every author may draw the basic materials of his work without restriction." In his opinion, the "dramatic structure" on which the majority had focused so much attention—the obsessed authoritarian ship's captain consumed by his sense of superiority and authority—was a common movie sea story. He gave as examples *Mutiny on the Bounty* (1935), with Charles Laughton, as the obsessed captain, and Clark Gable, as his lieutenant[1] and *The Sea Wolf* (1941), with Edward G. Robinson, as Wolf Larsen, the obsessed captain.[2]

For Justice Traynor, while "the individual writer should have ample protection for his literary enterprise . . zeal to protect him should not lead to straitjacketing producers against what appears here to have been but a legitimate exercise of their own freedom of enterprise in an open field." Justice Schauer also dissented. "'The Ghost Ship' sailed," he wrote, "but I think neither it nor its author was engaged in piracy; and I think upholding

---

1. Not to be confused with the 1962 remake of the film with Trevor Howard as the obsessed captain and Marlon Brando as his antagonist.

2. In *The Sea Wolf*, Edward G. Robinson plays a cruel captain who has his sailors beaten for any pretext. *See* the Internet Movie Database, www.imdb.com.

the judgment in this case supports a result which approaches closer to piracy than did any act of the defendants."

Just a few years later, in 1953, the California Supreme Court was given another opportunity to take up this same question. In *Weitzenkorn v. Lesser*, Ilse Lahn Weitzenkorn had written a literary work entitled "Tarzan in the Land of Eternal Youth," about the already familiar Tarzan character. She sent it to Sol Lesser at his request. Lesser later produced a motion picture called *Tarzan's Magic Fountain* (1949), which was distributed by R.K.O. Pictures. Weitzenkorn sued, claiming that when she sent her work to Lesser there was an understanding "that she would be compensated for the value of the work and that she would receive screen credit as an author if the studio used all or any part of it." She asked for $50,000 as the compensation she should have received, and also $100,000 in damages for the theft of her work. On the studio's motion, the trial court dismissed Weitzenkorn's complaint. She appealed and the California Supreme Court accepted her case.

The court determined that, in order for her to claim damages for plagiarism, there had to be substantial similarity between the movie and her work. Although there were some similarities, particularly in the combination of the characters, Tarzan, Jane, and Cheetah in an African locale, and in the general concept of a fountain of eternal youth, in terms of form and manner of expression, the two works were very dissimilar. Moreover, the court did not find much novelty or originality in these common themes.

But the court believed that Weitzenkorn might still have a case and the similarity requirement might be less, if she could show that a contract existed between her and the studio. If she could prove that Lesser had agreed to pay her for her work if the studio used it, or any part of it, regardless of its originality, then the studio would be obliged to honor the contract. So the question was: did the studio use it?

Weitzenkorn could not produce a written agreement because there was none. She claimed that there was an express oral agreement that the court should recognize. The court used the same analysis to evaluate the strength of Weitzenkorn's case as it had in *Golding*. Was there a similarity between her work and the film and was her idea original? Because her concept was not truly original—Tarzan, Jane, and Cheetah in Africa was, after all, a fairly common theme in books and movies at the time—the court concluded that, to have a cause of action against the studio, she would have to show that there was "substantial similarity" between the motion picture and the "protectable portions" of her work. After reviewing the two, the court concluded that there was in fact no similarity, other than the unoriginal surface elements, between them.

Because the court could find no obvious plagiarism, due to the absence of similarity, it had to fall back on the question of whether or not there was an agreement, even if Weitzenkorn could produce no written contract. The court concluded that she did not have to produce an express written contract if she could prove in some other way that Lesser had agreed to pay her for her work.

Weitzenkorn claimed that after she submitted her work to the studio at Lesser's request, he retained it for a long enough time to become completely familiar with its contents. In theory, these acts might be sufficient to prove an implied contract (that is, a contract implied to exist based on Lesser's conduct) or a quasi contract. According to the court, a "quasi contract," unlike a true contract, would not be based on the apparent intention of the parties to undertake an obligation to each other or on a promise made by one party to another. Rather, this was an obligation created or implied for reasons of justice, that is, because of a benefit conferred on or accepted by a party. In that case, the party becomes obligated to pay the other. But the court was not certain that this was Weitzenkorn's situation and they believed that she would have the same problem of proof as she had in trying to prove plagiarism. If there was no similarity between her work and the motion picture, it was hard to see how Weitzenkorn had conferred any benefit on the studio or how Lesser had *used* any of her property.

The court concluded that the only avenue to recovery that Weitzenkorn had was to prove the existence of an agreement. Although skeptical that she would be able to do so, the court sent her case back to the lower court in order to allow her to submit any supporting evidence that she might have.

Justice Carter dissented from the majority opinion. These cases always involve a balancing of equities. Just as the dissenting justices in *Golding* had expressed concern that the court's zeal in protecting the writer might hamper the ability of filmmakers to produce movies, Justice Carter was worried about the fate of writers in the harsh Hollywood milieu. "Authors," he said, "anxious to find a market for their work, are not in an advantageous bargaining position" to insist that the one to whom the composition is submitted sign a contract agreeing to pay compensation if the work is used. He believed that plots are and should be protectable. But he was in the minority.

This back and forth between the rights of authors to protect their work and the rights of studios to take advantage of the free flow of ideas continues to this day. Some would argue, however, that in California, at least, there is a bright line rule, and it is that expressed in the next case that the California Supreme Court considered on this issue, *Desny v. Wilder*.[3]

---

3. 46 Cal. 2d 715 (1956). *See* Reel 14, The Conversation.

The Conversation

Desny v. Wilder, 46 Cal. 2d 715 (1956)

Show business is worse than dog-eat-dog. It's dog-doesn't-return-other-dog's-phone-calls.

From *Crimes and Misdemeanors*,
produced and directed by Woody Allen (1989)

In certain types of poker, such as Texas hold'em, each player is dealt two private "hole" cards that are kept hidden from the other players. At showdown, each player plays the best five-card hand he or she can put together with any of the five "community" cards that are on the table and one or two of the "hole" cards in his or her hand. The player who can improve a hand on the board generally wins. Obviously, having an "ace" card as a "hole" card creates an advantage. The term "an ace in the hole" derives from poker terminology and means having an advantage that is hidden from others.

In 1951, Paramount Pictures released the movie, *Ace in the Hole*, starring Kirk Douglas as a frustrated down-on-his-luck big city newspaperman who is now working as a reporter for a small paper in Albuquerque, New Mexico. The film was written, produced, and directed by Billy Wilder. Wilder was a successful Hollywood screenwriter and director, originally from Austria, who had immigrated to Hollywood in 1933 following the rise of Adolf Hitler in Germany. He was noted for film comedies, such as *Ninotchka* (1939) (in collaboration with Ernst Lubitsch), films noir, most famously as the director of *Double Indemnity* (1944) (for which he received an Academy Award nomination), and serious dramas, such as *The Lost Weekend* (1945) (for which he received Best Director and Best Screenplay Oscars) and *Sunset Boulevard* (1950). In other words, he was a serious and creative screenwriter who had several major successes under his belt when he produced *Ace in the Hole* (1951). This latter film was to prove to be a disappointing experience for Wilder on many fronts. It was Wilder's first solo film[1] and not only did it fail at the box office, it was a disaster.[2] Critics disapproved of it,[3] although it has more recently gained a critical following. Paramount, the studio that released the film, changed its name at the last minute to *The Big Carnival*, without Wilder's consent. And as a final blow, it became the subject of a nasty lawsuit in which a screenwriter named Victor Desny accused Wilder of plagiarism, a suit that impugned Wilder's integrity and reputation for originality.[4]

Ace in the Hole plays on the expression derived from poker, by creating a scenario where the main character, a newspaper reporter, has an advantage that others don't suspect. The film was inspired by two well-known real life events. In 1925, a Kentucky man named Floyd Collins was trapped inside a sand cave for two weeks, following a landslide. A Louisville newspaper sent its reporter to the scene and his coverage turned this parochial event into a national tragedy, when despite heroic rescue efforts, Collins died. In 1949, a little girl in San Marino, California, fell into an abandoned well and thousands came to witness her rescue. But she also died.

---

1. Sikov, Ed, *On Sunset Boulevard: The Life and Times of Billy Wilder*, Hyperion, New York, 1998, p. 311.

2. Sikov, p. 325.

3. Sikov, p. 326. Sikov quotes a review from the May 7, 1951, edition of the *Hollywood Reporter*: "Ruthless and cynical, *Ace in the Hole* is a distorted study of corruption and mob psychology that, in this reviewer's opinion, is nothing more than a brazen, uncalled for slap in the face of two respected and frequently effective American institutions—democratic governments and the free press."

4. Sikov, p. 327

In the movie, the newspaper reporter, Chuck Tatum, exploits the plight of a New Mexico man, who is trapped in a cave, as his hidden ace in a high stakes game to restart his stalled career. Tatum is a brilliant but cynical reporter whose short temper and lack of respect for authority has landed him in trouble at a number of papers. He arrives in Albuquerque having just been fired from his last reporting position. The local newspaper editor gives him a job covering local events. Tatum heads out to Los Brios to report on the annual rattlesnake roundup. But on the way, he happens on a dramatic event: Leo Minosa (played by Richard Benedict) is trapped in a cave inside an ancient burial ground. The local Native Americans believe and have convinced Leo that the cave collapsed on account of the anger of their ancestors' spirits against him because he has been raiding the cave for artifacts that he sells in the truck stop and diner that he operates near the cave site. Tatum begins to write a series of articles intertwining the Native Americans' beliefs with the tragic story of Leo trapped in the cave while his loving wife, Lorraine (played by Jan Sterling), waits anxiously for her husband to be rescued.

In fact, Lorraine is anything but the faithful wife. A cheap-looking blonde stuck in a nowhere place, she wants nothing more than to leave Leo and to find a better life in the big city. She and Tatum both understand that Leo's story, if played right, can be a ticket out of there for both of them. When Tatum learns that the rescuers can free Leo in less than a day by going in from the back of the cave and shoring it up, Tatum makes a deal with them to drill instead from above in order to give him a week to milk his story. He colludes with the local sheriff to isolate the location where Leo is buried and to keep other reporters away. Lorraine agrees to allow visitors to camp outside the police barricades and makes money by charging admission for entry and by serving them in the diner. It is a carnival atmosphere. In fact, to make this point, eventually a real carnival shows up in the desolate area now packed with hundreds of sightseers, complete with a Ferris wheel. Tatum is very close to success—a big payoff for the story and a new job with a big name newspaper—but he overplays his hand and loses his "ace in the hole" when Leo becomes ill in the dank cave atmosphere and dies.

Following the movie's release, Victor Desny claimed in his lawsuit that he had provided Wilder with the idea for a film based on the Floyd Collins story. He demanded $150,000 in damages.[5]

According to Desny, in November 1949, he telephoned Wilder's office at Paramount and told Wilder's secretary, Rosella Stewart, that he wanted to propose a movie based on the Floyd Collins story. Desny asked her if he could send a copy of the treatment that he had prepared. When she learned that it was 65 pages, Stewart told Desny to prepare a synopsis because Mr. Wilder would not read such a long treatment. Two days later, Desny telephoned Wilder's office again and told Stewart that the synopsis was ready. She asked him to read it over the phone while she took it down in shorthand. Desny did so. During the conversation, according to Desny, Stewart also told him that she thought the story seemed interesting. Desny supposedly then told her that Wilder could use the story, but only if he paid Desny "the reasonable value of it." She reportedly answered that "if Billy Wilder of Paramount use[d] the story, 'naturally' they would pay him for it." During all this time, Desny never spoke with Wilder, only with his secretary.

Desny's only other contact with Wilder's secretary was in July 1951, when he called to protest the alleged use of his story in Wilder's film, *Ace in the Hole*. When he filed his lawsuit,

---

5. Sikov, p. 327.

Desny made clear that he was not suing Wilder for plagiarizing his idea but rather because Wilder promised to pay Desny for the reasonable value of the use of his idea and story synopsis if he used them and that Wilder had, in fact, used them.

Wilder's attorneys responded that not only did a verbal plot summary not constitute a formal story submission, but the account of Floyd Collins's death in the Kentucky cave was a historical incident that had been widely publicized and therefore was in the public domain. As such, Desny could not claim any property interest in it. In December 1953, the trial court judge, Stanley Mosk, agreed and ruled in favor of Wilder and Paramount. Desny appealed.

In August 1956, the California Supreme Court reversed Judge Mosk's ruling. In its opinion, the court considered three issues: What rule should apply when an idea is provided to another? Should a synopsis or a plot description ever be viewed as a literary property? And if so, what recovery would be appropriate for that type of literary property?

Wilder's counsel conceded that the act of disclosing an idea, if it was in fact the bargained-for exchange for a promise, may be consideration to support that promise. (In other words, if I say I will tell you my idea if you will pay me for it, and there is a promise to pay before the idea is provided, then once the idea is provided, you have to pay me for it.) But Wilder argued that the subsequent use of an idea is not sufficient to support a promise to pay for such use. He maintained that Desny disclosed his material before Wilder did, or could do, anything to indicate his willingness or unwillingness to pay for it.

The court did not accept this line of reasoning. While accepting that "ideas are as free as the air," they cannot be used by the entertainment industry until someone makes the industry moguls aware of them. "It cannot be doubted that some

189

ideas are of value to a producer." It is true that an idea cannot be viewed as property because someone else may think of the same idea and because "our concept of property implies something which may be owned and possessed to the exclusion of all other persons." However, the court held that if a person provides a valuable idea to a producer "who voluntarily accepts it knowing that it is tendered for a price," that person who provided the idea should "be entitled to recover."

The court acknowledged that this presented a "hazard" to film producers who received many unsolicited submissions of scripts on public domain materials that the producers could well have discovered on their own. But Desny's situation was different, the court believed, because here the person who generated the idea presented it to the producer on the understanding that the producer would be willing to pay for it. In that case, the parties have made an express contract, "or, under these circumstances, as some writers view it, the law itself, to prevent fraud and unjust enrichment, will imply a promise to compensate."

In order to infer such a promise, it is not enough that the writer submitted an unsolicited proposal. It must be based on circumstances known to the producer at or preceding the time when the disclosure of the idea is made and the producer must voluntarily accept the disclosure, knowing those circumstances and facts under which the idea was offered. In other words, unless the producer has an opportunity to reject the idea that is offered, he cannot be said to accept. If an author "blurts out his idea without having first made his bargain, [he] has no one but himself to blame." No court will enforce a claim for payment for an idea where the demand for compensation is made after an unconditional disclosure of the concept, that is, "the law will not imply a promise to pay for an idea from the mere fact that the idea has been conveyed, is valuable, and has been used for profit."

As the court saw it, the fact that Desny made two phone calls to Wilder's office was significant. No contract to pay for the Floyd Collins idea was formed when Desny first called and told Wilder's secretary his basic idea to make a movie based on the account of Collins's tragic death. At that time, Wilder was free to use that idea "as he saw fit," to develop it through the studio's own research function, and to make it into a useable script. In fact, the court acknowledged, Wilder may have actually done that.[6]

But there were two calls and in the second conversation, Desny read his synopsis to Wilder's secretary, who took it down in shorthand. If Wilder used Desny's synopsis, the court said, then he could be found to have implicitly agreed to pay for whatever value it had. As the court saw it, the two telephone conversations, with the secretary taking down the synopsis, "appear[ed] to have been parts of a single transaction and must be construed as such." Paramount and Wilder argued that neither Wilder nor his secretary were authorized to negotiate contracts to procure scripts for the studio. But the court did not accept this. An obligation for Paramount to pay for Desny's story could nevertheless have been created "if in fact Wilder and Paramount used Desny's synopsis to make the film." It would be untenable, the court found, for Paramount to allow its employees, Wilder and Stewart, to procure literary material and to use it, all the while disavowing their authority to act as the studio's agents.

In short, Desny had no copyright, did not claim any copyright or other ownership interest in the screenplay for *Ace in*

---

6. According to Sikov, Wilder began preparing to make *Ace in the Hole* in October 1949, one month before Desny called Wilder's secretary. A radio writer, Walter Newman, suggested the script idea to Wilder and he took it. It was about a cave, an accident, and a cynical newspaper reporter. Wilder liked it. Sikov, p. 311.

the Hole, and yet was able to prevail in the California Supreme Court on the basis of an implied contract: he offered it, they took it and used it. Therefore, they were obligated to pay Desny for its value, even though the story line was in the public domain.

After this ruling in favor of Desny, Wilder's attorneys settled with him in August 1956, paying him $14,350 for his idea.[7]

So for Desny, as for Wilder, *Ace in the Hole* did not work out to be the valuable property that either of them would have hoped. Desny received one-tenth of his initial demand, while for Wilder, the movie lost money. Moreover, he was forced to accept one further insult at the hands of the studio. Wilder's next film for Paramount, *Stalag 17* (1953), was a hit and Wilder anticipated receiving a share of the film's profits. However, Paramount recouped some of the money that *Ace in the Hole* had lost from Wilder's share of the profits from *Stalag 17.* Despite all the disappointments, Wilder knew that he had made a good film[8]—it was just too far ahead of its time.[9]

---

7. Sikov, p. 328.

8. Sikov, p. 327. Sikov quotes Wilder as saying, "It's the best picture I ever made."

9. Despite criticism that has been leveled at the California Supreme Court for its rulings that protect ideas that cannot be copyrighted, by allowing writers the ability to recover on various implied contract and promissory estoppel theories, the rule of *Desny v. Wilder* has endured for over fifty years. There was some discussion at the time the federal Copyright Act of 1976 was passed (17 U.S.C. §§101-1331), which expressly denies copyright protection for ideas and specifically preempts claims made under state law that duplicate copyright infringement claims (17 U.S.C. §301(a)), that a federal court would view *Desny* as an attempt at such duplication. (*See* Kulik, Glen L., "Copyright Preemption: Is This The End of *Desny v. Wilder?*", 21 Loy. L. A. Ent. L. Rev. 1, 14 (2000).) However, in a recent Ninth Circuit decision (*Montz v. Pilgrim Films & Television,* 606 F. 3d 1153 (9th Cir. 2011), aff'd en banc, 649 F. 3d 975 (9th Cir. 2011), cert. denied, *Pilgrim Films v. Montz,* No. 11-143 __ U.S. ___ (Nov. 7, 2011), a federal appellate court held specifically that an implied contract claim under California law was not preempted by federal copyright law because it flows from an agreement and understandings different from copyright protection. The court said, "the *Desny* innovation serves to give some protection for those who wish to find an outlet for creative concepts and ideas but with the understanding that they are not being given away for free. Without such legal protection, potentially valuable creative sources would be left with very little protection in a dog-eat-dog business." 649F. 3d at 981.

Part V

The Movie Industry from the 1960s to the 1980s
The Rise of Independent Producers

With the two major legal developments of the postwar years—the collapse of the studio system after the *de Havilland* case and the breakup of the Majors after the *Paramount* decision—independent film producers began to play a larger role in Hollywood. Even before the *de Havilland* ruling, some stars had held a measure of power in Hollywood. In the 1920s, Mary Pickford, Charles Chaplin, and other partners in United Artists had produced their own films, in which they also performed. But successes such as these were a rarity. Before the *de Havilland* case, most stars were held to seven-year contracts with little to no control over the films in which they were cast. A few, such as Bette Davis, who were represented by the powerful Hollywood agent, Lew Wasserman, were able to negotiate more lucrative contracts and a share of the profits.[1]

After the war, and with changes made to the system in the wake of the *Paramount* decision, actors as well as agents played a much greater role in film development, often working hand-in-hand with independent film producers. One early example was the partnership between the actor James Stewart, and his agent, Lew Wasserman. After Stewart's success on Broad-

---

1. Mae West and The Marx Brothers also had contracts that provided them a percentage of gross profits. Thompson & Bordwell, p. 336.

way in the play *Harvey*, he and Wasserman developed a screen adaptation of the play, with Stewart playing the lead, earning a fee plus a percentage of the gross. They also sold a "package" to Universal of another film, *Winchester '73* (1950), a western directed by Anthony Mann, with Stewart as the lead. This time, Stewart received no up-front fee but half of the profits from the movie. The film was very successful and made Stewart a wealthy man.[2]

The 1960s were a watershed decade for the movie industry. By the end of the 1950s, studios were still producing the films that historically made money, "road-show pictures"— long, lavish productions that were released initially in just a few select movie houses in major cities (such as New York and Los Angeles), charging higher prices. After this exclusive run had played out, then the films would be moved into a greater number of theaters. A successful film, such as *The Ten Commandments* (1956) or *Ben Hur* (1959), would have had a run that lasted several years, generating significant revenues for studios and justifying the cost of their production. However, if not successful, they could significantly affect the studio's bottom line, impacting its ability to invest in other smaller but better films.[3]

By the 1960s, this model was wearing thin, but the studios continued to make the motion pictures that had been their paradigm for success: war movies, westerns, "generally with aging stars and increasingly threadbare and recycled plots,"[4] and romantic comedies with reliable box office stars, such as Doris Day and Rock Hudson, as well as "road show" films, such as *Cleopatra* (1963), *The Longest Day* (1962), and a remake of

---

2. Thompson & Bordwell, p. 336.

3. Harris, Mark, *Pictures at a Revolution: Five Movies and the Birth of the New Hollywood*, New York: The Penguin Press, 2008, p. 45.

4. Harris, p. 10.

Mutiny on the Bounty (1962).[5] Musicals, like Disney's *Mary Poppins* (1965), Warner Bros.' *My Fair Lady* (1964), and Twentieth Century Fox's *The Sound of Music* (1966), remained the lifeblood of the studios in the 1960s.[6]

However, the industry saw changes on many fronts. As competition to the Hollywood studios, a wealth of innovative films were coming into the United States from abroad, in particular those of the French directors François Truffaut and Jean-Luc Godard, themselves influenced by earlier Hollywood movies. Films such as Truffaut's *Jules et Jim* (1962), Godard's *À Bout de Souffle* (Breathless) (1960), and Fellini's *La Dolce Vita* (1960) attracted audiences not just in New York and Los Angeles, but in college towns and urban areas across the United States, and these had a strong impact on young movie producers in the United States.

Where the studios still retained control was in film distribution. But by 1960, the "package-unit approach"—where an agent or an independent producer would obtain rights to a story, commission a script, pull together the talent (director and main actors), and sell it as a package to a studio—had become a commonly used method for film development and production. The agent Lew Wasserman put together several films in this manner in the 1950s in cooperation with his client, Alfred Hitchcock, which were big successes, such as *North by Northwest* (1959), *Rear Window* (1954) (co-produced with James Stewart, who played the lead),[7] and the thriller, *Psycho* (1960). Other direc-

---

5. *Cleopatra* was a prime example of what was wrong with the mega-studio production. It was at the time the most expensive film ever—costing more than $40 million—and it was one of the longest, with over four hours' running time, and to top it off, it was a bust at the box office. Harris, p. 9.

6. Harris, p. 75.

7. *See* Reel 25, A Never-ending Story, for a discussion of the legal case, *Stewart v. Abend*, involving this movie.

tors and stars also struck out on their own; John Ford and Otto Preminger are well-known examples. Ford's Argosy Pictures produced the popular nostalgic Irish film *The Quiet Man* (1952), starring John Wayne and Maureen O'Hara, and Preminger produced several adaptations of best-selling novels, such as *Anatomy of a Murder* (1959), *Exodus* (1960), and *Advise and Consent* (1962). The actor Kirk Douglas took on the epic *Spartacus* (1960), putting together the star-filled cast. By the 1960s, a wide range of stars, producers, and studios played together in various combinations under this "package" model. A studio might acquire a movie that had been filmed and edited (or almost fully edited) by a producer or director, originate its own film (through an acquired or commissioned script), or accept a package assembled by an independent producer, an actor's production company, or an agent (or any combination of actor, producer, and agent).[8]

This model allowed independent producers, directors, and actors to shape their own movie projects, selecting the bodies of work in which they wanted to be involved and engaging their own scriptwriters, without having to accept the studio-imposed staff, crew, or actors.[9] United Artists was the first of the major studios to embrace this economic method of movie production, providing financing, publicity, and distribution in return for a negotiated share of the profits.[10] Other studios eventually followed, although their progress toward this way of working was slowed by the reluctance of the old-line movie moguls to accept change. But as Bob Dylan was singing, "the times are a-changin'." The moguls were being edged out by a new corpo-

---

8. Thompson & Bordwell, p. 680.

9. Harris p. 34.

10. "From the beginning of the 1960s to the end of that decade, even as the overall number of Hollywood films declined sharply, so-called independent production at the majors quadrupled." Harris, p. 41.

rate mentality at the studios. At the end of 1966, Jack Warner, founder and head of Warner Bros., sold a third of his shares in the company to an independent production company, Seven Arts.[11] Darryl Zanuck at 20th Century Fox was the last mogul still in power but he had turned the day-to-day studio operations over to his son, Richard Zanuck.

As the role of the independent producer expanded in the 1960s, the movie business attracted people who enjoyed the process of putting together—packaging—disparate functions to produce a motion picture, and who, in return for relatively low base compensation, enjoyed a relatively high percentage of the film's gross receipts. The producer sought out these experiences not just because they held out the prospect of great financial reward, but because of the satisfaction gained from having created a successful whole from initially very disconnected parts: finding a concept or a novel to be adapted, locating a director, booking stars, tracking down other talent—not just cast, but also crew (cinematographers, screenwriters, film editors, sound technicians, etc.). No amount of compensation could replace this satisfaction.

Some of the more innovative and successful films of the 1960s were the result of this new creative synergy among the independent producers, actors, and their agents. The industry was in flux and the films that were made and succeeded during that decade show it. In truth, it has been pointed out that the films of that era reflect the so-called "generation gap" described by historians of the time.[12] The old Hollywood was represented by the successful musicals and westerns. But there also was the new Hollywood, represented by a younger generation of actors and filmmakers, who made movies that, for example, parodied

---

11. Harris, p. 266.
12. Harris, pp. 102-103.

the old standards, such as the comic western, *Cat Ballou* (1966) that starred both the new generation, represented by Jane Fonda as the title character, and the old, in the person of Lee Marvin (who won an Academy Award for his performance).[13] These filmmakers, heavily influenced by the French New Wave (represented by Truffaut and Godard) and by the movies of Ingmar Bergman, attempted to make motion pictures that were American but with a self-consciousness that pulled from past history and yet were situated well in the present.

Bonnie and Clyde (1967) was representative of this generation's movie culture. Scripted entirely by two writers with Godard's *Breathless* in mind, and with the hope of luring François Truffaut in as its director, it was received coolly by its studio financier, Warner Bros., and particularly the studio head, Jack Warner, as well as most established film critics, but not by the newer generation of commentators—Pauline Kael[14] and Roger Ebert.[15] Moreover, the film was very warmly received on college campuses and in Europe, as were its stars, Warren Beatty and Faye Dunaway.[16] A popular French musician of the

---

13. Harris, p. 382.

14. Pauline Kael wrote, "*Bonnie and Clyde* is the most excitingly American movie since *The Manchurian Candidate*. . . . Though we may dismiss the attacks with 'What good movie doesn't give offense?,' the fact that it is only good movies that provoke attacks by many people suggests that the innocuousness of most of our movies is accepted with such complacence that when an American movie reaches people, when it makes them react, some of them think there must be something the matter with it." "*Bonnie and Clyde*," *The New Yorker*, October 21, 1967, reprinted in Schwartz, Sanford, ed., *The Age of Movies, Selected Writings of Pauline Kael*, Library of America, 2011, pp. 154-173.

15. Roger Ebert wrote, "'Bonnie and Clyde' is a milestone in the history of American movies, a work of truth and brilliance. It is also pitilessly cruel, filled with sympathy, nauseating, funny, heartbreaking, and astonishingly beautiful. If it does not seem that those words should be strung together, perhaps that is because movies do not very often reflect the full range of human life." "*Bonnie and Clyde*," *Chicago Sun-Times*, September 25, 1967, found at rogerebert.com, http://rogerebert.suntimes.com/apps/pbcs.dll/article?AID=/19670925/REVIEWS/709250301, last accessed December 30, 2011.

16. Harris, p. 391.

time, Serge Gainsbourg, in 1968 recorded a song he had written in honor of the movie, with the same title, "Bonnie et Clyde."[17]

The films of the 1960s reflected the angst and disorientation of the decade, which began with the inauguration and assassination of President John F. Kennedy and ended with the assassinations of Martin Luther King, Jr. and Robert Kennedy, the traumatic bloodshed of the Vietnam War, and the promise of the experimentation to come in the 1970s and 1980s. They reflect the desire for conformity and stability and at the same time the rebelliousness and irreverence of the nation's youth.[18] Thus you have during the decade between 1961 and 1969, the release of comfortable movies such as *The Absent-Minded Professor* (1961), *Mary Poppins* (1964), and *Camelot* (1967) along with other more disturbing films, such as *Dr. Strangelove* (1964), *Bonnie and Clyde* (1967), *Cool Hand Luke* (1967), and *Midnight Cowboy* (1969). *Romeo and Juliet* was released the same year, 1968, as *Rosemary's Baby*. By the end of the 1960s, Americans were facing a future where uncertainty prevailed but opportunity beckoned, and this trend was reflected in the films introduced during that time period in American cinema.

---

17. Duet with Brigitte Bardot, recorded 1968, Mercury (France).
18. Starr, *California*, p. 287-289.

Fatal Attraction
The Taming of the Shrew

Blaustein v. Burton, 9 Cal. App. 3d 161 (2d Dist. 1970)

**I know that we are both dangerous
people, but we are fundamentally nice.
I mean we only hurt each other.**
Richard Burton[1]

I n the 1960s and 1970s, Elizabeth Taylor and Richard Burton
were the "in" couple—the most talked about and written
about—the most sensationalized film stars of their time. They
were larger than life, a fiery couple, constantly feeding the tab-
loid media with their parties, their excesses, her jewels (including a 19-carat Krupp and a 69.42-carat Cartier diamond), and,
yes, their brawls. From the time they met, co-starring in *Cleopatra* (1963)—with Taylor in the name role and Burton playing the
ancient legend's second lover, Marc Antony (Rex Harrison having played the role of Julius Caesar, her first)—sparks flew and
the stage was set for the Liz and Dick soap opera. The headlines,
which at first had been set in motion by 20th Century Fox's public relations machine headlining Taylor's striking beauty and
the kohl makeup that emphasized her azure eyes, soon turned
negative as news spread that the romance between Cleopatra
and Marc Antony was not play acting and that the two stars,
both married to other people, had begun an illicit affair. Tay-

---

1. Bragg, Melvyn, *Rich: The Life of Richard Burton*, London, Hodder & Strough-
ton, 1988, p. 309, quoted in Harris, *Pictures at a Revolution*, p. 117.

lor already had received bad press in the United States as the spoiler in the breakup of the storybook marriage between Eddie Fisher and America's darling, Debbie Reynolds. But this time the scandal was international, when the couple's very public affair on location in Italy drew condemnation from the Vatican and Taylor abandoned Fisher (whom she soon after divorced) to live with and eventually marry Burton.

But this scandal, albeit damaging to the prospects for the film, did no long-term harm to the bankability of the two stars and they were very much in demand in the 1960s. The couple appeared together in several post-*Cleopatra* films, including *The Sandpiper* (1965) and *Who's Afraid of Virginia Woolf* (1966). This latter film was a huge success.[2] They began to take a more proactive role in choosing and producing themselves the films in which they wanted to perform and they were very much involved in preproduction and production decisions, for better or for worse. This included the production of Franco Zeffirelli's adaptation of *The Taming of the Shrew* (1967). Their decisions were not always beneficial, for themselves or for those who came into contact with the two. One of these latter was Julian Blaustein, who sued the couple in 1967 over *The Taming of the Shrew*.

Blaustein had been involved in the movie business in various roles since 1949. He was no neophyte. He established his career as an independent producer by putting together the package for *Broken Arrow* (1950) and selling it to Twentieth Century Fox. He also produced *The Day the Earth Stood Still* (1951) and *Khartoum* (1966). However, he is best known in legal circles not for his productions but for taking on the Burtons.

---

2. The "lure of seeing Elizabeth Taylor and Richard Burton behind closed doors doing something 'for adults only' proved irresistible to audiences." Harris, p. 184. This was the second-highest grossing film of the year.

In 1964, he conceived the idea of producing a film based on the Shakespearean comedy, "The Taming of the Shrew," with the lead roles of Petruchio and Katharina (Kate) played by Burton and Taylor, and with the Italian stage director, Franco Zeffirelli, as the director. According to the facts presented at trial, in April 1964, Blaustein met with Hugh French, Richard Burton's agent, to ask whether the Burtons would be available and if they would be interested in working on a film that Blaustein wanted to produce. He pitched a concept that he had developed, based on the Shakespeare play but with three what he considered to be innovative twists. First, Shakespeare had used a "play within a play" device that Blaustein thought ought to be eliminated. Second, he had the idea of including in the film version two key scenes—that of the wedding and the wedding night—that occur offstage in the play. And finally, he suggested that the movie be filmed in Italy, in the actual settings that Shakespeare described. French told Blaustein that, to his knowledge, the Burtons had not discussed making a motion picture together based on the Shakespeare play and that he would arrange for Blaustein to meet with them to discuss the idea.

Blaustein traveled to New York and while there attended the opening of a Broadway production of "Hamlet" on April 9, 1964, in which Richard Burton played the title role. French introduced Blaustein to Burton at that time as "the man who had been talking about 'The Taming of the Shrew.'" However, the promised meeting with both Burtons did not take place because Richard Burton was preoccupied with his stage performance. Blaustein then traveled to London where he met with John Van Eyssen, Franco Zeffirelli's agent. Zeffirelli was at the time best known as an Italian stage director, and not as a film director.[3] Blaustein

3. He would later become known for his very successful film of Shakespeare's *Romeo and Juliet* (1968).

discussed with Van Eyssen his idea for a film of *The Taming of the Shrew* with the Burtons as lead characters. Van Eyssen agreed to contact Zeffirelli with the idea. The three men later met in Paris in May 1964, where Blaustein had an opportunity to describe his concept in detail. However, at the time, Zeffirelli expressed concerns that the Burtons might not be willing to work with him because he was not known as a director in the United States.

While in London, Blaustein called Richard Burton's agent, French, several times and arrangements were made for him to meet the Burtons in New York at the end of May. But when Blaustein arrived, the Burtons were not available to meet with him. He returned to Los Angeles, where he met with his lawyer, Martin Gang. Gang's law firm also represented the Burtons. Blaustein relayed his idea to Gang and expressed his frustration at not being able to get a meeting with the Burtons. Gang agreed to try to arrange the meeting.

Gang contacted Aaron Frosch, the Burton's New York lawyer, who agreed to arrange a meeting, which finally took place on June 30, in New York. At the beginning of the conversation, Burton commented that it seemed a good idea for the Burtons to make the film and he added, "I don't know how come we hadn't thought of it." At the meeting, the parties also discussed details, including Blaustein's concept (which included his ideas for changes from the Shakespeare play), the idea of using Zeffirelli as the film's director, and the possible cost of production. At the conclusion of the meeting, Burton stated that they "should plan on doing" the film. He added, "Let's plan to go ahead now. Elizabeth and I would like to do this. We think Zeffirelli is a good idea. We will accept him." He then told Blaustein to work out appropriate arrangements with Frosch, their attorney in New York.

After the meeting, Blaustein contacted Gang and authorized him to work with Frosch to structure a deal to do the picture, telling him, "It's a picture that I want badly to do." He then went back to London to continue discussions with Zeffirelli and his agent. He reported to Gang in a July 7 letter that these talks were going well and that they were making progress.

On his return to Los Angeles, Blaustein then discussed the terms of the deal with Mickey Rudin, a partner in Gang's law firm, who was also representing the Burtons in connection with the film project. In an August 1964 telephone call, they discussed financial terms: percentage share of gross receipts, guaranteed fees, and the like. Rudin agreed to get back to Blaustein once he had had an opportunity to discuss these with the Burtons. But then Blaustein heard nothing until that December. He assumed at the time that this was because the Burtons, who were busy, were not yet ready to make a commitment.

On December 30, 1964, Rudin and Gang met with Blaustein in Gang's office in Los Angeles where they advised Blaustein that his position in the project was in jeopardy. They also advised him at the time that he really could do nothing about that because he had "no legal rights" in the concept or the project. At the time—this was his lawyer advising him after all—he "simply accepted that."

After a March 1965 meeting in Dublin where Richard Burton was making another picture, Rudin telephoned Blaustein to let him know that he "might not be the producer if the picture is ever made" but that "there would be a reward for [his] contribution to the project." Blaustein sent a letter to Rudin and Gang where he told them that he was not going to "try the case" with his own attorney but he continued, "it's important to me, Mickey, that you understand that I can never consider any such payment to be a satisfactory substitute for the function that has been denied me on a project that I initiated." On April 27, 1965, Gang wrote a letter to Blaustein, stating, "There is no question in anybody's mind that this was your idea, of 'Taming of the Shrew,' and bringing Zeffirelli in was your idea, and this is so recognized by all the principals, including Mr. Burton and Mr. Zeffirelli."

In December 1965, Blaustein heard rumors that a "deal" was being put in place for the production of *The Taming of the Shrew* involving the Burtons and Zeffirelli and was informed by his attorney, Gang, that discussions to this effect were taking place with Columbia Pictures to produce the film. Blaustein wrote to Gang in January 1966 suggesting that Columbia be informed of his participation in the project, but Gang dissuaded Blaustein from contacting Columbia, since by doing so, he "might upset the possibility of any deal being made because Columbia wouldn't want to get involved in litigation . . . and it would be best not to upset the apple cart." On this advice, Blaustein refrained from contacting Columbia.

As he suspected, however, a film based on "The Taming of the Shrew" starring Richard Burton and Elizabeth Taylor and directed by Franco Zeffirelli, financed and distributed by Columbia Pictures, opened in March 1967. Rudin, Gang's law partner, had represented the Burtons in negotiations with Columbia. The movie eliminated the play within a play device from Shakespeare's work, and contained the two key scenes, the wedding and the wedding night, that Blaustein had suggested (rather than have them take place offstage, as in the play). And the film was photographed on location in Italy, although not in the exact locales that Shakespeare had referred to in the play. Blaustein received no payment from the participants nor did he receive any screen credit.

Hurt and angry by this betrayal not only by the Burtons and

Zeffirelli, but by his own lawyer, Blaustein sued the Burtons and Zeffirelli in Los Angeles Superior Court on November 14, 1967, for breach of contract and unjust enrichment.

At trial, the Burtons defended by arguing that there was nothing unique about the idea of making a film based on "The Taming of the Shrew." Indeed, two former movie icons as much in the public eye if not more so than the Burtons—the former King and Queen of Hollywood, Douglas Fairbanks and Mary Pickford—had made that film in the 1930s.[4] They also pointed out that there was nothing unique about a non-American directing English-speaking actors in a film. Zeffirelli was not unfamiliar with Shakespeare and, in fact, he later claimed that he had originally proposed making a film of "The Taming of the Shrew" with the Italian actors, Marcello Mastroianni and Sophia Loren. But his London agents told him that he needed to work with British actors to have credibility for his film, and they thought of the Burtons.[5] Moreover, as a legal matter, they argued, Blaustein's negotiations with the Burtons, through their attorney, had not resulted in any coproduction or joint venture agreement to make the film. In fact, there was no written agreement of any sort with the Burtons. Just conversations.

The trial court agreed with the Burtons— there could be no breach of contract without a contract—and granted the Burtons' motion for summary judgment. Blaustein appealed.

On appeal, he argued that there were issues of fact whether there was a contract between him and the Burtons and that he should be entitled to prove his case. They responded that in any event his lawsuit was barred by California's two-year statute

---

4. *The Taming of the Shrew* (1929).

5. LoBianco, Lorraine, Article, "The Taming of the Shrew," Turner Classic Movies, found at http://www.tcm.com/tcmdb/title/3751/The-Taming-of-the-Shrew/articles.html, last accessed August 17, 2011.

of limitations because if there was a contract and a breach of that contract, Blaustein had first learned of the breach in early 1965 when Rudin informed him that he might not be the film's producer. Furthermore, they contended, New York law should apply, because Blaustein's discussions with the Burtons had taken place in that state, not California (and under New York law, Blaustein would have to prove that his idea was unique or novel; California did not have such a requirement to prove a breach of contract). And to further object, they also pointed out that there was no contract because there was nothing in writing.

The appellate court disagreed. Relying on *Golding* and *Weitzenkorn*,[6] as well as *Desny*,[7] the court ruled that Blaustein's idea of a film based on Shakespeare's play, "The Taming of the Shrew," was one that could be protected by contract, under either California law or New York law. Even though there was no written agreement, a contract might be implied, based on either the conduct or the words of the parties or both. A jury might conclude that, from the negotiations and the conduct of the parties and those of their agents, there was an implied contract, even if there was no express agreement. In other words, the Burtons may have made an implied promise of payment conditioned on their subsequent use, in return for Blaustein's act of disclosing his idea, not in return for his promise to disclose the idea.

Blaustein had stated in his affidavit: "I made the disclosures and rendered the services with the expectation and understanding that in the event the defendants used my ideas and went forward with the production of a film version of 'The Taming of the Shrew,' I would be engaged as a producer of the film at

---

6. Golding v. R.K.O. Pictures, Inc., 35 Cal. 2d 690 (1950) and Weitzenkorn v. Lesser, 40 Cal. 2d 778 (1953). *See* Reel 13, The Players: Idea Submission Cases.

7. Desny v. Wilder, 46 Cal. 2d 715 (1956). *See* Reel 14, The Conversation.

my then going rate, and receive the usual screen credits, or I would receive the monetary equivalent of such compensation or credit."

The court noted, "Since it appears from the record that Blaustein shared his ideas and the Burtons elected not to engage him as a producer of the film, all that remains to be done is payment by the Burtons." The court determined that the Burtons' assertion that a *written* contract did not exist was irrelevant. "Where a contract has been fully performed by one party and nothing remains to be done except the payment of money by the other," the court continued, it is not necessary that the contract be in writing. It was also not relevant that Blaustein and the Burtons had not even discussed the financial terms of the arrangement. Furthermore, because Blaustein was a professional producer, it defied reason that he would have approached the Burtons' agent to float an idea simply for the pleasure of doing so, or for the purpose of making the Burtons happy.[8]

There was the issue that Blaustein had waited to file his suit until November 1967, after the movie was released and more than two years after he had learned from his lawyer in March 1965 that the Burtons did not intend to use him on the film. Did Blaustein sit on his rights and therefore let too much time pass? The court believed that the answer depended on when the Burtons could be held to have used Blaustein's concept. That might have been when a script embodying the idea was written or it could have been when the film was first released in theaters, because it would be that event that would have destroyed any further marketability of the idea. If that were the case, then since the movie was first released in March 1967, Blaustein

---

8. Crabb, Kelly Charles, *The Movie Business: The Definitive Guide to the Legal and Financial Secrets of Getting Your Movie Made*, New York, Simon & Schuster (2005), p. 476.

would have been well within the two-year period when he filed his lawsuit in November 1967.

In the end, the filming of *The Taming of the Shrew* turned out to have mixed results for all parties and to be a disappointment as well. Blaustein did not get to produce the movie he had so longed to make. For Zeffirelli, the film did not receive the critical acclaim that his production of *Romeo and Juliet* would receive the next year. The Burtons put $1 million of their own money into the project and waived their combined salaries (which would have amounted to more than $2 million), electing to take a percentage of the gross. The movie was a financial success: it initially grossed $7 million when first released domestically, but when it reached international markets, it grossed over $12 million.[9] However, the reviews by the critics, even those who claimed to have liked the movie, were disappointing. *Variety* called it "a boisterous, often over-stagey frolic."[10] Bosley Crowther, the film critic for *The New York Times*, called it a "totally wild abstraction of the Bard for purposes of a fast return engagement between the Burtons in a florid and fustian film" that in the end "all grows a bit tedious."[11] Wilfred Sheed in *Esquire* had harsher words, particularly in his assessment of Elizabeth Taylor's acting ability. Calling her fixed in the skills she had at ten, never having progressed beyond that, he said, "Of Miss Taylor, there is little to say. She will never really be adequate to any classical role."[12] Ouch.

---

9. LoBianco, TCM Article.

10. Variety staff review Saturday, December 31, 1966: found at http://www.variety. com/review/VE1117795446?refcatid=31 last accessed August 17, 2011.

11. Crowther, Bosley, film review, "Burtons Arrive in 'Taming of the Shrew': Shakespeare Gets Lost In Film at Coronet," *The New York Times*, March 9, 1967, found at http://movies.nytimes.com/movie/review?res=9504E2D71E3BE63ABC4153D FB566838C679EDE last accessed August 17, 2011.

12. Sheed, Wilfred, film review, *Esquire Magazine*, 1967 quoted in LoBianco, TCM Article.

Perhaps the biggest lesson that the Burtons should have learned was from the past: Mary Pickford and Douglas Fairbanks divorced shortly after they filmed *The Taming of the Shrew* in 1929. Their marriage was already breaking up when they made the film but certainly the subject matter—that of a tempestuous relationship between husband and wife—was not ideal to establish a rapport between a feuding couple. For the Burtons, history eventually repeated itself. They divorced in June 1974, seven years after the film was released.[13] It took a few years, but the bad luck caught up with them.

And the lesson Blaustein should have taken away from the experience is this: in Hollywood, you have to watch your back, because even your own lawyer cannot be trusted, especially when his partner is representing your adversary.[14]

---

13. They remarried in 1975 but then divorced again in July 1976.

14. It is to be assumed that Blaustein waived the conflict of interest in having the same law firm represent both him and the Burtons in the production contract negotiations because it does not appear that Blaustein raised what otherwise would have been a violation of California legal ethics rules. Whether or not he waived the conflict, it does not appear that Blaustein's attorney served him well or protected his interests in this matter.

Born to Dance

Parker v. Twentieth Century Fox Film Corp.,
3 Cal. 3d 176 (1970)

> **Don and Chorus: Gotta dance!**
> **Gotta dance! Gotta dance!**
> **Don: Broadway rhythm's got me,**
> **ev'rybody dance!**
> Gene Kelly as Don Lockwood, in *Singin' in the Rain* (1952)

Shirley MacLaine Parker (Shirley MacLaine) is a well-known actress who has appeared in many films of all genres.[1] Her biggest breakthrough came in 1960 when she was cast opposite Jack Lemmon in Billy Wilder's *The Apartment*. But she can sing and dance as well as act and has always been admired for her versatility. The same year that she played the serious role of suicidal Fran Kubelik in *The Apartment*, she also performed the part of Simone Pistache, opposite Frank Sinatra and Maurice Chevalier, in the musical comedy, *Can-Can* (1960). In 1961, she played opposite Audrey Hepburn in the drama, *The Children's Hour*, directed by William Wyler, followed by comedy roles in *My Geisha* (1962) and *Irma La Douce* (1963), another Billy Wilder film, cast in the title role opposite Jack Lemmon.

In August 1965, she signed a contract with Twentieth Century Fox to play the lead in the planned production of a motion picture to be called *Bloomer Girl*, based on the 1944 Broadway

---

1. She was born Shirley MacLean Beaty and is the older sister of actor Warren Beatty.

musical of the same name. She was to receive $53,571.42 per week for fourteen weeks, for a total of $750,000. Filming was to begin in May 1966. However, just before shooting was scheduled to start, Fox decided not to make the picture after all and in April 1966 notified her that the movie would not be made. Fox did not provide an explanation for the cancellation, although given the timing, there are several possible reasons.

At the time *Bloomer Girl* was in production, Fox was struggling. By the mid-1960s, the Hollywood studios in general and Fox in particular were facing a time of uncertainty.[2] After the studio's co-founder, Darryl Zanuck, had returned to manage it following significant losses, largely from its disastrous $40 million bet on *Cleopatra* (1963), he shut down the production company, laid off many employees, and installed his son, Richard, as head of production.[3] The studio then proceeded cautiously to rebuild itself. But by 1965, it had already made a commitment to produce *Dr. Dolittle* (1967), another musical, and there was a premonition in Hollywood, after a run of several successful films in that genre—namely *My Fair Lady* (1966), *Mary Poppins* (1965) and *The Sound of Music* (1966)—that perhaps too many studios were jumping onto the musical theater bandwagon and that it perhaps was time to slow down. Because Fox had made one bet already with *Dr. Dolittle*, there was likely less of an appetite at the studio for another musical to be released in the same time frame.

And then there was the subject matter. *Bloomer Girl* was based on the life of Amelia Bloomer, a suffragette who lived in the mid-nineteenth century. She also was an abolitionist. It is likely that the studio realized too late (after signing MacLaine)

---

2. Harris, *Pictures at a Revolution*, p. 2.
3. Harris, pp. 43-44.

that in a time of social upheaval—with civil rights protests, the challenges to segregation in the south, and the beginning of the women's liberation movement—this was not a film that it would be able to release below the Mason-Dixon line, or in other more conservative communities. For a studio trying to reestablish itself slowly, producing family-oriented, feel-good types of movies such as *The Sound of Music* and *Dr. Dolittle*, the story of a feminist antiabolitionist in *Bloomer Girl* may have been just too much controversy for the studio to take on.

In any event, Fox cancelled the production. "To avoid damage" to MacLaine, the studio instead offered her the leading actress role in *Big Country, Big Man* for the same compensation, to be filmed in Australia. (*Bloomer Girl* was to have been shot on location in California where MacLaine lived.) While *Bloomer Girl* was to have been a musical, *Big Country, Big Man* was to be a western. The roles would have been very different: Amelia Bloomer was a suffragist and MacLaine would have been the sole lead; the female lead in *Big Country, Big Man* would have been a secondary role to the male lead in what was essentially a man's movie. MacLaine was given a week to accept this alternate role. She let the offer lapse and then sued Fox to recover the agreed-upon guaranteed compensation provided for in her contract.

Fox answered her complaint that she was not entitled to recover any money because she had failed to mitigate her damages. She would have been made whole with the same compensation, Fox asserted, if she had not unreasonably refused to accept its offer of the female lead in *Big Country, Big Man*. MacLaine's attorneys made a motion for summary judgment against Fox, which the court granted. She was awarded the $750,000 plus interest. Fox appealed and the case ultimately was decided by the California Supreme Court.

In the appeal, the only issue was whether MacLaine should have mitigated the damages by accepting the substitute offer of the leading lady role in *Big Country, Big Man*. The appellate court ruled no. It was clear that MacLaine's refusal to accept Fox's tendered substitute employment could not be applied to reduce her damages because the offer of the female lead in that western was of employment that was both different and inferior. There was actually no factual dispute about that conclusion: the parties agreed on exactly what those differences were. *Bloomer Girl* was to be a musical revue calling on MacLaine's talents as a dancer as well as an actress. The film was to be made in Los Angeles. On the other hand, in *Big Country, Big Man*, MacLaine would have performed a straight dramatic role in a western-type movie, taking place in an opal mine in Australia. The court stated, "The female lead as a dramatic actress in a western-style motion picture can by no stretch of imagination be considered the equivalent of or substantially similar to the lead in a song-and-dance production."

In addition, the court noted that the substitute offer proposed to eliminate or substantially reduce certain approval rights that MacLaine had negotiated in her original *Bloomer Girl* contract. For example, the agreement had specified that MacLaine approved the director who had been chosen for *Bloomer Girl* and that, in case he failed to act as director, she was to have the right to approve any substitute director. Furthermore, the contract provided that MacLaine was to have the right to approve the dance choreographer selected for the film, and also gave her the right of approval of the screenplay. In short, the offer was for inferior employment with reduced prerogatives that was not at all the equivalent. The appellate court accordingly affirmed the $750,000 judgment in MacLaine's favor.

In retrospect, from a simple contract law perspective, this

case seems like a "no brainer." The studio breached its agreement with MacLaine and did not have a better movie to offer her. The only role available was both different and inferior. Given their seemingly weak position in this case, one wonders why studio executives decided to contest her claim. It is an important fact that, in offering MacLaine this other role, Fox also tried to renegotiate other business terms that had been part of her original agreement, such as the right to approve a change in director and the right to approve the screenplay. One might ask why Fox attempted to do this and why studio executives persisted in taking this position all the way to the California Supreme Court. The answer to this question, one suspects, is simple: power.

It is important to take note of the historical period in which this rift between MacLaine and Fox took place. At the time, the major motion picture studios were confronted with the growing influence of independent producers and, more importantly, of the actors and directors who were producing their own films. Just twenty years before, stars had been the employees of the studios under seven-year contracts that obliged them to accept any role the studio chose to thrust upon them or face suspension (which lengthened the term of the employment contract). Twenty years before that, Jetta Goudal had been ostracized in the industry for daring to take on Cecil B. DeMille.[4] The *DeHavilland* case[5] and the *Paramount* decision[6] had done much to liberalize the studios and to give actors a much bigger say not only in the roles they would accept, but also in how the film would be produced and who would direct their perfor-

---

4. Goudal v. DeMille, 118 Cal. App. 407 (2d Dist. 1931). *See* Reel 6, *A Star is Born.*

5. De Havilland v. Warner Bros. Pictures, 67 Cal. App. 2d 225 (2d Dist. 1944). *See* Reel 8, *A Dangerous Woman.*

6. United States v. Paramount Pictures, 334 U.S. 131 (1948). *See* Reel 9, *The Studios' Last Stand.*

mance (sometimes taking on the directing position themselves) and what lines they would say. Instead of controlling the entire process, studios had been relegated to being part of a production team, sometimes handling only the movie's marketing and distribution functions. By the 1960s, this change should have been accepted by studio executives, but the old-line moguls, such as Jack Warner at Warner Bros. (the studio that had lost its suit with Olivia de Havilland), and Darryl Zanuck at Fox, were slow to grasp the import of this growing independence and were eager to put stars in their place.

In this context, it is easy to understand why the *Parker* case had to be decided by the California Supreme Court. Who would have control and power over the direction of the industry was very much at stake. "The men running the movie business used to have the answer; now it had slipped just beyond their reach, and they couldn't understand how they had lost sight of it."[7] Even when they were not producing their own films, actors were demanding greater control over their careers and their image, by insisting on approval rights over essential elements of the film and over who would form the team that would bring it to the screen. The clauses in MacLaine's contract that gave her these types of approval rights were critical terms. It is as likely as not that Fox's attempt to renegotiate these when it offered her a supposedly substitute role in *Big Country, Big Man* were as much the critical factor in her decision to sue Fox as the insulting offer of an inferior part (with the claim that it was the equivalent) or the deprivation of her guaranteed salary.

By the 1960s, having this type of approval right in a film contract symbolized as much as a high compensation package—although that counted too—the importance and value of the

---

7. Harris, p. 2.

star in the motion picture business. For a performer to accept a contract without those rights might well have been taken as a sign that the star's clout was slipping and, in an industry where perception and image are everything, this could easily have affected the parts and compensation the actor would be offered in future films. MacLaine was at a high point in her career when she accepted the lead role in *Bloomer Girl*. She needed to take on Fox and to win the case in order to make a statement. In the same light, Fox could easily have taken the court's adverse ruling as one more sign of its diminishing importance in the motion picture industry.

One last note. Fox campaigned hard and *Dr. Dolittle* surprisingly was among the 1967 nominees for Best Picture at the Academy Awards in 1968. It did not win.[8] One wonders what would have happened if Fox had chosen to stay with *Bloomer Girl* and to produce that movie instead of *Dr. Dolittle*. From all accounts, it sounds as if the story of Amelia Bloomer would have been an entertaining and timely musical, with Shirley MacLaine providing a full range of fun and entertainment to the audience, while *Dr. Dolittle* is generally considered to be a bore.

---

8. The Academy of Motion Picture Arts and Sciences, The 40th Academy Awards (1968) Nominees and Winners, found at http://www.oscars.org/awards/academy awards/legacy/ceremony/40th-winners.html.

Intermission 6

A New Leaf:
Who Should Have Control
Over the Finished Work?

Elaine May has had a storied career in Hollywood that many would envy. She is a respected screenwriter, director, and actress, who has been responsible for award-winning films, such as *Heaven Can Wait* (1977) which she cowrote with Warren Beatty (who also starred in the film),[1] as well as some which are, rightly or wrongly, considered great disasters, most notably, *Ishtar* (1987).[2] She is also known for her strong creative spirit and her willingness to take on big studio bosses who she believed did not sufficiently respect the director's ultimate control over the film editing process. The best known example is her battle with Robert Evans, then Vice President of Paramount Pictures, at a time when he was at the height of his power at the studio, having just released the box office hit, *Love Story* (1970).

May had been a successful comedienne, connecting in Chicago with future director Mike Nichols. The couple relocated to New York in the 1960s and quickly became the successful comedy team of Nichols and May, arriving on Broadway with a very successful show, "An Evening with Mike Nichols and Elaine May." Soon after their partnership broke up, they both moved on to filmmaking, Nichols with his successful movies, *Who's Afraid of Virginia Woolf* (1966) and *The Graduate* (1967), and May with a series of films, beginning with *A New Leaf* in 1971. This movie, which she wrote, directed, and starred in (with Walter Matthau)[3] was very funny, very well-received by critics, and ultimately was nominated for two Golden Globes (Best Comedy and Best Actress). And it was a film that May came to hate, so much that she sued Paramount and Evans to prevent the movie's release. Her complaint? That the film that she delivered to Paramount for release was drastically recut, reedited, and shortened without her consent, making it into a very different movie from what she had intended. She argued that it had been "butchered," that it was, as reedited, a "cliché ridden, banal story," and that it would be "a disaster" if the film were to be released. After seeing the studio cut, she said, "I made a film about a man who commits two murders and gets away with it. In this new version, the murders have been eliminated."[4]

May's writing and directorial talent was in creating very funny movies that move quickly from comedy to bathos to tragedy, all the while retaining a dark humor. Her original version of *A New Leaf*—with the two murders—was three hours long; by eliminating subplots, including the infamous murders, Paramount was able to shorten the running time and avoided releasing a film with the troubling (in Hollywood) conclusion of a man getting away with murder.

Even in its shortened form, many critics loved it. Roger Ebert wrote that the movie was "hilarious, and cockeyed, and warm," even though he argued that the director's editorial judgment should have been respected.[5] Vincent Canby at *The New York Times* called it "a beautifully and gently cockeyed movie. . . . The entire project is touched by a fine and knowing madness." But he also said, "Not having seen Miss May's version, I can only say that the film I saw should be a credit to almost any director, though, theoretically at least, Miss May is right. The only thing that gives me pause is the knowledge that its success will probably be used in the future as an argument to ignore the intentions of other directors—but with far less happy results."[6]

In the plot, Henrietta (played by May) is a wealthy single botanist whose dream is to have a fern or a leaf named after her. Matthau plays Henry, an aging bachelor who has squandered his own fortune and has no ability to work. Therefore, he needs to find a wife with money and, voilà, he meets Henrietta. Once he marries her, he immediately makes plans to do away with her, studying toxicology in order to create a nondetectable poison. In May's plot, Henry discovers that Henrietta is being blackmailed by her lawyer and another man. He gets rid of them by poisoning

Intermission 6 (continued)

them. He gets away with these criminal acts, but in the end he is obliged to spend his life as Henrietta's husband—which May intimated was like a "life sentence"—as punishment. Once the cuts were made, completely eliminating the murders, the ending seems a rather sentimental story of redemption. For unexplained reasons, having produced a poison, Henry never uses it, but somehow learns to endure life with his rich wife. This was not at all what May intended for the film, and certainly was not reflective of her world view.

May sued Paramount in an effort to prevent the movie's release in its edited form or at least to have her name removed from the film credits. She claimed that "Paramount . . . took her black comedy away from her." Paramount responded that May had not lived up to her contract, had "failed to perform her duties as a director in a timely . . . and professional manner, resulting in substantially increased costs." The trial court ruled against May. She vowed to appeal, wishing at least to have her name taken off the credits, but the appeal was never filed.[7] She had apparently moved on.

May immediately took on her next project—directing the critically and commercially successful *The Heartbreak Kid* (1972), with Charles Grodin, Jeannie Berlin (May's daughter in real life), and Cybill Shepherd, which tells the funny-sad story of a goofy, clumsy new bride, Lila (played by Berlin), who, while stuck in her hotel room in Miami Beach recovering from a nasty sunburn acquired on the first day of their honeymoon, loses her husband to the glamorous Shepherd. May also wrote and directed *Mikey and Nicky* (1976) with Peter Falk as Mikey and John Cassavetes as Nicky, and, of course, the notorious *Ishtar* (1987), with Warren Beatty and Dustin Hoffman. This last was a box office disaster, with a $55 million production budget and a box office gross of $12.7 million. However, in later years, both Hoffman and Beatty defended the movie.[8]

Curiously, had Elaine May sued Paramount in France over the cuts made to *A New Leaf*, or conversely, if U.S. courts protected moral rights, May likely would have been far more successful in her suit against Paramount than she was in New York.[9]

1. And for which she was nominated in 1978 for a best screenplay Academy Award.

2. For Elaine May, a new Hollywood term was coined — "movie jail" — referring to someone whose perceived failure as a director was so profound, she would not be allowed at the helm of a movie production again, for a very long time, if ever. Unfortunately for May, and probably movie viewers, this is the case; May has not directed a new film since *Ishtar* was released.

3. This was the first time a woman performed all three functions in the same movie.

4. Kanfer, Stefan, "Cinema: An Anthology of Gaffes," *Time*, March 29, 1971, found at http://www.time.com/time/magazine/article/0,9171,944338,00.html, last accessed July 21, 2010.

5. Roger Ebert, "*A New Leaf*," April 6, 1971, rogerebert.com, found at http://rogerebert.suntimes.com/apps/pbcs.dll/article?AID=/19710406/REVIEWS/104060301, last accessed October 15, 2011.

6. Canby, Vincent, "Love Turns 'New Leaf' at Music Hall," Movie Review, *The New York Times*, March 12, 1971, found at http://movies.nytimes.com/movie/review?res=9C00E7D71131E73BBC4A52DFB566838A669EDE, last accessed October 26, 2011.

7. Kanfer. *See* note 4 above.

8. Biskind, Peter, *Star: How Warren Beatty Seduced America*, New York, Simon and Schuster, 2010, p. 382. Dustin Hoffman was quoted as saying, "*Ishtar* was a B minus, C plus comedy," but "There's a spine to it; isn't it better to spend a lifetime being second rate at what you're passionate about, what you love, than be first rate without a soul. That's magnificent, and that's what she was after. I'd do it again. I just wish it had worked out better."

9. *See* discussion at Reel 26, The Sculptor — *Huston v. La Cinq*.

The Curious Case of Obscenity and the Supreme Court

United States v. A Motion Picture Entitled "I am Curious-Yellow," 404 F. 2d 196 (2d Cir. 1968); *Wagonheim v. Maryland State Board of Censors,* 255 Md. 297, 258 A. 2d 240 (1969); aff'd *Grove Press v. Maryland State Board of Censors,* 401 U.S. 480 (1971)

I know it when I see it.

Justice Potter Stewart, discussing obscenity, from *Jacobellis v. Ohio,* 378 U.S. 184 (1964)

I n the first half of the twentieth century, courts showed a reluctance to overturn established precedent regarding claims of film censorship, leaving the *Mutual Film* decision[1] in place long after social mores had moved in a more liberalized direction. In the second half of the century, after the 1957 *Burstyn* decision,[2] the Supreme Court issued a series of opinions that deferred more to First Amendment rights, even for more controversial books and movies.

In *Burstyn,* the Court had told state and local censorship boards that they needed to justify their use of prior restraint in blocking the exhibition of films, although greater leniency was shown to those boards when there was a question of obscenity.

---

1. Mutual Film Corporation v. Industrial Comm'n of Ohio, 236 U.S. 230 (1915). *See* Reel 5, This Film Is Not Yet Rated—Censorship of Movies.

2. Joseph Burstyn, Inc. v. Wilson, 343 U.S. 495 (1952). *See* Reel 12, The Cardinal—The Catholic Church and Movie Censorship.

But obscenity remained a concern in a large number of cases, particularly because Hollywood, New York, and other metropolitan centers in the United States were taking even greater liberties in what was filmed. This was a time of liberalization on all fronts—in education, in art and literature, in racial and gender attitudes—and the movies of this era were reflective of these societal changes. In 1967, in *In the Heat of the Night*, a film about racial tensions in the South, for the first time a black man (played by Academy Award winner Sidney Poitier, as a northern police detective), struck a white man in a movie, and got away with it.[3] That same year, Michelangelo Antonioni released *Blow-Up*, with nude scenes, and without an MPAA seal, and the film was exhibited in numerous theaters across the country without repercussion. Also in 1967, films such as *The Graduate* (the story of a recent college graduate who has an affair with his girlfriend's mother) and *Bonnie and Clyde* (chronicling the escapades of two 1930s gangsters, featuring extreme violence) both vied for the Best Picture Oscar at the Academy Awards. And two years later, *Midnight Cowboy* (1969) (the story of two down-and-out men on the mean streets of New York, depicting drug use and male prostitution) won three Academy Awards, including Best Picture.

These movies appealed to younger audiences—baby boomers now college-aged who were making their own film-viewing decisions, which studios noticed.[4] Other, even more risqué films followed, such as *Easy Rider* (1967), *The Last Picture Show* (1971), *A Clockwork Orange* (1971) and *Last Tango in Paris* (1972).

But at the same time, local communities looked askance at the overtly sexual content that was showing up in films. They

---

3. Harris, *Pictures at a Revolution*, p. 336.
4. Thompson & Bordwell, p. 515.

wanted to ban movies that they considered to be obscene. In 1957, the Supreme Court attempted to protect First Amendment rights for works of literature and art, while still allowing obscenity, which did not merit constitutional protection, to be banned.[5] Samuel Roth, who ran a literary business in New York, was convicted of violating a criminal statute that prohibited sending "obscene" materials through the mail. He had mailed advertisements for a publication called *American Aphrodite*, containing literary erotica and nude photography. In an opinion upholding the conviction, Justice Brennan set out a standard under which a work could be evaluated to determine if it was obscene. This would be, the Court said, a work "utterly without redeeming social importance" that appeals to the "prurient interest" of "the average person, applying contemporary community standards." The Court was essentially trying to define what was in reality indefinable. This ruling applied specifically to books and magazines, not films per se.

In a later decision, also involving a book, the Court attempted to give greater clarity to *Roth's* definitional scheme. In *Memoirs v. Massachusetts,*[6] the Court set up a three-pronged test to determine obscenity: does the dominant theme, taken as a whole, appeal to a "prurient interest in sex"? Is the material "patently offensive" because it "affronts contemporary community standards" in the representation of sexual matters? Is the material "utterly without redeeming social value"? In that case, the Court concluded that a 1749 novel by John Cleland, entitled *Fanny Hill: Memoirs of a Woman of Pleasure*, could not be banned in Boston because, even though it met, in the Court's view, the first two prongs of the *Roth* test, the book could not be shown to be completely without social value.

---

5. Roth v. United States, 354 U.S. 476 (1957).
6. 383 U.S. 413 (1966).

In the meantime, a different type of movement to overturn obscenity laws was also taking place in the courts. Movie distributors and theater owners were continuing to challenge state and local censorship laws, which were still on the books in a number of states and towns, including New York. Even though one would have thought the power of local censors to have been greatly diminished after the *Burstyn* decision,[7] this was not the case. In those areas where censorship boards still operated, before a film could be shown within the geographic area over which a board had jurisdiction, the censor had to issue a license. The delays were costly and aggravating. A number of cases went to the Supreme Court, including two brought by Times Film Corporation,[8] but the Court in split decisions continued to hold that a licensing scheme that required a film exhibitor to submit a film for review before screening was not a prior restraint on speech. This left courts to rule in each individual case to determine whether the specific rule infringed on constitutional rights.

In a case arising out of Maryland (the last state to disband its censorship board), a Baltimore theater owner, Ronald Freedman, desiring to test the board's authority, elected to show an innocuous French film, *Revenge at Daybreak* (1952), about the Irish revolution[9], without first obtaining a license from the Maryland board.[10] In a unanimous decision, the Court finally responded to the problems censorship boards were causing film distributors and exhibitors—particularly the delays in releasing films in certain locales—and ruled that censors had to act quickly.

---

7. *See* Note 2 *supra.*

8. Times Film Corp v. City of Chicago, 355 U.S. 35 (1957) and Times Film Corp. v. City of Chicago, 365 U.S. 43 (1961).

9. The original title of the film was *La jeune folle.*

10. "The Law: Censoring the Censors," *Time,* Friday, Mar. 12, 1965, found at http://www.time.com/time/magazine/article/0,9171,839397,00.html.

If they did not promptly issue a license, then the theater was free to show the movie. It would then be up to the censors who had delayed to "go to court to restrain showing the film."[11] In the aftermath of this decision, most states and cities that still had censorship statutes were forced to either revise them or revoke them. Maryland rewrote its law completely and it survived legal challenges until it was voluntarily rescinded in 1981.[12]

In 1971, the Supreme Court was given an opportunity to refine its rulings on obscenity in relation to films when it was confronted with an appeal from a Maryland Court of Appeals decision involving a risqué Swedish film, *I Am Curious (Yellow)* (1967), directed by Vilgot Sjöman, a protégé of Ingmar Bergman. The dispute started in 1968 when Grove Press had attempted to bring the movie into the United States for theatrical exhibition. It was seized by U.S. Customs officials in New York City, who refused to release the film for distribution in the United States.[13] This movie had been reviewed by critics who considered it a serious, artistic film, with a contemporary motif of "youth challenging social, political and sexual conventions."[14] But the film also had overt sexual themes, nudity, and very graphic sex scenes. At the trial, the local jury judged it to be obscene.[15]

On appeal, the Second Circuit Court of Appeals reversed the jury's verdict on the ground that, under standards set out by the Supreme Court in *Roth* and *Memoirs*, the picture could not be kept out of distribution.[16] But the decision (two to one) was

---

11. Freedman v. Maryland, 380 U.S. 51 (1965). *See* Wittern-Keller & Haberski, p. 161.

12. Wittern-Keller & Haberski, p. 162.

13. Under Section 305 of the Tariff Act of 1930, 19 U.S.C. §1305 (1964).

14. Wittern-Keller & Haberski, p. 172.

15. United States v. A Motion Picture Film Entitled "I Am Curious-Yellow," 285 F. Supp. 465 (S.D.N.Y. 1968).

16. United States v. A Motion Picture Film Entitled "I Am Curious-Yellow," 404 F. 2d 196 (2d Cir. 1968).

not uncontroversial. The three-judge panel issued three separate opinions.

Judge Hays, who wrote the majority opinion, got the film's theme about the search for identity and understood that it chronicled the life of a young girl trying to work out her role in a changing social, political, and economic world. But he also realized that a "fairly large part of the film is devoted to the relations between the girl and her young lover," as he stated obliquely. As he pointed out, there was nudity. There were several scenes depicting sexual activity in various circumstances, "some of which are quite unusual," he observed dryly. In an understatement, he noted "It seems to be conceded that the sexual content of the film is presented with greater explicitness than has been seen in any other film produced for general viewing." The question was whether, "going farther in this direction than any previous production, the film exceeds the limits established by the courts."

The government argued that sexual content in books should be treated differently than sexual conduct in movies, because in movies the actual conduct "can be seen and heard." "Nudity and sexual activity in motion pictures," the government argued, "bear a close resemblance to nudity and sexual activity in a public place." The court agreed that "obviously, conduct of this type," that is, in a public place, "may be forbidden." But there was a difference between public activity and movies. "In the motion picture," the court pointed out, "the material is part of an artistic whole and is limited with and related to the story and the characters which are presented."

Judge Hays also noted that, under *Burstyn*, a motion picture, like a book, was entitled to First Amendment protection. Only if it was obscene, as determined using the three-pronged definitional standard for obscenity established by the Supreme Court in its *Memoirs* decision, could the film's release into theaters be prohibited. In his view, moreover, even though the jury at the trial had found *I Am Curious* to be obscene, "obscenity" was not a question of fact to be put before a jury. It was rather an issue of constitutional law to be decided by the judge in the case. Otherwise, much as in cases where books have been judged, many juries might find a literary classic, such as James Joyce's *Ulysses*, to be obscene, but to ban it would raise serious constitutional issues.[17]

Using the Supreme Court's three-pronged test, Judge Hays determined that the movie *I Am Curious* could not be classified as obscene. Even though he could give some weight to the jury's finding that the film was "patently offensive" because it affronted "contemporary community standards," as they—the representatives of that community—saw it, the movie did not meet the other two of the three grounds. Although sexual content was an important part of the movie, and even one of its principal themes, the court could not say that "the dominant theme of the material, on the whole appealed to a 'prurient' interest in sex." Whatever the dominant theme of the movie was, Judge Hays noted, it was "certainly not sex." And he also decided that *I Am Curious* was not "utterly without redeeming social value." While acknowledging that he was no expert in film, based on film critics' and professors' expert testimony at trial, he could say that *I*

---

17. This might have been the case in the 1960s, but *Ulysses* created a controversy when it was first brought into the United States in the early 1930s. The book was initially published in serial form in an American magazine called *The Little Review*, which was mailed to subscribers by Sylvia Beach, the owner of the novel's publisher, Shakespeare & Co., in Paris. The serialization was halted in 1922 over charges of obscenity. A test case was brought in the Second Circuit and in *United States v. One Book Called Ulysses*, 5 F.Supp. 182 (S.D.N.Y. 1933), the federal district court determined that the book was not obscene. This decision was confirmed by the appellate court in *United States v. One Book Entitled Ulysses by James Joyce*, 72 F.2d 705 (2nd Cir. 1934). In *United States v. A Motion Picture Film Entitled "I Am Curious-Yellow*, Judge Hays cited *Roth v. United States* for the comparison to *Ulysses*, 354 U.S. 476. 497-98 (1957), concurring opinion of J. Harlan.

Am Curious did "present ideas" and did "strive to present these ideas artistically."

Accordingly, the court ruled that the movie fell within the realm of intellectual endeavors that the First Amendment was designed to protect and could not be banned under U.S. tariff law. Justice Friendly concurred in this majority opinion, but not happily. In his opinion, he stated clearly that he found the film to be offensive, but he felt, with "no little distaste," that he had to follow the Supreme Court's standard for defining obscenity. Chief Justice Lumbard had no such qualms. He dissented, stating that he would have banned the movie because, even using the Supreme Court's test for obscenity, the film was utterly without social value. He saw no plot in the movie and therefore could not understand how the sexual content in it arose from that nonexistent plot or advanced it. Nor could he see that it reflected anything other than a desire on the part of the director to shock and titillate the audience.

Once the Second Circuit issued its reluctant 2–1 decision, the film that the government had seized could then be exhibited in theaters across the United States, except, of course, where there were local censors. *I Am Curious* was found to be obscene by the local authorities in a number of states, including California, Georgia, Michigan, and Missouri, and several cities, including Boston and Baltimore.[18] Even though the Second Circuit had found the film to be constitutionally protected, the Maryland Appeals Court, using the same definitional scheme from *Roth* and *Memoirs* that the majority in the Second Circuit had used, came to the opposite conclusion, finding *I Am Curious* to be utterly without social value.[19] The Maryland court

---

18. Wittern-Keller & Haberski, p. 173.
19. Wagonheim v. Maryland State Board of Censors, 255 Md. 297, 258 A. 2d 240 (1969).

determined that it was their duty to make "an independent constitutional judgment" on the question. In these justices' view, there was no doubt that the film was obscene, and furthermore, as one of the justices put it, it was "a crashing bore." Essentially, the court believed that, although some experts may have claimed the film to be a work of art, "it was time to draw the line against pornography" masquerading as art.[20]

Grove Press appealed this decision and, in 1970, the U.S. Supreme Court agreed to hear the case. A bevy of supporters of the movie submitted briefs, urging the Court to adopt the Second Circuit's decision and overturn the Maryland court. Had Justice Douglas, a strong supporter of constitutional rights, taken part in this review, it is likely that these petitioners would have had their way. However, he had recused himself from consideration of Grove Press's appeal. The other eight members of the Court split evenly and issued a one-line opinion, affirming the judgment of the Maryland court.[21]

As a result of the earlier Second Circuit decision, however, which was not addressed by the Supreme Court, *I Am Curious (Yellow)* was distributed into most cities and states in the United States and, as Grove Press's lawyer, Edward de Grazia, stated in his submittals to the Maryland court, the movie was exhibited in hundreds of theaters "in 40 states to more than 5 million people."[22] The notoriety of the legal dispute, which lasted for over three years, probably increased ticket sales by sparking the curiosity of moviegoers, wondering what all the fuss was about. Only the curious people of Baltimore were left out.

20. Wittern-Keller & Haberski, p. 174.
21. Grove Press v. Maryland State Board of Censors, 401 U.S. 480 (1971).
22. Wittern-Keller & Haberski, p. 174.

Intermission 7

Publicity and the Movies:
The Movie Poster

Production, distribution, and marketing—these are the
three functions that bring a movie to life and ensure that the
moviegoer will see it on a screen in a wide number of theaters,
and that the film will enjoy a large audience. Since the early days
of cinema exhibition, one means that has enticed people to see
a film has been the movie poster. Whether an image of a dancing
Fred Astaire and Ginger Rogers seeming to float in the air in a
publicity poster for *Swing Time* (1936); the anxious but resigned
faces of Humphrey Bogart and Ingrid Bergman advertising
Casablanca (1942); the early poster of Carl Laemmle presenting
The Phantom of the Opera (1925) with an image of Lon Chaney
seeming to lurk underneath the watery sewers of Paris; a photo
of a swimsuit-clad Betty Grable hugging a beach ball to arouse
anticipation for *Moon Over Miami* (1941); the image of a hulking
John Wayne in *Hondo* (1953) ("First she was afraid he'd stay—
then she was afraid he wouldn't"); or a smiling, bejeweled Audrey
Hepburn looking out at her prospective audience for *Breakfast
at Tiffany's* (1961) (in a poster that does not present her name in
the credits—everyone knows who she is), these iconic posters
command significant prices at art auctions and studios are ever
vigilant in protecting their intellectual property rights in these
posters and their designs. These posters have outlived their initial
purpose—to entice audiences to be among the first to see the
new movie—but live on as evidence of the popularity of those
films, and as art work subject to licensing fees for the studios.

It is ironic that one legal case that put the studios on
the opposite side in a dispute over the value of an artist's
concept involved a movie poster where the studio "borrowed"
a design from a cover illustration for an edition of *The New Yorker*
magazine. In March 1976, Saul Steinberg created a well-known
illustration of a myopic New Yorker's view of the world, where
a few select streets of the city loom large and locales further

away, such as New Jersey, California, and the rest of the world are shown as insignificant. This cover was imitated by Columbia Pictures to create a promotional poster for the film *Moscow on the Hudson* (1984), which tells the story of a Russian saxophonist who defects while in a circus performing in New York City, and, speaking little English, is forced to make a new life.

The poster and *The New Yorker* cover are not exactly alike— the *Moscow on the Hudson* poster has a comparable insular view of New York, but instead of looking west, toward California and beyond, the Columbia poster looked east, with Europe and Moscow as distant locales. Imitation is the highest form of flattery, as they say. However, unfortunately for Columbia, the design for the poster so closely resembled the famous Steinberg cover that a federal district court determined that the studio had infringed Steinberg's copyright and it had to be changed.[1]

1. Steinberg v. Columbia Pictures Industries, Inc., 663 F. Supp. 706 (S.D. N.Y. 1987).

Back to the Future

Lugosi v. Universal Pictures, 25 Cal. 3d 813 (1979);
Guglielmi v. Spelling-Goldberg Productions,
25 Cal. 3d 860 (1979)

> **Count Dracula: To die, to be "really" dead, that must be glorious!**
> **Mina Seward: Why, Count Dracula!**
> **Count Dracula: There are far worse things awaiting man than death.**
> From *Dracula* (1931)

I n the 1960s and 1970s, when actors were more and more conscious of their image, and gaining greater control over how they would be portrayed in motion pictures and in the publicity for those films, two back-to-back California Supreme Court cases involving actors from a much earlier time in the history of the cinema emphasized why achieving and maintaining that control was critical. These cases determined the rights of the heirs to two well-known icons from the early cinema—Bela Lugosi, most famous for his portrayal of Count Dracula in a film adapted from Bram Stoker's famous novel, and the iconic Rudolph Valentino, the silent film heartthrob.[1]

In September 1930, Lugosi, already a well-known film actor noted for his distinctive nose and voice, and Universal Pictures concluded an agreement for the production of the film *Dracula* (1931). The contract gave Universal the right to reproduce and use "and give publicity to the artist's name and likeness."

---

1. *See* Intermission 1, Scandals in Hollywood: Selling Movies and Hiding the Foibles of the Stars.

Lugosi died in 1956. In 1966, Hope Linninger Lugosi and Bela George Lugosi, the widow and surviving son of Bela Lugosi, sued Universal, alleging that after their husband's and father's death, the studio had taken property that the Lugosis had inherited from Bela Lugosi. They charged that, from 1960 on, Universal had entered into various licensing agreements that authorized the licensees to use the Count Dracula character on various consumer products, such as children's toys, clothing, Halloween masks, pencil sharpeners, and even a candy dispenser. The Lugosis sought to recover any profits that Universal had made from the licensing agreements and to prevent the studio from entering into any new contracts, without the Lugosis' consent.

The issue was whether, when he signed his movie production contract with Universal, Bela Lugosi had granted to Universal the merchandising rights in his portrayal of Count Dracula, or whether any of those rights were retained by Bela Lugosi and therefore were passed on to his heirs at his death. The trial court had agreed with the Lugosis, finding that Universal was licensing the "uniquely individual likeness and appearance of Bela Lugosi in the role of Count Dracula" (not another of the actors who had played Dracula in other films based on the *Dracula* novel).[2] The court therefore concluded that Lugosi during his lifetime had a protectable property or ownership right in his facial characteristics and the individual manner of his likeness and appearance as Count Dracula, that this property or owner-

---

2. Because Bram Stoker had failed to register his copyright for his 1897 novel in the United States, it had always been in the public domain there. In England and other countries that had signed on to the Berne Convention, the novel passed into the public domain in April 1962. The film, *Dracula*, in which Lugosi appeared, was copyrighted after the studio purchased the motion picture rights from Florence Stoker, Bram Stoker's heir. The trial court found that, even though Universal held a copyright in the movie, the character, Count Dracula, as described in Stoker's novel, was in the public domain in the United States.

ship right was of such character and substance that it did not end at Bela Lugosi's death but instead passed on to his heirs, and therefore that they had the sole right to this property under Lugosi's will.

Universal appealed. The case ultimately came before the California Supreme Court, which issued a divided opinion with the majority written by Justice Stanley Mosk and the dissent by Chief Justice Rose Bird. The majority ruled that, once protected by law, the right of a person to use his name and likeness is a right of value upon which a person can capitalize by selling licenses. However, because Lugosi did not create in his lifetime in his name and likeness a "*right* of value" which could have been transmuted into *things* of value, his heirs could not claim any right. Such a "right of value," the court ruled, to create a business, product, or service of value is protectable only during a person's lifetime; it did not survive Lugosi's death.

The court based its ruling on then California law governing rights of privacy, or publicity, as it is sometimes called. This law generally protects persons from intrusion into their seclusion or private affairs, public disclosure of embarrassing private facts, so-called "false light publicity"—placing the person in a false light in the public eye[3]—and appropriation by others, for their advantage, of that person's name or likeness.[4] The court ruled that this statute, which provided for damages for unauthorized commercial use of another person's "name, photograph, or likeness," under specified conditions, did not create any right that could be passed on to a person's heirs. This right of publicity, the court pointed out, is a *personal* right that does not extend

---

3. *See* discussion of this concept at Reel 27, Shipwrecked—The Billy Tyne Story and *A Perfect Storm, Tyne v. Time Warner Entertainment*, 336 F. 2d 1286 (11th Cir. 2003).

4. Then Cal. Civ. Code §3344, adopted in 1971.

to members of the person's family, unless their own privacy was invaded also. Justice Mosk, in his majority opinion, worried what the consequences would be if the court were to rule otherwise. "May the remote descendants of the historic public figures obtain damages for the unauthorized commercial use of the name or likeness of their distinguished ancestors? If not, where is the line to be drawn, and who would draw it?"

Thus, the court ruled, under California law, upon Lugosi's death, anyone, related or unrelated to Lugosi, "with the imagination, the enterprise, the energy, and the cash could, . . . have impressed a name using Lugosi's name, and made or lost money from the enterprise, depending on the value of the idea. After Lugosi's death, his name was in the public domain."[5]

Justice Mosk went further in disappointing the hopes of Lugosi's heirs. They had no right as Lugosi's successors to control the commercialization of a likeness of a fictional character, Count Dracula, that their husband and father had portrayed for compensation in the movie. Justice Mosk noted, "merely playing a role . . . creates no inheritable property right in an actor, absent a contract so providing . . . neither Lugosi during his lifetime nor his estate thereafter owned the exclusive right to exploit Count Dracula any more than Gregory Peck or his heirs could possess . . . exclusivity to General MacArthur, George C. Scott to General Patton, James Whitmore to Will Rogers and Harry Truman, or Charlton Heston to Moses." This was not to say, he insisted, that in some cases protection could be available to any original creation of a fictional figure played exclusively by its creator, such as the Little Tramp character originated by Charles Chaplin. But Justice Mosk did not believe that Bela

---

5. The court did not address the issue, because it was not before them, whether anyone other than Universal could have built a business coupling Lugosi's name with that of Dracula.

Lugosi created Dracula—although many film enthusiasts would disagree with him on this point—any more than countless other actors had created Hamlet, for example.

According to Justice Mosk, because Lugosi played Dracula under an employment contract that gave Universal the right to exploit the actor's "poses" and "appearances" and because, under California employment law, everything that an employee acquires by virtue of his employment, except for his compensation, belongs to the employer, it seemed clear that as between Lugosi—an employee who was hired and paid "handsomely" by Universal—and the studio, the product of that employment and all residuals flowing from such employment belonged to Universal. The heirs should have no greater right now than Lugosi would have had in his lifetime.

Chief Justice Bird, writing in dissent, strongly disagreed with the majority in this case. As she saw it, although the role of Count Dracula had been performed by a number of actors both before and after Bela Lugosi, Lugosi's portrayal of Dracula *was* distinctive, so distinctive that in the minds of many, when someone mentioned Dracula, they heard Lugosi's voice and they saw his likeness (it was as much his likeness as that of Dracula). Lugosi had invested his own identity into the role, in the same manner as Charlie Chaplin had "become" the Little Tramp, or as, later, she said Carroll O'Connor had become Archie Bunker in the popular television show, *All in the Family*. She noted that substantial publicity value existed in the likeness of each of these actors. As she saw it, "the professional and economic interests in controlling the commercial exploitation of their likenesses *while portraying these characters* were identical to their interests in controlling the use of their own 'natural likenesses'" [emphasis added]. And Lugosi's likeness in his portrayal of Count Dracula was the same. "Universal did not license the use of an undifferentiated Count Dracula," when the studio agreed to the use of Lugosi's likeness on candy dispensers and t-shirts. It was rather "the distinctive and readily recognizable portrayal of Lugosi as the notorious Transylvanian count." And Justice Bird also believed that the right to exploit one's own likeness could be inherited, because it was a proprietary interest in the value of one's own likeness, that is, a commercial right, not a personal one, such as the right of privacy.

Justice Bird further did not agree that Lugosi's 1930 employment agreement granted Universal the right to license Lugosi's portrayal of Count Dracula in the sale of commercially merchandised products. She noted in her dissent that in 1936, six years after the contract was made, Universal requested and received Lugosi's permission to use in its production of *Dracula's Daughter* a wax likeness of Lugosi's portrayal of Count Dracula from the original *Dracula* movie. If the 1930 contract had granted Universal the broad right to use Lugosi's likeness, as the studio had asserted in this case, then it would neither have needed nor sought Lugosi's consent in 1936.

Immediately after rendering the *Lugosi* decision, in December 1979, the California Supreme Court took up this same right of publicity question in a companion case.[6] This time, the dispute centered on the rights of the heir of a famous silent film actor. Jean Guglielmi was the nephew of Rodolfo Guglielmi,[7] more familiarly known as Rudolph Valentino, the world-renowned silent movie star who died in 1926, at the height of his fame. On November 23, 1975, Spelling-Goldberg presented a televised "fictionalized version" of Valentino's life, in a film entitled *Legend of Valentino: A Romantic Fiction.*

---

6. Guglielmi v. Spelling-Goldberg Productions, 25 Cal. 3d 860 (1979).

7. His full name was Rodolfo Alfonzo Raffaello Pierre Filibert Guglielmi di Valentina d'Antonguolla.

The film, advertised as a work of fiction, purported to show the life and loves of the famous Italian actor who became one of Hollywood's first romantic film stars. The film's producers used Valentino's name, likeness, and personality without obtaining the prior consent of Guglielmi. He sued, complaining that the producers had misappropriated Valentino's "right of publicity." He claimed that, as Valentino's legal heir, he was the present owner of that right. He maintained that, by incorporating Valentino's identity into the film and related advertisements, the producers were able to earn a larger profit from the film than they would have if they had not been able to use Valentino's name.

Spelling-Goldberg demurred, denying as legal matter that Guglielmi had any cause of action against them on account of their use of Valentino's name or likeness in the fictionalization of his life. The trial court agreed. The case came to the California Supreme Court as a companion to the *Lugosi* case.

In a very brief opinion, Chief Justice Bird affirmed the lower court's ruling, relying on the *Lugosi* decision, but also on First Amendment considerations. Guglielmi had not claimed that the fictional work defamed or violated either his or Valentino's right to privacy. Rather he argued that the work infringed on Valentino's right to publicity, which he had inherited. According to Justice Bird, Guglielmi would have had a right to sue the producers if, first, Rudolph Valentino had had a right of publicity in the commercial use of his name, likeness, and personality that could be transferred to his heirs and, second, if they impermissibly infringed on that right.

Based on her dissent in *Lugosi*, Justice Bird believed that, as to the first condition, a prominent person had a substantial economic interest in the commercial use of his name and likeness that she believed was entitled to protection and should be able to be inherited, at least for a period of fifty years after the individual's death. The main question was whether the film about Valentino's life *impermissibly* infringed on his right to publicity. She was concerned about the conflict between a right of publicity claimed by the film star and the First Amendment right that the producers had to freedom of expression.

Guglielmi contended that the film was not entitled to constitutional protection as free expression because it incorporated Valentino's name and likeness into a work of fiction for financial gain, where the producers knew that the film falsely portrayed Valentino's life. For the Chief Justice, whether these factors outweighed the producer's constitutional rights was a crucial issue. The fact that the film was a work of fiction would not negate these rights—entertainment is entitled to the same constitutional protection as political or philosophical treatises. She also did not believe that the fact that the film had been made for commercial purposes would overcome these rights. First Amendment protection is not limited to those who publish for free. However, she questioned whether the use of Valentino's name and likeness in the film was necessary or was it incorporated into the film solely to make it more profitable? Guglielmi argued that it was the latter. However, Justice Bird hesitated to go down that road. Requiring an author to justify the use of a celebrity's identity in a particular publication had the potential of chilling the exercise of free speech and could become a form of censorship.

Fiction writers may "weave into the tale persons or events familiar to their readers . . .. The right of publicity derived from public prominence does not confer a shield to ward off caricature, parody and satire," she stated. Rather, prominence invited creative comment. And for Justice Bird, this was the case with respect to the Valentino film. He had been an immensely popular Hollywood star. As she noted, his life and career in the cinema coincided with an important cultural and historical event, the debut of the feature film. He was a screen idol, a legend, a symbol of romance. In short, she concluded, "his lingering persona is an apt topic for poetry or song, biography or fiction. Whether . . . [the film] constitutes a serious appraisal of Valentino's stature or mere fantasy is a judgment left to the reader or viewer, not the courts."

Guglielmi also claimed that the film was not entitled to constitutional protection because the producers acted with "knowledge or reckless disregard of the falsity" of their broadcast. This appeared to be an effort on his lawyer's part to import an "actual malice" standard of liability from defamation cases into the right of publicity.[8] Justice Bird saw this analysis as misguided. "In defamation cases, the concern is with defamatory lies masquerading as truth." With a work of fiction, on the other hand, "there is no pretense." No fiction—by the very fact that it is fiction—has any obligation to be faithful to the historical truth. "Therefore," she said, "where fiction is the medium," as alleged by Guglielmi, "as is evident in the film's title, *A Romantic Fiction*, it is meaningless to charge that the author 'knew' that his work was false." In short, Justice Bird concluded, the right of publicity did not "outweigh the value of free expression." She also ruled that, because the use of Valentino's name and likeness in advertisements for the film was "merely an adjunct to the exhibition of the film," such use did not infringe on any of Valentino's rights, no more than the film did.

In reaction to the *Lugosi* and *Guglielmi* cases, the California legislature amended the state's Civil Code to create a right for heirs to enforce a famous person's right of publicity after

---

8. "Actual malice" was established as a standard for proving defamation of public figures by the U.S. Supreme Court in The New York Times Co. v. Sullivan, 376 U.S. 254 (1964).

that person's death.[9] The statute allows for damages against any person who uses a "deceased personality's" name, voice, photograph, or likeness "in any manner, on or in products, merchandise or goods" or for the purpose of advertising or selling any of them, without the prior consent of the deceased celebrity's heirs. Damages are a minimum of $750 and are to be calculated based on the gross revenue derived from the use. These are considered to be property rights that are freely transferable, whether the transfer occurs before or after the death of the deceased person. These rights are applicable to any transfer after January 1, 1985,[10] and are intended to continue for seventy years after the death of the personality.[11]

The statute contains, however, a "literary work" exception: the use of a deceased personality's name or voice or likeness in plays, books, magazines, newspapers, musical compositions, films, radio or television programs, original works of art, and any advertisement of any of these works, is not prohibited by the statute provided "it is fictional or nonfictional entertainment, or a dramatic, literary or musical work."[12] However, the statute allows an heir to prove that the use is so directly connected with the product or merchandise that it is actually an advertisement.[13]

This statute would have allowed the Lugosi's action against Universal to move forward had it been in effect, but not Guglielmi's, because the Valentino film in the *Guglielmi* case would have fallen under the "entertainment" exception. However, the

---

9. Cal. Civ. Code §990, enacted in 1988 and amended in 2007 as §3344.1: "Deceased Personality's Name, Voice, Signature, Photograph or Likeness in Advertising or Soliciting."

10. Cal. Civ. Code §3344.1(b).

11. Cal. Civ. Code §3344.1(g).

12. Cal. Civ. Code §3344(a)(3).

13. Cal. Civ. Code §3344(a)(3).

statute would not permit, it seems, a "movie" that is produced solely to sell a product (such as an infomercial), using a famous personality's name or likeness. Or so it would seem. However, in 1997, a federal appeals court in California nevertheless disallowed an heir's effort to prohibit the use of a deceased celebrity's likeness.[14] The court held that the use of the image of Fred Astaire in a series of dance instruction videotapes was exempt from liability under California's statute because the tapes were covered by the "film" exemption contained in the law. The court concluded that this exemption applied even if the use of the Fred Astaire film clips at the beginning of each tape was an advertisement.

---

14. Astaire v. Best Film & Video Corp., 116 F.3d 1297 (9th Cir. 1997).

Copycat

Smith v. Montero, 648 F. 2d 602 (9th Cir. 1981)

> **Trinity: Well, I'm not lookin' for trouble.**
> **Bambino: You never knew how to**
>   **do anything else.**
> Terence Hill as Trinity with Bud Spencer
> as Bambino in *My Name is Trinity* (1970)

One film genre that has had a surprising longevity is the western. Whether in the Tom Mix silent films or the movies of John Ford in the 1930s through the 1950s—such as *Stagecoach* (1939), *My Darling Clementine* (1946), *Fort Apache* (1948), *She Wore a Yellow Ribbon* (1949), *Rio Grande* (1950), or *The Searchers* (1956), to name just a few—the cowboy has held an iconic place in movie history. Even though serious westerns were produced throughout the twentieth century, they also have been parodied, imitated, and spoofed from the beginning of cinema, such as in Buster Keaton's very funny *Go West* (1925), about a young man who falls off a train, decides to become a cowboy, and ends up herding 1,000 head of cattle to Los Angeles. European moviegoers were particularly enchanted with this genre and the etiology of the western was a much discussed subject in the French *Cahiers du Cimema*.[1]

In the 1960s, the Italian director, Sergio Leone, produced a series of westerns, including *A Fistful of Dollars* (1964), *For a Few Dollars More* (1965) and *The Good, the Bad and the Ugly*

---

1. *See, e.g.*, Hillier, Jim, "American Cinema" *Cahiers du Cinéma, Volume I : The 1950s. Neo-Realism, Hollywood, New Wave*, Routledge Library of Media and Cultural Studies, p. 82.

(1966), that played on European enthusiasm for this genre. He also tossed movie stereotypes on their head by, for example, casting typical good guy Henry Fonda as the lawless gunslinger Frank in *Once Upon a Time in the West* (1968). Commonly known as "spaghetti westerns" (because of their Italian origin), Leone's films portrayed a West that was harsher, more "realistic" than that which had been presented in pre-1960s Hollywood westerns. These movies, shot in locations in Spain showing wide arid vistas that rivaled Ford's Monument Valley, used an international cast and made their American stars, Clint Eastwood and Charles Bronson, world famous.

These films, influenced by and parodying themes in earlier Hollywood westerns, were themselves subject to imitation and parody, particularly in the popular Italian "Trinity" movies—*They Call Me Trinity* (*Lo Chiamavano Trinità*) (1970) and *Trinity Is Still My Name* (*Continuavano a Chiamarlo Trinità*) (1971)—directed by another Italian, Enzo Barboni. These films made two Italian actors famous, at least in Italy: Carlo Pedersoli and Mario Girotti. Pedersoli had started his career in serious motion pictures, appearing as a member of the Praetorian guard in *Quo Vadis* (1951), which was filmed in Italy. In 1967, he changed his name to Bud Spencer (in homage to his favorite American actor, Spencer Tracy, and his favorite American beer, Budweiser) and teamed up with Mario Girotti, whose screen name was Terence Hill, to appear in a number of immensely popular buddy films in the 1960s and 1970s. Hill and Spencer became internationally known stars and their western spoofs paved the way for Mel Brooks's *Blazing Saddles* (1974).

The success of these films led Producioni Atlas Cinematografia (PAC), an Italian film company, to make its own imitations of the successful *Trinity* movies. For these films, an American actor, Paul L. Smith, and an Italian, Antonio Cantafora, were cast in the lookalike Bud Spencer and Terence Hill roles. Paul Smith was not new to the movie business. A former professional athlete, Smith's first acting role was in *Exodus* (1960), which was shot in Israel. He is more famous for his performance as the sadistic Turkish prison guard in *Midnight Express* (1978), but he also had small roles in *Dune* (1984) and *Red Sonya* (1985).[2] However, between *Exodus* and *Midnight Express*, there were the buddy movies and the spaghetti western spoofs. One of these was *Simone e Matteo: Un gioco da ragazzi* (1976), which portrayed two inept mobsters, Butch and Toby, trying to steal guns. Smith played Butch and Cantafora, under his screen name, Michael Colby, played Toby.[3]

Smith's contract with PAC at the time *Simone e Matteo* was filmed provided that he would receive star billing in the screen credits and advertising for the movie. This obligation was to be included in all agreements that PAC made with distributors of the film. PAC licensed the rights to distribute the movie in the United States, under the title *Convoy Buddies*, to Edward Montero and his distribution company, Film Ventures International. When Film Ventures got the film, however, instead of giving screen credit to Smith and Colby, Montero renamed Colby (the Terence Hill lookalike) as Terence Hall and Smith (the faux Bud Spencer) as Bob Spencer in both the movie credits and the advertising for the movie. Either Montero was obviously trying to carry the spoof one step further and play off the public's familiarity with Terence Hill and Bud Spencer, or he was hoping that the public would be confused and believe that they were watching another of the famous *Trinity* movies. In any event,

---

2. *See* Paul L. Smith, Biography, found at www.fandango.com/paull.smith/bio graphy/p111942.

3. *See* description of the film at the Internet Movie Database, http://www.imdb. com/title/tt0073713/.

Smith did not get the joke, and he sued in federal district court in Los Angeles, saying that "The only thing an actor has is his name and if that's taken away, he has nothing."[4]

Smith claimed that in switching the names, Montero had damaged his reputation as an actor and that as a result he had lost specific employment opportunities. He also argued that Montero's actions in changing his name in the screen credits was deceptive and violated the Lanham Act.[5] The trial court dismissed the case, ruling that Smith did not have a valid Lanham Act claim. Montero had not deceived moviegoers by misusing Smith's name. Smith's problem was not that his name had been misused; it was that it had not been used at all. Smith appealed.

Section 43(a) of the Lanham Act prohibits using a "false designation of origin or any false designation" in connection with any goods or services.[6] Smith argued that Montero violated Section 43(a) by using a false designation or representation in the film credits and in its advertising with another actor's name instead of Smith's. The district court had dismissed Smith's claim because that section of the Lanham Act was intended to govern merchandising practices "in the nature of, or economically equivalent to, palming off and/or misuse of trademarks and trade names."

The appellate court found this interpretation to be too limiting and contrary to established case law. The statute was intended to prevent not just palming off or falsely representing goods in commerce but also "reverse palming off"—removing or obliterating the original trademark to resell goods produced by

---

4. Quoted in an interview with a former employee of Film Ventures International, found at the Unknown Movies website, www.badmovieplant.com/unknownmovies/reviews/fvi.html.

5. *See* Intermission 8, The Lanham Act—Trademark Law and Preventing Deceptive Behavior in the Industry.

6. 15 U.S.C. §1125(a).

someone else. Smith argued that removing his name and substituting a false name closely resembling another famous actor's name constituted reverse passing off. Montero responded that the protection afforded by the Lanham Act was limited to "sales of goods" and did not extend to claims that a motion picture shown to the public might contain false information as to origin.

The appellate court did not accept this limitation. The Lanham Act explicitly condemned false designations in connection with "any goods or services" and had been held to apply to motion pictures. Because Montero not only had removed Smith's name from all credits and advertising but had also substituted a name of his own choosing (which was imitative of another famous actor's name), this did amount to reverse passing off, much as if a distributor removes a manufacturer's name from a product and substitutes his own. "As a matter of policy, such conduct, like traditional palming off, is wrongful, because it involves an attempt to misappropriate or profit from another's talents and workmanship," as well as to deprive the original person of the value of his own name and goodwill that would stem from public knowledge of the true source.

Consequently, the court ruled that Smith had a valid claim, noting that

> "in the film industry, a particular actor's performance, which may have received an award or other critical acclaim, may be the primary attraction for moviegoers. Some actors are said to have such drawing power at the box office that the appearance of their names on the theater marquee can almost guarantee financial success. Such big box office names are built, in part, through being prominently featured in popular films and by receiving appropriate recognition in film credits and

advertising. Such actors' fees for pictures and indeed, their ability to get any work at all, is often based on the drawing power their name may be expected to have at the box office, being accurately credited for films in which they have played would seem to be of critical importance in enabling actors to sell their 'services,' i.e., their performances.

Was it true that the inclusion or exclusion of Paul Smith's name from the marquee of *Convoy Buddies* (or more likely from the DVD box cover) had any impact on his obtaining a role in *Midnight Express*? Having a film credit for a role in a spoof of a spoof does not seem as important as if, for example, Tom Cruise's name had been left off the film credits for *Top Gun* (1986). On the other hand, fans of the real Terence Hill and Bud Spencer most certainly would have been disappointed when they popped the disc into their DVD player and discovered that Terence Hall and Bob Spencer were not the famous *Trinity* stars.

Intermission 8

The Lanham Act: Trademark Law and Preventing Deceptive Behavior in the Industry

The Lanham Act[1] has as its purpose to prevent consumer confusion as to the source of a product and to prevent unfair competition, as well as to protect trademark owners by preventing others from taking advantage of the owner's goodwill and from deceiving consumers as to the origin of the products sold under those trademarks. Trademark owners generally call upon the Act to prevent others from infringing on their marks, that is to prevent another producer from using a mark that looks like or is confusingly similar to the protected mark in connection with the marketing or sale of goods or services that are similar to those of the trademark owner. It also helps prevent the mark from being "blurred" or "tarnished."

Blurring occurs when the public associates a trademark with someone else's goods or services and this association "impairs the distinctiveness of the famous mark.[2] "Tarnishment" creates an association between the protected mark and goods or services of another that could harm the reputation of the famous mark.[3] For example, in 2003, the owners of the well-known Victoria's Secret lingerie shops sued the proprietor of a shop selling sex toys, called "Victor's Little Secret," claiming that the use of that similar brand tarnished the more famous lingerie brand.[4]

One concern among trademark owners is the practice of "palming off" and "reverse passing off." "Passing off" or "palming off" occurs when someone imitates or otherwise uses a famous mark to sell his or her goods, pretending that they came from the famous source. An example would be the sellers outside baseball stadiums or soccer playoff games, marketing cheap t-shirts branded with the logos of the teams playing inside. In 1946, the Lanham Act incorporated "passing off" as a form of unfair competition.[5]

Intermission 8 (continued)

"Reverse passing off" occurs when the original trademark is removed from a product, or masked, and the product is either sold unbranded or worse, with a different mark which prevents the consumer from associating the product with the manufacturer's own mark. The *Smith v. Montero* case was an important decision to recognize reverse passing off as a behavior for which damages could be awarded under the Lanham Act.[6]

More recently, an attempt was made by a work's creator to use, without success, the concept of "reverse passing off" to prevent a video maker from passing off a reissuance of a television series as its own work, without attribution to the original creator.[7]

After World War II, General Dwight D. Eisenhower wrote a book chronicling his war experience, which was published by Doubleday under the title *Crusade in Europe*. Doubleday licensed the film rights to the work to Twentieth Century Fox, for a television series with the same title. Time/Life under license from Fox made the series, which aired in 1949. In 1975, Doubleday renewed its copyright in the book, but Fox failed to renew its rights in the film. In 1988, Fox reacquired the television rights to the book and gave New Line Home Video and SFM Entertainment the exclusive rights to distribute videos of the 1949 television series.

However, at approximately the same time, Dastar Corp., realizing that Fox had allowed its copyright in the 1949 series to lapse and that the film was now in the public domain, released its own set of videos, using the original series with only minor modifications. Dastar gave no credit to Fox or anyone else. Fox, New Line, and SFM sued Dastar for copyright infringement, claiming a violation of Fox's copyright in the television rights to the book and also claiming that, by selling videos of the series "without proper credit," Dastar was guilty of "reverse palming off" under Section 43(a) of the Lanham Act.

The case reached the U.S. Supreme Court in 2003, where, in an almost unanimous decision (with only one abstention—

Justice Breyer—who recused himself), the Court ruled that the Lanham Act could not be used to prevent unaccredited copying of a work in the public domain. In the majority opinion, Justice Scalia perceived the "reverse passing off" argument as an attempt to "resurrect an expired copyright." As the Court saw it, the parties bringing this suit were not really creators, but rather companies that had let their copyright protection lapse. They wanted to retain the exclusive distribution rights that they thought they still had and prevent Dastar from selling its own version. In discussing the Lanham Act claim, the Court noted that it was doubtful that Fox and its friends would have been content with Dastar selling its video if the company had given the studio and the others the "proper credit" that they were demanding. At least one commentator has noted that this case illustrates the need for Congress to reconsider what place "moral rights"—the personal rights, as opposed to economic rights, that artists have in their creations—should have under U.S. law.[8]

---

1. The Trademark Act of 1946, as amended by 15 U.S.C. §§1125 et seq.

2. 15 U.S.C. §1125(c)(2).

3. 15 U.S.C. §1125(c)(2)(C).

4. Moseley v. V Secret Catalogue, 537 U.S. 418 (2003).

5. Lanham Act of 1946 §43(a), as amended, 15 U.S.C. §1125(a).

6. Smith v. Montero, 648 F. 2d 602 (9th Cir. 1981); See Reel 19, Copycat. *See also*, Wright, Catherine Romero, Comment, "Reverse Passing Off: Preventing Healthy Competition," 20 Seattle U.L. Rev. 785 (1997), found at digitalcommons. law.seattleu.edu/cgi/viewcontent.cgi?article=1517&context=sulr.

7. Dastar Corp. v. Twentieth Century Fox Film Corp., 539 U.S. 23 (2003).

8. Mortensen, Rick, "D.I.Y. After Dastar: Protecting Creators' Moral Rights Through Creative Lawyering, Individual Contracts, and Collectively Bargained Agreements," Vanderbilt Journal of Entertainment and Technology Law, Vol. 8:2:335 (2006), found at http://litigation-essentials.lexisnexis.com/webcd/ app?action=DocumentDisplay&crawlid=1&srctype=smi&srcid=3B15&doctype=cit e&docid=8+Vand.+J.+Ent.+%26+Tech.+L.+335&key=5959b7af8bdf275f1c33c55c 88a61696. *See also*, Intermission 3, Moral Rights: A Different Way of Viewing Artistic Works.

Part VI

Trends in the Movie Industry Post-1980

The last decades of the twentieth century (and the beginning of the twenty-first) saw tremendous changes in the film industry which were reflective of transformations in society in general during that same time period. In the movie business, these were distinguished by three social and economic megatrends—rapid technological innovation, business consolidation, and globalization—as well as an increasing legal awareness of intellectual property rights, in particular that of copyright. In addition, this time period saw increasing tension between copyright and First Amendment rights, between copyright protection and the promotion of creative transformative expression.

Technological advances had a major impact on all aspects of the film industry, from the way movies are made to their very subject matter, as well as how, when, and where motion pictures are exhibited. In the late 1970s, two new technologies were introduced, both of which profoundly affected the public's entertainment and film-viewing habits. The first of these was satellite and cable television, which vastly increased the number of channels available to the American public, and which provided another outlet for movie studios to exhibit recent films, after their first runs in theaters. The second was the home videocassette recorder.[1]

In the early 1980s, two rival Japanese companies began to distribute in the United States devices that enabled televi-

---

1. Thompson & Bordwell, p. 680.

sion audiences to record programs—including televised movies— from their TV sets onto tapes to view later at their leisure. Although these devices—the Sony Betamax and the videocassette recorder (VHS system)—are considered primitive by today's standards (in an era where video streaming over the Internet is commonplace), at the time, this technology revolutionized the way movie fans watched films, enabling them to record their favorite motion pictures, to create their own private film libraries, and to rewind tapes to savor the best scenes. The studios, of course, felt threatened by this shift in control over the movie-viewing experience and took legal action in an effort to block the new technology. Having failed in this effort, they soon recognized opportunities to create new revenue streams (by selling prerecorded VHS tapes). By 1987, videocassette rentals and sales accounted for half of major film companies' domestic revenues.[2]

By the end of the 1990s, just when the market was saturated with videocassette rentals, a new technology, the digital video disc (DVD) was introduced and rapidly replaced videocassette recorders in most people's homes. This trend was aided by an ever-decreasing price structure for DVD players and by the higher picture and sound quality that this format allowed. This in turn led to advancements in home theater technology as viewers upgraded their systems, with bigger and better quality television sets (particularly after the introduction of flat screen plasma and high-definition (HD) sets). People built home film libraries, purchasing their favorite movies on DVD. Studios began adding special features to DVDs, such as movie trailers, interviews with the director and actors, omitted scenes from the editing process, behind-the-scene tours of the makeup rooms

2. Thompson & Bordwell, p. 680.

and computer graphics studios, and other background detail. "By 2000, home videos were yielding the studios an annual $20 billion worldwide revenue stream, three times the North American box-office income."[3]

Alas for Hollywood, the world did not stand still. If the 1990s and early 2000s can be characterized as the era of the DVD (and in this sense the newer Blu-Ray technology—using a disc that must be purchased or rented, usually with a high premium, in order to view a motion picture on one's television set—can be viewed as an extension of the DVD), then the time period since the late 2000s could be called the "post-DVD era" or the "virtual era," or what some refer to as the "weightless economy." Just as greater numbers of consumers every year abandon brick-and-mortar stores in favor of online shopping and now download their favorite music and video games, as well as a wide variety of apps for their iPhones and iPads, and read books, newspapers, and magazines in electronic format, so they also now "stream" their movies. And what they want is access to their chosen form of entertainment—whether music, news, or movies (and especially movies)—at the times they want, by the means they want, in the format they want, and at the right price point. This trend has presented a challenge to the film industry and its basic economic model.

From the earliest days of the cinema, the industry has controlled the time frames for movie release: there is an initial release into a select number of theaters (a "limited release"), generally in time for a holiday or just before the end of the calendar year (to be in time for Academy Award nominations), then, shortly after a media blitz of advertising to build anticipation, the film is released into a wider number of cinemas nation-

---

3. Thompson & Bordwell, p. 681.

wide (the "national release window"), followed by an international release. The invention of television created a new release window for the industry. Films that had finished their theatrical run could be reintroduced to the public through a television premiere. Cable provided better opportunities for viewing films on television. A movie at the end of its theatrical run could be given exclusive viewing slots on paid premium channels, such as HBO or Showtime. Pay-per-view created yet another revenue-enhancing release window, as did the development of the DVD.

For years, viewers accepted the studio release windows as a given. But no more. Now that they have experienced other viewing opportunities, they are no longer content to trek to a movie theater to see the first run of a film or else wait for the DVD release, for example. For a number of reasons, people are not rushing out to theaters to see every newly released movie. For one thing, they may not want to stand in line and see the movie with a crowd. Having purchased high-end equipment in order to create "home theaters"—complete with large screen HD or plasma sets, surround sound, and comfortable seating—they want to use them.

At the same time, the viewing experience in theaters has deteriorated; it no longer has the same appeal. Gone are the Egyptian palaces and ornate cinemas of the 1920s. They have been replaced with the Multiplex, which may seem bigger because ten or more movies can be exhibited there at the same time, but which generally have more compact auditoriums, smaller screens, and often thin walls. And audiences, perhaps more used to behaving as if in their own homes, have become noisy and disruptive. I first noticed this when I took my son to see *Crouching Tiger, Hidden Dragon* (2000) on opening night. I thought that perhaps because this movie, an action film, was in Chinese, people felt more comfortable yelling at the screen because they could not understand the dialogue. But no. Movies are now no longer just motion pictures; they have become events, much like basketball games or boxing matches. As such, they must be seen when first released, during the opening weekend, if at all. Moreover, a film is judged by its box office take during those critical first hours after the big theatrical release. If it fails, it quickly drops off the marquee, to reappear if at all only during the later DVD release window. As a result, smaller, more intimate, movies and art films that take time to grow on audiences and develop a following through word-of-mouth do not have a chance in this environment. They close after only a short run in a limited number of theaters, or are released straight to DVD. These movies are better viewed in the more intimate, quieter world of the home theater.

Besides better appreciating the viewing ambiance they have created for themselves in their home theaters, today's moviegoers have neither the patience nor the attention span to tolerate the arbitrary release timeline dictated by the studios. They fail to understand why they have to wait several months before they can see a movie that is being heavily advertised outside of the cinema. And it is a business model that is at odds with marketing conventions. Most consumer products companies succeed by gearing their products toward the desires and tastes of their consumers, and then by promptly making the products as widely available in as many venues as possible. In the movie industry, quite the opposite occurs. After weeks of creating a "buzz" around a new release through movie trailers and advertising in a wide range of media, including television, the Internet, Facebook, and apps on mobile devices, the studios then delay the actual release for several months while the film is shown on just a few screens, sometimes only in New York and Los Angeles. This was perhaps a good business practice in the days when the only way to see a movie was at a local cinema. But today, the consumer asks herself: Why should I care about a new movie if I can only see it in theaters in two cities and I don't live there? And why should I pay attention when it is released in more theaters when I have other forms of entertainment to distract me? By the time a "must-see" movie makes it to DVD or a cable channel, the momentum has passed. Those who elected to avoid the crowds at the multiplex have moved on. Unlike the moviegoers of the 1920s and 1930s, for whom an outing at the cinema was frequently a way to escape a hot urban apartment or to relieve the boredom of a small rural town, today's viewer has just too many choices for entertainment that are immediate and hassle-free.

As the industry has witnessed disappointing attendance numbers at the box office, the result has been a nascent trend to "collapse the release window." For the past several years, studios have experimented with concurrent releases of films in a variety of media, notably in theaters but also through video-streaming services. Some studios are forming alliances with distributors of video-on-demand (VOD), such as cable companies, to simultaneously release a film in theaters and in VOD format. From a business perspective, collapsing the release window in this manner has a desirable result for movie producers, especially those who are part of media conglomerates that include cable companies, because it affords them greater control over the exhibition and revenue streams from the movies—something they lost when studios were forced to divest their theaters as a result of the *Paramount* decision in 1948. Early VOD release also allows studios to reach the home viewer without going through the traditional DVD sale window, enabling them to avoid the cost of DVD production and distribution. This ultimately provides studios with greater profits from a movie than through DVD sales, because they generally receive a bigger share of the revenue from VOD than from DVDs, largely due to fewer middlemen; the DVD retailer is cut out of the economic chain with VOD.

Of course, as the market tightens and the studios regain greater control over the entire movie production chain—production, distribution, and, once again, exhibition—the antitrust concerns that were raised in the *Paramount* decision could once again come into the forefront. However, this time, as opposed to sixty years ago, the world has drastically changed from the days when movies were perceived to be Americans' primary source of entertainment. If movies become too expensive due to overly restrictive studio control, they may also become irrelevant to the viewing public. In the end, this is all speculation. It is far too early in this rapidly changing technological environment to gauge what the next new trend in the film industry will be.

The development of digital technology in the latter part of the twentieth century also changed the way films were shot and how they were exhibited in theaters. Until the last few decades, movies were produced in an analog medium. The cinematographer captured on a strip of film a continuous imprint of light and sound waves. But by the late 1980s and 1990s, use of digital technology (capturing information in a binary form of ones and zeros) was making headway. The first major innovation in this area was the use of motion-control-systems—computer-governed cameras that repeated frame-by-frame movements over miniatures or models. First used in the filming of *Star Wars* (1977), this process soon became a basic methodology for creating special effects shots and has been extensively used in most science fiction and action films from that time forward. Sound recording and reproduction by means of digital audio tape have become standard. With the introduction of faster computers with greater memory, their use in movie production—not just for special effects in action films, but also to correct scene color, for example—became standard.

Digital technology also has changed animation through use of computer graphics imaging (CGI). This has led to more and more realistic movies created entirely through use of computers. In 1995, *Toy Story*, the first completely CGI feature film, was produced by Pixar and released by Disney, followed by *A Bug's Life* in 1998, and *Toy Story 2* in 1999. These films were very successful and led the way to an entirely new genre of motion pictures—animated films for adult viewers as well as children, exemplified by the immensely popular *Ratatouille* (2007), *WALL-E* (2008) and *UP* (2009).

Another recent technological change in cinema is the use of stereoscopic filmmaking, or 3D technology. The concept of 3D is not new in itself. In the 1950s, movies were sometimes exhibited presenting offset images that were perceived as three-dimensional when viewed through special glasses. This never really caught on, however. The movie *Avatar* (2009) brought about a renewed interest in 3D technology. Filmed with stereoscopic cameras, the movie presents two offset images separately seen by the movie viewer's left and right eye. These images combine in the viewer's brain and leave the perception of 3D depth without glasses. The movie's director, James Cameron, has predicted that eventually motion pictures shot in 3D will become the norm (much as sound technology became the norm in the 1930s).[4]

The second megatrend of the late 20th Century, consolidation, has impacted the film industry, much as it has impacted

---

4. "James Cameron: Pushing The Limits Of Imagination," Fresh Air from PBS station WHYY in Philadelphia, Interview with *Avatar* director, James Cameron, February 18, 2010.

the manufacturing, finance, and banking industries. By the late 1990s, all of the major studios were part of large conglomerates.[5] This trend is exemplified by the saga of two successful studios from the early twentieth century, Metro-Goldwyn-Mayer, or MGM, and United Artists. MGM was founded in 1924 when Marcus Loew, owner of the Loew's theater chain, merged Metro Pictures, Samuel Goldwyn's Goldwyn Pictures Corporation, and Louis B. Mayer Pictures. By 1969, MGM had been acquired by a wealthy financier, Kirk Kerkorian, who valued the company not for its film production and distribution history and capabilities but rather for its vast Southern California real estate holdings. This was an era when California real estate prices were booming and Kerkorian planned to benefit from a divestiture of MGM's properties. At the same time, he downsized studio operations.

In 1967, United Artists, the legendary studio of Charles Chaplin and Mary Pickford, was sold to Transamerica Corporation, a large conglomerate known for its insurance businesses. In 1981, Transamerica sold United Artists to Kerkorian. Shortly after, in 1986, Kerkorian in turn sold both MGM and United Artists to media mogul Ted Turner. Turner resold the two studios back to Kerkorian that same year, but retained ownership of the extensive MGM film library.

In 1990, Italian financier Giancarlo Parretti bought the combined MGM/UA Company with the financial backing of the French lender, Crédit Lyonnais, in a financially troubled transaction. Crédit Lyonnais was forced to take control of the company in 1991 as it stood on the brink of bankruptcy. This lender promptly sold the business back to Kerkorian. In the 1990s and early 2000s, MGM engaged in a series of costly acquisitions using leveraged financing, as was common in that era.

---

5. Thompson & Bordwell, p. 681.

Already struggling under a heavy debt load, in 2004 the company was acquired by a consortium of Sony Corporation, Comcast Corporation, and several private equity investors. In 2005, these investors took MGM private in a deal that saddled the studio with an even greater—in fact overwhelming—debt burden.[6] In 2006, United Artists, still part of MGM, was put under the management of actor Tom Cruise and his production partner, Paula Wagner, who became head of that studio. Not able to handle the insurmountable debt load, MGM filed for bankruptcy protection in late 2010, emerging in early 2011 with new management but a still uncertain future. It nevertheless announced ambitious plans for the production of two anticipated films for 2012—*The Hobbit*, a prequel to the very successful *Lord of the Rings* trilogy, and a new James Bond movie.[7]

In much the same way, other legendary studios of the twentieth century were moved like chess pieces from one corporate "home" to another, once they were sold by the moguls who founded them to conglomerates seeking to diversify their assets. This has led to great uncertainty in the business. The earliest acquisitions led to strange bedfellows, as companies purchased businesses that seemed to have no relationship to one another. This was part of a larger trend affecting not just the movie industry. In the 1980s and 1990s, large holding companies acquired portfolios of such disparate subsidiaries as beverage companies, cereal producers, pesticide manufacturers, and cleaning products makers. Thus, Coca-Cola owned Colum-

---

6. "MGM Files for Bankruptcy Protection," Dealbook, *The New York Times*, Nov. 3, 2010, found at http://dealbook.nytimes.com/2010/11/03/m-g-m-files-for-bankruptcy/, last accessed July 17, 2011.

7. Howell, John, "23rd James Bond movie due 2012 despite MGM bankruptcy," *Science Fiction World*, Nov. 10, 2010, found at http://sciencefictionworld.com/films/science-fiction-films/661-23rd-james-bond-movie-due-2012-despite-mgm-bankruptcy.html, last accessed July 17, 2011.

bia Pictures, the Canadian wine-and-spirits business Seagram's owned a controlling interest in MCA/Universal, and Transamerica, the insurance conglomerate, owned United Artists. The more recent trend for the movie industry is toward mega-media conglomerates. 20th Century Fox, for example, is part of Fox Filmed Entertainment, which in turn is owned by News Corporation. Warner Bros. is part of Time Warner. Paramount Pictures is owned by Viacom, Universal Studios by NBC Universal Media, and Columbia Pictures by Sony Corporation.

This consolidation in the industry has changed the way movies are made. Movie producers have grown more conservative in their choices of where they will invest their money. There is much less willingness on the part of studio executives to take risks and to bet on untried ideas. Financial decisions in particular are made by senior executives who might have experience overseeing a wide range of industries and yet who have no particular affinity for, or background in, film production. Additionally, movies are created by and produced by younger filmmakers for a younger audience than was formerly the case. These two developments have converged in the blockbuster movie, relying on special effects and oriented toward young men and teenagers. This in turn has led to a tendency to repeat prior successes rather than bet on a new idea. MGM announced plans to release the twenty-third James Bond movie in 2012, on the safe assumption that the public will pay money to see it. Sequels and prequels with bankable stars have become common. If *Toy Story* and *Toy Story 2* were popular, then *Toy Story 3* will be also. People liked the first *Pirates of the Caribbean* movie, and they also attended the second. Therefore, it is assumed that they will go see the third and probably a fourth. And so on.

The quality of movies has suffered—at least partly as a result of these two tendencies—as bets continue to be placed on the tried and the true, even as the original concept becomes trite and worn. California historian Kevin Starr has called this the "dumbing down" of motion pictures, although he attributes the blame precisely to the fact that "the nation's primary dream machine, Hollywood," no longer makes films for adult audiences, but rather has been putting forth movies "primarily for an adolescent and young-adult audience."[8] According to Starr, the poster child for this trend is the movie *Titanic* (1997), which was filled with special effects, had blockbuster stars, won eleven Academy Awards, including Best Picture, and made a phenomenal amount of money for its producer and distributors. But in Starr's opinion, echoing that of other film critics,[9] the film was "devoid of complexity, subtlety, grace, or compassion." It did not need any of these. As Starr notes, "from a business perspective—in a business targeted toward teenagers—*Titanic* could be considered a work of genius."[10]

Unfortunately, an industry that gears its successes to business trends will also lose out when those trends change. Or when an economy crashes. For example, since the 2008 global economic crisis, U.S. box office revenues have gone down even as ticket prices have gone up. Young people, the primary audience for the studios since the late 1990s, no longer have the disposable income to support the motion picture industry on their own. As one commentator has explained, "as bad as the economy is for adults, it is worse for teenagers. . . . The teenaged audience is becoming picky. That's a nightmare for

---

8. Starr, Kevin, *Coast of Dreams: California on the Edge, 1990-2003*, Alfred A. Knopf, New York, 2004, p. 42.

9. *See, e.g.,* Turan, Kenneth, "'Titanic' Sinks Again (Spectacularly)," *Los Angeles Times*, December 19, 1997, found at http://articles.latimes.com/1997/dec/19/entertainment/ca-39, last accessed December 27, 2011.

10. Starr, Kevin, *Coast of Dreams*, p. 44.

studios that are used to pushing lowest-common-denominator films."[11]

As the major studios retrenched into the safe realm of blockbusters and prequels, other filmmakers, whose work is aimed at more adult audiences, gained increased visibility. The accessibility of computer and digital technology, as well as open-source film editing software, have enabled small independent filmmakers to create quality, low-budget films. Although many of these fail to gain a significant enough following to be recognized, some do, particularly if their films are picked up by distributors after winning accolades at festivals, or more recently, after having been touted in social media. Established actors and actresses, having gained fame and wealth by appearing in blockbusters, seek to develop and demonstrate their acting range by performing in these smaller films, often on a low or no-fee basis, with a profit participation. At times they are the screenwriters or the producers. Newcomers to the industry have been able to establish themselves through developing and producing an independent film.

The independent movie industry has received a big boost from the proliferation of film festivals over the last thirty years. Some, such as Toronto or Sundance, are now meccas where newly debuted movies can be discovered, picked up for distribution by major studios, and achieve financial success, particularly when compared against their comparatively low production budgets. Sundance started as a local art film festival in Salt Lake City, Utah, in the late 1970s. Named in honor of festival chair and actor Robert Redford and the role that he played in *Butch Cas-*

---

11. Barnes, Brooks, "A Year of Disappointment at the Movie Box Office," The New York Times, December 25, 2011, found at http://www.nytimes.com/2011/12/26/business/media/a-year-of-disappointment-for-hollywood.html?bl, last accessed December 27, 2011.

sidy and the Sundance Kid (1969), the Sundance Festival was one of the first to cultivate newly discovered filmmakers in the United States. Each January, the festival, in the ski resort of Park City, Utah, draws Hollywood celebrities as well as corporate sponsors. A number of well-regarded and disparate independent films, such as *Sex, Lies and Videotape* (1989), *Reservoir Dogs* (1992), and *Little Miss Sunshine* (2006), premiered at Sundance.

Another film genre that has matured in the last few decades, owing greatly to the availability of low-cost filmmaking and film editing technology and the increasing number and influence of film festivals, is the documentary. For example, the acclaimed award-winning Errol Morris movie, *The Fog of War: Eleven Lessons from the Life of Robert S. McNamara* (2003), was first screened at Cannes. Michael Moore's *Fahrenheit 9/11* (2004), a controversial film questioning the U.S. government's decision to send troops into Iraq in 2003, was also screened at Cannes, receiving the festival's coveted Palme d'Or award. It achieved blockbuster status in its genre, grossing over $200 million, a record for a documentary.[12] Certainly many of the more successful documentaries—in terms of both critical acclaim and strong revenues—have also broached timely subjects. Witness *Fahrenheit 9/11*, a film about the Iraq war premiering less than a year after the invasion. Former Vice President Al Gore's *An Inconvenient Truth* (2006), discussing the science of climate change, was a successful Academy Award-winning movie.[13]

---

12. Epstein, Edward Jay, "Paranoia for Fun and Profit: How Disney and Michael Moore Cleaned Up on Fahrenheit 9/11," *Slate*, Tuesday, May 3, 2005, found at http://www.slate.com/articles/arts/the_hollywood_economist/2005/05/paranoia_for_fun_and_profit.html, last accessed December 27, 2011. Epstein notes that the film was an "event" that "took in more than $228 million in ticket sales worldwide," and made another $30 million in royalties on sales of 3 million DVDs.

13. Lovgren, Stefan, "Al Gore's 'Inconvenient Truth' Movie: Fact or Hype?" *National Geographic*, May 25, 2006, found at http://news.nationalgeographic.com/news/2006/05/060524-global-warming.html, last accessed December 27, 2011.

And more recently *Expelled: No Intelligence Allowed* (2008), with Ben Stein as narrator, was surprisingly successful because it reached an audience that was receptive to the topic: intelligent design versus Darwinian evolution, as well as because the topic provoked controversy. *Expelled* was also the subject of an important federal case interpreting the fair use exception to Copyright Law.[14] The willingness of courts to liberally expand the application of the fair use doctrine during the first decade of the twenty-first century has enabled film producers to make documentaries at far less cost than was the case when rights to even very short clips from movies or songs had to be purchased in order to sign on a distributor (so essential to the success of any film).[15]

The third economic and social megatrend that has profoundly affected the movie industry in the last few decades has been the globalization resulting from trade agreements and the growth of multinational businesses. This has intensified the corporate movie studios' tendency to aim for blockbuster hits at the expense of artistic quality. As consumers in other parts of the world have rapidly adopted American culture, whether in the form of clothes (such as blue jeans), food (McDonald's and other fast food), and music, they have eagerly flocked to see American movies. "During the 1980s, foreign ticket sales often equaled domestic box-office sales. Schwarzenegger and Stallone movies pulled in bigger crowds abroad than at home."[16] But these had to be blockbusters—action thrillers or science fiction movies—where dialogue was minimal and special effects and

---

14. Lennon v. Premise Media Corp., 556 F. Supp. 310 (S.D.N.Y. 2008).

15. *See* Donaldson, Michael C., "Fair Use: What a Difference a Decade Makes," Journal of the Copyright Society of the U.S.A., Vol. 57, No. 3, Spring 2010, p. 331.

16. Thompson & Bordwell, p. 683.

cool graphics ruled. They were predictable but they sold; in fact, they sold well.

The emphasis on profitability and the bottom line had another effect on the film industry. Studios learned that motion pictures did not have to be made in Hollywood. They could be filmed on location in other countries, whose governments often offered generous tax incentives to influence the decision, for much less than in Southern California. Sites in Vancouver and Toronto, in Canada, as well as locations in Poland and other Eastern European countries, have become popular less-expensive filming venues. Much as in the early twentieth century, when East Coast and Chicago-based filmmakers flocked to Southern California to benefit from its many advantages—reliably good weather and easy-going business climate, as well as trained staffs of actors, writers, and technicians[17]—the trend in the early days of the twenty-first century has been to disperse away from Los Angeles. Being in Hollywood is no longer considered to be necessary. In fact, the successful director Roman Polanski, a fugitive from California justice for more than thirty years,[18] has proved that good, well-received movies, including the Academy Award-winning *The Pianist* (2002), can be produced and distributed by American studios without the filmmaker ever setting foot in the United States.

From a legal perspective, perhaps the most important development in the last few decades has been the change in the requirements of Copyright Law coupled with ambivalent public attitudes with respect to the rights of copyright holders. From the perspective of the movie industry, by the end of the twentieth century, Copyright Law had never been stronger in acknowl-

---

17. Starr, Kevin, *California*, pp. 274-276.
18. *See* Reel 29, And Justice for All—*Polanski v. Superior Court*, 180 Cal. App. 4th 507 (2d Dist. 2009).

edging the rights of creators, especially when one considers that just 100 years before, the rights of filmmakers to any copyright protection at all was at best fragile, dependent on the willingness of courts to assume that Congress would have wanted movies to be as protected as photographs. By the end of the twentieth century, the terms of copyrights acquired as early as the 1920s had been extended to almost the middle of the twenty-first century by congressional action.[19] However, at the same time, never had those holding copyrights been so threatened by willful infringers. For the new technologies that have proved to be so beneficial to the filmmaking process have also made copyright infringement easy and prevalent.

---

19. The Sonny Bono Copyright Term Extension Act, Public Law 105-298, October 27, 1998, 112 Stat. 2827, extended the terms of all existing copyrights by twenty years, and changed the basic term for new works to the life of the author plus seventy years. *See* Intermission 10, Derivative Works and Copyright Duration.

The Transformers

Sony Corporation of America v. Universal City Studios, Inc., 464 U.S. 417 (1984)

> **Jeffrey Goines: There was this guy, and he was always requesting shows that had already played. Yes. No. You have to tell her before. He couldn't quite grasp the idea that the charge nurse couldn't make it be yesterday. She couldn't turn back time."**
>
> Brad Pitt, as Jeffrey Goines,
> from *Twelve Monkeys* (1995)

After the disruptions to their business model caused by the *Paramount* decision,[1] which broke up the vertically integrated production, distribution, and exhibition system controlled by the major film studios, the Hollywood studios were settling into the new business model where they produced or acquired films from independent producers or funded a package deal assembled by an independent producer or agent. They still controlled major sources of revenue through distribution channels and through secondary markets, such as cable television channels—like Home Box Office (HBO) and Showtime—to which they licensed movies that had completed their runs in theaters.[2] Although the cable stations also produced some of their own content, they nevertheless represented a new and profitable source of revenue to the studios.

---

1. United States v. Paramount Pictures, 334 U.S. 131 (1948).
2. Thompson & Bordwell, p. 680.

This comfortable system was disrupted in the late 1970s by the advent of a new technology, the video recorder. In 1975, Japan's Sony Corporation began marketing its Betamax home videocassette recorder (VCR) and Matsushita introduced its Video Home System (VHS) soon after. Before this invention, viewers could only see movies at the time they were shown on television or at the movie theater when they were released. You could not have a sleepover party, as my teenage daughter did once, that consisted of a Michael J. Fox marathon. What a luxury it was when Sony first introduced video technology into the American home. Now people could watch movies when they wanted to see them and were no longer dependent on movie theaters and television broadcast schedules. Sales of the two video recording devices increased throughout the 1980s as prices for the equipment decreased, so that by 1988 most U.S. households had a VCR.[3]

The Sony Betamax recorder had several features: a separate tuner on the system enabled it to record a broadcast from one station while the television set was tuned to a different channel, thus permitting the viewer to watch two simultaneous feature broadcasts—one "live" and the other, which was recorded at the same time—for later viewing. Tapes could be reused and the programs could be erased after viewing. The recorder had a timer, allowing the equipment to be activated and a program recorded even when the viewer was not at home. The Betamax also had a "pause" and "fast forward" feature, enabling the viewer to skip commercial advertisements. These were all new technological innovations in the 1980s.

Naturally, Hollywood studios, conservative by nature, were wary of this new technology precisely because of these features;

---

3. Thompson & Bordwell, p. 680.

they allowed people to tape movies from television (including from the cable stations to which the studios were frequently licensing films). As Hollywood saw it, the freedom to watch films taped from television on one's own schedule and to build a film library at a cost no greater than the price of a blank tape, or to rent or buy a videotape from one of the many video rental services that were springing up across the country, meant that viewers would have less desire to go out to watch a new movie in theaters.

Rather than wait to see whether these concerns would bear out, in 1976, Universal Studios and the Walt Disney Company, among others in the movie industry, sued Sony and its distributors to stop the sale of the VCR machines on the grounds that the taping infringed the studios' copyrights in their films. They argued that, because Sony was manufacturing and selling the Betamax, a device that could potentially be used for copyright infringement, the company was liable for any infringement committed by its purchasers.

The district court ruled in favor of Sony in 1977, finding that the average number of people who had a Betamax machine used it to record a program so that they could watch it at a time other than when it was being televised.[4] This practice is known as "time shifting." The court concluded that noncommercial recording of movies for home use was considered to be a "fair use" under U.S. Copyright Law and therefore did not infringe. It was also determined, however, that a substantial number of persons had accumulated libraries of tapes with movies recorded from television. But the court emphasized that the material that was broadcast over television was free to the public, the use itself was noncommercial, and the activity was a private

---

4. Universal Studios v. Sony Corporation, 428 F. Supp. 407 (C. D. Cal. 1977).

use, entirely within the home. Moreover, the court found that this device served a public interest by increasing access to television programming, due to the ability to time shift. Even when an entire copyrighted work was recorded, the court regarded it nevertheless to be a "fair use" because it found "no accompanying reduction in the market" for the studios' original work.

The court also determined that even if this home use was an infringement, Sony was not liable for it because the company had no direct involvement with the Betamax purchasers who recorded copyrighted works. Sony's advertising was silent on the potential for copyright infringement. However, its instruction pamphlet contained a warning: "Television programs, films, videotapes, and other materials may be copyrighted. Unauthorized recording of such material may be contrary to the provisions of the United States Copyright Laws." The district court thus found that Sony merely sold a "product capable of a variety of uses, some of them allegedly infringing." The studios did not agree with this reasoning, of course, and appealed.

The lower court's decision was reversed by the appellate court, which held that Sony could be liable for "contributory infringement," because its device's main purpose was for copying.[5] This was based on the contention of the studios that some individuals had used Sony's Betamax videotape recorder to record some of the studios' copyrighted works that had been shown on television and this use by these individuals infringed the studios' copyrights. Because Sony had marketed the Betamax machines for just this purpose, Sony was liable for the copyright infringement committed by its customers.

---

5. Universal Studios v. Sony Corporation, 659 F. 2d 963 (9th Cir. 1981). The court relied on the U.S. Supreme Court decision in *Kalem Company v. Harper Brothers*, 222 U.S. 55 (1911), which had held that a person who contributes to infringement by others can be held liable for "contributory infringement." *See* discussion at Reel 3, The Great Race—The "Ben Hur" Case.

To the Ninth Circuit, home use of the Betamax was not a "fair use" because it was not "productive." For the appellate court, it seemed clear that the cumulative effect of mass reproduction of films made possible by the Betamax would inevitably diminish the potential market for the studios' works. The Betamax, in the court's opinion, could not be compared to the "staple articles of commerce," such as photocopying machines, because unlike a photocopier, the Betamax did not render any substantial legitimate benefit. The judges believed that the "primary purpose" of the Betamax was reproducing television programming and virtually all such programming was copyrighted, even if some copyright owners might not object to this type of copying of their works.

The case arrived in the Supreme Court, where in a 5-4 ruling, in 1984, the Court reversed the Ninth Circuit, finding that Sony, as a manufacturer of a home recording machine, could not be held liable for contributory copyright infringement on account of potential illegal uses by its purchasers, because the device was sold for legitimate purposes and had substantial noninfringing uses.

Justice Stevens, in rendering the majority's decision, looked first to the purpose of the Copyright Act: to encourage and reward creative work but to "ultimately serve the cause of promoting broad public availability of literature, music and the other arts." Even "when technological change has rendered its literal terms ambiguous," Justice Stevens believed, the Copyright Act "must be construed in light of this basic purpose."

The studios, in their briefs to the Court, went back to that earlier movie copyright case, the *Kalem* decision,[6] as their prin-

---

6. Kalem Company v. Harper Brothers, 222 U.S. 55 (1911). *See* discussion at Reel 3, The Great Race— The "Ben Hur" Case.

cipal support. In *Kalem*, they noted, the Court had held that a producer of an unauthorized film adaptation of a copyrighted book, *Ben Hur*, was liable for his sale of the movie to jobbers, who in turn arranged for the commercial exhibition of the film, because he contributed to the infringement. They argued that, under *Kalem*, supplying the "means" to accomplish an infringing activity and encouraging that activity through advertisements was sufficient to establish liability for copyright infringement. Justice Stevens did not see how *Kalem* supported this premise. He noted that the producer in *Kalem* did not merely provide the "means" to accomplish the copyright infringement; the producer supplied the infringing work himself. Sony did not do this. Betamax equipment had a broad range of potential uses.

Justice Stevens noted that in other situations in which vicarious liability had been imposed, the person who contributed to the infringement "was in a position to control the use of the copyrighted works by others and had authorized the use without permission from the copyright owner." In this case, the only contact between Sony and Betamax purchasers was at the moment of sale. And there was no evidence that any Betamax purchaser was influenced or encouraged by any Sony advertising materials. There was no precedent in copyright law, Justice Stevens noted, for holding a manufacturer liable for contributory infringement because it had "constructive knowledge" that its customers might use the equipment to make unauthorized copies of copyrighted material.

The Court ruled that if the Betamax equipment was capable of substantial noninfringing uses, then its manufacturer would not be liable simply because it could also be used for infringing uses. Like the district court, Justice Stevens saw that the ability for private, noncommercial time-shifting in the home was one significant potential noninfringing use that satisfied this standard. He noted that other copyright holders—whose programs appeared on television and were available for copying with the Betamax—welcomed the practice of time-shifting. For example, Fred Rogers, who had a popular children's program, "Mister Rogers' Neighborhood," on Public Television stations, believed that time-shifting increased the number of viewers for his show. Because these copyright owners benefited from the practice, the studios could not be permitted to frustrate others' interests, the Court ruled. In an action for contributory infringement, the copyright holder cannot prevail unless the relief sought affects only his copyrighted work.

Justice Stevens also agreed that time-shifting, even if an entire work was copied, was a fair use. If time-shifting merely enables a viewer to watch a show or film that he or she had been invited to watch in its entirety by the broadcaster, then the fact that the entire work is reproduced to be watched at a different time would not change a finding of fair use. And finally, Justice Stevens did not believe that the studios had demonstrated convincingly that time-shifting would have a negative effect, agreeing with the district court that "any harm from time-shifting was speculative and, at best, minimal."

The decision was split 5-4. Justice Blackmun, writing for the minority, did not agree with the Court's opinion that home copying of a copyrighted motion picture was a "fair use." According to Justice Blackmun, fair use is "a form of subsidy." It creates an exception to the Copyright Act to allow another, such as a scholar, a critic, or a news reporter, "to make limited use of the author's work for the public good." Justice Blackmun did not consider the making of a videotape recording for home viewing as a productive use that justifies an exception to the studios' copyright protections. He also noted that while some used the machines solely for time-shifting, other were not erasing the tapes they recorded but instead were building a video library, at the studios' expense. As he saw it, unlike a scholar or a critic, the customary beneficiaries of the fair use exception—home viewers—added "nothing of their own." He did admit "that there are situations where permitting even an unproductive use would have no effect on the author's incentive to create, that is, where the use would not affect the value of, or the market for, the author's work." He used the example of a person making a photocopy of a magazine or newspaper article to send to a friend. However, he believed that the impacts on the motion picture industry from this new technology were as yet unknown and he believed it to be unreasonable to require the studios to prove that they had suffered harm from the Betamax device, for, he noted, this "may be impossible in an area where the effect of a new technology is speculative."

Luckily for the studios, Justice Blackmun's view did not hold the day, for in the end they benefited from the new video technologies as much as, if not more than, others. It was true that the decision was a boon to the home video market because it created a safe haven for the new technology, and the others that would soon follow—the Digital Video Disc or Digital Versatile Disc (DVD) and digital video recorder (DVR) devices. But it also significantly benefited the entertainment industry. Although some people elected to stay home to watch movies that they had recorded on their VCRs, as the quality of television sets improved in the 1980s and 1990s, viewers demanded a better quality movie than they could make from a televised production, and the sale of prerecorded movies proved to be extremely profitable for the industry. Just as the studios' fears that television would harm the industry had proved unwarranted—as licenses of films to network television became a fruitful source of revenue, and the advent of premium cable channels opened another window of opportunity in the 1970s and 1980s—"so movies on tape became another way for studios to earn still more money."[7] In the end, the studios had had little reason to panic and, instead of speculating about all the potential harm they could suffer, it would have been better for them if they had jumped on the bandwagon sooner. In the 1990s, new video rental outlets (including national chains such as Blockbuster) provided a lucrative outlet for studios, allowing them to keep movies in the public eye for a "second run" after they had finished their theater runs. And older films that were decaying in studio libraries were given a new life, on tape.

"The Majors also discovered that many viewers would buy video copies," and this provided yet another unforeseen source of revenue to the studios, especially after they lowered the price of the tapes. "By 1987, over half of major film companies' domestic revenues were flowing from videocassette rentals and sales. Soon video income was twice that yielded by theatrical releases."[8] Studios would have seen none of these new sources of revenue had they been successful in the *Sony* Betamax litigation in suppressing this new technology. The introduction of the new DVD technology in the mid-1990s proved to be even more lucrative. This technology was more difficult to copy—and therefore pirate—than videocassettes. And films could be released in regional formats, thus preventing DVDs from being sold in countries where a first-run film had not yet opened in the theaters.[9]

Sony did not fare as well, despite having won the case. Even though movie connoisseurs argued that Betamax was a better format, its competitor technology, the VHS, was simpler and

---

7. Thompson & Bordwell, p. 680.
8. Thompson & Bordwell, p. 680.
9. Thompson & Bordwell, p. 680.

less expensive to manufacture, which meant a lower price for consumers. Furthermore, the Betamax initially could record tapes that lasted only sixty minutes. This was not long enough to record most movies. The standard recording length for VHS tapes was three hours. Sony eventually adapted and offered tapes with longer recording time but by then it was too late. Particularly at a time when most consumers rented movies, stores preferred to carry and studios preferred to release films in only one format and the greater choice of films in the VHS counters drove the ultimate success of the VHS format.[10] By the late 1990s, videocassette sales and rentals had diminished substantially as studios and consumers changed over to DVDs. As manufacturers lowered prices for the players and movies on disc could be purchased cheaply, often for between $15 and $30 each, and sometimes less, VHS rapidly became passé.

---

10. *See* http://www.mediacollege.com/video/format/compare/betamax-vhs.html.

Funny Money
Creative Accounting in Hollywood

Buchwald v. Paramount Pictures Corporation,
Case No. C706083 (Cal. Sup. Ct. Tentative Decision
[First Phase], January 31, 1990; Tentative Decision
[Second Phase], December 21, 1990; Statement
of Decision [Third Phase], March 16, 1992[1]

**If we all do our jobs, we will each be
rewarded according to our just desserts.**
The Spanish Prisoner (1997)

In 1982, Art Buchwald, a humorist, political satirist, and writer prepared a screen treatment for a movie in which he proposed that Eddie Murphy would play the lead role. With his friend Alain Bernheim, who intended to produce the film, he pitched the concept to Paramount, where at the time Eddie Murphy was under contract. Paramount was interested in the idea and optioned the treatment in 1983; both Buchwald and Bernheim signed the standard studio contract at that time. Under these agreements, if the studio decided to use the treatment to make a film, both men would receive a specified percentage of the net profits from the film.

Paramount commissioned a number of scripts based on Buchwald's treatment from several screenwriters but nothing

---

1. Published as Appendices A, B, C, in O'Donnell, Pierce and McDougal, Dennis, *Fatal Subtraction: The Inside Story of Buchwald v. Paramount, or How Hollywood Really Does Business*, Doubleday, 1992 (paperback edition, Dove Books, 1996).

seemed to gel. Paramount finally decided to abandon the project in March 1985. In May 1986, Warner Bros. optioned Buchwald's treatment. However, in the summer of 1987, Paramount began to develop a movie that was rumored to be based on a story by Eddie Murphy. The movie was to be directed by John Landis, the director that Buchwald and Bernheim had suggested when they pitched the film. The story idea seemed similar to Buchwald's treatment as well as to the rejected studio script that had been based on it. In January 1988, Warner Bros. cancelled its plans to produce a film based on Buchwald's concept, citing the comparable Paramount project. Later that year, Paramount released *Coming to America* starring Eddie Murphy and affording sole screenwriting credit to Murphy.

There were similarities between Buchwald's treatment and the film, although the two were not identical. Both were modern-day comedies in which the main character—the role envisioned by Buchwald for Eddie Murphy in his treatment and played by Eddie Murphy in the film—is an extremely wealthy and well-educated member of royalty from a fictional African kingdom. In both stories, he arrives in a large American city on the East Coast. Both stories contain "fish out of water" and "love triumphs over all" themes. In both stories, events in the hero's home country in Africa leave the character alone, without the royal cushion, and he is required to experience the realities of an American inner city. In both cases, he comes out in the end a better man because of these experiences. In each story, the hero falls in love with a young American woman, marries her, and returns home with his new queen to his African kingdom. There are other smaller similarities also. In both works, for example, the hero has to work for a time in a fast-food restaurant and in each he manages to foil a robbery attempt with a mop.

Buchwald was neither paid nor was he given a screenwriter

credit in the movie. Both he and Bernheim sued Paramount for breach of contract in Los Angeles Superior Court. He did not sue for copyright infringement, even though he had registered a copyright for his 2-1/2 page movie treatment. To claim infringement, he would have had to prove that this treatment and the screenplay for *Coming to America* were "substantially similar," which would have been difficult, as there were, despite the similarities, many differences between the two.[2] Nor did he claim plagiarism or misappropriation of his idea. To make this claim, he would have had to sue the person claiming to be the screenwriter—that is, Eddie Murphy—and he did not want to do that, mainly because he blamed Paramount and not Murphy for his ill treatment.[3]

This was a basic breach of contract case. Both agreements with Paramount signed by Buchwald and Bernheim provided that Paramount would compensate them if a movie "based upon" Buchwald's treatment was made. For the trial court then, the important question was whether *Coming to America* was "based upon" Buchwald's treatment. Unfortunately, there was no definition of that expression in the contracts.

Buchwald maintained that, once a studio begins "development" of an idea on which it has an option, the various drafts and scripts that are created during that process are all "based upon" the original concept, even if the final screenplay bears little resemblance to the original treatment. Further, he asserted, if the screenplay is abandoned, but a later work is produced that has material points of similarity, the author of the original treatment can fairly claim that the later screenplay is "based upon" the original idea.

---

2. Buchwald's attorney wrote, "Art wrote a political satire. Paramount made a romantic comedy." O'Donnell, *Fatal Subtraction*, pp. 18-19.

3. O'Donnell & McDougal, p. 45.

Paramount disagreed but in the first phase of the trial the judge, Judge Schneider, accepted Buchwald's theory. Judge Schneider was very specific that this case was not about whether Eddie Murphy made substantial contributions to the movie's screenplay. The court was convinced that he had. Further, Judge Schneider made clear that no one had alleged nor did he believe that Murphy had stolen any part of Buchwald's treatment. He believed that the only issue in this case was whether any part of Buchwald's original idea had been used and if so, then Paramount had breached its contract with Buchwald by basing a later screenplay on Buchwald's original treatment without compensating Buchwald as required by the agreement.

The problem for Paramount was that the studio had deliberately kept the term "based upon" vague in the standard contract, without defining any parameters. This required a trial court judge in hindsight to provide that interpretation. And since the "based upon" language was in a standard contract prepared by the studio's attorneys, where there was a dispute as to its meaning, the court under California law was required to interpret the language against the party who wrote it. The judge noted that the studio could have structured its compensation scheme differently depending on whether or not the project was abandoned and then reprised in a different form, or with perhaps a descending percentage depending on the length of time between the submission of the idea and the release of the final film.

In the second phase of the trial, Buchwald and Bernheim challenged the compensation provided for in their contracts, which entitled them as writer and as producer of any film based on Buchwald's work to share in the *net* profits of the production. When the issue came up at trial, Paramount representatives produced evidence showing that despite the fact that *Coming to America* had grossed $288 million at the box office, there were no "net" profits at all. Once the production, distribution, and marketing costs were deducted from the gross, nothing was left. Hence, Buchwald and Bernheim were owed nothing. At trial, Buchwald and Bernheim asked the court to throw out the net profits calculation that the contract required.

Judge Schneider thought it odd that these men should have been surprised by the calculation of net profits generated by the movie. He noted that, although there may be creative people who do not understand the difference between gross and net profits, this should not have been the case for either Buchwald or Bernheim. However, he found it likely that they did know but really had no choice. As Judge Schneider said, "If a producer such as Bernheim (or a writer like Buchwald) wished to work in Hollywood, he would have to accept the standard studio terms." And that meant that they had to accept a contract that provided, with very few exceptions, that creative persons were to participate in the film's "net profits" only. These terms are rarely negotiated, and their calculation is set out in such a way that even a very successful Hollywood movie will rarely generate any net profits.[4] As Judge Schneider noted, the formula for calculating net profits in the contract allowed items to be charged to gross receipts for which "no justification, under any sort of sensible accounting system, could be found." These included charges for interest expense (even when no interest was paid or incurred), overhead charges on overhead, and percentages applied to the gross receipts to reflect certain types of costs that bore no relation to those actual costs. The effect was, in short, to double

---

4. In *Fatal Subtraction*, the authors quote from Eddie Murphy's deposition in the case, where he used the term "monkey points" to refer to a share of "net profits." When asked what he meant by this, he replied that these were "stupid points, in that you are stupid to take them because there won't be any. You sit there with your points going Eeeh, eeh, eeh, eeh, eeh. . ." p. 200 (Dove edition).

count and overcount the costs that the studio actually incurred. In the movie industry, this method of accounting, which would be unorthodox at best for any other business, is derisively called "Hollywood accounting."

Bernheim and Buchwald asked the court to rule that this formula for accounting net profits was "unconscionable" and therefore invalid. In order for a contract to be considered unconscionable, it cannot merely be one-sided, or a stupid deal for the disadvantaged party. The terms have to be "unduly oppressive," so unfair as to deprive the other side of any bargaining power, essentially offered on a take-it-or-leave-it basis. In *Buchwald*, the court found the terms in the standard studio contract to be this oppressive and the relative bargaining power of the parties to be so unequal that the result was "no real negotiation" and "an absence of meaningful choice."[5] Consequently, these terms were found to be unenforceable.

Although Judge Schneider struck down the unconscionable net profits calculation provisions of the contracts, he did not award the two men "benefit of the bargain" damages because, he reasoned, Paramount would never have agreed to the percentage of net profits provided for in the agreement (approximately 19 percent) if the term were to have been defined according to generally accepted accounting principles. Instead, he awarded both men the fair market value of the services they rendered—$150,000 to Bernheim and $150,000 to Buchwald.[6]

Rather than appeal the trial court's judgment and risk an adverse appellate court judgment—in particular with respect to the "unconscionability" ruling—and the wave of lawsuits from

5. O'Donnell & McDougal, Appendix B, pp. 568-69 (Dove edition).
6. According to Buchwald's attorney, O'Donnell in *Fatal Subtraction*, the two men and their attorneys incurred nearly $3 million in expenses. He admitted that he wrote the book in an effort to recoup some of those costs.

disgruntled screenwriters and producers that would likely follow, the studio instead entered into a confidential settlement agreement with Buchwald and Bernheim.

This case provides a vision into the cynical world of modern Hollywood where even the most talented people are treated as pawns on a chessboard, and where people are valued on the basis of what they can bring to the table today and how hard they, or their agents, can negotiate. It is an insight into a world where there is no loyalty: writers, directors, producers are treated alike and act accordingly, moving from studio to studio seeking the best deal, or, for many, any deal, depending on where they stand in the Hollywood pecking order. It is a world where agents, managers, and attorneys are involved at each stage of the relationship and friendship seems to count for little. And yet so many want to be part of it; if they have an idea or a treatment, they only want a chance to submit it, because it could just be the next blockbuster.

All About Eve
The Fickle Director
and the Demanding Star

Welch v. Metro-Goldwyn-Mayer Film Co.,
207 Cal. App. 3d 164 (2d Dist. 1988)

> **You think that because I'm a movie star
> I don't have feelings. Well you're wrong.
> I'm an actress. I've got all of them!**
>
> (Goldie Hawn as Elise in *First Wives Club* (1996)

fter the *De Havilland* case and the *Paramount* decision, actors had a growing amount of power and influence over the types of roles they would play and the way they were treated on the set. By the 1980s, many had followed the lead of innovators such as Bette Davis and later Warren Beatty and had established their own production companies in order to take control of their careers. The terms of their engagement for a film performance were covered in detailed contracts with the studios and the actors' production companies.

One thing that did not change since the early days of the cinema was the fickleness of movie producers and directors and their ability since before the *Goudal* case was decided[1] to terminate contracts of stars they found to be too demanding. And once they had done so, they did not hesitate to respond to

---

1. *See* Reel 6, A Star is Born, Goudal v. DeMille Pictures Corp., 118 Cal. App. 407 (2d Dist. 1931).

any breach of contract claim made by the star by blaming her and branding her as "difficult." Hollywood is also replete with tales—both in screenplays and real life—of aging stars who are replaced by ambitious younger ones. *All About Eve* (1950) tells the story of a mature Broadway star, played by the redoubtable Bette Davis (who also in real life was branded as one of those difficult ones), who is befriended, and ultimately finds herself upstaged by, a younger actress, played in the film by Anne Baxter.

And for a true chronicle, there is the story of Raquel Welch, an aging star trying to prove her worth in serious films, and Debra Winger, a new face in the movie business, eager to claim bigger and better dramatic parts. In this case, unlike the film *All About Eve*, neither star appeared to bear animosity toward the other until decisions were made that brought them into competition with each other through no actions of their own, but rather because of manipulation and hardball tactics of the studio.

By 1980, Raquel Welch had appeared in approximately thirty films. In her first motion pictures, such as *One Million Years BC* (1966), where she appeared as a scantily clad buxom prehistoric woman, she was generally typecast as a sex symbol. This was the case even in films where she received good reviews, such as *The Wild Party* (1975) and *Kansas City Bomber* (1972). She won a Golden Globe for her performance in *The Three Musketeers: The Queen's Diamonds* (1973), playing a sexy lady-in-waiting to the French queen. At forty years old, she was seeking to break out as a serious actress, but had a reputation as a strong-willed professional who sometimes clashed with directors.

Debra Winger was a talented young actress who, in 1980, had just completed her first break-through performance in the role of Sissy, John Travolta's wife, in *Urban Cowboy* (1980). She would later move into memorable roles in films such as *An Officer and a Gentleman* (1982), opposite Richard Gere, and *Terms of Endearment* (1983), a Best Picture winner. In the early 1980s, she was a sought-after actress. She also gained a reputation for being demanding, although this would not have been as evident in 1980 when she was first being introduced to a broader movie-going public.

In early 1980, successful Academy Award winners Michael Phillips and David Ward,[2] developed a film package based on John Steinbeck's two novellas about life in California's Monterey Bay, *Cannery Row* and *Sweet Thursday*. Ward had written the screenplay and planned to direct the film; Phillips was to be the movie's producer. They selected Nick Nolte to portray the leading male character and were seeking a strong actress to play the lead female role, that of Suzy, the prostitute. Various well-known actresses were considered for the part, including both Raquel Welch and Debra Winger.

Welch was eager for the opportunity and made several important concessions to get it. She even agreed to audition for the part, something that was not usually required of an established actress. She was cast in the role and in October 1980, her production company, Raquel Welch Productions, signed a contract with Metro-Goldwyn-Mayer (MGM)—which had accepted the Ward-Phillips project and agreed to finance it—to provide Welch's services for the movie. Under the standard "play-or-pay" clause in her contract, the studio had the right to terminate her from the film at any time but her fee was a guaranteed $250,000 (with payments to be divided into weekly increments during filming), which the studio was obliged to pay in full unless she failed to fulfill her obligations under the agreement. Welch

---

2. For *The Sting* (1973).

agreed to be available for rehearsals and wardrobe fittings for the two-week period before shooting began.

But Welch for her part had negotiated several concessions from the studio. The studio was required to provide her with a fully equipped "star-type" trailer on the set for makeup purposes. She also was to have her choice of hairdresser and makeup artist, on first call to her, as well as a wardrobe assistant. And she requested additional consideration in morning call times. In general, the other actors had a morning call time at 7:00 or 7:30 a.m., and set calls at 8:00 or 8:30 a.m., whereas Welch had requested and was allowed two hours for makeup and hair, but she had a preparation routine that included an additional hour for yoga and exercise. Accordingly, she had a makeup call time at 6:30 or 7:00 a.m., with a set time three hours later.

Welch was initially provided a trailer that was too small, leaving insufficient room for makeup in front of a mirror. She was then provided a larger trailer with a makeup mirror and chair but this still did not meet her needs because it was too narrow and became overcrowded when her assistants were preparing her for her set calls. Her makeup artist could not move around without climbing over either Welch or the television set. The TV was eventually removed at Welch's request. She also asked for and received a small empty trailer for her daily yoga exercises.

Principal photography began on December 1, 1980, and Welch was first called for filming on Thursday, December 4, when the movie was already behind schedule and $84,000 over budget. Those first days, even though Welch arrived on time at 7:00 a.m. for her makeup call, she generally was not used until after lunch and sometimes late in the afternoon. The crowded conditions in her trailer remained a problem for her. Eventually, she requested and received permission to make up at her home until the trailer situation could be sorted out. The film's production manager delivered an MGM makeup mirror to her house for her use. Neither the producer, Phillips, nor the director, Ward, raised any objections to this new arrangement (although in testimony later in the trial, the production manager claimed that he had delivered the makeup mirror to her home not to allow her to do her makeup there but only to allow her to "get a head start on her makeup").

However, Phillips and Ward were not happy about Welch's making up at home and claimed to have agreed to it only to avoid a confrontation with her. They were also unhappy about her later set calls, because these required the director to begin filming each morning on scenes that did not require her presence, and this usually meant that the filming of her scenes would have to take place later in the day, which in turn cut down on the number of takes he could make of her scenes. The producer, Phillips, thought that three hours for makeup was extravagant and he believed that her late availability for shooting would cause problems when filming of her major scenes began. However, no one told Welch that she couldn't make up at home and the daily call sheets continued to allow her three hours for makeup. She was always on the set in time for her first call even though the director did not use her at the time. And Phillips even called Welch at home to compliment her on how good she looked in the dailies.

In the meantime, the production crew was experiencing significant cost overruns. In particular, several scenes in which Welch was not involved went greatly over budget. On Thursday, December 18, MGM studio heads met with Phillips to express their dissatisfaction with the dailies that he had provided (none of which involved Welch) and also with the fact that the film was over budget so early in shooting. They raised concerns about the experience level of first-time director Ward and wondered if this was causing the cost overruns. Phillips deflected criticism of Ward by blaming Welch, claiming that she was causing the production delays, which in turn were causing the costs to increase. He noted her unusual three-hour makeup period and the fact that she was making up at home (while failing to note that this had been a temporary arrangement for the prior three days while they located an adequate makeup trailer for Welch).

The studio heads became alarmed by Phillips's assertions, worrying that both Phillips and Ward were intimidated by Welch. It was against studio policy to allow an actress to make up at home both because it was an advantage for the production to have her available for rehearsal during the makeup period and because of the increased liability risks incurred when studio staff had to travel to her home to work. Phillips later claimed that at the time of his meeting with the studio executives, they told him to let Welch know that MGM intended to send her a letter notifying her that she was in breach of her contract unless she agreed to come to the studio the next morning for makeup. The meeting with studio heads had occurred on a Thursday. Phillips later claimed that he was also advised that this matter would not wait until the following Monday, but that Welch had to be notified that same day. The executives later testified to the contrary—that there had been no discussion at that time of sending any such "breach letter' to Welch and that Phillips had requested the meeting in the first place.

On that Thursday evening, after his meeting at MGM, Phillips claimed he called Welch and told her that studio executives believed that she was responsible for the production delays and that they would be sending her a notice that she was in breach of her contract. He informed her that the letter was being sent out that evening. He also claimed that he told her that she had to be at the studio the next morning for makeup. Welch later asserted that she had not received the message and was surprised the next day (Friday, December 19) when her makeup artist and hairdresser did not arrive at her home. Her husband drove her to the studio and she arrived one hour earlier than her set call and without any delay. She performed as requested throughout the day.

In the meantime, Phillips reported to MGM management that Welch had disobeyed his instruction to make up at the studio that morning. He also called Welch's agent, Michael Levy, to tell him that the studio was sending his client a notice of breach. This was the studio's first contact with Levy, even though the usual first step in resolving a serious problem with a movie star would be to call her agent. Phillips told Levy that the studio was pressuring him even though Welch had caused no delays. At the request of studio management, MGM's general counsel sent a letter to Welch that Friday morning, stating that Welch was in substantial breach of her obligations under her agreement with MGM, which also contained a threat to terminate its agreement with her.

Welch learned that the letter had gone out that day but continued working through that Friday afternoon. Her agent, Levy, called MGM's President, David Begelman, and was told not to tell him how to run his business. Levy agreed that Welch would arrive at the studio at 6:30 a.m. on Monday morning for two hours of makeup. He thought that the problem had been resolved. At the end of the day's filming, Welch was shown a long-unused studio makeup room that she accepted.

Phillips and Welch did not talk on Friday. Over the weekend, he left an urgent message on her answering machine. She asked her agent to return the call. Phillips and Levy had a series of conversations that weekend, during which Phillips asked to meet with Welch. She promised through her agent that she would meet with him at 9:00 a.m. on Monday morning. Phillips allegedly told others that he wanted Welch to be on edge because they would be shooting a tense scene on Monday.

On Sunday morning, studio executives informed MGM's general counsel that neither Welch nor her agent had unequivocally committed to follow the studio's orders. Phillips called the film's director, Ward, and told him that the studio might replace Welch because she had failed to meet with Phillips that weekend. Ward was unhappy, as he had never suggested that Welch should be terminated. But, in fact, by Sunday afternoon, MGM President Begelman had decided to terminate Welch because she had disobeyed his order to make up at the studio on Friday morning and had refused to talk with Phillips over the weekend. Welch's lawyer called Welch to give her the bad news. She was devastated. By this time, about 1/6 of her scenes had been shot.

On Monday, December 22, Welch received the letter from MGM informing her that the employment agreement was terminated due to her failure to comply with her contract obligations. She responded with a letter demanding payment from MGM of $194,444, which was the balance of the guaranteed fee that was owed pursuant to the agreement. MGM refused to pay and Welch sued.

Now, you may ask, why would a studio so precipitously terminate the contract of an actress in a film that was already running behind schedule and that was experiencing cost overruns, especially where it did not really appear that she was the cause of the film's troubles? And even if she had caused delays, why would the studio terminate her after she had agreed, through her agent, to give up the special treatment—late call time, three hours for makeup—that allegedly was causing the delays. It did not seem to make sense; it appeared almost as if the studio was inventing problems just to fire her from the film. But why would the studio executives want to do that? This is where the plot thickens.

Welch was replaced by Debra Winger in the movie. Winger received $150,000 to play the role. It cost almost $200,000 to replace Welch with Winger and to reshoot the scenes in which Welch had appeared. How had the studio managed to bring Winger in so quickly after terminating Welch?

To understand this, we need to go back to that same fateful weekend when Phillips, Levy, and Welch's attorney were negotiating the makeup situation and the supposed "breach letter." During that same time period, as the evidence in the trial revealed, Phillips and MGM executives were also engaged in a series of secret meetings with representatives of Debra Winger. As early as the Thursday prior to Welch's termination, David Chasman, a studio executive, had inquired of Winger's personal manager whether Winger could be available to start a film on short notice and was informed that she was available.

During that weekend, when MGM President Begelman made the decision to terminate Welch, Chasman called Winger's manager and told her that Welch had left the cast of *Cannery Row* and that the studio wanted Winger to return to Los Angeles (she was on vacation for the holidays) as soon as possible. Winger accepted the offer. On either Saturday or Sunday, Winger's manager engaged her attorney to negotiate a deal with MGM for Winger to appear in the movie. The deal was negotiated that weekend and was signed that Monday. On that Sunday night, Winger called her agent to let him know that she was replacing Welch on the film. At the trial, all the MGM executives denied that there had been any discussions with Winger before they terminated Welch that Monday, but the evidence contradicted those denials.

Welch received numerous inquiries from the press once the news of her termination became public. Many people assumed that she had failed to show up for work, which was generally the reason why actresses are removed from a film. Industry newspapers reported that she had been fired. An article recounting the incident appeared in the April 2, 1981, issue of *Rolling Stone*, a magazine with a weekly circulation at the time of over 700,000, with a wide readership in the motion picture industry. According to the article, the film's director, Ward, stated that Welch had been a "casting mistake" who was not necessarily a bad actress but who was not delivering a performance that he could live with. MGM President Begelman was quoted as saying that the studio "had a general feeling she had not lived up to her contract. We had no alternative. It is up to executives to tell people in this business we will not stand for that. The producer gave her appropriate directions and she failed to obey." These were words that he later most certainly came to regret.

By the time Welch's case came to trial, she had not made another movie and to date has not had a major role in any motion picture (although she has had small parts in films such as *Legally Blonde* (2001)). She had obtained a reputation in the industry as someone who was not dependable. In contrast, she had made six films between 1973 and 1980, with compensation ranging between $150,000 and $350,000.

In her lawsuit against MGM, Welch alleged that Phillips had conspired with the studio executives to interfere with MGM's contract with Welch in order to replace her with another actress without having to pay her the guaranteed fee in her contract. She claimed that they tried to make it appear that she, rather than Phillips or Ward, was responsible for the picture's budget problems. She sought $194,444 in actual damages (the amount of the guaranteed fee remaining to be paid under her contract at the time she was terminated) and $5 million in punitive damages for the contract interference. The jury voted in her favor, awarding her the balance of her fee, as well as $500,000 in punitive damages against Phillips and $3,750,000 in punitive damages against MGM. Ward was exonerated.

Welch also sued MGM for breach of the implied covenant of good faith and fair dealing—in other words, for bad faith dealing. For this count, the jury awarded her $400,000 in lost contract benefits, $1 million in lost promotional income, $750,000 for damage to reputation, and $3,750,000 in punitive damages. And Welch also sued for slander, based on Begelman's statement to the *Rolling Stone* reporter. For this statement, the jury awarded $300,000 in compensatory damages against Begelman, $150,000 in punitive damages against MGM, and $2,500 in punitive damages against Begelman.

MGM appealed.

On appeal, MGM argued first that Welch could not claim a conspiracy between Phillips and MGM because Phillips was acting as MGM's agent and MGM could not interfere with its own contract. As a general rule, a party to a contract can be liable for interfering with that contract if he conspires with a third party to breach it. But Phillips argued that he could not be considered a third-party conspirator with MGM executives because he was the studio's agent. Thus, his activities were "privileged." In other words, he claimed to be entitled, with an impersonal or disinterested motive, to endeavor to protect the interests of his principal—that is, MGM—by counseling the breach of the contract with a third party that he reasonably believed to be harmful to his employer's best interests. According to the court, this so-called privilege applies when the agent acts solely in the principal's interest and does not apply when the agent acts solely in his or her own self interest. MGM and Phillips argued that Phillips was acting with mixed motives. By acting as he did, he may have benefited himself, but he also helped MGM. These types of actions should also be privileged, they asserted.

The court disagreed. First, the court believed that Phillips was acting in his own self interest: Welch's evidence at trial, which the jury must have believed in order to render its verdict, suggested that Phillips was reacting to the threat of losing his own job and the resulting damage to his career by making Welch the scapegoat for the film's budget problems. Even though others may have had their reasons for replacing Welch, this appeared to be Phillips's main motivation. If the jury had believed that Phillips had provided MGM truthful information or that he had desired to benefit MGM, it would not have found him to be liable. The fact that they did shows that they believed that he acted in his own self interest and his actions were therefore not privileged.

On the bad faith argument, the jury's verdict also showed that they believed Welch's version of events. When Welch filed her lawsuit, her attorney tacked on a request for punitive damages because, from the start, MGM had adopted a "stonewall," "see you in court" attitude toward her. MGM complained about the punitive damage award. But the court pointed out that, as this was a bad faith discharge case, Welch was entitled to claim and to receive punitive damages. And it was clear to the court that the evidence presented at trial more than supported her case. Whatever the parties' motivations—whether Phillips's desire to protect himself from removal from the film because of its spiraling production costs, or MGM executives' need to demonstrate their power in dealing with demanding film stars, or MGM's "buyer's remorse" over a bad casting decision and desire to put a different actress into the role—the result was a conspiracy to falsely blame Welch for the movie's problems and to create a pretext for firing her so that MGM would not have to pay her the fee that was guaranteed under her contract.

As the court saw it, MGM's bad faith was further evidenced by the numerous facts brought out at trial: the false statements by MGM witnesses about the timing of their negotiations with Debra Winger, which were contradicted by both Winger's manager and her attorney; Phillips's informing Welch and her lawyer on Thursday night that a breach letter was going out even though she had not yet disobeyed the studio's makeup order for Friday morning; the failure to contact Welch's agent, Levy, before threatening Welch, even when MGM's expert testified that problems with a star were usually handled through the agent; Phillips's insistence, contrary to Welch's agent's testimony, that he was never told that Welch had agreed to use the new makeup room on Monday; Phillips's insisting that Welch refused to meet with him over the weekend when her agent had been in constant communication with him and Welch had agreed to a Monday morning meeting; and the abrupt firing on Sunday without waiting to see if she would fulfill her promises for Monday and at a time when most of the terms of Winger's contract to replace her in the film had already been agreed to.

The court intimated that there seemed to be something more to the studio's insistence that Welch make up at the studio that Friday morning rather than allowing her time to check out the new makeup room at the studio. This was especially troubling where she had been allowed to make up at home, had never been late for filming (which is what should have been important to the studio), was upset from Phillips's threat of a breach letter, and was facing her first major dialogue scene on that Monday. Although the court did not state it outright, there

311

was an implication in its assessment of these facts that the studio executives had intentionally set Welch up so that they could replace her.

The court seemed equally perturbed by the slander evidence. To them, MGM President Begelman's quote in *Rolling Stone* magazine was egregious.[3] MGM dismissed it as merely an expression of Begelman's opinion, maintaining that there was no evidence of malice. This latter was important because in order to prevail, because she was a public figure, Welch had to prove not only that Begelman had slandered her, that is, stated something false about her that would tend to cause injury to her reputation, but also, even if the statement were false, that it had been made with knowledge of its falsity or with reckless disregard for the truth.[4]

The court found that, although Begelman's statement included words that sounded like an expression of opinion (such as "we had a general feeling"), it also described facts ("she failed to obey") that had been communicated to him, as the head of the studio, by the movie's producer. Not only did the court believe it reasonable for the jury to conclude that Begelman was stating a fact that was false, but there also was, in the court's view, sufficient evidence to support the jury's finding of malice because Begelman knew that Welch had complied with her obligations and that he, in conjunction with other studio executives and with Phillips, had manufactured a pretext to fire her. Therefore, he must have known that his statement to the *Rolling Stone* reporter was false. It was a grandiose statement by a man trying to give an impression of strength and toughness in dealing with a star, and without caring about the damage that those

---

3. "We had a general feeling she had not lived up to her contract . . . we had no alternative. . . . The producer gave her appropriate directions and she failed to obey."
4. The New York Times Co. v. Sullivan, 376 U.S. 254 (1964).

words in a public interview might wreak on the actress's future career prospects. These are the type of heedless statements that executives later come to regret and that make general counsels cringe.

MGM particularly objected to the various monetary awards, which when tallied up, came to close to $10 million. They disputed, for example, the $1 million award for loss of professional income in the bad faith count. MGM argued that Welch did not have a reasonably certain future as a serious film actress. The court disagreed, believing that the compensation was justified: Welch had received significant income as an actress prior to entering into her contract with MGM and she had received no film offers after her firing from *Cannery Row*. Based on the compensation that film stars were making at the time of the trial, $1 million was not unreasonable.

MGM also claimed that prior to signing her contract with the studio, Welch had been considered to be a difficult actress and therefore she suffered no damage by Begelman's slander. But there again, the court disagreed. Even if she had been considered to be difficult prior to performing in *Cannery Row*, she was still considered to be a professional actress. After her dismissal, she became known as a contract breaker who had been fired from a film because she did not show up for work.

Finally, MGM objected to the $7 million in punitive damages. But the court pointed out that this amount was half what Welch had requested and amounted to only 3.6 percent of MGM's net worth at the time of trial. The court acknowledged that MGM had lost money on the movie and that the $500,000 damage award levied against Phillips (for conspiracy to induce breach of contract), was $300,000 more than the $200,000 production fee that Phillips received from MGM. But the court had no sympathy for any of the defendants, especially when balancing their "complete disregard of the likelihood that the unjustified firing would ruin Welch's film career," against "the relatively high actual damages that she suffered" and the permanent damage to her reputation.

In the end, everyone lost out in this case. The court's statement about Welch's future film career prospects proved to be prophetic. Even though the lawsuit vindicated her position that she had been set up to take the fall for others' mistakes, her reputation as a problematic star was cemented and her multimillion dollar judgment against MGM did not help her. In fact, if anything it labeled her as trouble. After the suit, she performed on stage, notably in *Woman of the Year* on Broadway, and in television programs, but she did not achieve her desire to be considered as a serious film star.

Cannery Row opened in early 1982 to dismal reviews. The movie was a major box office failure and MGM lost close to $16 million. *The New York Times'* film critic commented that Welch should have felt happy that she was fired from the film,[5] although it is certain that Welch would never have seen it that way.

There was no evidence that Debra Winger knew any of the circumstances surrounding Welch's firing at the time she was engaged to perform in *Cannery Row*. She would have had no reason to suspect the falsity in MGM's assertions that Welch had left the film. She appears to have been an innocent beneficiary of MGM's manipulation. But she was left to pick up the pieces of an expensive and already botched film production. Fortunately, she was able to overcome the bad press from this flop and went

---

5. "Miss Welch should send a large bouquet of roses to whoever is responsible," said Vincent Canby in *The New York Times*. Canby, Vincent, "The Fanciful Dropouts on 'Cannery Row,'" Movie Review, *The New York Times*, February 12, 1982, found at http://movies.nytimes.com/movie/review?res=9807E3D71038F931A25751C 0A964948260, last accessed October 15, 2011.

on to star in several more memorable films that brought her two Academy Award nominations—for Best Actress in *An Officer and a Gentleman* (1982) and in *Terms of Endearment* (1983).

But her career petered out soon after. After performing in several unsuccessful films, she took a break from film acting just when she was at the top of her career, and returned only intermittently afterwards. She played the lead roles both in *A Dangerous Woman* and *Shadowlands* in 1993, receiving her third Best Actress nomination for her performance in this latter film. More recently, she played the role of Anne Hathaway's mother in *Rachel Getting Married* (2008). Ironically, in her years in Hollywood, Winger also gained a reputation as a "difficult" and "demanding" actress. From Goudal to de Havilland, from Bette Davis to Raquel Welch and Debra Winger, Hollywood studios have always had problems trying to rein in and control the talented actresses who have appeared in their films. When the motion picture is successful, the complaints are minor, but studio executives rush in to affix blame when the movies fail.

Shall We Dance?

Rogers v. Grimaldi, 875 F 2d 994 (2d Cir. 1989)

My mother told me I was dancing before I was born. She could feel my toes tapping wildly inside her for months.

Ginger Rogers[1]

Remember, Ginger Rogers did everything Fred Astaire did, but backwards and in high heels.

Bob Thaves, *"Frank and Ernest"* (1982)

Through their incomparable performances in Hollywood musicals, they established themselves as paradigms of style, elegance, and grace. They were so popular and recognized that even today their identities are readily called to mind simply by hearing their first names—Ginger and Fred. This case involved the conflict between Ginger Rogers's right to protect her celebrated name and the right of others to express themselves in their own artistic work. When Rogers brought this case in New York, the court had to decide whether Rogers could prevent the use of the title "Ginger and Fred" for a fictional movie that was only obliquely related to Ginger Rogers and Fred Astaire.

By the 1980s, Ginger Rogers had been an international celebrity for more than fifty years. Her fame was established principally in a series of films from the 1930s in which she

---

1. *See* Ginger Rogers Official Website, http://gingerrogers.com/about/quotes.html.

costarred with Fred Astaire, including *Top Hat* (1935), *Swing Time* (1936), and *Shall We Dance?* (1937). Her name had "enormous drawing power" in the entertainment world. Only once, other than in her show business career, did she license her name for a commercial enterprise; this was in the mid-1970s when she agreed to allow J.C. Penney to produce a line of Ginger Rogers lingerie. She also wrote her autobiography that she hoped to sell for an adaptation as a movie.

In March 1986, a film created and directed by the famous Italian filmmaker, Federico Fellini, entitled *Ginger and Fred* (1986), was released in Italian theaters. The film told the story of two fictional Italian cabaret performers, Amelia and Peppo, who in their heyday imitated Ginger Rogers and Fred Astaire and who became known as "Ginger and Fred." The film focuses on a televised reunion for Peppo and Amelia many years after their retirement from the stage. The movie's producers described the movie as a "bittersweet story of these two fictional dancers and as a satire of contemporary television variety shows" in Italy. And as anyone who has ever watched variety shows on Italian television knows, it would take a lot of raucous behavior to satirize shows that are parodies of themselves.

The film opened to mixed reviews and had only a brief run in theaters in the United States.

Shortly after the motion picture opened in the United States, Ginger Rogers sued the producers, seeking to prevent the showing of the film. She claimed that they had violated Section 43(a) of the Lanham Act[2] by creating the false impression that the film was about her or that she had sponsored or endorsed it, or was

---

2. Section 43(a) created liability for "Any person who shall affix, apply, or annex, or use in connection with any goods or services . . . a false designation of origin, or any false description or representation . . . and shall cause such goods or services to enter into commerce." 15 U.S.C. §1125(a) (1982).

otherwise involved in the film. She also argued that the movie violated her right of publicity by appropriating her name for a commercial venture, and finally that the movie defamed her and violated her right to privacy by portraying her in a false light.

After two years of discovery (longer than the actual time the movie played in U.S. theaters), the defendants entered a motion in the trial court for summary judgment against Rogers. She objected, citing a market research survey that showed that the title "Ginger and Fred" misled potential moviegoers into thinking that the movie was about Ginger Rogers and Fred Astaire. She also provided anecdotal evidence of confusion, including the fact that when publicists for the U. S. distributors for the movie— MGM and United Artists—first heard about the film's title and before they saw the movie, as they prepared for distribution in the United States, they had begun gathering old still photos of Rogers and Astaire for possible use in the advertising campaign. The trial court granted the motion for summary judgment, finding that the filmmakers' use of Rogers's first name in the film's title and screenplay was an exercise of artistic expression and was not intended to serve a commercial purpose. Because it was not commercial speech, the false advertising prohibition of the Lanham Act (in Section 43(a)) did not apply and the film was entitled to First Amendment protection. These protections override any state law right of publicity claim. And the trial judge also rejected Rogers's "false light" claim.[3] Rogers appealed.

The appellate court was concerned that the district court's approach could "unduly" narrow the scope of the Lanham Act as it applied to movie titles. The court saw the need for balance: "Movies . . . are . . indisputably works of artistic expression and deserve protection. Nevertheless, they are also sold in the com-

---

3. Rogers v. Grimaldi, 695 F. Supp. 112, 120-121 (S.D. N.Y. 1988).

mercial marketplace like other more utilitarian products, making the danger of consumer deception a legitimate concern that warrants some government regulation.. . . . Poetic license is not without limits." The court noted that it is well-established where a title of a movie or a book has acquired secondary meaning— that is, where the title is sufficiently well-known that consumers associate it with a particular author's work—the holder of the rights to that title may prevent the use of the same or confusingly similar titles by other authors. And, they continued, "Indeed, it would be ironic if, in the name of the First Amendment, courts did not recognize the rights of authors to protect titles of their creative work against infringement of other authors."

Nevertheless, the court knew that First Amendment concerns had to play a role in this analysis. "Titles," they said, like the artistic works they identify, are of a "hybrid nature, combining artistic expression and commercial promotion." The title serves a dual role: it can be integral to the filmmaker's creative expression, but it also can be "a significant means of marketing the film to the public." "The artistic and commercial elements of titles are inextricably intertwined." Rogers's attorneys wanted the court to take First Amendment concerns into account only when the title is intimately related to the subject matter of the work, such that the author has no alternative means of expressing that subject matter. The appellate court did not wish to accept such an absolute standard, as it would not provide adequate leeway for artistic expression. Consequently, the court determined that the Lanham Act should only apply to artistic works where there was a real threat of consumer confusion that would outweigh the public interest in free expression. As a result, a title using a celebrity's name would be prohibited under the Lanham Act only when it has no artistic relevance at all to the underlying work or, if there is some small bit of artistic relevance, then the title explicitly misleads the public as to the source or content of the work.

Even a title that might implicitly suggest that a named celebrity had endorsed the work or had a role in producing the film, whether or not false, would, the court believed, be protected under the First Amendment if that title was artistically relevant to the work. It might be a different story if the title were explicitly misleading—for example, if the title of Fellini's movie had been "The True Story of Ginger and Fred." But that was not the case. And, the court noted, most consumers are not easily deceived by a movie's title; they "are well aware," the court said, "that they cannot judge a book by its cover," or a movie either.

In accordance with this analysis, the appellate court concluded that the title "Ginger and Fred" was not false advertising because it had artistic relevance to the film's content. The protagonists in the movie had been known as "Ginger and Fred" when they performed on stage. Thus, these names had not been arbitrarily chosen just to exploit the publicity value of their real life counterparts. The court also did not accept Rogers's claim that the title misled consumers into thinking that the film was about her and Astaire. Although some people, seeing the movie title, might think that the film was a biography about the two film stars, the title was also truthful in referring to the main characters in the film who were known to their audiences as "Ginger" and as "Fred."

The court believed that there was an ironical intent in the producer's choice of these two names. In an affidavit, Fellini had explained that Rogers and Astaire were to him a "glamorous and care-free symbol of what American culture represented" in the 1930s and 1940s that contrasted sharply with "the harsh time which Italy experienced" during that same time period. In the film, Fellini also sought to contrast "this elegance and class to the gaudiness and banality of contemporary television." Because of this, the court concluded, the title did not mislead; in fact, "it is an integral element of the film and the filmmaker's artistic expression."

The court also did not accept Rogers's claim that the producers had violated her right of publicity. Rights of publicity are governed by state law. The court did acknowledge a curious issue. In New York, where Rogers brought her suit, courts have ruled that claims related to these rights would be governed by the laws of the claimant's residence because these rights are personal property. Because Rogers lived in Oregon at the time she brought her suit, Oregon law should have governed her claim. However, at that time, there was no Oregon case law on point. And Oregon did not have a right of publicity statute. The court was in a quandary as to how to resolve this case. Should they presume that Oregon law would be the same as New York law? Or should they look to the laws of other states as well? The court elected to do the latter.

The common law right of publicity, where it exists, grants celebrities an exclusive right to control the commercial value of their names and prevents others from exploiting them without permission. Because it was more expansive than the Lanham Act, courts generally recognized the "need to limit the right to accommodate First Amendment concerns." The court noted that both New York and California courts, citing this concern for the right of free expression, refused to extend the right of publicity to bar the use of a celebrity's name in the title or text of a fictional or semi-fictional book or movie.[4]

---

4. *See, e.g.*, for New York: Hicks v. Casablanca Records, 464 F. Supp. 426 (S.D. N.Y. 1978); Frosch v. Grosset & Dunlap, Inc., 75 A. D. 2d 768, 427 N.Y.S. 2d 828 (1st Dept. 1980); and Guglielmi v. Spelling-Goldberg Productions, C.J. Bird concurring, 25 Cal. 3d 860 (1979).

The court believed that an Oregon court, given the opportunity, would follow in the same direction, especially considering Oregon's well-known "concern for the protection of free expression."

Rogers also claimed that the film portrayed her in a false light by depicting the dance pair in the movie in a tawdry and "seedy" manner. The court dismissed this claim out of hand, noting that the movie was not about Rogers but rather about a couple of fictional characters who were nicknamed "Ginger" and "Fred" by their sentimental Italian audience and whose only comparison to the real Ginger and Fred was that both pairs danced. Otherwise, the protagonists represented the real film stars only in their dreams. The court said, "We know of no state law that provides relief for false-light defamation against a work that clearly does not portray the plaintiff at all."

Intermission 9

What's in a Name?: Movie Titles and How to Protect Them

A title can make a major difference to the success of a motion picture. However, protecting movie titles from copying by others can be difficult, because they cannot be copyrighted. Film producers must look to trademark law for protection, but this also presents difficult challenges. Although it is possible to obtain a federal trademark registration for films, a single movie title is not permitted to be registered—only a series.[1] To obtain a registration with the Patent and Trademark Office (PTO), there must be at least one sequel to a movie to qualify for registration of a series.[2] The doctrine applies regardless of how distinctive the title is. Single work titles are deemed to be "inherently descriptive" or "inherently generic" and thus incapable of the necessary distinctiveness required for trademark registration.[3] And even if the single work title has acquired a secondary meaning— essentially, a significant recognition among the public, it will not be eligible for registration.[4]

However, if a single work title has acquired a secondary meaning, Section 43(a) of the Lanham Act[5] may provide protection, if consumer confusion would be created by duplicate titles. Once a film is associated in the consumer's mind by its title, such as *Gone With the Wind* (1939), then that title has acquired a secondary meaning. Consumer confusion can be shown through consumer surveys and advertising reports. A generic title would not acquire secondary meaning, which is why there have been several recent films bearing the same or comparable titles. For example, *Crash* (2005), an Oscar-winning film about the intersecting lives of several inhabitants of Los Angeles, has the same title as *Crash*, David Cronenberg's much darker 1996 movie. Generally, courts are hesitant in applying trademark law protections to titles because of free speech and freedom of expression concerns.

This was the situation in *Rogers v. Grimaldi*[6] where Ginger Rogers was unable to prevent the producers of an Italian film, *Ginger and Fred*, from using her name in a movie title. The court applied an "artistic relevance test" to determine whether the use of a particular title merits First Amendment protection— in other words, is the title relevant to the content of the work? Infringement may only be found if the use of the title is "explicitly misleading."[7]

Use of a multiparty agreement through the Title Registration Bureau of the Motion Picture Association of America (MPAA) is another way that film producers obtain protection for their titles.[8] The Title Registration Bureau has existed since the 1920s. It was set up under the auspices of the Motion Picture Producers and Distributors of America (MPPDA) under the Hays Office in order to allow member film production and distribution companies to preserve specific film titles for their use. The Title Registration office helped protect its members through self-enforced rules intended to prevent duplication of titles (and kept unscrupulous parties from intentionally sowing confusion).

Unfortunately, the large studios registered potential titles, whether or not they intended to ever make a movie with the registered names. This was yet another means by which the major studios were able to hinder the ability of independent film producers to succeed in the marketplace. These unused movie titles became bargaining chips. Allegedly when Charles Chaplin obtained a copyright for a film that he had initially named *The Dictator*, he discovered that Paramount had registered that title with the MPPDA. Paramount demanded a $25,000 payment in exchange for transferring its right to the title to Chaplin. Rather than pay, he changed the name of his movie and released it as *The Great Dictator* (1940).

With so many titles tied up, independent producers, who were becoming increasingly vocal in the 1940s, demanded reform of the registration system. As a result of these reforms, in a system that continues to this day,[9] a member pays an annual subscription fee, with an additional charge per title

Intermission 9 (continued)

registration. A subscriber is entitled to permanent registration of up to 500 titles that are based on an original screenplay. Unlimited titles to films based on an underlying work (such as a novel or short story) may be registered permanently. Only titles of movies that have been released in theaters in the United States may otherwise be registered permanently. Prospective titles for unreleased films can be registered in one-year intervals until the film is made. Subscribers receive a published list of every newly registered title. Once a title is published, objections must be filed within a set time period. Companies then negotiate among themselves, and these often result in the exchange of one title for another. Most of the disputes over titles seem to be worked out without the need to accelerate.

However, the Title Registration Bureau only protects titles that are registered by its members, which generally consist of the major studios and other producers who have been willing to subscribe. Moreover, the registration only protects titles against use by other Bureau members. Nonmembers are not subject to the MPAA's rules.[10] This limitation is demonstrated by an interesting case arising out of Indian courts.

In August 2008, Warner Bros. filed a lawsuit against the production company, Mirchi Movies, complaining about the similarity between the title to its Harry Potter movies—such as *Harry Potter and the Sorcerer's Stone* (2001) and *Harry Potter and the Goblet of Fire* (2005)—and Mirchi's Bollywood film, *Hari Puttar: A Comedy of Terrors*. This latter movie tells the story of a ten-year-old boy, Hari Puttar, who moves from India to Britain and then is left behind when his family leaves on vacation. He discovers two burglars attempting to steal a secret formula invented by Hari's scientist father.[11] Mirchi responded to Warner's complaint that there was very little similarity between Hari Puttar and Harry Potter, explaining that Hari is a popular Indian name and that "puttar" means "son" in Punjabi. (Apparently, versions of the authentic Harry Potter movies were also released in India, with Harry's name translated to Hari Puttar.) Warner Bros.

claimed that the title was confusing. Mirchi responded that it had obtained a valid trademark for the title of their Hari Puttar film in 2005 in India.

In September 2006, the court in Delhi rejected Warner Bros.' suit, saying that readers of the Harry Potter books, the more likely viewers of these films, would be sufficiently able to distinguish between the two works.[12]

1. The title of a single movie is treated as the title of an individual product, which is generally not eligible for trademark protection. Only a series of products from a single source, such as sequels, can be protected under trademark law. See In re Cooper, 254 F. 2d 611 (C.C. P. A. 1958), cert. denied 358 U.S. 840 (1958).

2. Trademark Examination Guide 04-06: "Registrability of Marks Used on Creative Works," §IV.1 (Nov. 14, 2006), available at www.uspto.gov/trademarks/resources/exam/examguide4-06.jsp; Trademark Manual of Examining Procedure §1202.08 (4th Ed. 2005), available at tess2.uspto.gov/tmbd/tmep-4ed/.

3. Herbko Int'l, Inc. v. Kappa Books, Inc., 308 F. 3d 1156 (Fed. Cir. 2002).

4. A movie cannot have a secondary meaning with the public before it is released. See In re Cooper, above. For further discussion of this topic, see Handel, Jonathan L., "Mark My Words," Los Angeles Lawyer, April 2008, pp. 22-28. According to Handel, In re Cooper, (see Note 1 supra) has been consistently followed by the courts.

5. Lanham Act of 1946 §43(a), as amended, 15 U.S.C. §1125(a).

6. Rogers v. Grimaldi, 875 F 2d 994 (2d Cir. 1989); See discussion at Reel 23, Shall We Dance?

7. See Timbers, Kerry L. and Huston, Julia, "The 'Artistic Relevance Test' Just Became Relevant: The Increasing Strength of the First Amendment as a Defense to Trademark Infringement and Dilution," TMR Vol. 93, p. 1278 (2003), found at http://www.inta.org/TMR/Documents/Volume 93/vol93_no6-a4.pdf.

8. See Memorandum of the Title Committee of the Motion Picture Association of America, Inc. (May 1, 2007); McCarthy, Edward Robert, "Comment: How Important Is a Title? An Examination of the Private Law Created By the Motion Picture Association of America," 56 U. Miami L. Rev. 1071 (July 2002).

9. The Society of Independent Motion Picture Producers (SIMPP), "What's In a Name: The Little Known Secret of Title Registration in Hollywood," excerpt from Aberdeen, J.A., Hollywood Renegades, found at www.cobbles.com/simpp_archive/title-registration_intro.htm.

10. Handel, p. 24.

11. The plot of this movie seems to resemble the popular Home Alone (1990) movie rather than a Harry Potter film.

12. See "Warner Bros Lose Hari Puttar Case," BBC News, Sept. 22, 2008, found at news.bbc.co.uk/2/hi/7628948.stm, and "Warner Brothers' Case Against Mirchi Movies Dismissed," Screen Daily, 23 September 2008, found at http://www.screendaily.com/warner-brothers-case-against-mirchi-movies-dismissed/4041001.article, last accessed August 18, 2011.

The Stunt Girl

Von Beltz v. Stuntman, Inc.,
207 Cal. App. 3d 1467 (2nd Dist. 1989)

> Eli Cross: Well, we need something,
>   Sam, and damn well you know it.
>   Something better.
> Sam: Better? How better?
> Eli Cross: Something less boring.
>   Something crazier.

Peter O'Toole, as Eli Cross, and Allen Garfield,
as Sam, from *The Stunt Man* (1980)

From the early days of cinema, dramatic action has been portrayed through various stunts. Audiences are entertained by the sense of excitement and danger, created by exploits and activities that are often as dangerous as they appear on the screen. Silent film stars such as Harold Lloyd and Buster Keaton performed many of their own, but early on, other more athletic performers were substituted, replacing a movie's top-billing actors to perform activities considered too hazardous for the stars to undertake. These men—and women—would ride in the runaway carriages and war party raids in classic westerns, for example. Later on, they would fly the airplanes and helicopters in war movies and drive the cars in high-speed chase scenes. It was—and remains—dangerous work, and accidents are not infrequent. Sometimes innocent bystanders are injured, or even killed. In 1984, the actor Jon-Erik Hexum died after accidentally shooting himself in the head, when the wadding from a blank cartridge in a pistol that fired blanks shattered his skull on the set of the television series "Cover-Up."[1] In July 1982, actor Vic Morrow and two small children were killed on the set during the filming of *Twilight Zone: The Movie* (1983), when a stunt involving a helicopter went tragically awry.[2]

Heidi von Beltz was an enthusiastic participant in the movie industry in the 1980s. A natural athlete, she combined stunt work in pictures with acting and modeling, and guest appearances in television shows, such as *Charlie's Angels.* She had had professional stunt experience, including driving a stunt car in *Smokey and the Bandit II* (1980). An attractive blonde, she was performing as a double for actress Farrah Fawcett on the set of the movie *The Cannonball Run* (1981), riding as a passenger in an Aston Martin, when something went terribly wrong and the car crashed into a van. Von Beltz suffered a broken neck.[3]

This was and still is considered one of the worst accidents in film history.

After the accident, von Beltz sued the movie's director, Hal Needham, and Stuntman, Inc., for damages resulting from her injuries. At the trial, the jury found both parties to be negligent and, having assessed von Beltz's damages to be $7 million, awarded her 65 percent of that amount, determining that she had been contributorily negligent to the extent of 35 percent. However, the jury also deducted the amount that she had already obtained in settlement from other parties involved in

---

1. "Jon-Erik Hexum's Fatal Joke," *Entertainment Weekly*, Oct. 14, 1994, found at http://www.ew.com/ew/article/0,,304026,00.html, last accessed October 21, 2011.

2. Cummings, Judith, "Director Standing Trial For Deaths On Film Set," *The New York Times*, July 23, 1986, found at http://www.nytimes.com/1986/07/23/us/director-standing-trial-for-deaths-on-film-set.html?scp=4&sq=Vic%20Morrow%20death&st=cse, last accessed December 13, 2011.

3. Kennedy, Dana, "Heidi von Beltz: Soul Survivor, stuntwoman Heidi von Beltz, paralyzed in a 1980 movie-set accident, tells her remarkable story," *Entertainment Weekly* (ew.com), April 1996, found at http://www.ew.com/ew/article/0,,292113,00.html, last accessed December 22, 2011.

the movie's production, including the production company, Cannonball Productions, Inc.—approximately $4.5 million—leaving her with an award of $0. All parties appealed.

Hal Needham was a former stunt person who had become a successful motion picture director. He was the president and sole shareholder of Stuntman, Inc., which was the so-called "loan-out" company that contracted out Needham's services as a director. He had formed the production company, Cannonball Productions, Inc., to produce *The Cannonball Run*. Cannonball Productions hired several persons, including von Beltz, to perform stunts in the film.

The movie was shot on location in Los Angeles, Georgia, Florida, and Las Vegas. The accident happened in a desert area near Las Vegas on June 25, 1980. On that day, von Beltz had been assigned to ride as a passenger in a 1962 Aston Martin, which was itself a double for another Aston Martin used elsewhere in the movie, and which had no seat belts. When the vintage sports car was delivered to the movie set, the stunt driver, Jimmy Nickerson, checked it out and noted that it had defective steering, bad tires, and a malfunctioning clutch. Needham had to delay the filming of the stunt to allow time for the car to be repaired. Whether or not the car was in fact fully repaired was an issue in dispute. Nickerson also had observed that the car had no seat belts and asked that they be installed. But they were not.

As a passenger in the car, von Beltz was assigned to operate a smoke machine placed behind the car's bucket seats, in order to create special effects. She was not included in the conversations that Needham held with the car drivers where he discussed his plans for the stunt.

In the first take, the driver, Nickerson, drove the Aston Martin south on the highway encountering on the way five northbound cars driven by other drivers. As planned, the Aston

Martin cut across in front of this opposing traffic, onto the opposite shoulder of the road, passing the incoming cars, and then returned to the highway, continuing south. The cameramen had set their lenses to create the illusion that the vehicles were passing closer together than they actually were. This stunt was performed perfectly.

However, Needham was dissatisfied with the effect created in the first take and decided to try something more adventurous. The second take began about thirty minutes after the first one had been shot. Before shooting this second take, Needham told the stunt drivers to speed up. He also wanted the Aston Martin to weave in and out of the oncoming cars in a serpentine fashion. An escape route was planned that required Nickerson to turn to the right. Nobody told von Beltz that the second take would be different from the first.

During the second take, the Aston Martin traveled at about fifty miles per hour. Nickerson realized that he was going to collide with one of the northbound stunt cars, a Ford van, but he was going too fast to be able to either take the planned escape route or avoid a collision with the van. Both Nickerson and von Beltz were injured in the accident, but von Beltz's injuries were the more serious; she was permanently and totally paralyzed from the neck down.

Customarily, stunt persons have ultimate control over their stunts and provide their own safety equipment. They are entitled to "stunt adjustments," which are based on the stunt's degree of risk. Stunt persons also may refuse to perform a stunt, or may require the stunt coordinator or the film's production manager to make safety equipment available. However, if a stunt person refused or hesitated to participate, his or her employment on the movie might be terminated.

Evidence at the trial showed that, on the set of *The Can-*

nonball Run, there were ten extra car seat belts, which could have been installed upon request. Other stunt persons on the movie set had even ordered that "five-point" safety harnesses be installed in stunt vehicles, even when these were already equipped with ordinary seat belts, before driving in those cars in the movie. Apparently, seat belts or harnesses could have been installed in twenty minutes. Von Beltz's expert testified that if she had been wearing a lap-shoulder belt at the time of the collision, her injuries would have been no more serious than fractured ribs.

Needham contended in his appeal that he was not liable to von Beltz because, by performing in a movie stunt, she had assumed the risk of being injured. This is known as the "fireman's rule" which holds that firemen, police officers, and other professionals, such as zoo veterinarians, who engage in hazardous activities in the normal course of their duties, have assumed the risk of known dangers and therefore are barred from recovery for injuries. Needham argued that a stunt person assumes the risk in exactly the same manner as a fireman or a policeman. He claimed that when von Beltz accepted employment as a stunt person, she implicitly assumed the risk of injury.

The court rejected this contention. They determined that they did not need to decide the question as to whether, as a matter of law, the fireman's rule would apply to movie stunt persons in general because, according to the facts presented in the case, von Beltz did not *fully* know the hazards she faced. The court noted that ordinarily a movie stunt is not like an athletic contest or a horse race—or a fire—where there are spontaneous, opposing, and sometimes hostile forces at play. Movie stunts are usually to some extent planned or choreographed events, although some are better planned or choreographed than others, just as some are more dangerous than others.

The court noted that a professional stunt person might be presumed to have expertise or physical agility that minimizes the hazards of a movie stunt. Nonetheless, the stunt person normally performs a stunt knowing that the danger has not been entirely eliminated. Where a stunt person has full awareness of the hazards he or she faces, it may be possible to conclude that, under the circumstances, he or she has assumed the risk of injury. However, where a movie director or producer changes the nature of the stunt without letting the performer know, and by doing this increases the risk or otherwise alters the risk without the stunt person's acquiescence, the director or producer may be held liable for any injuries that result because of the increased or altered risk. And when, in such circumstances, a stunt goes awry, as it did in this case, who is more negligent than another has to be left for a jury to decide in the resulting litigation.

In von Beltz's case, she had established that Needham did not inform her that he was changing the way the stunt in the second take would be performed. Therefore, she did not know that the stunt would be materially different and riskier than the one in which she had participated in the first take. Had she known, she could either have declined the stunt or requested that seat belts be installed. Instead, she participated in the stunt not knowing that her driver, Nickerson, was going to drive head-on into opposing traffic and weave through it in a serpentine fashion. She was not told that all of the stunt cars would be moving at a faster speed. Certainly, the court reasoned, this stunt had more hazards than the first one. Because von Beltz was not informed of the new dangers that she faced, Needham could not claim that she had assumed the risk.

Von Beltz, for her part, contended that the jury was wrong in finding that she had been 35 percent negligent. She claimed that this allotment was not supported by the evidence. The jury had made a finding of contributory negligence because von Beltz had not taken the safety precaution of using a seat belt in the movie stunt. The court noted that it was a matter of common knowledge that seat belts can minimize injuries in car crashes. Von Beltz did not dispute that her injuries would have been less if a seat belt had been used. Two facts worked against her. First, von Beltz had been a stuntwoman on a prior film in which she had driven a stunt car. Second, in the filmmaking industry, it is customary for stunt persons to take responsibility for their own individual safety equipment when they perform a movie stunt. Also, many stunt persons request additional safety equipment and the evidence showed that there were ten seat belts available on the movie location that would have been installed at the request of a stunt person. Furthermore, during the filming of *The Cannonball Run*, and prior to the injury-producing stunt, other stunt persons on the set had successfully ordered the installation of five-point safety harnesses. Testimony showed that it would have taken approximately fifteen to twenty minutes to install the seat belts in the Aston Martin. The record also indicated that the use of a five-point safety harness is a common precaution taken by many movie stunt drivers.

Given that movie stunts seem dangerous and frequently are actually dangerous, it was obvious to the court that a stunt person has the responsibility to use appropriate and available safety equipment. Even before the first stunt in *The Cannonball Run*, the court noted that von Beltz knew that there were no seat belts in the sports car in which she was to ride. She could have requested a seat belt before that take was shot, but did not do so. Therefore, the jury was entitled to conclude, based on that evidence, that von Beltz had not exercised ordinary care when she failed to request a seat belt.

Needham also challenged the verdict by arguing that he was the alter ego to Cannonball Productions who was von Beltz's employer for this film. Under California's workers' compensation law, an employee's only remedy for injuries sustained on the job is the statutory benefits to which he or she is entitled.[4] However, the statutory restriction does not limit an employee's request to recover damages against persons who are not employees of the same employer. Needham maintained that, since he and von Beltz were both employees of Cannonball Productions, she was not entitled to sue him for negligence.

The question for the court was whether Stuntman, Inc., Needham's "general" employer, had loaned Needham to Cannonball Productions, thus creating a "special employment" relationship between Needham and Cannonball. In such a situation, the special employer, Cannonball, would be solely liable for Needham's job-related negligent acts, under the legal doctrine of *respondeat superior*.[5] However, the court did not see that the relationship between Needham and Cannonball had been set up as an employment relationship. Needham had testified at the trial that his services as a director for the film had been secured by means of a contract between Stuntman, Inc. and Northshore Investment, a financial backer for the film. Needham had signed that agreement on behalf of Stuntman (as its president). Stuntman paid Needham his compensation and reimbursed his employment-related expenses. The corporation, Cannonball Productions, was set up for the sole purpose of producing the movie and processing the income and expenses of that production. Cannonball paid Stuntman for Needham's services in the

---

4. Cal. Lab. Code §360.

5. Literally, "let the master respond," i.e., a common law legal doctrine that makes a person's employer responsible for the negligence of its employees occurring while the employee was acting within the scope of his or her employment.

form of contract fees paid by checks made payable to Stuntman. The court could not see, based on these facts, how Needham could claim to be Cannonball's employee. In fact, he seemed to have set up this complicated relationship structure precisely in order to avoid being treated as the movie producer's employee.

The court therefore determined that Stuntman and Needham were properly allocated liability for von Beltz's injuries.

After almost nine years of litigation, von Beltz, Needham, Stuntman, and Cannonball settled out of court for approximately $4.5 million. However, von Beltz's life, once that of a talented, athletic, energetic aspiring actress, was forever changed by this unfortunate accident. One good thing that came out of von Beltz's very public lawsuit against the movie's producers was the now-mandatory use of seat belts in all stunt cars. In addition, the Directors Guild has implemented a rule prohibiting directors from altering stunts on location, to prevent unfortunate on-the-spot decisions of the type that led to tragic mishaps on the set of *The Cannonball Run*.[6]

---

6. Kennedy, "Heidi von Beltz: Soul Survivor," Note 3 supra. In a recent case—*Angelotti v. The Walt Disney Co.*, 192 Cal. App. 4th 1394 (2d Dist. 2011)—a stuntman was injured during a stunt that involved falling from a height of approximately eighty-nine feet. His loan-out company, Skiddadle, Inc., had contracted with the film's producer, Second Mate Productions, Inc. The court held that Angelotti was the special employee of Second Mate and therefore his recovery was limited to the worker's compensation payment, under Second Mate's insurance.

Intermission 10

The Hollywood
Stunt Performer

The stunt—an exciting and frequently dangerous piece of action in a film—has been part of the motion picture since the early days of the cinema. Many of the earliest films were silent comedies that depended for their humor on physical routines modeled after those that had been the stock in trade in vaudeville routines for years—pratfalls, backward flips, actors narrowly missed by falling objects. The most famous of the silent film comedians, Charles Chaplin, Joseph "Buster" Keaton, and Roscoe "Fatty" Arbuckle, all had their start in vaudeville.[1]

In those early days, the "stuntman"—a person willing to put his own life or well-being at risk in order to protect the "star" from physical injury on the set—did not exist. The first stuntmen on films were the comedians themselves, such as Chaplin or Keaton. Buster Keaton was one of the most memorable of the silent film stars, not only in the films he made but also in his physical appearance. He was short and slight, with a sober deadpan look; he was known as the "Great Stone Face." But he had tremendous physical strength and abilities. In *College* (1927), he plays a brainy college student who attempts various sports in order to impress a girl, while only managing to seem a clumsy fool. When the girl of his dreams is held hostage in her dormitory, however, Keaton performs amazing acrobatics to rescue her, his efforts culminating when he succeeds in pole-vaulting a long distance into the open second story window of the house where she is being held. Although he had been one of the most popular and successful of silent movie stars—his film, *The General* (1926) is considered a classic—he made some very poor decisions in his personal and professional life. To the end, however, he retained his incredible physicality. In his last film, the role of Erronius in *A Funny Thing Happened on the Way to the Forum*, which was released shortly before his death in 1966, despite being ill with cancer, he still managed to perform several of his own stunts, which, given the raucous staging of that film, was no small accomplishment.

One could say that Harold Lloyd invented the high-risk movie stunt, when he balanced on rooftops and ledges in films like *High and Dizzy* (1920), where Lloyd plays a patient sleepwalking on a building ledge, high above the street. At that time, filmmakers didn't fake the scenes. When you see Lloyd clinging to the minute hand of a giant clock face that is coming off in *Safety Last* (1923)—above the traffic that is visible in the background—that shot was genuine. Although there may have been nets outside the frame, and staging from rooftops and platforms, there is no question that Lloyd is really hanging from the clock. He was a daredevil. The variations of his work are incredible. In *Girl Shy* (1924), Lloyd undertakes a hair-raising daredevil ride to prevent a wedding.[2] Lloyd was not afraid of physical risks, even when they were not necessary. For a publicity photo, he was pretending to light a cigarette with a prop bomb— a round, black object with a fuse. Unfortunately, the bomb was real and the explosion took off his right thumb and index finger. From then on, in all his movies he wore a glove that covered rubber fingers on his right hand, but continued to do stunts that required the use of his hand.

With the rise of the western in the silent and early sound era, a number of rodeo stars became movie stars and stuntmen. Tom Mix was the most famous of these. He had started out as a performer in Wild West Shows at ranches and fairs in Texas and other western states. In 1910, he joined Selig Pictures, to handle the horses used in films and act as a safety man.[3] He gradually moved into acting in silent westerns, moving on to Fox Films in 1917. He was considered one of the best silent film cowboy stars, but he insisted on performing his own stunts, which, although not that much different from his rodeo pieces, gradually took on a more thrilling pace. He was very courageous in his performances. In *The Big Diamond Robbery* (1929), he performed one stunt riding at a fast pace underneath a moving carriage.[4]

Another great western actor and stuntman was Enos Edward

Intermission 10 (continued)

Canutt, known as Yakima Canutt.[5] He started
out in rodeos as a teenager as a bronco rider and
became a star cowboy performer on the rodeo circuit.
He moved to Hollywood to work as a stunt double in
movies and started performing in westerns in the 1920s.
His most famous movie role was the lead in *The Devil Horse*
(1926), where he "undertook several hazardous stunts, including
a ninety-foot cliff top leap."[6] He performed in many silent
westerns, but the coming of sound ended his acting career.
He had survived influenza during the epidemic in 1918, which
left scars on his vocal chords; his voice was too weak to allow
him to perform in cowboy roles. When talking pictures became
the norm, Canutt made stunt work his full-time job.[7] Among his
more famous roles were as John Wayne's double in *Stagecoach*
(1939) where he crawled under the belly of the stage team, and
as Clark Gable's double in *Gone with the Wind* (1939). He was
the stunt coordinator for the 1959 production of *Ben Hur*,
directing the famous chariot race.[8]

From the 1970s forward, modern stunt technology
developed, opening the way for thrilling blockbuster films,
with dazzling special effects in movies such as *Jaws* (1975) and
Star Wars (1977). This was the era of the successful car stunt
movies—*Smokey and the Bandit* (1977) and *The Cannonball Run*
(1981), produced by a former stuntman and stunt coordinator,
Hal Needham. The 1980s saw a plethora of science fiction films,
including the sequels to *Star Wars*, *The Empire Strikes Back*
(1980) and *Return of the Jedi* (1983), as well as *E.T.: The Extra-
Terrestrial* (1982), all of which relied heavily on both live action
stunts as well as computer generated images. This technology
has allowed directors to shoot exciting scenes—fight scenes,
falls, car crashes, and explosions—that would have been too
expensive, dangerous, or simply impossible to perform with real
people. However, given movie viewers' taste for the real thrill,
it is likely that the realism of an actual stunt will always be in
demand, and this means there will always be a role for a good
stuntman, or stuntwoman, and there will always be danger.[9]

1. The American Experience, PBS, People & Events: Charlie Chaplin (1889-1977), found at www.pbs.org/wgbh/amex/pickford/peopleevents/p_chaplin.html.

2. According to the Internet Movie Database, stuntman Harvey Parry doubled for Harold Lloyd in several of the most dangerous shots in Lloyd films; however, Lloyd was always said to do his own stunts. According to Parry, for the clock face scene in *Safety Last*, "he did not want to detract from the danger of Lloyd's actual stunt work. Lloyd performed the majority of the stunts himself on the rigged facade over a small platform, which was built near the rooftop's edge and still had to be raised a great height to get the proper street perspective for the camera. The size of the platform did not offer much of a safety net, and had Lloyd fallen, there was the risk he could have tumbled off the platform." The stuntman also revealed that he doubled for Lloyd in the long shots of him climbing the building in the distance. http://www.imdb.com/title/tt0014429/trivia.

3. Brownlow, p. 305.

4. Brownlow, p. 305.

5. He received his nickname as a result of a misprint in a newspaper caption, where he was photographed with some men from Yakima, Washington, and the caption identified him as "Yakima Canutt." Brownlow, p. 355.

6. Brownlow, p. 357.

7. Brownlow, pp. 357-58.

8. Brownlow, p. 354.

9. In October, 2011, a stuntman died on the set of *The Expendables 2* (starring Sylvester Stallone, Bruce Willis, Arnold Schwarzenegger, Chuck Norris, and Jean-Claude Van Damme) and another was injured and taken to the hospital, during filming on the Ognyanovo dam near Elin Pelin in Bulgaria. The men apparently were performing a stunt in a rubber boat that involved an explosion. The Sofia Echo, October 28, 2011, found at http://www.comingsoon.net/news/movienews.php?id=83659&offset=10, last accessed December 22, 2011.

A Never-ending Story

Stewart v. Abend, 495 U.S. 207 (1990)

These [judges] are all yawning, for no crumb of amusement ever falls from Jarndyce and Jarndyce (the cause in hand), which was squeezed dry years upon years ago.

Charles Dickens, *Bleak House*

Readers of Charles Dickens's novel *Bleak House* are familiar with *Jarndyce vs. Jarndyce*, the notorious case in equity that had endured in the courts for so long that the heirs to the original parties—long dead—continued to engage in battle for the ever-dwindling fortune. This is Dickens's satire of the nineteenth century British court system. In the movie industry, a similarly long-enduring battle over rights established by parties long dead continues to this day. It is the story of the revered Alfred Hitchcock film, *Rear Window*, and curious aspects of U.S. copyright law.

It all began in the last century. In 1942, a well-known writer of mystery short stories, Cornell Woolrich, published "It Had to Be Murder," in *Dime Detective Magazine*. The magazine's publisher obtained the rights to first-time publication of the story and Woolrich retained all other rights. In 1945, he agreed to assign the motion picture rights in this story, as well as in several other short stories he had written[1] to B. G. De Sylva Productions for $9,250. This agreement gave De Sylva broad rights for

---

1. Several of these stories were produced by Alfred Hitchcock as episodes of the television series, *Alfred Hitchcock Presents:* "The Big Switch" (1956), "Momentum" (1956), "Four O'Clock" (1957), "Post Mortem" (1958), and "The Black Curtain" (1962).

the film exploitation of this short story. At the time, the Copyright Act provided authors a 28-year initial term of copyright protection with, upon application, an additional 28-year renewal term. Woolrich agreed to renew the copyright to his stories at the appropriate time and to assign the same motion picture rights to De Sylva Productions for the 28-year renewal term. De Sylva's rights were later acquired by Paramount and MCA.

In 1953, actor James Stewart and director Alfred Hitchcock formed a production company, Patron, Inc., which acquired the motion picture rights in "It Had to Be Murder" from Paramount and MCA and, with Paramount, Patron produced and distributed the motion picture version of Woolrich's story, entitled *Rear Window*.

Rear Window is very closely based on Woolrich's story. In the story, Hal Jeffries, a man with a broken leg, is confined to his New York City apartment and can only move from his bed to a chair near the window of his second-floor bedroom. To pass the time, he observes the comings and goings of his neighbors in the building opposite his window. He fixates on one couple (Mr. and Mrs. Lars Thorwald). Mrs. Thorwald, he notices, appears to be in poor health and her husband is very attentive to her. After several days, Jeffries notices that she has disappeared. He believes that Thorwald has murdered her. He telephones an old friend, Detective Boyne, to report his suspicions and Boyne investigates. Following a lead that Mrs. Thorwald's belongings have been shipped to the countryside, the police encounter a woman who identifies herself as Mrs. Thorwald. The disappearance solved, Boyne stops his investigation.

Undeterred, Jeffries then enlists the assistance of his servant, Sam, to obtain proof of the murder. Sam slips a note under Thorwald's door that reads, "What have you done with her?" On seeing the note, Thorwald becomes agitated and Jeffries observes him pacing his apartment nervously. His pacing close-ly parallels that of a realtor who is showing a newly renovated apartment two floors above Thorwald's. Thorwald's reaction to the note convinces Jeffries that Thorwald is a murderer.

To obtain more concrete evidence of the murder, Jeffries telephones Thorwald, pretending to be a blackmailer, and he convinces Thorwald to meet him in a local park. When Thor-wald sets out to meet the blackmailer, Jeffries sends Sam to Thorwald's apartment to make it appear that the apartment has been searched, so that Thorwald will believe that the black-mailer has obtained evidence of a murder. Sam does this. When Thorwald returns, Jeffries phones him, pretending to have dis-covered evidence. But Thorwald does not believe him. Then Thorwald unexpectedly telephones Jeffries and, on hearing his voice, realizes that Jeffries is his blackmailer. After the phone call, Jeffries suddenly recalls the moment when Thorwald was pacing back and forth in his apartment while the realtor, two floors above, was creating a mirror image. He remembers that, when passing from the kitchen to the living room, the realtor's height relative to the window frame had changed while Thor-wald's had remained the same. Jeffries realizes that this was because, as part of the renovations to the apartment that the realtor was showing, a raised kitchen floor had been poured in concrete for decorative effect. Jeffries deduces that Thorwald buried his wife's body in the still wet concrete in that upper floor apartment when it was under renovation.

Jeffries tries to telephone Detective Boyne but his line goes dead. Thorwald has come around to his building and has cut the phone line. Jeffries realizes that Thorwald is coming to kill him. Unable to escape because of his cast, Jeffries hides in a rug on the floor and places a bust sculpture on his shoulder, hop-ing that in the dark Thorwald will not notice him. As Thorwald enters the room, he shoots at the bust. But just then, Detective Boyne rushes in behind him. Thorwald escapes out the window, climbs to the roof of his own building and then shoots into Jeffries's apartment. Detective Boyne returns fire and strikes Thorwald, who plunges to his death.

Jeffries then tells Boyne the plot: Thorwald had been poisoning his wife but kills her outright when she discovers what he has been doing. He then concocts a scheme with another woman to suggest that his wife has gone upstate. This woman was planning to stage the wife's suicide. In the closing lines of the story, a doctor arrives to remove the cast from Jeffries's leg and comments that Jeffries must have been bored while sitting around his apartment with nothing to do.

The story line of *Rear Window*, as fans of the movie will attest, very closely resembles this plot. Photojournalist, L. B. "Jeff" Jeffries, played by James Stewart, is incapacitated with a broken leg and spends the long hours observing his neighbors in an apartment building across a courtyard. There are several differences in the plot of the movie from that of the short story. For example, in the film, Jeffries can see down from his window to the garden below. He notices a little dog whose owner lowers him from an upper story apartment in a little basket to run around the garden. The puppy seems fascinated by one area in particular, which arouses Jeffries's suspicions.

In the film, the servant, Sam, is replaced by Jeffries's fiancée, Lisa Fremont, played by Grace Kelly, and his visiting nurse, Stella, played by Thelma Ritter. Boyne is replaced by detective Thomas Doyle. The park where Jeffries sets a rendezvous with Thorwald (played by Raymond Burr) becomes a bar down the street. And the film's ending is much more dramatic. Jeffries's girlfriend, Lisa, is arrested by the police while snooping around Thorwald's apartment. Jeffries calls Doyle to ask him to intercede to get Lisa out of jail. When Thorwald comes into his apartment, instead of wrapping himself in a rug, Jeffries grabs his camera and a box of flashbulbs. When Thorwald comes toward him, Jeffries sets off the flash, blinding Thorwald for a few seconds. Eventually, Thorwald takes hold of Jeffries and tries to push him out the open window. Hanging from the ledge, Jeffries calls for help and Lisa and Detective Doyle, accompanied by the police, rush in. Just as Jeffries slips, the police are able to break his fall. Thorwald confesses to the murder of his wife, and the police take him away.

Rear Window premiered on August 4, 1954, at the Rivoli Theatre in New York City and was distributed by Paramount through 1983. This film enjoyed a long-time success (becoming the fifth grossing film of 1954) and became one of the more popular of Alfred Hitchcock's films. The screenplay for the film was nominated for an Academy Award.

Unfortunately, Woolrich died in 1968, before he could obtain the rights in the copyright renewal term, as he had agreed with De Sylva. He died without a surviving spouse or any children. He left his property, including the short story rights, to the Claire Woolrich Memorial Scholarship Fund, administered by his executor, Chase Manhattan Bank (now JPMorgan Chase), for the benefit of Columbia University. On December 29, 1969, Chase renewed the copyright in the story, "It Had to Be Murder." However, instead of assigning the motion picture rights to Paramount or Patron, as Woolrich had agreed to do in his earlier rights assignment to De Sylva, Chase assigned the renewal rights to Sheldon Abend for $650 plus 10 percent of all proceeds from the exploitation of the story. Sheldon Abend was a literary agent who represented the estates of important persons, including George Bernard Shaw, Tennessee Williams, and David O. Selznick, as well as Cornell Woolrich.

In 1971, when the movie *Rear Window* was broadcast on the ABC Television Network, Abend notified Hitchcock, Stewart, and MCA, the owners of the *Rear Window* movie rights, that he owned the renewal copyright for Woolrich's short story and that their distribution of the movie without his permission infringed his copyright. Despite this notice, Hitchcock, Stewart, MCA, and their distributor, Universal, entered into a second license with ABC to rebroadcast the film. In 1974, Abend filed suit in federal district court against them, alleging copyright infringement. He dismissed his suit shortly afterwards in return for a payment of $25,000, for permission to continue the broadcast.

Three years later, in 1977, the Second Circuit Court of Appeals decided *Rohauer v. Killiam Shows, Inc.,*[2] holding that the owner of the copyright in a derivative work (such as in a motion picture based on a copyrighted short story) may continue to use the existing derivative work according to the original grant from the author of the preexisting work even if the grant of rights in the preexisting work lapsed. Several years after, in 1984, apparently relying on *Rohauer*, Stewart, Hitchcock, MCA, and Universal released the motion picture, *Rear Window*, in a variety of media, including new 35 and 16 millimeter prints for theatrical exhibition in the United States as well as on videocassettes. Thus the film was widely exhibited in theaters, over cable television, and through videocassette rentals and sales.

That same year, Abend had approached Steven Spielberg, then at Universal, proposing to license the "Rear Window" story for a remake of the *Rear Window* film as a segment of a television program Spielberg was then producing entitled "Steven Spielberg Presents Amazing Stories," which consisted of episodes based on fantasy and horror stories from the 1940s and

---

2. 551 F. 2d 484 (2d Cir. 1977), cert. denied 431 U.S. 949 (1977).

1950s. Abend made clear to Spielberg that he expected compensation for any use of either the short story or the film. Spielberg informed Abend that he was not interested in remaking the *Rear Window* film.

On the rerelease of *Rear Window*, Abend again sued the movie's producers (Stewart, Hitchcock, and MCA), as well as its distributor, Universal, this time in Federal District Court for the Central District of California instead of the Second Circuit (likely to avoid the effect of the *Rohauer* decision). Abend claimed that the rerelease of the movie infringed his copyright in the short story because the producers' right to use the story during the renewal term had lapsed when Woolrich died before he could register for the renewal term and transfer his renewal rights to the film's producers. Abend also contended that by rereleasing the movie at that time, they were interfering with his right in the copyright renewal, including the right to produce a remake of *Rear Window*. He claimed that, after he approached Steven Spielberg with his proposal, he had sought to contract with the cable television station, Home Box Office (HBO), to produce a television version of the story, but that Universal had informed HBO that neither Abend nor HBO could use the title "Rear Window" for any televised remake of the movie. He also argued that Universal's rerelease of the original movie had interfered with his right to make other derivative works.

Both parties moved for summary judgment and the district court granted Universal's motion, relying on *Rohauer*, as well as on the fair use defense presented by the studio. Abend appealed to the U.S. Court of Appeals for the Ninth Circuit.

In his appeal, Abend argued that, because he had obtained the renewal rights in the short story from the author's successor, Chase, free and clear of any purported assignments of any interest in the copyright, Universal's distribution of the film, *Rear*

Window, without authorization, infringed his renewal copyright. Universal responded that it had the right to continue to exploit *Rear Window* during the twenty-eight-year renewal period because Woolrich had agreed to assign to the original producer the renewal rights in the story. The defendants also relied on *Rohauer*, where the Court of Appeal for the Second Circuit had held that statutory successors to the renewal copyright in a pre-existing work could not "deprive the proprietor of the derivative copyright of a right . . . to use so much of the underlying copy-righted work as already has been embodied in the copyrighted derivative work, as a matter of copyright law."

The Ninth Circuit rejected the reasoning in *Rohauer*, concluding that, even if the preexisting work had been incorporated into the derivative work, use of the preexisting work was infringing unless the owner of the derivative work held a valid grant of rights in the renewal term. Stewart and Hitchcock had received from Woolrich only an expectation that the renewal rights would be assigned, but this never happened. Upon Woolrich's death, his successor, Chase, became "entitled to a renewal and extension of the copyright," which Chase secured. It then chose to assign the existing rights in the copyright to Abend instead of Stewart and Hitchcock.

Universal appealed to the U.S. Supreme Court, which affirmed the Ninth Circuit in a split decision. Justice Sandra Day O'Connor wrote the majority opinion, pointing out that Section 24 of the 1909 Copyright Act (which was in effect at the time Woolrich originally assigned his copyright to De Sylva) and Section 304 of the 1976 Copyright Act (in effect at the time the case was brought)[3] were intended to provide authors a "second bite at the apple," so to speak, allowing them another opportunity to

---

3. 17 U.S.C. §304(c). See Intermission 10, "Derivative Works and Copyright Duration."

obtain compensation for their works. It was, Justice O'Connor pointed out, a means to protect authors as well as their widows and orphans that had been in the Act since 1831, when Congress changed the provisions that had been in the law that had allowed authors to assign their contingent interest in the renewal term at the time of the original copyright assignment.[4] In her opinion, these 1831 provisions created "an entirely new policy, . . . vesting an absolutely new title in the writer and his heirs" at the time of renewal. In this way, Justice O'Connor noted, "Congress attempted to give the author a second chance to control and benefit from his work." Congress also intended, she noted, "to secure to the author's family the opportunity to exploit the work if the author died before he could register for the renewal term."

The Second Circuit, in *Rohauer*, had created an exception, trying to balance the equities. That court believed that "a person who, with the consent of the author, has created . . . a motion picture film" and has contributed something "as great or greater than the [work of] the original author, would have no truly effective way to protect himself against the eventuality of the author's death before the renewal period," since there was no way of telling who would be the surviving widow, children, or next of kin, or the executor until that date arrives. The equities did seem skewed in the case before the Supreme Court. On the one side was Alfred Hitchcock, a legendary film producer, who had taken a relatively unimportant pulp detective story and from it had created a critically acclaimed film, and on the other was neither a widow nor an orphan but the powerful executor, Chase Manhattan Bank, which, instead of honoring the commitments of the deceased, had sold the renewal option to the author's agent, for a pittance.

---

4. Copyright Act of February 3, 1831, ch. XVI, 4 Stat. 436.

Major Hollywood studios filed friend of the court briefs in this case, arguing that upholding the Ninth Circuit's decision would undermine one of the policies of the Copyright Act—the dissemination of creative works—because many fewer works would reach the public. If the Court were to follow this "second opportunity" reasoning, without allowing a *Rohauer* exception for derivative works, the demands of holders of copyrights in the original work, such as Abend,[5] would be so exorbitant that a negotiated accommodation would be impossible.

However, Justice O'Connor was not persuaded. She believed that "an initially high asking price does not preclude bargaining." She assumed that Abend was asking for a share of the proceeds because he wanted to profit from the distribution of the work, not because he wanted to prevent the work from being shown. She pointed out that the Copyright Act already created a balance because the term of a copyright was limited. On the other hand, she noted, "nothing in the copyright statutes would prevent an author from hoarding all of his works during the term of the copyright." A copyright owner can refuse to license the copyright to anyone, and thus prevent any exploitation of the work.

Justice O'Connor concluded that in this case the grant of rights in Woolrich's story had lapsed and therefore the movie producers' rights to use those portions of the story that were incorporated into *Rear Window* had expired. It was up to those owners of the movie's copyright to negotiate a deal with Abend under which the movie could continue to be distributed and exhibited. She also ruled that the rerelease of the movie had infringed on the ability of Abend to market new versions of the story.

---

5. Abend apparently had demanded 50 percent of the future gross proceeds from *Rear Window*.

Justice Stevens, joined by Justice Rehnquist and Justice Scalia, dissented from this opinion. Justice Stevens observed that the Copyright Act confers on an entire derivative work—not just the new material contained in that work—the status of all other works of authorship, that is, new original works, the right to copyright protection. The original work and a derivative work made with the consent of the author of the original work are both given independent copyright protection. Therefore, he concluded, Congress intended the original author to be able to sell the right to make the derivative work that could be distributed during the full period of the derivative work's copyright protection.

As a result of this case, the Copyright Act was amended to provide an option of automatic renewals for works published between 1964 and 1977.[6] Congress also added to the law provisions to allow owners of rights in derivative works to continue to use and to distribute the derivative works even after the termination of the copyright assignment.[7]

But because *Rear Window* and Woolrich's short story were both created before the 1976 Copyright Act, they were unaffected by these legislative changes. As a result of this litigation, on December 12, 1991, Abend entered into a settlement agreement with the defendants, which provided for payment to Abend for past and future uses of the short story, as embodied in the *Rear Window* film, and for the right to continue to distribute the movie, but which also restricted Universal's right to use the works, except as specifically licensed for distribution (that is, without any further right to exploit the movie, such as in a sequel). This

---

6. Under the automatic renewal provisions, renewal vested on either of two dates: when the registration was filed or, if no registration was filed, at the beginning of the renewal term. Copyright Renewal Act of 1992 §304(a)(2)(B).

7. 17 U.S.C. §304(a)(4); see also 17 U.S.C. §203(b)(1).

superseded the original assignment from Woolrich and restricted Universal to a "nonexclusive license" to continue to use the short story as embodied in the existing *Rear Window* film. A May 12, 1992, settlement agreement also gave Universal the right to use excerpts of the short story, film clips from the film, and the title "Rear Window," for display in Universal theme parks.

The agreements explicitly provided that Abend owned the exclusive right to use and exploit the short story, including the right to exclusively market the story for a remake of the film. These agreements also provided that the 1954 film would not be distributed, exhibited, or performed during the three-year period from November 1, 1996 to October 31, 1999, to allow Abend to exploit new film adaptations of the short story.

But this was not the end. For Abend, it was only the beginning. In 1996, Abend again communicated with Steven Spielberg and Universal about a potential license to use the short story for a remake of the *Rear Window* film, starring Christopher Reeve. Reeve had been a popular screen star, best known for his performances as the title character in *Superman* (1978), *Superman II* (1980), and *Superman III* (1983), who had been paralyzed after a horse-riding accident in 1995.[8] Abend thought that he would be perfect for the role of the incapacitated observer in a *Rear Window* movie. However, on November 18, 1996, the attorneys for the Hitchcock Trust wrote to Abend to object to any remake of *Rear Window* by Abend, threatening to enforce the Trust's right to prevent any such remake. Spielberg and Universal elected not to participate in the movie remake that Abend had proposed.

Abend then licensed the story to RHI Entertainment (Hallmark Entertainment) to create a made-for-television movie

---

8. Christopher Reeve died in 2004 at age 52.

entitled *Rear Window*, which was broadcast on ABC Television on November 22, 1998, starring Christopher Reeve and Darryl Hanna. Reeve portrayed Jason Kemp, a paralyzed man living in a high-tech home who witnesses a crime. The film did not generate the enthusiastic response that the original Hitchcock film had.

In 2000, after the expiration of the three-year "stand still" agreement with Abend, Universal distributed a rerelease of the original *Rear Window* film as a Collector's Edition DVD, with new subtitles, interviews, and a rerelease trailer narrated by James Stewart. Royalties were paid to Abend.

By 2008, all of the parties to the original rights assignment—Woolrich, Stewart, and Hitchcock—were dead,[9] as well as Abend,[10] and by all rights the lengthy litigation should have come to an end. Abend had profited well from his initial payment of $650 to Chase Manhattan Bank in 1969. But no. This was not to be. Although Abend was dead, his litigiousness lived on. In 2008, the Abend Revocable Trust sued Universal, Paramount, Dreamworks, and producer Steven Spielberg, in federal district court in New York, for infringing the copyright to the 1942 Woolrich story, claiming that a newly released movie, *Disturbia* (2007), was based on that original story. The suit also alleged that the film infringed on the copyright for the Alfred Hitchcock film, *Rear Window*. This latter claim was thrown out in May 2009.

In *Disturbia*, a troubled teenager, Kale, is confined to his suburban home under house arrest and spends his time spying on his neighbors. He notices strange behavior by one neighbor—named Turner—and, after learning that several women in the area have disappeared, concludes that Turner must be the culprit. He enlists the help of two friends, a girl, Ashley, with whom

---

9. Alfred Hitchcock had died in 1980, and James Stewart died in 1997.
10. Sheldon Abend died in 2003.

he has a romantic relationship, and a buddy, Ronnie. After some more spying, a couple of break-ins into Turner's home, and the near-murder of his own mother, Kale is able to rescue his mother and be released from house arrest. The film ends with Kale and Ashley kissing, while Ronnie videotapes them.

On September 21, 2010, the judge assigned to the case threw out the lawsuit, ruling that "no reasonable trier of fact could find the works substantially similar within the meaning of the copyright law."[11] Even though the district court acknowledged similarities between the Woolrich story and *Disturbia*, the court thought those similarities revolved mainly around the concept or idea—a male protagonist confined to his home spies on neighbors to stave off boredom and in doing so discovers that one of the neighbors is a murderer—and not the expression of that idea. As between the expression of the idea in "It Had to Be Murder" and in *Disturbia*, the court found wide differences in the setting (one a New York City apartment, the other a suburban California neighborhood), the protagonists (one an adult man, the other a teenager), and the murderer (one a married man who kills his wife, the other a serial killer of young single women). And because it is only the expression of an idea that is protected by copyright law, the court concluded that the short story and the Spielberg movies were only similar on a very abstract, conceptual level, such that "no reasonable trier of fact could find the works substantially similar." Therefore, no infringement existed.

That should have been the end of it all, but no. Much like *Jarndyce vs Jarndyce*, at the time of this writing Abend's litigious spirit lives on. The Abend Trust does not give up so easily. In a 68-page complaint filed on October 28, 2010, in California

---

11. The Sheldon Abend Revocable Trust v. Spielberg, 748 F. Supp. 2d 200 (S.D.N.Y. 2010).

Superior Court in Los Angeles, the Trust claimed that Universal breached the 1992 settlement agreement by distributing and advertising *Disturbia*, by not removing elements of the original Woolrich story from *Disturbia*, and by developing a marketing plan for the new film that plays on the similarities between the original *Rear Window* film and *Disturbia*. This time, however, instead of including Steven Spielberg in the suit, the Abend Trust has pulled the Alfred Hitchcock Trust into the litigation, because it was a party to the 1992 settlement agreement that the Abend Trust uses as the basis for this particular court battle. In this case, the Abend Trust has requested unspecified compensatory, exemplary, and punitive damages.[12] The crux of the Abend Trust's suit is that the settlement agreement did not give Universal the right to "further exploit" the ideas in the *Rear Window* story without payment or permission.

Thus, even though the creative spirits—Woolrich, Hitchcock, and Stewart—behind the classic *Rear Window* are long gone, like a bad zombie movie, the Abend Trust holds onto its "rights" and will continue to bring increasingly craven and useless litigation to "protect" them. This is the case even though Sheldon Abend, during his lifetime, never contributed any creative spark to either the original story or the film, but rather purchased rights for a mere $650 through what appears to have been an astute manipulative maneuver on his part while he was acting as agent for Woolrich.

---

12. Thompson Reuters News and Insights, "Debate over Rights to Hitchcock Classic Far From Being in Rear Window," found at http:newsandinsight.thompsonreuters. com/California/legal_materials/Court_filings/2010/11-november/debate_over_rights_ to_hitchcock_classic_far_from_being_in_rear_window/, last accessed August 21, 2011. *See* also website for the Law Offices of Clay M. Townsend, P.A., Current Cases, found at http://www.townsendfirm.com/current-cases.htm, last accessed August 21, 2011. See Complaint and Summons, The Sheldon Abend Revocable Trust v. NBC Universal, Inc., et al, Case No. BC 448409, Superior Court of the County of Los Angeles, filed October 28, 2010, found at http://www.townsendfirm.com/Summons.pdf.

Intermission 11

Derivative Works
and Copyright Duration

Many disputes in the movie industry revolve around
the question of whether or not a film is derived from someone
else's material and if so whether that material is entitled to
copyright protection.

As we have seen, courts are frequently faced with situations
where an idea, a concept, or a treatment, are presented to a
movie producer and then used in a film without recognition or
compensation to the originator. The rule is generally that an
idea or concept is not protected by copyright law in the United
States, although compensation may nevertheless be required
to be paid if there was some sort of contract, either express
or implied, between the originator and the producer. With a
treatment, copyright protection may be available if the treatment
is substantial enough to be considered the *expression* of an
idea and not just an idea. Then the courts will look to see if there
is substantial similarity between that treatment and the film's
screenplay and if the movie's producer or the screenwriter had
access to the treatment before the screenplay was written.

Stewart v. Abend [1] was a case where a derivative work was
created from copyrighted material. Each work had independent
copyright protection, but the derivative work depended on the
ongoing permission from the owner of the original copyright to
use that original work. It is one thing where the original work has
passed into the public domain (when the copyright for the original
work has expired) before the copyright for the derivative work
expires. But it is another story where, as in *Stewart v. Abend*, the
copyright for the original work had to be renewed and the owner
of the original copyright failed to assign the renewal rights in that
original work to the owner of the derivative work. The author of
the derivative work had a valid copyright in the derivative work,
but was powerless to further exploit that work or enjoy any of the
benefits of the copyright without a license to continue to use the

original work. This unfortunate person was at the mercy of the owner of the copyright to the original work and generally, after having paid once for the rights when the derivative work was created, had to settle for more onerous terms in order to continue to exhibit and exploit a work that had already been created. Justice O'Connor justified this result as a means for |an author and his widow and orphans to renegotiate terms to an assignment and to capture some additional benefit from that original copyright. She recognized that the original copyright owner may have had little bargaining power in the assignment negotiations when the potential value of his or her work was unknown.

When looking at the facts of *Stewart v. Abend*, these considerations were, however, lacking and the equities, it seems, ought to have been skewed in the other direction. Woolrich, the original copyright owner, was known in the motion picture industry and appeared to have negotiated fairly sophisticated agreements for his original short stories, leaving, it appears, a considerable estate to Columbia University. And, after his death, Sheldon Abend, who did not contribute anything creative to the original work, was able to negotiate a hard bargain with the owner of the rights to the movie, *Rear Window*, all for an investment of a mere $650.

It seems in retrospect that Justice O'Connor was too blasé in her assessment of the situation in that case in assuming that the parties could come to terms without extortion because Abend would be eager to see the movie, *Rear Window,* continue to be exploited. On the contrary, he did not want to see the classic film exhibited because he intended to produce his own remake, taking advantage of the goodwill from the title of Hitchcock's film to market his own movie. When dealing with a man as litigious as Abend, coming to terms that would be fair to the parties without ongoing disputes proved to be impossible.

Congress recognized the problem and made a series of amendments to the Copyright Act after this case was decided in an effort to rectify the situation. But there is still tension between

Intermission 11 (continued)

the copyright holder and those who would seek to exploit that original work to create new works. Part of the problem arises from the continuous extensions to copyright terms established by the Copyright Act since 1978. Another is the right of termination and recapture that was enacted under the 1978 Copyright Act (which is unique in U.S. intellectual property law).

The 1790 Copyright Act provided for a fourteen-year term for works published with notice, running from registration, which could be extended for another fourteen years, if a renewal was timely filed.[2] In 1831, the initial copyright term was extended to twenty-eight years, but the renewal term remained at fourteen years.[3] Congress also included a new provision in that Act specifying that if the author had died before the end of the initial twenty-eight-year term, the right of copyright renewal passed to his widow or orphans.[4] Section 16 of the 1831 Act expressly enlarged the term of copyright for those authors who had obtained copyrights prior to the enactment of the 1831 Act, so that their copyright terms would equal those for authors of future works.[5]

In 1909, Congress made further revisions to the Copyright Act, maintaining the initial copyright period of twenty-eight years but extending the renewal term to twenty-eight years as well.[6] The 1909 Act provided that, in addition to living authors, the widows, widowers, children, executors, or next of kin of deceased authors could exercise the renewal right.[7] Section 24 of the 1909 Act provided that copyrights already in existence would be extended "such that the entire term shall be equal to that secured by [the] Act, including the renewal period."[8] (It was not until 1912 that motion pictures were accorded copyright protection under U.S. law.)[9]

Meanwhile, in other parts of the world, there is a general consensus that the term of a copyright should be at least a life plus fifty years. This was required by the Berne Convention for the Protection of Literary and Artistic Works, an international copyright treaty that was first adopted in 1886[10] and which the

United States finally joined in 1989.[11] It was not until the Copyright Act of 1976 was enacted that the term of copyright in the United States was brought into line with that in those countries that were members of the Berne Convention.[12] This Act provided for a term of the life of the author plus fifty years for works created or published after January 1, 1978. During the interim period before 1978, there was a dual system for copyrighted works: any work published prior to 1923 was considered to be in the public domain; any works published after 1923 were entitled to a copyright for a limited term. After 1978, federal statutory copyright protection was available for all works fixed in a tangible media, including pre-1978 works that were still protected by copyright at that time.[13] The basic term of a copyright was extended from a total of fifty-six years (including renewal term) to a basic term of the life of the author plus fifty years.

The 1976 Copyright Act added another provision having an impact on assignees and licensees of copyrights. This law enabled authors (and their heirs and executors) to terminate their assignments and to recapture their copyrights within a five-year window, beginning thirty-five years from the date of the initial assignment or license (or if the grant covers the right of publication of the work, the period begins at the end of thirty-five years from the date of publication of the work).[14] This right is not unlike the right established as early as the 1831 Copyright Act that was the subject of *Stewart v. Abend* allowing authors and their widows and orphans to recapture the copyright at the time of renewal. However, under this Act, the right to terminate a copyright assignment specifically does not apply to an authorized derivative work created after the original assignment and before the termination.[15]

In 1998, the Sonny Bono Copyright Term Extension Act[16] extended the terms of all existing copyrights by twenty years, and changed the basic term for new works from the life of the author plus fifty years to the life of the author plus seventy years.[17] In the case of a joint work, the term now lasts for seventy years after the death of the last surviving author.[18] For new anonymous

Intermission 11 (continued)

and pseudonymous works created after January 1, 1978, the term is ninety-five years from the first year of publication or 120 years from the year of creation, whichever expires first.[19] For works created but not published or registered before January 1, 1978, the term lasts for the life of the author plus seventy years, but in no case would it have expired sooner than December 31, 2002.[20] If the work was published before that date, the term would not expire before December 31, 2047.[21] The Act also extended the total term of pre-1978 works that were still in their original or renewal copyright term to a total of ninety-five years from the date that the copyright was originally secured.[22]

As a result of these latest revisions to the Copyright Act, well-known works that would have long ago passed into the public domain, such as Margaret Mitchell's novel, *Gone with the Wind*, and Walt Disney's original animated film cartoons featuring Mickey Mouse, still enjoy copyright protection long after the deaths of their original creators. In the case of *Gone with the Wind*, for example, under prior law, Mitchell's original copyright extended for twenty-eight years from 1936, when the work was first published, until 1964. Mitchell's estate renewed the copyright in 1963 for a renewal term that should have expired in 1992 (twenty-eight years from 1964 to 1992). The 1976 Copyright Act added nineteen years to the renewal term, in other words, extending the copyright for *Gone with the Wind* to 2011. But the Sonny Bono Act added another twenty years to that renewal term, so that the copyright for this novel has now been extended until 2031. The copyright for the short story, "It Had to Be Murder," on which the film, *Rear Window*, was based, was extended by Sonny Bono until 2037, plenty of time for Sheldon Abend's estate to find new reasons to litigate.

---

1. *See* Reel 25, A Never-ending Story—*Stewart v. Abend*, 495 U.S. 207 (1990).

2. Copyright Act of 1790, Act of May 31, 1790, ch. 15, Section 1. The 1790 Act, which sought "the encouragement of learning," provided that the author of a map, chart, or book or his assignee would have a copyright for a term of fourteen years from the date of compliance with certain notice, deposit, and recordation

procedures. The 1790 Act also provided that, if the author survived the initial term, he or his "executors, administrators or assigns" could renew the copyright for a renewal term of fourteen years.

3. Copyright Act of 1831, Act of February 3, 1831, ch. 16, Sections 1 and 2.

4. Copyright Act of 1831, Act of February 3, 1831, ch. 16, Section 2.

5. Copyright Act of 1831, Act of February 3, 1831, ch. 16, Section 16.

6. 1909 Amendments to the Copyright Act, Act of March 4, 1909, ch. 320, 35 Stat. 1075 (1909), Section 23.

7. 1909 Amendments to the Copyright Act, Act of March 4, 1909, Section 23.

8. 1909 Amendments to the Copyright Act, Act of March 4, 1909, Section 24.

9. 1912 Amendments to the Copyright Act, Act of August 24, 1912, Section 5(l) and (m).

10. Berne Convention for the Protection of Literary and Artistic Works, Sept. 9, 1886, revised, Paris, July 24, 1971, 25 U.S.T. 1341 (1988).

11. Berne Convention Implementation Act of 1988, Pub. L. No. 100-568, 102 Stat. 2853, 2857, October 31, 1988.

12. Public Law 94-553, October 19, 1976, 17 U.S.C. §§101 et seq. (1994 & Supp. 2000).

13. 17 U.S.C. §304.

14. 17 U.S.C. §203(a).

15. 17 U.S.C. §203(b)(1).

16. Public Law 105-298, October 27, 1998, 112 Stat. 2827.

17. 17 U.S.C. §302(a).

18. 17 U.S.C. §302(b).

19. 17 U.S.C. §302(c).

20. 17 U.S.C. §303(a).

21. 17 U.S.C. §303(a).

22. 17 U.S.C. §304(a).

The Sculptor

Huston v. La Cinq, Cass. Civ. 1re (28 mai 1991);
Turner Entertainment Co. v. Huston,
CA Versailles, civ. ch., 19 décembre 1994[1]

I wanted to shoot in black and white like a sculptor chooses to work in clay, to pour his work in bronze, to sculpt in marble.[2]

John Huston, speaking of *The Maltese Falcon* (1941)

John Huston was a writer, director, and actor responsible for a number of iconic films during his long career in the film industry. Among his more famous works are *The Maltese Falcon* (1941), *The Treasure of the Sierra Madre* (1948), *Key Largo* (1948), *The African Queen* (1951) and *The Asphalt Jungle* (1950).[3]

He is noted as an innovator in the "film noir" genre, which was an offshoot of the gangster films of the 1930s and 1940s, and inspired by the "hard-boiled detective" fiction "pioneered by" writers such as James M. Cain and Dashiell Hammett.[4] Gangster films generally chronicled the rise of a ruthless mobster to power, followed by his arrest or death. In the late 1940s, these mutated to the "film noir," which is a term applied by French film critics when discussing a number of Hollywood films made

---

1. Translated from the French in Ent. L. Rep., March 1995 at 3.
2. Quoted at http://www.unclaw.com/chin/teaching/iip/turner.pdf.
3. Increasingly unhappy over the House Un-American Activities Committee and "moral rot" in the United States, Huston moved to Galway, Ireland, in 1952, and became an Irish citizen in 1964.
4. Starr, *California*, pp. 281-283.

during and shortly after World War II and released abroad after 1945.[5] "Noir" in French means "black" or "dark," but also can have the connotation of "gloomy" or "shadowy." Film noir refers to the stylistic manner in which these movies were shot as well as to the "bleakness and emotional disconnect" that these films evoked.[6]

One of the original films in this genre is Huston's *The Maltese Falcon*, released in 1941. This movie was based on the Dashiell Hammett novel about a private eye embroiled in a mystery involving shady international characters seeking a stolen statuette supposedly made of gold. It depicts betrayal and cynicism, where the detective-hero, Sam Spade, "asked nothing of anyone and expected even less."[7] Historian Kevin Starr wrote that Humphrey Bogart in this film gave "one of the most riveting performances of his career."[8] While many of these films were crime stories, they often also contained social commentary.

Huston's *The Asphalt Jungle* (1950) is considered a classic in the film noir genre. The movie was produced by Metro-Goldwyn-Mayer (MGM), a division of Loew's Inc., at a time when Huston was under a contract of employment with Loew's. Like *The Maltese Falcon*, this film too is a tale of betrayal and double crosses, where no one can trust anyone else, and there are no heroes.

In the film, a character named Doc (played by Sam Jaffe) has just been released from prison and immediately seeks out accomplices to carry out a heist—a million dollar burglary of a jewelry store—that he had plotted before his release. He recruits a tough guy named Dix (played by Sterling Hayden),

---

5. Thompson & Bordwell, p. 233.
6. Starr, *California*, p. 284.
7. Starr, *California*, p. 283.
8. Starr, *California*, p. 283.

and Gus (played by James Whitmore), a bar owner. The robbery is a success and Doc and Dix take the jewels to a fence, named Emmerich (played by Louis Calhern). Unfortunately, Emmerich claims not to have enough money to pay the burglars outright, hoping that they will leave the jewels behind for him to sell on his own (thus cutting them out). This does not happen and Doc keeps the loot. Even though the heist had gone very well, the aftermath devolves into bad blood among the men, moving from double cross to double cross, with each person acting in his own self-interest, and with the police on the tail of the thieves. In the background are the dark, grimy streets of New York City, as much a character in the film as the robbers.

Creating one of the best and last of the films noirs, Huston intentionally shot the movie in black and white, even though color technologies were available. Although color initially had been used primarily for comedies and musicals, certainly by the early 1950s, more than half of Hollywood films—even serious dramas—were being shot in color.[9]

In the 1970s and 1980s, there was a trend to "colorize" older movies that had originally been filmed in black and white. This was from the start a controversial enterprise. John Huston was one of many directors who assailed this practice, saying "It's not color, it's like pouring 40 tablespoons of sugar water over a roast."[10]

In 1986, film critics Gene Siskel and Roger Ebert devoted a special episode of their television show, "Siskel & Ebert," to address the colorization movement, which they called "Hollywood's New Vandalism."[11] "It's about money," Siskel asserted

---

9. Thompson & Bordwell, pp. 328-29.
10. Thompson & Bordwell, p. 341.
11. Siskel & Ebert & The Movies—Colorization, "Hollywood's New Vandalism" (1986), found at www.youtube.com/watch?v=YpT1DkBOngo.

flatly. He explained that network television would not show classic black-and-white films during prime time unless they could be offered in color. "They lock up people who attack paintings and sculptures in museums, and adding color to black-and-white films, even if it's only the tape shown on TV, . . . is vandalism nonetheless," Ebert added.[12] "What was so wrong about black and white movies in the first place? By filming in black and white, movies can sometimes be more dreamlike and elegant and stylized and mysterious. They can add a whole additional dimension to reality, while color sometimes just supplies additional unnecessary information."[13]

Unfortunately, Huston's work was not immune from the colorization trend. *The Asphalt Jungle* was directed by Huston while he was under contract to Loew's, whose MGM division originally produced and distributed the film. Huston had coauthored the screenplay with Ben Maddow, who also was employed by Loew's as a salaried writer. On May 2, 1950, Loew's registered the copyright for the film. This registration was renewed in 1977. On September 26, 1986, the copyright was transferred to Turner Entertainment Co., by virtue of a merger with MGM that included the transfer of ownership of MGM's movie library and connected rights to Turner.

Turner had a number of black-and-white films that it had acquired in the transaction colorized, including *The Asphalt Jungle*, and it registered a copyright for the colorized version of this movie. When it was broadcast on television in the United States, John Huston was very upset by what he viewed as the

---

12. "Hollywood's New Vandalism," found at www.youtube.com/watch?v=Ch35RK ILGtQ.

13. "Hollywood's New Vandalism," found at www.youtube.com/watch?v=6t91-JBI-Cw+feature=related.

defacement of his work. He called it "cultural butchery."[14] Huston died in 1987.

Turner contracted with a French television network, the Fifth French Television Channel ("La Cinquième Chaîne," familiarly known as "La Cinq") to broadcast the colorized version of *The Asphalt Jungle* in France on June 26, 1988. John Huston's heirs, Angelica, Daniel, and Walter Huston objected to this broadcast, as did Huston's cowriter, Ben Maddow, and a number of French screenwriters', actors', and directors' guilds.[15] The Huston heirs and Maddow sought an injunction from a French court to prevent this broadcast of the colorized version of the film, arguing that it would be a violation of the author's moral right, which was aggravated in their opinion by the fact that John Huston had opposed the colorization of his works during his lifetime.

On June 24, 1988, a judgment was entered in favor of the Huston heirs and Maddow, suspending the broadcast. The court stated that colorization of a black-and-white film constituted an infringement on the moral rights of the authors and their heirs if the colorization was not specifically authorized.[16] The injunction was sustained the next day by the Paris appellate court.[17] Some months later, the same initial court confirmed the injunction, forbidding the broadcast of the colorized version.[18]

---

14. Quoted by Roger Ebert, in "Hollywood's New Vandalism," found at www.youtube.com/watch?v=YpT1DkBOngo.

15. Including the Société des Auteurs et Compositeurs Dramatiques, the Société des Réalisateurs de Films, the Syndicat Français des Artistes interprètes.

16. *Angelica Huston et autres c. Société d'exploitation de la Cinquième Chaîne de Télévision*, Tribunal de Grande Instance de Paris, 24 juin 1988.

17. *Société d'exploitation de la Cinquième Chaîne de Télévision c. Angelica Huston et autres*, Cour d'Appel de Paris, 14 chambre, S.A. référée, 25 juin 1988, published in J.D.I. 4, 1988, p. 1010ff.

18. *Angelica Huston et autres c. Société d'exploitation de la Cinquième Chaîne de Télévision*, Tribunal de Grande Instance de Paris, 23 novembre 1988, published in J.D.I. 4, 1988, p. 1010ff.

In its decision, the court applied French law because the judges believed that moral rights of authors, as part of basic human rights, were of higher importance than contract or copyright law and further that the protection of moral rights of authors did not depend on the laws of the country of origin of the work. The Hustons would not have been able to obtain such a judgment had the court applied U.S. law because "moral rights" of authors would not have been taken into account in a U.S. court.[19] In the United States, because neither the Hustons nor Maddow held any copyright or other property right in *The Asphalt Jungle*, they had no say in how the film would be treated. However, under French law, they were so entitled. This was because, under French law, a creative work is deemed to contain the personality of the author. In other words, in creating *The Asphalt Jungle*, John Huston and Ben Maddow had imbued this film with an original and personal character that transcended the legalistic notion of who held the "rights" to the work. Copyright is a property right whereas the author's "moral right" is an extension of the author himself.

The French court did not accept that any system of law would hold that corporate entities (whether MGM or Turner Entertainment) could be either the author or the director of a film.[20] For this court, corporations were not persons and it was illogical to think, and no one would even try to claim, that *The Asphalt Jungle* was directed by Turner Entertainment or that

---

19. Moral rights of authors are provided for in Article 6bis of the Berne Convention for the Protection of Literary and Artistic Works; See Gilliam v. ABC, 538 F. 2d 14, 24, 26 (2d Cir. 1976), where the court specifically ruled that copyright law did not recognize moral rights of authors.

20. Under U.S. copyright law, although the two men, Huston and Maddow, wrote the screenplay, it was considered a "work made for hire," that is, they were paid to write it and therefore, Loew's, the party that paid them to write it, owned the copyright to it. But they still are credited as the screenwriters and director in the film credits.

this company wrote the film's screenplay.[21] Unlike a property right, a moral right is not transferable, which explains why the author always retains a moral right over a work even after the copyright has been transferred to another party. The court further held that in France, Huston was and would always be considered to be the film's creator, and, through his estate, he was entitled to assert his moral rights. And, it held, because part of Huston's fame was in his unique use of black and white to create an atmosphere in a film that interplayed with its theme and plot, this same atmosphere would be jeopardized by colorization.

Turner Entertainment appealed to the court of appeal in Paris, which reversed the lower court judgment on July 6, 1989, ruling that the author of *The Asphalt Jungle*, under U.S. law, was Turner, as the successor to Loew's, and that because U.S. law should have been applied, neither John Huston's heirs nor Ben Maddow had a moral right to the work. The court further authorized the Cinquième Chaîne to broadcast this colorized version of the film. The judgment did require that a warning notice be provided to television viewers, advising them that they could, if they chose, use the color control device on their television sets out of respect for the memory of John Huston.

In resolving the conflict in this manner, the court weighed in favor of U.S. law, which was the law of the jurisdiction where the film was first exhibited. The court noted that the colorization of the film was an adaptation permitted under U.S. law and that Turner had properly registered its copyright for this version in 1988. Under the "work-made-for-hire" provisions of U.S.

---

21. "Quelque soit le système choisi, la volonté des cocontractants ne saurait masquer le fait que constitue la création, qu'ainsi, nul ne saurait soutenir qu' "Asphalt Jungle" a été réalisé par T.E.C. et que cette entreprise a écrit le scenario de ce film."

Copyright Law, the copyright owner could do what it wanted with the film.[22]

The Huston heirs and Maddow did not give up, but appealed this judgment to the Cour de Cassation in Paris, the highest court in the French judiciary.[23] On May 28, 1991, the Cour de Cassation reversed the Paris appellate court, cancelling every part of its judgment, stating that its ruling violated French law.[24] The court stated unequivocally that "no mark can be leveled against the integrity of a literary or artistic work regardless of the country in which this work was first created. The person who is the author, by the sole fact that he is the creator, enjoys a moral right granted in his favor by French law. These laws are mandatory."

Following French legal procedure, the Cour de Cassation then returned the case to a court of appeal, the "Cour de Remand," this time in Versailles, for retrial. Turner provided the same argument to the court in Versailles as it had in Paris: John Huston's heirs could not claim the status of a foreign author (with a moral right) in France because Turner (by assignment from Loew's) was the sole author of the work under the laws of the country in which *The Asphalt Jungle* was created, the United States. They could not claim that French law protected them with respect to a right that they did not have. Moreover, Turner

22. *Société Turner Entertainment c. Angelica Huston et autres,* Cour d'Appel de Paris, quatrième chambre, S.B., 6 juillet 1989, published in J.D.I. 4, 1989, p. 979-1004.

23. This court does not rule on the merits of a case but solely determines whether the lower courts correctly applied the law based on the facts. See http://www.courde cassation.fr/about_the_court_9256.html. If the court determines that they have not, then the matter is referred back to a Cour d'Appel, generally not the same that previously decided the case and never with the same judges. Herzog, Peter, with the collaboration of Weser, Martha, "Civil Procedure in France," Columbia University School of Law Project on International Procedure, Hans Smit, Director and Editor, Nighoff, The Hague: Netherlands, 1967, p. 158.

24. Section 1.2 of the Law of 64-689 of 8th of July 1964 and Section 6 of the Law of 11th of March 1957.

argued, as the legal author of the work, it had all the rights to introduce a colorized version of the film, which was in effect merely an adaptation of the movie, not a mutilation.

In their response, the Huston heirs asked the court to consider the judgment of the Cour de Cassation, which had held that they had, as John Huston's heirs, a moral right under French law. They noted that the Berne Convention[25] required that the application of moral rights to a cinematographic work be decided according to the law of the country where the protection is claimed, which in this case was France. This was because U.S. law only protects economic rights and not moral rights,[26] and also because there were no reciprocal agreements between the two countries governing the moral rights of authors.

The Cour de Remand in Versailles issued its judgment in December 1995. Although it was true that Turner held a valid copyright to *The Asphalt Jungle*, this court ruled, on the one hand U.S. law focuses exclusively on the protection of economic rights without any reference to the creative act underlying the work, while on the other hand, French law provides that "the author enjoys the right to respect for his name, his status, his work. This right is attached to his person; it is perpetual, inalienable, and inprescribable. And after death, it is accorded to the author's heirs." According to the court, even though the Huston heirs were not entitled to seek protection of a copyright they did not own, John Huston and Ben Maddow, who were indisputably the coauthors of the screenplay, and John Huston, as the director of the film, *The Asphalt Jungle* (having created it), were nevertheless under French law vested with the corresponding

---

25. Article 14bis (2) of the Berne Convention for the Protection of Literary and Artistic Works.

26. Law of 8 juillet 1964. If the United States had had a comparable law in effect providing for the protection of moral rights, that law could have been applied.

moral right, which is immutable. The court therefore disagreed with Turner's contention that, as the undisputed owner of all economic rights to the film, it had the right to adapt the work and to colorize the film without the authors' permission.

The court pointed out that the aesthetic use of black and white in films had earned John Huston his fame. In 1950, when color technology was already widespread and another option was available, John Huston shot *The Asphalt Jungle* in black and white, following a deliberate aesthetic choice, because he considered it best suited to the character of the work. There-fore, the court ruled, the colorization of the film without autho-rization and control by the authors or their heirs amounted to a violation of the creative activity of its makers, even if it may have satisfied the expectations of a certain public for commer-cially obvious reasons. This colorization infringed the moral right of the film's creators. Accordingly, for the damage that the Hustons and Maddow suffered, the court awarded them 400,000 FF (or approximately $100,000).

Moreover, the court ruled that the lower court had been correct in prohibiting La Cinq from showing this modified ver-sion of the film. Because, contrary to the lower court's ruling, La Cinq had broadcast the movie (as authorized by the Paris court of appeal) without waiting for the final judgment of the Cour de Cassation, this broadcast was also a direct and definite violation of the authors' moral right. The court accordingly directed La Cinquième Chaîne to pay the Hustons and Maddow an addition-al 200,000 FF (approximately $50,000) as damages.

Finally, Turner was required to pay the full costs of the appeal.[27]

---

27. Cour d'Appel de Versailles, Arrêt du 19.12.1994, R.G. No. 615/92, published in RIDA avril 1995, no. 164, p. 389, commented by Kérévan, A.

Shipwrecked
The Billy Tyne Story and *A Perfect Storm*

Tyne v. Time Warner Entertainment,
336 F. 2d 1286 (11th Cir. 2003)

> Linda Greenlaw: [warning Billy over the radio]
> Billy? Get outta there! Come about! Let it-
> let it carry you out of there! What the hell
> are you doing? Billy! For Christ sake!
> You're steaming into a bomb! Turn around
> for Christ sake! Billy, can ya hear me?
> You're headed right for the middle of
> the monster! Billy?... [starts crying]
> Linda Greenlaw: ... Oh, my God!
>
> Mary Elizabeth Mastrantonio as Linda Greenlaw,
> in *A Perfect Storm* (2000)

Some movies are entirely fiction—original screenplays invented by a screenwriter or adaptations based on other works of fiction, such as a play or a novel. Other movies—documentaries—are factual, telling a true story through interviews, news clips, and other techniques. Documentaries recount through film an event, such as an election in *Primary* (1960), about the 1960 Wisconsin Primary campaign between John F. Kennedy and Hubert Humphrey for the Democratic Party nomination for President of the United States; the aftermath of a mass murder at a high school in Columbine, Colorado, in Michael Moore's *Bowling for Columbine* (2002), which analyzes America's penchant for gun violence; or an interview with former Secretary of Defense Robert McNamara in Errol Morris's *The Fog of War* (2003), which provided the director with an opportunity to explore lessons learned from the Vietnam War.

There are some movies, however, that exist in between a true work of fiction and a documentary; these are fictionalizations of real events such as the life of Beethoven in *Immortal Beloved* (1994), the story of John Nash, a Nobel prize-winning economist, in *A Beautiful Mind* (2001), or more recently, the founder of Facebook in *The Social Network* (2010). *The Perfect Storm* (2000) was such a movie.

In the fall of 1991, the swordfishing vessel, the "Andrea Gail" left Gloucester, Massachusetts, heading for the fishing grounds in Canada's Grand Banks in the North Atlantic. There were six crew members on board, including the captain, Billy Tyne. Their timing was bad: while they were heading back to Gloucester, several intense weather patterns combined into what meteorologists described as a "perfect storm," with winds that howled past 90 miles per hour and seas that towered to 100 feet, and the Andrea Gail was caught in it.[1] The vessel sank somewhere off the Massachusetts coast, apparently with the whole crew aboard, and its remains were not found. All six crew members— Capt. Billy Tyne, crewmen Bobby Shatford and David Sullivan of Gloucester, Dale Murphy and Michael Moran of Florida, and Alfred Pierre of New York—were presumed to have been killed. The storm and its impact were widely reported in newspapers and on television. Based on these stories, as well as personal

---

1. Jagodzinski, Rob, "The Perfect Storm," *The Gloucester Times*, June 3, 2008, found at http://www.gloucestertimes.com/andreagail/x645305794/The-Perfect-Storm, last accessed October 3, 2011.

interviews with weather reporters and members of the crew's families, in 1997 Sebastian Junger published the best-selling nonfiction account, entitled *The Perfect Storm: A True Story of Men Against the Sea.*

That same year, Warner Bros. purchased the rights to produce a motion picture based on Junger's book. This film, *The Perfect Storm*, was released in 2000. It portrayed the lives and deaths of Billy Tyne (played by George Clooney) and his mate, Dale Murphy (played by John C. Reilly). The movie also depicted brief portrayals of Tyne's and Murphy's children and other family members, including Tyne's ex-wife. Warner Bros. did not seek out the permission of any of these individuals for the portrayal of Tyne, Murphy, or any of them in the film, nor did they receive any compensation from the film's producer.

Unlike Junger's book, the movie did not claim to be a true story but rather a "dramatized" account of the storm and the reactions of the men on board the Andrea Gail during the storm, even though none of them lived to authenticate it. In the film, the crew has come into port, after a poor outing. Tyne announces that he is going back out to try his luck again, even though it is already October and late in the season. Five men agree to join him, including Murphy, played by Reilly, and a young sympathetic crew member, Bobby, played by Mark Wahlberg. While Tyne is portrayed as a competitive and impetuous loner, Murphy is shown as a recently divorced devoted father. At first the men catch little, so they sail further east, past their usual fishing grounds, with Tyne choosing to ignore the storm warnings behind him. Finally, their luck improves and the fish begin to bite. They haul in a good catch but then the ice machine fails. The only way to save the catch is to hurry back to shore. But between the Andrea Gail and Gloucester is the confluence of two powerful weather fronts and a hurricane. Should they head home through the storm of the century? Or should they wait it out and lose the catch?

The crew fatefully underestimates the strength of the storm, despite repeated warnings from other ships. When the Andrea Gail loses her antenna, another fishing boat, captained by Linda Greenlaw (played by Mary Elizabeth Mastrantonio), calls in a "May Day" warning. The Andrea Gail is buffeted by the storm. In the last shot of the boat, the viewer sees two men thrown overboard, and the remaining crew attempting to turn the vessel just as it is hit by an enormous rogue wave. The ship fails to ride the wave and sinks. Back on shore the fearful women wait, but the Andrea Gail will never return to Gloucester.

There is no doubt that the film took liberties in recounting the lives of the crew both during the time at sea and even before they set sail from Gloucester. For example, Clooney's character, Billy Tyne, was depicted as a down-on-his-luck swordboat captain who, like Captain Ahab in *Moby Dick*, was obsessed with the next big catch. He also was portrayed as a man with a volatile temper. In one scene, for example, he is shown berating his men for wanting to return to port in Gloucester. This scene was obviously invented. Warner Bros. took other liberties in depicting the relationships the men had with their families.

Although the movie did not hold itself out as being factually accurate, the following statement appeared in the opening credits: "THIS FILM IS BASED ON A TRUE STORY." However, the closing credits contained a disclaimer stating that the events had been dramatized.

On August 24, 2000, Erica Tyne and Billie Jo Francis Tyne, the two daughters of Billy Tyne, and Dale Murphy, Jr., the son of Dale Murphy, Sr., as well as other members of the Tyne and Murphy families, sued Warner Bros. in federal district court in Florida, under Florida's commercial misappropriation law and common law, for false light invasion of privacy, seeking $10 million in damages.[2]

Florida's statute[3] governing "commercial misappropriation," stated that "no person" was permitted to "use another's name [or] likeness," without "the consent of that individual . . . for commercial advertising purposes." There was an exception in the Florida law that allowed the use of names when the situation was a "newsworthy event" covered by the news media. Arguing that the Florida statute did not apply to the use of Tyne's and Murphy's names or likenesses in *The Perfect Storm*, Warner Bros. moved for summary judgment. On May 9, 2002, the district court ruled in the studio's favor, holding first, that the term "commercial purpose" in Florida's statute was not intended to apply to the use of a person's name or likeness in an expressive medium, such as a novel or a movie, and second, that the film, *The Perfect Storm*, did not constitute a false light invasion of privacy.[4] The Tynes and Murphy appealed to the Court of Appeals for the Eleventh Circuit.

The problem that the Tynes faced in the Eleventh Circuit where their case was decided was a prior Florida state court decision, *Loft v. Fuller*,[5] that seemed to contradict their argument. *Loft* had specifically limited the Florida statute to prevent only the unauthorized use of people's names "to directly promote" a product or service. The *Loft* court had ruled that uses elsewhere, such as in a novel or a movie, were protected by the First Amendment of the U.S. Constitution. The Tynes tried to differentiate their case from *Loft* by pointing out that, in *Loft*, the filmmaker had relied on newspaper accounts of the

---

2. *The Perfect Storm* had grossed over $150 million.
3. Fla. Stat. 540.08.
4. Tyne v. Time Warner Entm't Co., 204 F. Supp. 2d 1338 (M.D. Fla. 2002).
5. 408 So. 2d 619 (Fla. 4th DCA 1981).

events portrayed in the movie in question and that was why the First Amendment applied. Here, they argued, Warner Bros. had depicted events at sea and relationships among crew members and their families that had never been reported in the press and were intentionally fabricated. Because these depictions were "knowingly false," they argued, they should not be protected by the First Amendment.

Because the Tynes questioned a state court's interpretation of a state law, the Eleventh Circuit chose not to issue a ruling on this question but instead referred the parties to the Florida State Supreme Court. This court issued its decision on April 21, 2005,[6] ruling that the district court in *Tyne* had correctly interpreted Florida law: the purpose of the Florida statute was limited to direct promotions or advertising using a person's name, and otherwise the First Amendment protected works of artistic expression, such as movies, plays, books, and songs.[7]

The Eleventh Circuit also tackled the Tynes' right of privacy claim. The two daughters had maintained that the movie portrayed their father, Billy Tyne, in a false light. Even though they admitted that generally children do not inherit a false light privacy claim under Florida law, they contended that the court should recognize their own, individual, "relational" right of privacy. This was premised in the personal invasion of privacy that they had experienced when their father was publicized in a false light. They asserted that the movie "falsely vilified" their father as an "obsessed boat captain" and that this portrayal was "egregiously painful and injurious."

The district court had found the Tynes' argument to be

---

6. Tyne v. Time Warner Entm't Co., 901 So. 2d 802 (Fla. 2005).

7. In a follow-up ruling, the Eleventh Circuit then affirmed the lower court's ruling interpreting the Florida statute, Tyne v. Time Warner Entm't Co., 425 F. 2d 1363 (11th Cir. 2005).

meritless.[8] Also, the children were not entitled to bring such an action on their father's behalf. Such a claim is, the court had held, "strictly personal and may be asserted only by the person who is the subject of the challenged publication." Relatives of a deceased person could not make such a claim "regardless of how close" their own relationship with the dead man. Both of the Tyne daughters argued that there was an exception to this rule when the relative suffers an independent violation of her personal privacy at the same time. Both Erica and Billie-Jo Tyne claimed to have suffered because they were portrayed in the movie—which was the case. But the court believed that, although the girls were depicted in the film, these appearances were of a very minor nature—once in a photograph in the wheelhouse of the Andrea Gail and once attending their father's memorial service. In neither scene did the actresses portraying the girls speak any lines at all. And both scenes were actually factual: Billy Tyne kept his daughters' photograph in the wheelhouse of the boat and the girls did attend their father's memorial service. Therefore, the movie did not portray either girl in a false light. And because there was no independent violation of their *own* privacy rights, they could not maintain a claim for the invasion of their father's privacy.

The appellate court agreed with the district court's analysis on this subject, noting that the only reason courts grant a recovery for a "relational false light claim" is where the relative has been humiliated by the film and where the defendant's conduct toward the dead person is "egregious." In this case, the court could not see that the movie's portrayal of Billy Tyne descended to such a level. And so, despite their many years of litigation, moving from district court to appellate court to state court and

---

8. 204 F. Supp. 2d 1342.

back again to appellate court, the Tynes recovered nothing on their $10 million claim.

The Tyne children suffered three times. Having first lost their father at sea in a disastrous storm, they then had to endure the pain of seeing him portrayed on screen as a man very different from the one they had known. And finally, seeking some sort of redress in court, they had to wait years to hear from justices in a distant court that the insult inflicted on their father was not that significant and that they had no claim for damages against a studio that had not even consulted them before making a movie purporting to show their father's last days. They learned the often hard lesson of tort law: not all wrongs have a remedy; not every pain inflicted will result in a damage award.

The Pirates of the Internet

Metro-Goldwyn-Mayer Studios v. Grokster, Ltd., 545 U.S. 913 (2005)

> **Sean Parker: Well, I founded an Internet company that let folks download and share music for free.**
> **Amy: Kind of like Napster?**
> **Sean Parker: Exactly like Napster.**
> From *The Social Network* (2010)

Just when movie studios had grown comfortable with a technology that they had initially viewed as threatening—video recording and DVDs—something new was invented that posed an even greater threat to their bottom line: the innovative technologies that enabled the sharing of music and videos over the Internet. Using the capabilities of peer-to-peer networks (P2P), those who wanted to watch a movie without going to a theater or renting or buying a DVD were able to simply download the film from the Internet for free and watch it over their computers (or even burn it to a CD or DVD to watch on television).

P2P networks operate by means of computers communicating directly with each other, rather than through a central server. Their advantage over information networks is precisely this absence of a central computer server to manage the exchange of information or files among users. As a result, the high bandwidth communication capacity for a server is not necessary nor is there any need for costly server storage space. Since copies of a file may be available on many users' computers, file requests and retrievals may occur faster than with networks, and because file exchanges do not have to travel through the intermediary of a server, communication can take place between any computers that are connected, without potential disruptions due to server shutdowns. Because of these potential benefits in security, cost, and efficiency, many universities, government agencies, corporations, and libraries, among others, have recognized the value of P2P systems.

However, the primary use of P2P networks in the late 1990s and early 2000s seemed to be for music and video downloads without authorization. Two companies in particular—Grokster and Streamcast—provoked the wrath of the studios, largely because they had a substantial and growing popularity that over time could seriously harm the studios' business model. Both Grokster and Streamcast (through its Morpheus program) distributed free software that allowed computer users to share electronic files through P2P networks.

Grokster's software employed what was known as "Fastrack" technology, while Streamcast distributed the Morpheus software that relied on what was known as Gnutella technology. Users of both Grokster and Morpheus utilized a comparable process: a user would send a file request directly to other computers; search results were sent back to the requesting computers, and the user could then download the desired file from a peer's computer. Neither Grokster nor Streamcast were involved in this process. Neither had servers that could intercept the content of the search results.

A group of copyright holders consisting of movie studios and others, led by Metro-Goldwyn-Mayer (MGM), filed suit against Grokster and Streamcast in federal court in the Central District of California, requesting that the court order the two companies to stop distributing their free software, and seeking damages for the companies' users' copyright infringement, arguing that the two file-sharing businesses knowingly and intentionally distributed their software in order to enable users to infringe copyrighted works in violation of the Copyright Act.

While acknowledging that the users had directly infringed the studios' copyrights, the district court granted summary judgment in favor of the two software distributors,[1] based on the U.S. Supreme Court's decision in *Sony v. Universal City Studios, Inc.*[2] (the "Betamax decision"). The district court ruling was affirmed by the Ninth Circuit Court of Appeals[3] because, under the Betamax decision, P2P software had legitimate and legal uses. Under this ruling, the distribution of a commercial product capable of substantial noninfringing uses could not give rise to contributory liability for infringement unless the distributor actually knew of specific instances of infringement and failed to act to stop the infringing practices. The Ninth Circuit also noted that the software distributors did not materially contribute to their users' infringement because the users themselves searched for, retrieved, and stored the files of copyrighted materials, without any involvement by the distributors, other than their initial provision of the software. And the Ninth Circuit held that the distributors could not be vicariously liable—another theory put forth by MGM—because they did not monitor or control the software's use, had no right or ability to supervise the use, and had no duty to police the users' activities.

---

1. 259 F. Supp. 2d 1029 (C.D. Cal. 2003).
2. 464 U.S. 417 (1984); *See* Reel 25, The Transformers.
3. 380 F. 3d 1154 (9th Cir. 2004).

MGM appealed to the U.S. Supreme Court. This was a closely watched case, aligning computer and Internet technology companies and trade associations on one side and the recording industry, the Motion Picture Association of America, and movie studios on the other.

Justice Souter wrote the majority opinion. From the first, he acknowledged the overwhelming evidence of copyright infringement presented by MGM—that nearly 90 percent of the files available for download on Grokster's system were copyrighted works, and that billions of files were shared each month. Given this, "the probable scope of copyright infringement," he concluded, was "staggering." Grokster and Streamcast actually did not deny that users of their software employed it mainly to download copyrighted files. MGM had notified the companies that eight million copyrighted files could be obtained using the companies' software.

Justice Souter also noted that neither Grokster nor Streamcast were "merely passive recipients of information about infringing uses." He found the record to be "replete with evidence" that, from the moment Grokster and Streamcast began to distribute their free software, each one clearly voiced the objective that recipients use it to download copyrighted works, and each took "active steps to encourage infringement." Justice Souter noted that after Napster was sued for facilitation of copyright infringement, Streamcast actively pursued Napster users, giving away a software program called "Open Nap" to distribute copies of the Morpheus software and to encourage users to adopt it. Grokster took similar steps. Grokster also sent users a newsletter promoting its ability to provide particular, popular, copyrighted materials.

Finally, Justice Souter observed that neither Grokster nor Streamcast received any revenue from users—they gave their software away free of charge. The source of income for both companies was advertising, and the price to advertisers depended on the number of Grokster or Morpheus users who utilized the program. He pointed out, "while there is doubtless some demand for free Shakespeare, the evidence [showed] that substantive volume is a function of free access to copyrighted work." He admitted that there had to be a balance between protection for creative pursuits through copyright and promotion of technological innovation, by limiting copyright infringement liability. "The more artistic protection is favored," he said, "the more technological innovation may be discouraged." On the one hand, there is the fear "that digital distribution of copyrighted material threatens copyright holders as never before, copying is easy and many people (especially the young) use file-sharing software to download copyrighted works." He worried that "the ease of copying songs or movies using software like Grokster's or Napster's is fostering disdain for copyright protection." But these fears are "offset by the different concern that imposing liability, not only on infringers but on distributors of software based on its potential for unlawful use, could limit further development of beneficial technologies."

In this case, the Court saw the balance as needing to provide greater protection for copyright holders. However, while all members of the Court agreed that Grokster could be liable for contributory infringement because it intentionally induced or encouraged the users of its software to infringe on copyrighted works, they disagreed on whether this case was different from the *Sony* case.

Not that many years before, in *Sony*, the studios had claimed that Sony was contibutorily liable for infringement that occurred when VCR owners taped copyrighted programs because the company supplied the equipment that was used to infringe and knew that infringement would occur. However, to the studios' dismay, because a principal use of the VCR was "time-shifting"—taping a program for later viewing at a more convenient time—and because this was considered to be a non-infringing use, Sony was not held liable for the infringement that could take place by users of its equipment. In the Betamax decision, the Court held that because the VCR was "capable of commercially significant non-infringing uses," the manufacturer could not be faulted simply because the machine could also be used to infringe.

MGM hoped that, in *Grokster*, the Court would overturn or at least substantially limit *Sony*, by eliminating the "safe harbor" for technologies capable of substantial noninfringing uses.[4] But the majority of Justices did not see the need to go so far in *Grokster*. Because Grokster's and Streamcast's behaviors actively induced the infringement by the users of their software, they could be found to be liable without revisiting the holding of *Sony*. Justice Souter pointed out, for example, that Streamcast's advertising was aimed at Napster users while the *Napster* case was in the courts. He also noted that neither company attempted to develop filtering tools or other mechanisms that would diminish the users' infringing activities. He believed that "this evidence underscored Grokster's and Streamcast's intentional facilitation of their users' infringement." And finally, the companies' advertising pricing model—where the more the software was used, the more ads went out and the greater the advertising revenue—buttressed the evidence that the companies were actively encouraging the infringing activities. Although, as the Court noted, "this evidence alone would not justify an inference

---

4. *See* Samuelson, Pamela, "Three Reactions to MGM v. Grokster," 13 Mich. Tele-comm. Tech. L. Rev. ____ (2006), available at http://www.mttlr.org/volthirteen/samuelson.pdf.

of unlawful intent, when viewed in the context of the entire record, its import is clear."

Based on this theory of active inducement, the case was sent back to the district court for a trial based on the principles set out in the decision. On November 7, 2005, as part of a settlement with MGM, Grokster announced that it would no longer offer its P2P file-sharing service.[5] Settlement talks with Streamcast broke down and in further court proceedings, the district court ruled against Streamcast, granting MGM's motion for summary judgment on September 27, 2006, finding instances of "massive" copyright infringement on its P2P network and "overwhelming evidence of unlawful intent."[6] On October 16, 2007, the court issued a permanent injunction, requiring Streamcast to use filtering technologies while "preserving its noninfringing uses as feasible."[7]

Even though MGM won this case, in many respects, the studios lost the larger battle. Even the decision was not what they had sought. They believed that the Supreme Court would be so shocked by the extent of the unauthorized file-sharing activity that the Justices would revisit *Sony* and perhaps even strike down the protection that this decision afforded to technologies with substantial noninfringing uses.[8] But this was not to be. In fact, the studios were left in pretty much the same position after *Grokster* in their ability to challenge innovative technologies as they had been before.

5. Raysman, Richard and Brown, Peter, "File Sharing in the Post-Grokster World," THE NEW YORK LAW JOURNAL, Vol. 236, No. 70, Wednesday, October 11, 2006, found at http://www.thelenreid.com/resources/documents/10/106-File -Sharing.pdf.

6. Metro-Goldwyn-Mayer Studios v. Grokster, Ltd., 454 F. Supp. 2d 966, 971 (C.D. Cal 2006).

7. Metro-Goldwyn-Mayer Studios v. Grokster, Ltd., 518 F. Supp. 2d 1197 (C.D. Cal 2007).

8. *See* Reply Brief for Motion Picture and Recording Company Petitioners, Metro-Goldwyn-Mayer Studios v. Grokster, Ltd., No. 04-480 available at http://www.eff.org/IP/P2P/MGM_v_Grokster.

In a sense, in this area, the studios seem to be playing a game of "whack-a-mole." They were able to shut down Grokster and Streamcast, but other technologies have since replaced the software of these two companies—technologies that have proved to be more useful and less capable of detection than the earlier forms of P2P sharing. The most recent of these is "bittorrent" sharing, which debuted in 2001, but whose popularity took off in 2005, after the *Grokster* decision. Bittorrent sharing is a form of P2P sharing technology that is even more hated by the studios than Grokster and Morpheus were. "Bittorrents" (also known as "torrents") work by downloading small bits of files from many different Web sources at the same time, so that no single file can be traced to a single computer. Bittorrent networking may be one of the most popular activities on the Internet at the present time, that is, until it is replaced, as it is sure to be, by a new and even more disruptive technology. It is fairly safe to state that the motion picture industry will have its hands full for years to come as studios confront the new technologies that will be developed and that will most certainly disrupt their economic model.

The structure of the movie business is changing and, much as movie studios might try to fight these developments, it will continue to do so. The studios can become participants in innovation trends—as they have done when they have licensed films to services such as Netflix to stream into homes—even though this has alienated theater owners,[9] or they can be left behind.

---

9. Cieply, Michael, "Scuffle Over On-Demand Movies Portends Battles to Come," *The New York Times,* April 24, 2011, found at http://nytimes.com/2011/04/25/business/media/25vod.html?_r=1&ref=motionpictureassociationofamerica, last accessed July 9, 2011.

Intermission 12

Copyright Protection, Movie Piracy, and the Internet

Since the early days of the cinema, tension has existed between enforcement of copyright and protection of First Amendment rights, and between affording copyright holders strong protection for their work while limiting copyright in order to encourage innovation and creativity. Thus, Thomas Edison and Biograph battled over whether Edison had engaged in copyright infringement when he would "rip off" the plots of competitors' films and use them to stage his own productions.[1] Before the Copyright Law afforded protection specifically to motion pictures, the courts had to consider whether a movie was a dramatization of a work of fiction, requiring the film's producer to obtain a license from the holder of the book's copyright, or a fair use of that work.[2]

Early theft in the silent film era was practiced more by competitors in the industry than by the general public. And movie exhibitors were not always honest in their dealings with movie distributors. It was not unheard of for an exhibitor who had rented a movie for a certain number of days for a fixed fee to hold on to the film for a few days more in order to profit 100 percent from the additional days' showings. This was known as "bicycling."[3] There was no Federal Express at the time so it was harder to know what day a film had been sent back. And illegal screenings were not uncommon. The owner of several theaters might screen a movie rented for one theater and then show it surreptitiously in other theaters that he owned, or the film rented to one owner might be shared among several theater owners.[4] Movie producers would send spies into various regions to check on the integrity of their licensees. And, in a more obvious case of piracy, sometimes copies of the film would be stolen while the reels were in transport. These types of behaviors occur today— only in cyberspace.

Intermission 12 (continued)

What is one person's theft is another's fair use. The past several decades have seen a collision among the various competing interests involving copyright and both Congress and the courts have faced significant challenges in defining the scope of copyright protection. This is all in line with furthering the purpose of the Copyright Law, which is not so much to protect the interests of the creators per se as it is "to promote the Progress of Science and the Useful Arts,"[5] that is, to further creativity and knowledge. Sometimes it is feared that too much control is provided by current law to copyright holders, thus strangling the creative process.[6] At other times, copyright holders fear a culture that fosters a blatant disregard for their interests. In a recent *New York Times* article on the subject, an artist describes a younger generation that has grown up with the Internet as follows: "For the generation that I spend my days with, there's not even any ideological baggage that comes along with appropriation anymore."[7]

Because the purpose of copyright is not so much to protect the interests of authors and creators as it is to promote knowledge, their monopoly is limited when it conflicts with an overriding public interest, such as free speech rights or the encouragement of creative or intellectual pursuits, or technological innovation. Based on this understanding that there are certain "fair uses" of a copyrighted work that are beneficial to society, but without clear definition, Congress codified this exception to the law in 1976.[8] The purpose behind this legislation was to allow a limited use of copyrighted material without prior permission from the copyright owner and to provide "some guidance to users in determining when the principles of the doctrine apply."[9]

Accordingly, a balancing test consisting of four factors listed in section 107 of the Copyright statute is used to determine whether a particular use can be justified as a "fair use." These are 1) the purpose and character of the use, including whether such use is of a commercial nature or is for nonprofit educational purposes, 2) the nature of the copyrighted work, 3) the amount and substantiality of the portion used in relation to the copyrighted work as a whole, and 4) the effect of the use upon the potential market for or value of the copyrighted work. As a general rule, courts are more likely to find that a use is fair where it is for noncommercial purposes, the copied work is factual rather than creative, the amount taken is small or insignificant in proportion to the overall work, and the new work is transformative and not a mere copy or substitute for the copyrighted work.

Consideration is given to all four of the listed factors, although they may be given different weight depending on the circumstances. For example, in a recent case[10] analyzing whether the use of a clip from John Lennon's song, "Imagine," in a documentary film exploring the concept of intelligent design[11] was a fair use, the District Court for the Southern District of New York was most influenced by the fact that the use in question was transformative rather than a mere copy. "The more transformative the new work," the court stated, "the less will be the significance of the other factors, like commercialism, that may weigh against a finding of fair use."

Similarly, fair use is more readily found if the work for which the exception is claimed is factual, such as a scholarly or a scientific work, rather than a more creative work such as a novel or a photograph. "Courts are more willing to find a secondary use fair when it produces a value that benefits the broader public interest," the *Lennon* court noted. But the fact that the new work is creative does not necessarily weigh against a finding of fair use, depending on how the other factors balance out. As the *Lennon* court pointed out, the filmmakers in that case had a stronger argument in favor of fair use where they had only used fifteen seconds of a three-minute song, than if they had appropriated, for example, the entire piece, especially where the excerpt in question constituted a mere .27 percent of the film's one hour, thirty-nine-minute running time. It is logical that the more of the original taken, both in amount and substantiality, the greater the negative impact on the market

Intermission 12 (continued)

for the copyrighted work (which is the fourth factor to be considered).

The court did not agree with the plaintiffs—Yoko Ono Lennon and John Lennon's sons, Julian Lennon and Sean Ono Lennon—that the use of the excerpt from "Imagine" would harm the marketplace for licensing the song. Again, because of the transformative nature of the use in the film, the court could not see how inserting this short clip from the song into a documentary with a subject totally unrelated to commercialization of John Lennon's music would "usurp the market for licensing the song for traditional uses." The holding in the Lennon case had a strong and almost immediate impact on the documentary film industry in particular. Filmmakers, often with very tight budgets, suddenly felt liberated by this decision to use excerpts from copyrighted works in their movies, as they were freed from the often insurmountable burden of paying licensing fees to multiple parties. And, with greater judicial definition around the four "fair use" factors specifically as they related to a documentary film, distributors and financiers have become more willing to finance and distribute documentaries that lack license agreements, relying on legal opinions that the uses of excerpts from copyrighted works are fair uses bearing minimal risk of financially crippling infringement lawsuits. One commentator has noted that since 2008, when the Lennon case was decided, the number of documentary films screened at the Sundance Film Festival has grown exponentially.[12]

This is not to say that the law surrounding fair use is settled. Although for the past decade or so courts, much as in Lennon, have centered their determination on the transformative nature of the derivative work, at least one court recently rejected that argument in finding that Richard Prince, an artist who had used photos of Rastafarians by Patrick Cariou in a series of collages, could not rely on fair use to justify his infringement of the photographer's copyright.[13] Even though the works by Prince were transformative, the judge in the case found that they were not sufficiently so, particularly when this factor was weighed against the fact that Prince had taken a large amount of Cariou's work in order to produce his own. In issuing a summary judgment against Prince, she found that in a number of his paintings Prince had appropriated entire photos, and in the majority of his paintings he had appropriated the central figures depicted in Cariou's portraits. Consequently, the Court held that this use usurped the commercial market for Cariou's photos.[14]

A *New York Times* article discussing the decision and its impact on the art and media world noted that in some respects this and other fair use cases were perhaps irrelevant in the larger scheme of things, given the impact of the Internet over the past two decades. "If the case has had any effect so far," the author concludes, "it has been to drag into the public arena a fundamental truth hovering somewhere just outside the legal debate: that today's flow of creative expression, riding a tide of billions of instantly accessible digital images and clips, is rapidly becoming so free and recycling so reflexive that it is hard to imagine it being slowed, much less stanched, whatever happens in court."[15]

Piracy in the movie industry is not new—only the technologies used to achieve it. When Jack Valenti was head of the Motion Picture Association of America (MPAA), he appeared on the "60 Minutes" program on CBS Television, where he told Harry Reasoner that film piracy was "a cancer in the belly of the film business."[16] This was at the time that the VCR was introduced and the movie industry predicted that a calamity was just around the corner, once television viewers started building their movie libraries by taping films off television. The Supreme Court did not agree with this dire prediction in the landmark case in favor of this new technology.[17] In fact, at least one Justice believed that recording movies for home use was a "fair use," even though this was not at all transformative and entire copyrighted works were copied. Justice Blackmun, writing for the minority, disagreed, as he failed to understand how home movie viewing advanced the "Useful Arts." Of course, the disaster predicted by the studios did not transpire. Nor did a similar calamity occur when DVD

Intermission 12 (continued)

technology was introduced. In fact, the movie industry made very nice profits through the sale of films in DVD format. But what Valenti did not foresee was the even bigger problem for the industry— movie downloads over the Internet by digital pirates.

It is true that when the VCR was introduced, it did not take long for "bootleg" copies of tapes to be sold in flea markets and other cut-rate locales. These were later replaced by bootleg DVDs when the technology changed. Certain countries obtained a reputation for egregious levels of piracy, notably some Southern Mediterranean countries, such as Italy, as well as China.[18] With the advent of the Internet, the bootlegging world changed dramatically, to the increasing dismay of the movie industry. Since the 1990s, movie pirates have been "ripping" movies— that is, using camcorders to record movies as they are shown in theaters. Early results were of very poor quality. The sound initially was recorded by means of the camera's microphone, which would capture in the recording the various noises made by the audiences. This "problem" was rectified by the use of separate microphones at other showings and using the best of each. Once the copy was made, it was uploaded to the Internet and shared with millions of users. Downloaders, often college students and computer geeks, but also stay-at-home moms and other "law-abiding" people, worldwide, initially used software such as Grokster or Morpheus, but after the 2005 Supreme Court *Grokster* decision,[19] bittorrent sharing has become wildly popular, through Internet sites such as BitTorrent, CinemaTorrents, Torrentzap and the like.[20]

The movie industry has not sat back idly, but has moved on several fronts. In May 2011, the MPAA pushed for legislation that would allow American authorities to seek court orders directing domestic Internet providers, search engines, and others to stop doing business with foreign-owned sites that trade in pirated material. It would give greater power to copyright owners to sue pirates in federal court, using streamlined procedures to eliminate sites that have reappeared with different domain names or new owners after a violation.[21] The introduction of this legislation resulted in intense lobbying by the motion picture industry on the one hand and Internet service providers, search engines, on-line video services (such as YouTube), and Internet freedom advocates on the other. Due to intense lobbying and public awareness campaigns by new media activists in early 2012, action on the legislation was postponed until a compromise between the competing interests could be found.[22]

On another front, several movie producers have filed lawsuits in federal courts against bittorrent users who have allegedly downloaded movies copyrighted by these producers. The companies first seek out films on bittorrent sites and capture the IP addresses of the peers who are downloading or uploading pieces of the files. They identify the Internet service provider for each IP address from a public database and then generate a spreadsheet listing the IP address, the name of the service provider, and the date and time of the download. This spreadsheet is then saved as a pdf file and attached to a subpoena request filed with the court, to obtain from each service provider, anywhere in the United States, the name and address of the customer attached to each IP address. If the judge grants the subpoena request, then, armed with these names and addresses, the producers send out settlement demands to each of these alleged infringers. This is comparable to a much criticized tactic employed by the music recording industry a number of years ago, but this more recent effort is on a much broader scale.

Questions arise whether a federal judge in a particular circuit who issues such a subpoena has jurisdiction over an Internet service provider who is not doing business in that circuit where the judge is sitting, and further whether the judge would have jurisdiction over a customer of a service provider who may live hundreds of miles away. But apparently the gambit has proved successful for the studios that have tried it, for many customers have quietly paid settlement demands in the amount of thousands of dollars rather than risk the

Intermission 12 (continued)

expense of defending in a faraway court and a fine that could amount to hundreds of thousands of dollars.

The industry hopes that bittorrent users in the United States will stop the illegal downloads. However, the tactics the studios are using so far—legislative and legal action—may not be the most effective in stopping the activities of on-line users and could, in fact, be counterproductive. Because many of the films that have been downloaded using bittorrent technology have poor quality, it would seem that those who could afford the price of a DVD or Blue Ray or a video streaming service would not choose the poor quality of video downloads. It may be that the better strategy for the studios would be to concentrate on developing a business model that provides a satisfactory movie viewing experience (such as through streaming services) for their customers—including those who in the past watched movies in theaters or who bought DVDs—at a reasonable and fair price. Going after people who are engaged in illegal downloading activities—frequently students without the extra money to invest in a movie library at that time but who are enthusiastic about film, or others (such as busy parents) who cannot afford to go out to the movies—seems counterproductive. Not only does it distract from the development of new technologies and films that satisfy the consumer, which should be the studios' foremost concern. but it creates bad publicity for the industry while alienating young people who are the industry's best hope for future paying customers and who, once alienated, will simply turn to the newest technology that allows them to circumvent the industry's efforts. This is the reality of a dynamic digital world. The movie industry can try to coerce those who occupy it into accepting its model, or more likely, the industry will have to develop new commercial models that better exploit the changing technologies and ensure fair compensation for creators. Tightening the grips of copyright protection without acknowledging and accommodating this new reality runs the real risk of creating, as Justice Souter predicted in the *Grokster* case, a culture of disrespect for copyright, and of undermining creative activity.

1. American Mutoscope & Biograph Co. v. Edison Mfg Co., 137 Fed. 262 (D.N.J. 1905). *See* Reel 2, Trading Places—Edison and the Nascent Copyright Protection for Film.

2. Harper Brothers v. Kalem Company, 169 Fed. 61 (2d Cir. 1909); *aff'd* Kalem Company v. Harper Brothers, 222 U.S. 55 (1911). *See* Reel 3, The Great Race—The "Ben Hur" Case.

3. Broderick, Suzanne, Book Review, Segrave, Jerry, *Piracy in the Motion Picture Industry*, McFarland, 2003, Project Muse, Film & History: An Interdisciplinary Journal of Film and Television Studies, Vol. 34.1 (2004) pp. 87, found at http://muse.jhu.edu/journals/film/Summary/v034/34/broderick.html.

4. Broderick, Book Review.

5. U.S. Constitution, Article 1, Section 8.

6. Nocera, Joe, "A Tight Grip Can Choke Creativity," *The New York Times*, February 9, 2008, found at http://www.nytimes.com/2008/02/09/business/09nocera.html?pagewanted=all, last accessed December 28, 2011.

7. Stephen Frailey, an artist who runs the undergraduate photography program at the School of Visual Arts in Manhattan, quoted in Kennedy, Randy, "Apropos Appropriation," *The New York Times*, December 28, 2011, found at http://www.nytimes.com/2012/01/01/arts/design/richard-prince-lawsuit-focuses-on-limits-of-appropriation.html?pagewanted=1&_r=1&hp, last accessed December 28, 2011.

8. Section 107, 17 U.S.C. §107. See Electronic Frontier Foundation, Fair Use Frequently Asked Questions (and Answers), http://w2.eff.org/IP/eff_fair_use_faq.php, last accessed December 28, 2011.

9. HR Rep. No. 94-1476, at 65-66 (1975), reprinted in 1976 U.S.C.C.A.N. 5659, 5678-79.

10. Lennon v. Premise Media Corp., 556 F. Supp. 2d 310 (S.D.N.Y. 2008).

11. The movie—*Expelled: No Intelligence Allowed* (2008)—narrated by Ben Stein, consists of Stein's interviews with proponents of intelligent design and those arguing in favor of Darwin and evolution.

12. Donaldson, Michael C., "Fair Use: What a Difference a Decade Makes," Journal of the Copyright Society of the U.S.A., Vol. 57, No. 3, Spring 2010, p. 331.

13. Cariou v. Prince, 784 F. Supp. 2d 337 (S.D.N.Y. 2011). The case is on appeal to the U.S. Court of Appeals for the Second Circuit. Prince v. Cariou, Case No. 11-1197-CV, filed October 26, 2011. *See* Kennedy, Randy, "Court Allows Richard Prince to Appeal Copyright Decision," *The New York Times*, September 15, 2011, found at http://artsbeat.blogs.nytimes.com/2011/09/15/court-allows-richard-prince-to-appeal-copyright-decision/, last accessed December 28, 2011.

14. *See* "Richard Prince Retains BSF for Appeal in Closely Watched Copyright Suit," Boies, Schiller & Flexner, LLP In the News, found at http://www.bsfllp.com/news/in_the_news/000152. *See also* Bates, Stephen, "Richard Prince ordered to destroy lucrative artwork in copyright breach," *The Guardian*, March 23, 2011, found at http://www.guardian.co.uk/world/2011/mar/23/richard-prince-artwork-copyright-breach, last accessed December 28, 2011.

Intermission 12 (continued)

15. Kennedy, Randy, "Apropos Appropriation," *The New York Times*, December 28, 2011, found at http://www.nytimes.com/2012/01/01/arts/design/richard-prince-lawsuit-focuses-on-limits-of-appropriation.html?pagewanted=1&_r=1&hp, last accessed December 28, 2011.

16. Quoted in Broderick, Book Review.

17. Sony Corporation of America v. Universal City Studios, Inc., 464 U.S. 417 (1984). *See* Reel 20, The Transformers.

18. Broderick, Book Review.

19. Metro-Goldwyn-Mayer Studios v. Grokster, Ltd., 545 U.S. 913 (2005). *See* Reel 28, The Pirates of the Internet.

20. *See* http://netforbeginners.about.com/od/peersharing/a/torrent_search.htm.

21. SB 968, Protect IP Act (Preventing Real Online Threats to Economic Creativity and Theft of Intellectual Property Act of 2011), introduced May 12, 2011, by Senator Patrick Leahy of Vermont. This law was aimed at disrupting the business model of "rogue" websites, especially those registered outside the United States, which are "dedicated to infringing activities."

22. *See* Weisman, Jonathan, "After an Online Firestorm, Congress Shelves Antipiracy Bills," The New York Times, January 20, 2012, found at www.nytimes.com/2012/01/21/technology/Senate-postpones-piracy-vote.html, last accessed March 25, 2012.

And Justice for All

Polanski v. Superior Court,
180 Cal. App. 4th 507 (2d Dist. 2009)

> **Evelyn Mulwray: What were you doing there? [In Chinatown]**
> **Jake Gittes: Working for the District Attorney.**
> **Evelyn Mulwray: Doing what?**
> **Jake Gittes: As little as possible.**
> **Evelyn Mulwray: The District Attorney gives his men advice like that?**
> **Jake Gittes: They do in Chinatown.**
>
> From *Chinatown* (1974), directed by Roman Polanski

This is a case that could have been the plot of a Roman Polanski movie. Polanski has been acclaimed as one of the most innovative and brilliant film directors of his time. He also has been vilified as a child molester who fled the United States to escape punishment for his crime. As in a Polanski film, the truth, if there is a "truth" in all this, is not so evident or clear-cut.

Roman Polanski was born in Paris in 1933. His parents, Polish émigrés, returned to Poland just two years before Hitler's invasion of Poland, starting World War II. After the invasion, his parents were taken to concentration camps. Young Roman escaped the Warsaw ghetto and spent the war years wandering the Polish countryside, sheltering with Catholic families. In 1945, he reunited with his father (his mother had died in the concentration camp) and went to technical school, changing later to the Polish National Film School in Łódź in 1950.[1] He appeared in several short films before taking up directing, debuting with the critically-acclaimed *Knife in the Water* (1962). This film—the story of a quarrelling, unhappily married couple, who take a young hitchhiker along on a sailing trip—illustrates early on the moral ambiguity and uncertainty that are predominant in Polanski's films, whether *Rosemary's Baby* (1968), *Tess* (1979), or *Chinatown* (1974). This latter film, the story of fraud and corruption in Los Angeles, could be a parable for Polanski's own life, particularly those fateful years after his arrival in Hollywood in 1968.

At the time, he was a very successful and sought-after filmmaker, having earned box office success as well as critical acclaim with *Rosemary's Baby*. He was newly married to actress Sharon Tate and the couple was expecting their first child. But then everything fell apart for Polanski. In 1969, while he was away in Europe, his wife and several friends were brutally murdered during a home break-in by the infamous cultist Charles Manson and his gang.

Although stricken, Polanski returned to film directing almost immediately, making the award-winning *Chinatown* in 1974, starring Jack Nicholson and Faye Dunaway, for which he received a Best Director Academy Award nomination. He was rebuilding his life when he was arrested on charges that he had plied a thirteen-year-old girl with champagne and part of a Quaalude during a modeling shoot in 1977, and raped her. The child's mother had left her alone with Polanski in a Hollywood hills home during the photo shoot. He was initially indicted on six felony counts, including rape by use of drugs, child molesta-

---

1. Polanski's biography is found at http://www.imdb.com/name/nm000591.bio.

tion, and sodomy. Fearing the negative publicity of a high-profile trial, at the request of the child's family, the Los Angeles district attorney's office agreed to a plea bargain with Polanski and he pleaded guilty to a lesser charge of unlawful sexual intercourse. The remaining charges were dropped. The judge in the case, Judge Rittenband, sent Polanski to prison for a ninety-day psychiatric evaluation. But Polanski was released in forty-five days and then fled the country for France before sentencing, after the judge reportedly told the lawyers that he planned to send Polanski back to prison. Polanski has remained a fugitive since 1978.

When the Polanski case came up before the California Court of Appeal in 2009, the court stated that it "surely must be one of the longest running sagas in California criminal justice history." Polanski had asked the Superior Court in Los Angeles County to dismiss the criminal prosecution against him that had been pending since 1977. However, the trial court refused to consider Polanski's request until he returned to the United States and made a personal appearance in court. Polanski refused to do so.

Why Polanski fled and why he refused to return in 2009 is a "saga" as the appellate court described it that contains all the uncertainty, the ambiguity, and sense of futility and corruption that Polanski would have captured in a film, had it not been the saga of his own life. The facts are contained in various court documents, including declarations provided in 1978, 2008, and 2009, by Polanski's lawyer, Douglas Dalton, and the deputy district attorney who had prosecuted Polanski in 1977, Roger Gunson. They are amplified by interviews among the various parties, including Polanski, Dalton, Gunson, and the victim, Samantha Geimer, now an adult, and her attorney, Lawrence Silver, that were edited into a documentary film, *Roman Polanski: Wanted and Desired*, directed by Marina Zenovich, which aired on HBO in 2008. As seen in even the best light, it is a sordid tale involving a publicity-hungry judge, a biased district attorney, and allegations of corruption and misdealing. In other words, it is the Los Angeles portrayed in Polanski's *Chinatown*, where corruption wins out over truth and no one can get a fair shake. Or so it is likely what Polanski believed when he fled the country in 1978.

The facts in the court record were as follows: When Polanski agreed to the plea bargain negotiated by his counsel with the district attorney and the attorneys for the victim, he changed his plea of innocence to guilty on a single count. This plea could have led to a sentence of as many as twenty years in state prison, depending on a report from the probation department and the positions taken by the district attorney and the child's counsel. However, given the agreement of all the parties, Polanski was led to believe that the judge would impose, if anything, a light sentence and, more likely, probation. This is what all parties, including the victim's family, desired.

The probation report was ordered and it confirmed that Polanski was not a mentally disordered sex offender. At the sentencing hearing, Dalton, Polanski's lawyer, pleaded for probation while Gunson argued that Polanski should receive a sentence of some time in custody. The trial judge then ordered that Polanski be sent to prison in Chino, California, for a diagnostic evaluation. The judge stayed the order for ninety days to allow Polanski to complete a film that he was then directing. This order itself was a subject of internal controversy and dispute as the later court filings and the 2008 documentary disclose.

The diagnostic study, when completed, recommended that Polanski be placed on probation. However, on February 1, 1978, Polanski failed to appear in court for a scheduled hearing and it was later learned that he was in France. A warrant was issued for his arrest. On February 14, 1978, Polanski's attorney, Dalton, filed a verified statement moving that the trial judge, Judge Rittenband, be disqualified for cause because he was biased against Polanski. On February 21, 1978, Judge Rittenband consented to transfer the matter to a different judge.

The various subsequent court filings and statements in the 2008 documentary at once contradict, dispute, amplify, and add nuance to these basic facts. The appellate court noted in 2009 that while these were only allegations, they were supported by considerable evidence. Based only on the declarations of Polanski's attorney, Dalton, and the deputy district attorney, Gunson, each of which supported the other's statements (and which were made under penalty of perjury), the court surmised that in an evidentiary hearing, a court would conclude that they demonstrate "malfeasance, improper contact with the media concerning a pending case, and unethical conduct."

As so amplified, the case against Polanski becomes murkier, but it is clear that the judge in the case was out of control. Prior to ordering the diagnostic study in Chino, Judge Rittenband told attorneys Dalton and Gunson and the probation officer who were gathered in his chambers that the diagnostic study would constitute Polanski's punishment and that there would be no further incarceration. He also told them that he expected a favorable report from Chino. Both Gunson and the probation officer objected to this course of action, telling the judge that using a diagnostic study as a punishment was not permitted under the California penal code.[2] Nonetheless, Judge Rittenband maintained that he was going to take this action to incarcerate Polanski because he feared that Polanski would not be safe in county jail.[3]

---

2. The provisions that allow for a diagnostic study were Cal. Penal Code §1203.03.

3. In his answer to Dalton's motion to disqualify him, Judge Rittenband stated that he wanted to send Polanski to Chino because he was concerned that Polanski might be subject to an attack in county jail by inmates who traditionally dislike child molesters.

Judge Rittenband also told them that he believed that sixty days in Chino would be sufficient time in custody to constitute Polanski's punishment. Dalton further stated in his declarations that Judge Rittenband told him and Gunson to play out a charade at the hearing, with Dalton arguing in favor of probation and with Gunson arguing for incarceration. In 2008, Dalton amplified this statement, adding that Judge Rittenband told them that he had made up his mind to go this route and to have the diagnostic study be Polanski's full punishment as long as the prison returned a favorable report on the director, and, more importantly, the press was not told of the agreement. Because the judge had made up his mind, in his chambers that day he neither sought nor listened to recommendations from anyone in the room, despite the fact that both the child's family's attorney and the probation officer urged that Polanski not be ordered to serve any time in prison. Deputy District Attorney Gunson confirmed these assertions in his own declaration in 2009, stating that he "told Judge Rittenband that the diagnostic study was not designed to be used as a sentence, but Judge Rittenband said that he was going to do it anyway."

Was the judge just being "pigheaded"? Certainly so, but there was more to it. Part of the explanation was provided when the 2008 documentary was released. That film contained an interview with a former deputy district attorney named David Wells, who claimed to have initially handled the case, but who was removed because he "was too close to the investigation." He claimed in the interview to have nevertheless remained close to the proceedings and, because he was on friendly terms with Judge Rittenband, to have had a number of private conversations with the judge about the case because, he asserted in the interview, the judge was not knowledgeable about criminal law or criminal procedure. Wells further asserted in the film that he was "very miffed the way it turned out" because he felt that "the guy belonged in state prison." He claimed to have suggested to Judge Rittenband that he use the diagnostic study referral as a punishment for Polanski because Polanski would not be able to appeal it.[4]

According to both the court record and the 2008 documentary, during the ninety-day stay of the diagnostic study that Judge Rittenband had granted to allow Polanski to complete a movie in Europe that he was directing for producer Dino DeLaurentiis,[5] Judge Rittenband saw a newspaper photograph that had been taken at the Oktoberfest in Munich in 1977, showing Polanski smoking a cigar and seated among other revelers, including two young women. The judge ordered Polanski back to Los Angeles and held a hearing to determine whether he should revoke the stay. Polanski testified that he had been in Munich on a business matter related to the film and DeLaurentiis corroborated this testimony. According to the 2008 documentary, the photo and its depiction of Polanski carousing in Munich riled the judge. In the documentary, Deputy DA Wells also asserted that he had called the judge's attention to the photo of Polanski in Munich. "Look here," Mr. Wells claimed in the film

---

4. From Wells's interview, *Roman Polanski: Wanted and Desired*. After the documentary aired, Wells recanted part of his statements in the interview, saying that he never told the judge to send Polanski to prison. He said that he had made up the story to make it look better. "Key figure in Polanski documentary says he lied," Today, msnbc.com, October 1, 2009, found at http://today.msnbc.msn.com/id/33110308/ns/today-entertainment/t/key-figure-polanski-documentary-says-he-lied/#.T2-48tlnAxQ, last accessed July 16, 2011.

5. According to the 2008 documentary, Polanski's lawyers told the judge that he needed at least twelve months to finish the movie and the judge told them to ask for the stay to be extended in ninety-day increments because granting a year's stay would make him look bad in the media.

interview he told the judge, "he's flipping you off."[6] Wells later denied this.[7]

Whether or not Wells egged him on, Judge Rittenband rescinded the stay and sent Polanski to serve his ninety days in prison in Chino. However, Polanski was released early and the diagnostic study came back recommending parole. The judge was apparently miffed at the early release. In January 1978, there was another meeting in Judge Rittenband's chambers. According to Dalton's declarations, the judge announced that he considered the diagnostic study to be the worst he had ever seen—a "complete whitewash" of Polanski—and that he intended to send Polanski back to prison. But he also had "hatched a plan" that would give the appearance of showing toughness toward Polanski to the press, but with a modification of the sentence after Polanski had served forty-eight days, on the condition "that he would voluntarily agree to be deported from the United States."[8]

Dalton summarized the judge's new requirements in his 2008 declaration: 1) that Polanski would serve forty-eight additional days in prison, 2) that he would not be permitted to have a hearing on this additional sentence, 3) that he would agree to waive his rights to a deportation hearing and agree to "voluntarily deport himself," and 4) that no hearing would be permitted until after Judge Rittenband had announced the prison sentence

---

6. *See* Cieply, Michael, "Polanski Asks Prosecutor to Review Film's Claims," *The New York Times*, July 17, 2008, found at www.nytimes.com/2008/07/17/movies/17polanski.html?adxnni=1&fta=y&adxnnix=1310879943-3mN4SaisxonohZxwf23Qy D8A, last accessed July 16, 2011.

7. "Key figure in Polanski documentary says he lied," Today.msnbc.com, October 1, 2009, found at http://today.msnbc.msn.com/id/33110308/ns/today-entertainment/t/key-figure-polanski-documentary-says-he-lied/#.T2-48tlnAxQ, last accessed October 15, 2011.

8. Judge Rittenband was relying on a California Penal Code provision that would allow the sentencing judge to retain jurisdiction over the case for 120 days after sentencing. Cal. Penal Code §1158, now Cal. Penal Code §1170(d).

and "that even more serious consequences could be expected if a hearing were held." Dalton also pointed out that at no time did the deputy district attorney, Gunson, request any of these conditions. According to Dalton, Judge Rittenband told the two attorneys that no one was to tell the press that the judge would be permitted to modify the sentence and that he would only publicly state that Polanski was sentenced to prison for the term prescribed by the statute.

The parties reconvened the next day in Judge Rittenband's chambers, this time with Lawrence Silver, the family's attorney. Dalton was planning to request a hearing to try to change the judge's mind. But Judge Rittenband cut him off, telling him that nothing could influence him to change his position. When Gunson suggested that the judge simply sentence Polanski to ninety days in county jail with a forty-two-day credit for the time that Polanski had served while he was undergoing the diagnostic study in Chino, Judge Rittenband told them that the press would not be satisfied with a county jail sentence. For appearances' sake, he needed to send Polanski to state prison. In his 2008 declaration, Dalton noted that Judge Rittenband reneged on his promise that Polanski would receive probation at the conclusion of the diagnostic study because he had been the subject of "criticism" in the press.

Dalton suggested more time to confer with his client, but Judge Rittenband refused to postpone the hearing because "the press expected a hearing" and "they were going to have one." He also told Gunson and Dalton that they should be prepared to make their arguments at the hearing for and against incarceration as if they had no idea that the judge had already decided on his sentence. Both attorneys objected to the denial of Polanski's right to a presentencing hearing. They also objected to the lack of legal authority for Judge Rittenband's sentence and the conditions that he intended to impose. Judge Rittenband ignored these objections. He also cautioned Dalton that, if Dalton made a motion for a new trial, then the judge would rescind his agreement to modify the sentence and to release Polanski after forty-eight days. According to Dalton, on leaving the judge's chambers that day, both he and Gunson resolved not to participate in the charade, which was solely "for the benefit of the press and with the result already pre-determined by the judge."

It was obvious to both Dalton and Gunson that, throughout the process, Rittenband had been playing to the press and that he continued to do so. Dalton alleged that as early as June 1977, Judge Rittenband was giving press conferences about the pending case. In *People* magazine, Dalton contended, the judge was quoted as saying, "I've handled other celebrity cases and this just doesn't look like anything other than a routine rape case to me." He was further quoted, according to Dalton, as observing "from what I've been able to gather, public opinion is divided on who is at fault. There are those who think Polanski is a devil, and others who wonder why a mother would let her thirteen-year-old daughter go around with a forty-three-year-old film director anyway." Dalton also had a quote from the *Herald Tribune*, from an interview with the judge after the Munich photo appeared, in which the judge stated "that Polanski could be on his way to prison that weekend." The 2008 documentary also contained an interview with a local newspaper reporter who recounted how the judge would call him into his chambers to ask his opinion on matters related to the case.

In the documentary, Dalton stated that, after Polanski learned that Judge Rittenband had revoked his original agreements and—uncertain that the judge would honor his latest offer even if Polanski accepted all the new conditions—rather than face the prospect of a long prison sentence if the judge were to renege again, Polanski chose to flee. Dalton then made his motion to disqualify Judge Rittenband, not only for his failures to afford due process to Polanski (through his off-the-record decisions made in chambers and his charade to impress the media), nor solely for his inappropriate interviews with the press where it was obvious that he had prejudged the case before any evidentiary hearings were held, but also because of other inappropriate and unethical contacts.

In his 1978 declarations in support of his motion to disqualify, Dalton noted that on several occasions, Judge Rittenband would refer to the mail that he had received criticizing him for allowing Polanski to work on the film in Europe instead of sending him straight to prison. He also presented evidence that the judge took into account other claims and accusations that were not part of the court record, such as calls he received from a friend in London falsely claiming that a similar incident involving Polanski and an underage girl had occurred in Great Britain and other unsubstantiated claims that a friend of Polanski had arranged for him to meet the girl specifically for sex. Dalton also stated that, within days of Polanski's flight in 1978, Judge Rittenband had held a press conference, disclosing the details of his in-chambers discussions with the two attorneys, including his intention to impose a forty-eight-day prison sentence, followed by voluntary deportation.

In 1997, Dalton requested the assignment of the *Polanski* case to a new judge in order to potentially resolve the case. The matter was assigned to Judge Fidler. This judge indicated to Dalton and Gunson that he believed that a commitment made by a judge of the court should be honored and he therefore agreed that the period of time that Polanski was incarcerated in Chino while undergoing the diagnostic study would constitute his full punishment. He told Gunson and Dalton that if Polanski returned to Los Angeles, he would be booked and immediately allowed to be released on bail. He also agreed that once Polanski met with the probation department, the judge would conduct a hearing and terminate probation without Polanski having to serve additional time in custody. But Judge Fidler also required that the sentencing hearings be televised so that the public could know and understand all that had occurred in 1978. For Polanski, the prospect of televised proceedings was a deal killer and therefore he chose not to return to the United States, even with the assurance that he would not be incarcerated. According to Dalton, Polanski was not willing to face what would be a media circus, particularly because by 1997, he was married[9] and had two young children. And so, he preferred to remain a fugitive from justice rather than resurrect what was at the time a twenty-year-old case.

When the film *Roman Polanski: Wanted and Desired* aired in 2008, it caused an uproar because of its portrayal of blatantly unethical and inappropriate behavior by the judge (who was by then deceased) in the 1977 case and by Mr. Wells's statements. At that time, Dalton made a motion in Los Angeles Superior Court, asking the court on its own motion to dismiss the *Polanski* case or to allow another court to review it, because of the alleged judicial and prosecutorial misconduct (based on Wells's statements). At the same time, the victim, Ms. Geimer, now a grown woman, expressed her desire that the matter be concluded.[10]

On February 17, 2009, the court issued an order ruling that Polanski had to be present at any proceeding regarding his case.

---

9. To French actress Emmanuelle Seigner.

10. "Woman in case against Roman Polanski seeks dismissal," CNN Justice, January 12, 2009, found at http://articles.cnn.com/2009-01-12/justice/polanski.case_1_ samantha-geimer-mr-polanski-baby-and-chinatown?_s=PM:CRIME, last accessed July 16, 2011.

Under the "fugitive disentitlement doctrine," the court concluded that Polanski was not entitled to request relief from the court
while he remained at large. On May 4, 2009, Polanski's counsel
advised the trial court that Polanski would not appear at the
hearing. On May 7, 2009, the court's order took effect. On July 7,
2009, Polanski's attorneys filed an appeal.

In September 2009, the case took a bizarre turn. Polanski had been living publicly in France for the past thirty years,
traveling widely within Europe, and no effort had been made to
either arrest or extradite him. All this time, he was busy directing some very prominent and well-regarded films, including
Tess (1979) and more recently *The Pianist* (2002). He received
his first Best Director Oscar for *The Pianist* in 2003, but obviously did not attend the awards ceremony. Actor Harrison Ford
accepted the award on his behalf and traveled to Paris later to
present it to Polanski.

Suddenly, in the fall of 2009, the *Polanski* case came back
into the headlines. On September 27, 2009, without warning,
Polanski was arrested in Switzerland, where he had traveled
to attend the Zurich Film Festival where he was to be awarded the festival's lifetime achievement award. He chose to fight
extradition to the United States in Swiss courts. What had happened had a simple explanation. Embarrassed by the negative
publicity that the 2008 documentary had caused the Los Angeles
district attorney's office, which was exacerbated by Polanski's
attorneys' subsequent motion to dismiss the charges, like sleeping bears, the office pulled out the old arrest warrant and put
events in motion to achieve the stunning arrest in Switzerland.[11]

---

11. *See* Clark, Marcia, "Polanski's Lost Alibi," *The Daily Beast*, September 29,
2009, found at www.thedailybeast.com/articles/2009/09/30/polanskis-lost-alibi.html,
last accessed July 16, 2011. Marcia Clark, the former Los Angeles prosecutor in the
O.J. Simpson case, claimed to have telephoned some former colleagues to gain an
understanding of what had provoked this sudden activity in a thirty-year-old case.

In response to Polanski's decision to fight extradition, the district attorney's office in Los Angeles filed a supplemental brief in the proceedings on Polanski's appeal, asserting that Polanski's plan to oppose extradition constituted a forfeiture of his right to request relief from the court. At the same time, the victim's attorneys requested that the court dismiss the matter in order to end "the disruption, trauma, and personal invasion" that she claimed to suffer whenever public interest in the case resurged.

In the appellate division, the court first dismissed the district attorney's arguments that Polanski had waived his right to seek relief from the court, particularly because "of the very serious allegations of judicial and prosecutorial misconduct" that Polanski's lawyers had raised. However, the court nevertheless ruled that, while Polanski remained at large, regardless of whether he believed that his flight had been justified and necessary because of the trial judge's egregious conduct and violation of his rights, he was not entitled to relief until he appeared in court. The court also pointed out that Polanski could have and should have requested the dismissal of the charges much sooner. While he only recently had learned of the unethical role Wells may have played in the case by "ushering" Judge Rittenband "along a path of iniquity" because of his own "personal axe to grind" against Polanski, Polanski knew of Judge Rittenband's unlawful and improper conduct and had had ample time in the past thirty years to seek redress. Now, the court observed, with Judge Rittenband deceased, the ability of the justice system "to ascertain the truth" had been "negatively impacted."

Finally, the court concluded, instead of fleeing the country, Polanski had had other remedies to which he could have availed himself. He obviously did not do so because he feared that, despite California law that prohibited the judge's illegal actions, he would have been trapped by them and sent to prison. Even if that were the case, and the court was not unsympathetic to those fears, the court nonetheless believed that Judge Rittenband would have stayed his sentence of incarceration to allow Polanski to appeal. (Neither Polanski nor his attorney Dalton, who had had first-hand experience with Judge Rittenband's capricious behavior during those tense weeks in 1977, were nearly as optimistic that the judge would have acted so rationally. Dalton had advised Polanski—based on his recent experience with Judge Rittenband—that Polanski likely would face incarceration while the appeal was pending.) The court also failed to understand why Polanski had refused to return to Los Angeles in 1997 when Judge Fidler agreed to honor Judge Rittenband's earlier commitments. The court noted that this did not look like the behavior of a man "unfairly exiled" because he had "no remedy but flight in the face of alleged misconduct by the trial court," but rather a situation where a fugitive wants "also to direct the conditions under which that relief is dispensed." Polanski had choices and he chose to remain a fugitive.

At the same time, even in 2009, the court believed that Polanski was not without remedies. He could request to be sentenced in absentia or return to California and request that the court either dismiss the charges due to judicial misconduct or ask the court to honor the sentencing agreement that had been made at the time he fled. According to the court, the only remedy to which he was not entitled was to have all the charges dismissed and to be freed from all threat of further punishment while he remained in Europe outside the jurisdiction of the court.

However, in a final salvo, the court did not spare the district attorney's office, expressing its dismay at their refusal to address the misconduct in which Wells claimed to have engaged during his interview for the 2008 documentary. The court was shocked that a member of the prosecutor's office would have recommended the misuse of a sentencing tool as a punishment and "deliberately provoked the judge against a defendant based on a newspaper photograph and no other information." The court asked the district attorney's office to investigate and "take appropriate corrective action." The court also observed that if in its investigation, misconduct was found to have "tainted the proceedings against Polanski" sufficiently to warrant a dismissal of the case, then it should do so on its own motion. The court concluded by expressing a desire that the parties pursue a "long overdue resolution of this matter."

But that was not to be. On January 6, 2010, upon remand to the superior court, Polanski's lawyers followed the appellate court's advice and presented a notarized letter from Polanski in which he asked to be sentenced in absentia. The court scheduled a hearing, and on January 22, 2010, ruled that Polanski had to be present in court for sentencing.[12]

In July 2010, the Swiss Justice Minister announced that Switzerland would not send Polanski back to the United States for sentencing.[13] The Swiss officials had requested that the U.S. government provide records to determine whether or not Polanski's forty-two-day court-ordered psychiatric evaluation at Chino State Prison had constituted Polanski's whole sentence, as Polanski's attorneys had argued. "If this were the case," the Swiss authorities said in a statement, "Roman Polanski would

---

12. "Judge rules Swiss-based Roman Polanski must be present in U.S. court to resolve unlawful sex case," NYDailyNews.com, January 22, 2010, found at http://articles.nydailynews.com/2010-01-22/gossip/17943777_1_roman-polanski-harsher-sentence-lawrence-silver, last accessed July 16, 2011.

13. Cumming-Bruce, Nick and Cieply, Michael, "Swiss Reject U.S. Request to Extradite Polanski," *The New York Times*, July 12, 2010, found at http://www.nytimes.com/2010/07/13/movies/13polanski.html?src=mv, last accessed July 16, 2011.

actually have already served his sentence, and therefore both the proceedings on which the U.S. extradition request is founded and the request itself would have no foundation."[14] The requested documentation was not provided.

Polanski returned to France, where he remains and where he continues to direct movies. In a documentary previewed at the Zurich Film Festival in September 2011[15]—Laurent Bouzereau's *Roman Polanski: A Film Memoir*—Polanski commented about his career, the murder of his wife Sharon Tate, and the case. He stated, "She is a double victim: my victim, and a victim of the press."[16] And the victim, Samantha Geimer, in a March 2011 interview lays the blame squarely on the press and the courts as much as Polanski for the years of turmoil that they have caused her. "You shouldn't be damaged more by the court than by the crime," she said.[17]

---

14. Cumming-Bruce & Cieply, "Swiss Reject U.S. Request to Extradite Polanski."

15. Polanski was awarded the lifetime achievement award at the 2011 Zurich Film Festival that he missed receiving in 2009, due to his arrest. "'Roman Polanski: A Film Memoir' Is Surprise Addition To Zurich Film Festival," Deadline Hollywood, Tuesday, September 27, 2011, found at http://www.deadline.com/2011/09/roman-polanski-a-film-memoir-is-surprise-addition-to-zurich-film-festival/, last accessed October 7, 2011.

16. Murphy, Eileen, "Roman Polanski on Sex Case: 'Regretted it for 33 Years,'" ABC News, October 3, 2011, found at http://abcnews.go.com/blogs/entertainment/2011/10/roman-polanski-on-sex-case-regretted-it-for-33-years/, last accessed October 7, 2011.

17. Hopper, Jessica, "Exclusive: Roman Polanski's Victim Speaks Out on 34-Year Anniversary of Crime," ABC News, March 10, 2011, found at http://abcnews.go.com/US/gma-exclusive-roman-polanskis-victim-samatha-geimer-speaks/story?id=13103064, last accessed October 7, 2011.

A Foreign Affair

Golan v. Holder, 611 F. Supp 2d 1165 (D. Colo. 2009),
rev'd 609 F 3d 1076 (10th Cir. 2010), aff'd, 565 U.S.__ (2012)

**Danny: The truth is, I thought it mattered—
I thought that music mattered. But does it?
Bollocks! Not compared to how people matter.**

Pete Postlethwaite as Danny, in *Brassed Off* (1996)

H ad the *Shostakovich* case[1] been decided today rather than in the 1940s, the result would be different, because, even though the works of the Soviet composers were at that time in the public domain and available for the free use of the music department at Fox studios, the same works that were the subject of the movie *The Iron Curtain* were granted copyright protection in 1994 by the U.S. Congress in controversial legislation.[2] With copyright protection, Shostakovich and his colleagues would have had a more winnable case. Fox had used the compositions in question without obtaining the prior consent of the composers and this would have infringed their copyright. How and why did it happen that a work in the public domain suddenly had copyright protection?

The United States did not join the Berne Convention for the Protection of Literary and Artistic Works,[3] an international

---

1. Shostakovich v. Twentieth Century Fox Film Corp., 196 Misc. 67, 80 N.Y.S. 2d 575 (N.Y. Sup. Ct. 1948); *aff'd* 275 A.D. 692, 87 N.Y. S. 2d 430 (1949). *See* Reel 10, The Iron Curtain Descends.

2. Pub. L. No. 103-465, 103d Cong., 2d Sess., 108 Stat. 4809 (1994).

3. Berne Convention, Article 18, Sept. 9, 1886 (revised at Paris on July 24, 1971).

treaty first enacted in 1886, until 1988.[4] In April 1994, the United States signed the Uruguay Round General Agreement on Tariffs and Trade which formed the World Trade Organization. Included in this round of agreements was the Agreement on Trade-Related Aspects of Intellectual Property Rights (TRIPs).[5] The TRIPs agreement required, in part, that its signatories comply with Article 18 of the Berne Convention and thus extend copyright protection to all works of foreign authors whose term of protection had not expired in their native countries. A further act of Congress—the Uruguay Round Agreements Act (URAA)—was required to fully implement Article 18.[6] Section 514 of this Act[7] restores the U.S. copyrights of foreign authors who had lost those rights to the public domain for any reason other than the expiration of a copyright term.

Section 514 provided several "supplemental protections" for those who had previously made use of the former public domain works. They were "immunized" from liability for acts of copying that occurred before the restoration of the works' copyright and were entitled to continue copying, as long as the original author did not file a notice of intent to enforce his or her copyright.[8] They were also entitled to sell or otherwise use copies

4. Berne Convention Implementation Act of 1988, Pub. L. 100-568, §12, 102 Stat. 2853, 2860. When the United States joined the Berne Convention, the implementing legislation did not extend copyrights to any foreign works that were already in the public domain in the United States.

5. Uruguay Round Agreements, 1994, World Trade Organization, Annex 1C—Trade-Related Aspects of Intellectual Property Rights (TRIPS), http://www.wto.org/english/docs_e/legal_e/27-trips.pdf.

6. Berne Convention, Art. 18.

7. 17 U.S.C. §104A.

8. 17 U.S.C. §104A(d)(2). In order to enforce a restored copyright against a reliance party, a foreign copyright owner had to either file notice with the Copyright Office within twenty-four months of restoration (17 U.S.C. §104A(d)(2)(A)(i)). or serve actual notice on the reliance party (17 U.S.C. §104A(d)(2)(B)(i)). A reliance party is liable for infringing acts that occur after the end of a twelve-month grace period.

of works where the copyright was restored for one year.[9] And they could continue to exploit derivative works based on the foreign work, as long as a reasonable royalty was paid.[10] But on the other hand, after Section 514 became law, any copying of a work beyond the first year's grace period after notice of intent to enforce was filed and any continued use or sale of a derivative work based on the copyrighted material after this notice was filed, without payment of a royalty, was prohibited.

Richard Kapp,[11] a musician, and Lawrence Golan, a professor and conductor, among others, filed suit in September 2001, challenging Section 514 on Constitutional grounds. Their suit was dismissed in 2005 and the dismissal was upheld by the Tenth Circuit Court of Appeals for most of the claims, but reversed on the basis of the plaintiff's First Amendment challenge.[12] On remand, the lower court considered whether Section 514 interfered with Kapp's and Golan's First Amendment interest in using works in the public domain.

Kapp and Golan argued that, by granting these old works "restored" copyrights, Congress had traded away their rights of free expression in these public domain materials under the First Amendment, favoring the private interests of copyright holders and the heirs of foreign authors. Some of the foreign works

9. A reliance party is liable for infringing acts that occur after the end of a twelve-month grace period, starting from notice of restoration. 17 U.S.C. §104A(d)(2)(A)(ii) (I), 17 U.S.C. §104A(d)(2)(B)(ii)(I). Reliance parties may sell or otherwise dispose of restored works during this grace period (17 U.S.C. §109(a)), but they cannot make additional copies during this time. 17 U.S.C. §104A(d)(2)(A)(ii)(III), 17 U.S.C. §104A(d)(2)(B)(ii)(III).

10. Under Section 514, "a reliance party may continue to exploit that derivative work for the duration of the restored copyright if the reliance party pays to the owner of the restored copyright reasonable compensation . . ." 17 U.S.C. §104A(d)(3)(A) If the parties are unable to agree on reasonable compensation, a federal court will determine the amount of compensation. 17 U.S.C. §104A(d)(3)(B).

11. Kapp had produced, among other things, acclaimed recordings of Shostakovich's String Quartets.

12. Golan v. Gonzales, 501 F 3d 1179 (10th Cir. 2007).

that received copyright protection by Section 514 had been in the public domain in the United States for decades; some had been created as far back as the 1920s. Thousands of works were affected: musical compositions by not only Shostakovich but also by Prokofiev and Stravinsky, paintings by Picasso, the drawings of M.C. Escher, the writings of George Orwell and J.R.R. Tolkien, and some very famous films, including Fritz Lang's *Metropolis* (1927), Jean-Luc Godard's *À Bout de souffle (Breathless)* (1960), and Leni Riefenstahl's *Triumph des Willens (Triumph of the Will)* (1935).

In their suit, the plaintiffs claimed to have been put into a position of either having to pay for their previously royalty-free use, or stop using these works altogether. This affected orchestras wanting to perform, and recordings made by performers of, what had been public domain works that were now subject to someone else's restored copyright. It also frustrated the efforts of professors, such as in film schools, wanting to teach previously public domain works, classic film distributors required to remove works from their catalogues, and film preservationists and archivists—in other words, people who had relied on artistic works in the public domain for their livelihoods. As a result of the impact of Section 514, these people were either prevented from using the works or were required to pay licensing fees to the copyright holder—fees that were often cost-prohibitive.

On remand, the district court ruled in favor of the plaintiffs and against the government.[13]

The principle of public domain, as expressed by the Tenth Circuit when it overruled the original district court opinion,[14] is that once free of copyright protection, a work is available for

---

13. 611 F. Supp. 2d 1165 (D.C. Colo. 2009).
14. Golan v. Gonzales, 501 F 3d 1179 (10th Cir. 2007).

public use, which in turn inspires new creations, and makes copyright ultimately "the engine of free expression." As the district court noted on remand, one of the traditional "contours" of copyright protection "is the principle that once a work enters the public domain, no individual—not even the creator—may copyright it."

In defense of Section 514, the government gave three arguments. First, the law brought the United States into substantial compliance with its international treaty obligations under the Berne Convention. Second, it helped protect the copyright interests of U.S. authors abroad. Third, it corrected for historic inequities imposed on foreign authors who had been denied U.S. copyrights through no fault of their own.

The court admitted that Section 514 did provide some protection for reliance parties who had exploited the works prior to the copyright restoration for copies and derivative works beyond what a normal copyright would allow.[15] The court also expressed its belief that Congress had the discretion under the Berne Convention to except parties "who have relied upon works in the public domain," as the Tenth Circuit had suggested in its prior opinion.[16] The government had additionally argued that Section 514 was necessary to protect the works of U.S. authors from reprisal under the Berne Convention. But the district court pointed out that the Convention itself only allowed sanctions against a country that was not a signatory to the treaty and therefore provided no basis for sanctions to be levied against U.S. authors.[17] Likewise, the court did not find the

---

15. *See* note 10 supra.

16. 501 F 3d at 1176.

17. Berne Convention, Article 6 allowed sanctions only against a "country outside the Union that fails to protect in an adequate manner the works of authors who are nationals of one of the countries of the Union."

government's expressed concern about the economic impact caused by foreign piracy of copyrighted U.S. works to be persuasive, as it seemed that the countries where piracy was rampant did not participate in the Berne Convention.

Finally, the court was not persuaded by the government's third argument—that Section 514 served an important equitable interest in restoring copyright protection to authors of foreign origin who lost their U.S. copyrights through no fault of their own either because they failed to comply with U.S. copyright formalities or because the United States did not have copyright treaties with their nations at the time they created their works. In fact, the court was concerned because it seemed that Section 514 extended protections to foreign authors which were not afforded to U.S. authors even in their own country. The court found that this result "rather than correct an historic inequity," created "an inequity where one formerly did not exist." The court could not see how granting foreign authors copyrights in the United States while denying similar protection to U.S. authors "could constitute an important governmental interest." Accordingly, the district court granted Kapp's and Golan's motion for summary judgment, ruling that Section 514 violated their freedom of expression under the First Amendment.

This decision was appealed to the Tenth Circuit, and the Motion Picture Association of America, among others, joined as friends of the court to oppose Section 514. This was to no avail. In 2010, the Tenth Circuit reversed the lower court decision.[18]

The appellate court disagreed with the lower court's assessment of the governmental interest in advancing the rights of American copyright holders abroad. In the appellate court's view, these interests were at least as important or substantial

---

18. 609 F 3d 1076 (10th Cir. 2010).

as other rights and therefore entitled to "substantial deference." This was more so the case as it involved foreign affairs. The court took note of congressional testimony asserting that "billions of dollars" were lost each year because foreign countries were not providing copyright protection to American works that were in the public domain abroad.[19] The United States was subject to criticism because it was not honoring its obligations under Article 18 of the Berne Convention.

Golan's complaint was that, in enacting Section 514, Congress did not need to limit protection for those who had relied on the public domain for so long. But the appellate court understood Congress's desire to "set an example" for other countries to follow in copyright restoration. What the United States did would impact how other countries would decide to act in restoring copyright protection in those jurisdictions. And there had to be a balancing between the interests of U.S. copyright holders and the so-called reliance parties. In its analysis of that balancing, the court came to the conclusion that Section 514 does not unnecessarily burden the plaintiffs' First Amendment rights. As the court saw it, the burdens imposed on the reliance parties were congruent with the benefits Section 514 afforded to U.S. copyright holders.

Golan and the other plaintiffs had argued that there were less restrictive means of restoring foreign copyrights. For example, they observed that in Great Britain, when copyrights were restored, the statute afforded greater protections to reliance parties. Under that model, a reliance party is entitled, for example, to continue to use a derivative work that was created before the copyright was restored. The law allows a copyright holder

---

19. Quoting a statement by Eric Smith, former Executive Director and General Counsel of the International Intellectual Property Alliance at the congressional hearings prior to enactment of Section 514.

to "buy out" the creator of the derivative work.[20] In other words, the law in Great Britain allows copyright owners to "buy back" their rights immediately after copyright restoration.

The court did not see how this model was any less restrictive on speech than Section 514. In both instances, the copyright owner has the ability to terminate the reliance party's interests. The only significant difference that the court saw was that under the U.K. model, the reliance party received compensation from the copyright owner; under Section 514, the reliance party had to pay a "reasonable" royalty to the copyright owner in order to continue to use the work. Even the court had to acknowledge that a reliance party, such as Richard Kapp, who had created musical arrangements of former public domain pieces, would appreciate receiving compensation for the value of the derivative works that he had created and for which he was unable to pay the demanded royalties. However, even if the British approach was "arguably more protective of reliance parties' economic interests," the court was unable to say definitively that receiving compensation from the restored copyright owner was "substantially more protective of reliance parties' expressive interests."

The court therefore held that, because Section 514 advanced an important government interest and did not burden substantially more speech than necessary to advance that interest, it was consistent with the First Amendment.

Richard Kapp died in 2006 and thus failed to see the conclusion of his case. Lawrence Golan continued the battle. In October 2010, the Fair Use Project at Stanford University, representing Golan, filed a petition with the U.S. Supreme Court,

---

20. Citing Karp, Irwin, Final Report, Berne Convention Article 18 Study on Retroactive United States Copyright Protection for Berne and Other Works, 20 Colum.-VLA J.L. & Arts 157, 180 (1996).

appealing both Tenth Circuit decisions, arguing not only that the statute impinged on Golan's First Amendment right to free expression but also that, in enacting the URAA, Congress exceeded its authority under the Copyright Clause of Article I of the U.S. Constitution because the clause gives Congress no authority to grant copyrights to works that are already in the public domain. In its first ruling in 2007, the Tenth Circuit had disagreed, stating that Congress had that authority.

On March 7, 2011, the Supreme Court agreed to hear this case. For Golan and those who have supported him in his long journey to the Supreme Court, this was a significant matter of fairness. "This statute [URAA] throws into question one of the most basic premises of intellectual property: once a work of authorship is placed in the Public Domain, it belongs to the public, and remains the property of the public," explained Anthony Falzone, the executive director of the Stanford University Fair Use Project. "That principle was respected for more than 200 years, because it represents a critical limit on the intellectual property 'monopoly' the framers authorized. What Congress did here represents a huge departure from those basic principles with substantial constitutional ramifications."[21]

On January 18, 2012, the Court rendered its decision, holding that Section 514 did not exceed Congress's authority under the Copyright Clause and further that the First Amendment did not inhibit the restoration authorized by Section 514. Justice Ginsberg delivered the Court's opinion, joined by four justices. Justice Ginsberg reiterated the justifications that had been put forth by the government and accepted by the appel-

---

21. Albanese, Andrew, "U.S. Supreme Court Takes On Landmark Fair Use Case," Publisher's Weekly, Mar 08, 2011, found at http://www.publishersweekly.com/pw/by-topic/digital/copyright/article/46401-u-s-supreme-court-takes-on-landmark-fair-use-case.html, last accessed October 1, 2011.

late court, showing deference to the government's arguments in favor of adherence to the Berne Convention. Justices Breyer and Alito dissented. In his dissent, Justice Breyer questioned whether Congress's decision to remove works from the public domain actually furthered progress in science and the useful arts—which is the basis for Congress's authority to enact copyright term limits under the Copyright Clause. As he observed, "the statute" did "not encourage anyone to produce a single new work." On the other hand, he noted instances of the burdens placed upon libraries, music lovers, and book buyers who were, since the statute's enactment, forced to pay higher prices to acquire works that had previously been in the public domain. Justice Breyer worried that the effect of the law was to create a situation in which consumers would either have to pay more for things already in existence or might be unable to get them at all.

The concerns raised by Justice Breyer are real. Since the law was enacted, for example, local orchestras have complained of not being able to afford the royalties to perform a Shostakovich work, young children are no longer introduced to classical music through performances of Prokofiev's "Peter and the Wolf," and film archivists and scholars have no longer been able to obtain copies of important movies.

About the Author

Carol Robertson has been a practicing attorney for 30 years, including as a partner at a major San Francisco law firm and as corporate counsel with San Francisco Bay Area companies. In the course of her practice, Ms. Robertson has enjoyed a diverse legal practice, including matters related to new media, advertising and entertainment. She has taught French at the high school and college levels, and holds a BA and an MA in French Literature. She interrupted her studies toward her PhD in order to attend law school at the University of California at Berkeley (Boalt Hall School of Law), where she graduated in the top 10 percent of her class in 1980.

She has been a frequent speaker at professional seminars, workshops, conferences and conventions throughout the United States and Canada, on various business and legal subjects, and has taught English at the Law and Business School and at the College of Sciences at the Université de Pau, France. Ms. Robertson has been an adjunct professor at John F. Kennedy University in Pleasant Hill, California in the School of Management and in the Law School, where she has taught courses in Business Law, Business Ethics and Negotiation Techniques.

Ms. Robertson has been a film enthusiast since her childhood and enjoys a wide range of genres, from serious drama to romantic comedy, from the silent comedies of Buster Keaton or Charles Chaplin to recent releases, from an avant garde French or Italian film to a classic Ozu. Her favorite weekend activity is to pass the time with a good movie, preferably in the company of good friends, and accompanied by a glass of wine and a piece of dark chocolate or a bowl of popcorn.

Her love of movies translates to this simple equation: in so many of the films produced in the past 100 years, one is able at once to experience the movement and thrill of a life outside of one's own while at the same time contemplating one's own existence.

Index

M

N